1982

THE
ROOTS
OF
ETHICS
SCIENCE, RELIGION, AND VALUES

THE HASTINGS CENTER SERIES IN ETHICS

A Continuation Order Plan is available for this series. A continuation order will bring delivery of each new volume immediately upon publication. Volumes are billed only upon actual shipment. For further information please contact the publisher.

THE
ROOTS
OF
ETHICS

SCIENCE, RELIGION, AND VALUES

Edited by

Daniel Callahan
The Hasings Center
Hastings-on-Hudson, New York

and

H. Tristram Engelhardt, Jr.
The Kennedy Institute of Ethics
Georgetown University
Washington, D.C.

PLENUM PRESS · NEW YORK AND LONDON

ISBN 0-306-40796-5

Preface

OUR AGE IS CHARACTERIZED by an uncertainty about the nature of moral obligations, about what one can hope for in an afterlife, and about the limits of human knowledge. These uncertainties were captured by Immanuel Kant in his *Critique of Pure Reason,* where he noted three basic human questions: what can we know, what ought we to do, and what can we hope for. Those questions and the uncertainties about their answers still in great part define our cultural perspective. In particular, we are not clear about the foundations of ethics, or about their relationship to religion and to science. This volume brings together previously published essays that focus on these interrelationships and their uncertainties. It offers an attempt to sketch the interrelationship among three major intellectual efforts: determining moral obligations, the ultimate purpose and goals of man and the cosmos, and the nature of empirical reality. Though imperfect, it is an effort to frame the unity of the human condition, which is captured in part by ethics, in part by religion, and in part by the sciences. Put another way, this collection of essays springs from an attempt to see the unity of humans who engage in the diverse roles of valuers, believers, and knowers, while still remaining single, individual humans.

The essays in this volume address, as a consequence, the philosophical foundations of ethics, the importance and relevance of religion for ethical viewpoints, the ways in which science can illuminate our nature as knowers and valuers, and the extent to which moral psychology can account for our roles as scientists. In addition, the embedding of science in a nexus of moral obligation is explored. It is no accident, as these essays show, that there are interconnections among ethics, religion, and science. Nor is it an accident that we as a culture are recurringly brought to examine these interrelationships.

Over the last half a millennium, the West has repeatedly had its orientation to ultimate place and purpose shaken as a result of changes in the understanding of the possibility for knowing, valuing, and believing. Before the Reformation, the West for the most part shared a common view of morals and faith. There was a structure of values and of religious authority, which included modes for the resolution of disputes. Religion was thought to provide objective knowledge of fact and value. The Reformation shattered that certainty, putting in jeopardy claims to objectivity in religion. Numerous competing orthodoxies arose, each claiming the truth of its own viewpoint, many claiming the right of each individual to mediate directly with the deity and to interpret for himself the Holy Scriptures. The issue of the objective resolution of competing claims to religious truth became increasingly difficult, as the interchange in this volume between Alasdair MacIntyre and Paul Ramsey suggests, and as the article by David Burrell and Stanley Hauerwas argues with respect to moral claims generally. When Martin Luther nailed his 95 theses to All Saints' Church in Wittenberg on the eve of All Saints' Day, 1570, he marked a new era for the West and established many of the background presuppositions of these essays. That Halloween signaled the end of a consensus and the loss of commonly held ways of framing a moral consensus.

The changes of the Reformation did not occur alone, but in tandem with other cultural challenges. Exposure to other cultural viewpoints through the colonial and imperial adventures of Europe brought Europeans into contact with individuals holding radically different views of the nature of reality and of the important good of life. The question of objectivity in ethics, even outside religious grounds, was thus brought into question, fashioning the lineaments of the modern predicament, in which moral certainty seems elusive. In great measure, the loss of a moral orthodoxy and of an established sense of moral objectivity restored the conditions of the pre-Christian West. Much of the sense of crisis in moral philosophy reported in some of the essays in this volume reflects this loss of objectivity or intersubjectivity. A concrete ethic, as Burrell and Hauerwas argue, has become the deliverance of a particular moral story, rather than that of a formal moral system.

However, it is not simply that the pre-Christian absence of a moral consensus and orthodoxy has been restored to the West. The loss of orientation has been more profound. There is now an objective account to justify the sense of loss of orientation, provided in the same century as the Reformation: the loss of the Ptolemaic account of the cosmic centrality of the earth and therefore of man. The understanding of man's place in the cosmos was shaken. When Nicolaus Copernicus saw the first copy of his *De Revolutionibus orbium coelestium* on his deathbed on May 24, 1543, he saw a force for the uprooting of the Western viewpoint that was as substantial and profound as that of the Reformation. He had provided an understanding of the cosmos that dislodged man from his central place in creation and cast him adrift in a directionless universe within which there was no absolute point of reference to give final orientation. This profoundly upsetting truth, which Giordano Bruno embraced to his end, even when he was condemned by Pope Clement VIII and burnt in the Plaza of Flowers at Rome on February 17, 1600, is an appropriate metaphor for the value uncertainties of our modern age. The proposition that the universe was infinite and filled with innumerable worlds in great measure signaled the modern context for the problem of understanding man's place in nature. Bruno's cosmological thesis had ethical significance for it suggested the arbitrariness of any view of the place of man in the cosmos. And, as the interchange between Stephen Toulmin and Loren Graham suggests, the concern about the ethical implications of science, including cosmology, continues into this century.

Indeed, Stephen Toulmin points out that Charles Darwin and Russell Wallace further contributed to this metaphysical disorientation with the appearance of *The Origin of the Species* in 1859. Not only was the cosmos not designed around the earth as its center, but neither was man a product of divine design. In fact, man was no longer a creature but a product of evolution. Just as the earth's place in the cosmos was the result of blind chance, so too was man's place in nature. As the sociobiologists would indicate in the years to come, and as Richard Alexander argues by implication in his essay, so too are human moral dispositions the result of the blind forces of evolution.

Thus, on the one hand, the interplay of ethics and science has been puzzling and disturbing. On the other hand, this interplay is central to the modern human condition. It is for this reason that it was selected as the focus of the research project that produced the essays selected for this volume. From 1974 through 1978 The Hastings Center, with the support of the National Endowment for the Humanities, explored "the foundations of ethics and their relationship to the sciences." Those four years of research produced four volumes published by The Hastings Center, from which these essays were taken: *Science, Ethics, and Medicine; Morals, Science, and Sociality; Knowledge, Value and Belief; and Knowing and Valuing.* The result was a multidimensional geography of the nexus of science and ethics which displayed: (1) how concepts guide both science and ethics, not simply through their conceptual content, but through their metaphorical force; (2) how causal explanations are made available to account for the existence of moral dispositions so that science can appropriate ethics in part by giving an empirical explanatory account of ethics, and how ethics can offer a moral account of science, and in that way appropriate science as part of its domain; (3) that there are recurrent attempts to secure the objective status of some values by endeavoring to read them from the processes of nature (e.g., evolution); (4) that both science and ethics presuppose value judgments, so that there is is no crisp line to be drawn between an explanation and an evaluation, between value-neutral facts and fact-free values; and (5) that though both ethics and science can make claims of universal truth or applicability for their axioms, the articulation of both scientific and ethical assertions is heavily time-bound, placed within particular historical contexts. Further, as a result of pressing for the nature of the interplay of ethics and science, the nature of the foundations of ethics was itself explored, as the essays in the volume by Alasdair MacIntyre, Gerald Dworkin, Hans Jonas, and Daniel Burrell and Stanley Hauerwas attest.

The essays on the foundations of ethics, and the relationship of religion to those foundations, address the problem of fashioning convincing and encompassing moral viewpoints, of dealing with moral authority and moral autonomy, and of delineating convincing senses of moral obligation. For example, Hans Jonas addresses in his essay, "The Concept of Responsibility: An Inquiry into the Foundations of Ethics for Our Age," the problem of ethics in a technological age and the issues that that age raises regarding responsibility for the safety of mankind. Mankind, having become the lonesome master of this earth, is left with the task of developing a sense of obligation, as Jonas argues, *sub specie temporis*. Alasdair MacIntyre, Paul Ramsey, Gunther Stent, and Hans Jonas also explore where religion can help ground such a sense of responsibility. The result is that one faces the issue of whether religion can ground ethics, or whether ethics must ground religion in the sense of providing a basis for choosing among the moral claims of competing faiths. And in fact, as the interchange of Hans Jonas and James Gustafson suggests, the character of religious claims has itself changed over the last half millennium, leading at times to much more tentative contributions from theologians.

The interplay of science and ethics is explored in Stephen Toulmin's analysis of the moral psychology of science and of the sciences, which casts science within a larger moral account, and by Gunther Stent's argument for causal grounds of ethics in the deep structure of the human brain, which fixes ethics as an object of scientific study. This latter enterprise is pursued further by Richard Alexander, who provides a sociobiological account of societal laws and ethics. Thus both ethics and science, each in its own way, appropriate one another as objects of study. The interplay is thus one of dialectical, mutual illumination. Finally, the closing essays in the volume indicate conceptual links between ethics and science. John Ladd argues for the moral responsibility of the scientist, and Stephen Toulmin and Loren Graham explore the ways in which scientists have understood and can understand the interconnection of ethics and science. In closing with these essays, the volume signals the leitmotif of the modern age. Science is continually evoking ethical issues either directly or through refashioning our understanding of ourselves and of our state in the cosmos. Man is recurringly pressed to see how prevailing values can control science as well as be compatible with prevailing scientific views.

As this selection shows, the research from which these essays was drawn was necessarily interdisciplinary. This was unavoidable, for each discipline casts doubt upon the other and calls its charge into question. The analysis was, therefore, multiperspectival in enlisting philosophers, scientists, theologians, and historians. Though the deliverances of this undertaking are in part incomplete, in part fragmentary, and in part tentative, they suggest well that future explorations must similarly be interdisciplinary, for the questions and puzzles of the place of ethics and of science are in the end inseparable. This, though, should not be unexpected, given the history of the modern age, which was born out of intertwining ethical and scientific puzzles about the nature of the human condition. An understanding of the nature of man and the human condition will, as these essays show, be found not only in distinguishing but also in relating the grand human endeavors of valuing, believing, and knowing.

Daniel Callahan
The Hastings Center

H. Tristram Engelhardt, Jr.
Kennedy Institute of Ethics

Contents

II. Religion and the Foundations of Ethics

III. Science, Ethics, and Values

IV. Knowing and Valuing

I

The Foundations of Ethics

1

A Crisis in Moral Philosophy: Why Is the Search for the Foundations of Ethics So Frustrating?

Alasdair MacIntyre

THE NEED TO INQUIRE about the foundations of ethics arises intermittently; when it does arise, it generally represents a point of crisis for a culture. In different periods in the past of our own culture the oracles that have been resorted to in such situations have been of various kinds: Hellenistic cults, the *imperium* of Augustus, and the rule of St. Benedict all represent responses to such crises. But at least three times it has been the moral philosophers who have been summoned: in the twelfth century when "Ethica" took on the meaning transmitted to our word "ethics"; in the eighteenth and nineteenth centuries when a shared, secular rational form of moral justification was required to fill the place left empty by the diminution of religious authority; and now.

The ability to respond adequately to this kind of cultural need depends of course on whether those summoned possess intellectual and moral resources that transcend the immediate crisis, which enable them to say to the culture what the culture cannot—or can no longer—say to itself. For if the crisis is so pervasive that it has invaded every aspect of our intellectual and moral lives, then what we take to be resources for the treatment of our condition may turn out themselves to be infected areas. Karl Kraus's famous remark that psychoanalysis is a symptom of the very disease of which it professes to be the cure may turn out to have application to other disciplines.

I am going to argue that Kraus's remark applies to a good deal of work in recent and contemporary English and American moral philosophy. (Note that I am not at all suggesting that outside the Anglo-Saxon world they order these things better; *au contraire*.) I shall proceed in the following way: First I shall describe what I take to be the symptoms of moral crisis in our culture and their historical roots; secondly, I shall describe what I take to be the key features of recent moral philosophy; thirdly, I shall conclude from my description that such moral philosophy is essentially a reflection of our cultural condition and lacks the resources to correct its disorders; and finally, I shall inquire why this is so.

Symptoms of Moral Crisis

The superficial symptoms of moral disorder are not difficult to identify: what can be going on when the *New York Times* announces that ethics is now fashionable? What can be said of a culture in which morality is periodically "rediscovered"? Why is instant but short-lived moral indignation endemic among us? What are we to make of a society in whose *liberal* iconography a few years ago the diabolical face of Richard Nixon was counterbalanced by the angelic benignity of a Sam Ervin, it being for that purpose obliterated from consciousness that Senator Ervin had voted against every piece of civil rights legislation ever proposed in the Congress? What are we to make of those politicians and academics who have already so successfully forgotten what they did during the Vietnam War? Who now remembers the present President's response to Lieutenant Calley's courtmartial conviction?

What the answers to such questions establish is that overt moral stances in our culture tend to have a temporary and a fragile nature. These characteristics are, I suggest, rooted in the character of contemporary moral debate and contemporary moral conviction. It is a central feature of contemporary moral debates that they are unsettlable and interminable. For when rival conclusions are deployed against one another—such as "All modern wars are wrong," "Only anti-imperialist wars of liberation are justified," "Sometimes a great power must go to war to preserve that balance of power which peace requires," *or* "All abortion is murder," "Every pregnant woman has a right to an abortion," "Some abortions are justified, others not"—they are rationally defended by derivation from premises that turn out to be incommensurable with each other. Premises that invoke a notion of a just war derived from medieval theology are matched against premises about liberation and war derived partly from Fichte and partly from Marx, and both are in conflict with conceptions that count Machiavelli as ancestor. Premises about the moral law with a Thomistic and biblical background are matched against premises about individual rights that owe a good deal to Tom Paine, Mary Wollstonecraft, and John Locke; and both are in conflict with post-Benthamite notions of utility.

I call such premises incommensurable with each other precisely because the metaphor of weighing claims that invoke rights against claims that invoke utility, or claims that invoke justice against claims that invoke freedom, in some sort of moral scale is empty of application. There are no scales, or at least this culture does not possess any. Hence moral arguments in one way terminate very quickly and in another way are interminable. Because no argument can be carried through to a victorious conclusion, argument characteristically gives way to the mere and increasingly shrill battle of assertion with counterassertion. This is bad enough, but it is not all.

For if I have no adequately good reasons to give you to convince you that you should exchange your premises for mine, then it follows that I should have adopted my premises rather than yours, when I originally adopted my position. The absence of a shared rational criterion turns out to imply an initial arbitrariness in each one of us—or so it seems.

This conjunction of an inability to convince others and a sense of arbitrariness in ourselves is a distinctive characteristic of the American present. It provides a background against which rapid shifts of feeling become an intelligible phenomenon, against which it is less surprising to find so much moral self-consciousness combined with so little moral stability. It is unsurprising also that a need to inquire about the foundations of ethics arises, independently of any special concerns with particular areas of the moral life. What produced this condition?

Part of the answer is clear, even if only part: our society stands at the meeting-point of a number of different histories, each of them the bearer of a highly particular kind of moral tradition, each of those traditions to some large degree mutilated and fragmented by its encounter with the others. The institutions of the American polity, with their appeal to abstract universality, and to consensus, are in fact a place of encounter for rival and incompatible outlooks to a degree that the consensus itself requires should not be acknowledged. The image of the American is a mask that, because it must be worn by blacks, Indians, Japanese and Swedes, by Irish Catholics, New England Puritans, German Lutherans, and rootless secularists, can fit no face very well. It is small wonder that the confusions of pluralism are articulated at the level of moral argument in the form of a mishmash of conceptual fragments.

Key Features of Modern Moral Philosophy

There are three central features of modern moral philosophy: its appeal to intuitions, its handling of the notion of reason, and its inability to settle questions of priority between rival moral claims. I shall only be able to give a few examples to illustrate my claims, but I shall therefore take care to use examples that have a certain typicality and that enjoy a certain prestige. My final suggestion will be that modern analytical moral philosophy is essentially a ghost discipline; its contemporary practitioners are pale shadows of eighteenth- and nineteenth-century predecessors and their failures simply reiterate the failures of those predecessors.

One of the key ancestors of modern moral philosophy is of course Henry Sidgwick. It is Sidgwick whose use of the word "intuition" bridges the gap from its nineteenth-century to its twentieth-century usage. And it was Sidgwick who took it to be the task of moral philosophy to articulate, to systematize, and to bring into a coherent rational whole our prephilosophical moral intuitions, as does John Rawls nowadays—and as does J. O. Urmson and as did Sir David Ross. What is surprising is that, even when such authors acknowledge a debt to Sidgwick, they never notice his own conclusion: where he had hoped to find Cosmos, he had found Chaos. That is, they do not face the possibility that our prephilosophical intuitions do not form a coherent and consistent set and therefore cannot be systematically and rationally articulated as a whole. Yet the evidence is close at hand. Rawls constructs what he takes to be *the* concept of justice in terms of a set of principles of patterns of distribution; Nozick retorts with arguments starting from premises that are certainly as widely held as are Rawls's. From this he then is able to show that if his premises are conceded, the concept of justice cannot be elucidated in terms of any pattern of distribution. The structure of the debate between them is thus for all its philosophical sophistication at once reminiscent of the modes of everyday moral argument. Why should I accept Nozick's premises? He furnishes me with no reasons, but with a promissory note. Why should I accept Rawls's premises? They are, so he argues, those that would be accepted by hypothetical rational beings whose ignorance of their actual position in any social hierarchy enables them to plan a type of social order in which the liberty of each is maximized, in which inequalities are tolerated only insofar as they have the effect of improving the lot of the least well-off, and in which the good of liberty has priority over that of equality.

But why should I in my actual social condition choose to accept what those hypothetical rational beings would choose, rather than for example Nozick's premises about natural rights? And why should I accept what Rawls says about the priority of liberty over equality? Many commentators have identified a weakness in Rawls's answer to this latter question; but the weakness of Rawls's position is as clear when we consider the former question.

Rawls might suggest that if I do not accept his premises, I myself will fail as a rational person. This type of consideration has been central to the work of a number of other moral philosophers and notably to that of R. M. Hare, who has deplored

Rawls's appeal to intuitions and has urged that in the conception of moral reasoning alone can we find adequate means for discriminating those principles that we ought to accept from those that we ought to reject. But Hare is only able to carry through his project—which turns on the fact that I cannot consistently apply universal principles to others that I am not prepared to apply in like circumstances to myself—by excluding from it a class of agents whom he calls "fanatics," a class that includes Nazis who are prepared to embrace such principles as "Let all Jews be put to death and let this be done even if it is discovered that I am a Jew."

It follows that we do not discriminate moral principles, even on Hare's view, by logic or reason alone, but only—at best—by conjoining the requirements of logic or reason with the nonlogical requirement that moral agents shall not be, in Hare's special sense, fanatics. And there seem no good arguments for accepting this latter point and at least one good argument against it; surely to want political office-holders to hold such principles as "Let all incompetent political office-holders be deprived of office and let this be done even if it is discovered that I am incompetent." It is difficult not to see in this part of Hare's position a covert, even if mistaken, appeal to intuitions as clear as any in Rawls.

The moral that I want to draw is simple and twofold; intuitions are no safe guide, and the conception of reason—usually a conception of consistency, sometimes eked out by decision theory—employed in moral philosophy is too weak a notion to yield any content to moral principles. What is wrong with being morally unprincipled is not primarily that one is being *inconsistent* and it is not even clear that the unprincipled *are* inconsistent, for it seems to be the case that in order to be practically inconsistent one first needs to have *principles*. (Otherwise what is it about one that is inconsistent?) Consider those two charming scoundrels who lounge insolently at the entrance to modernity, Diderot's *Lui* in *Le Neveu de Rameau* and Kierkegaard's 'A' in *Enten-Eller*. Both boast that they abide by no rules. What have Rawls and Hare to say to them? Rawls and Hare might well answer—and I sympathize with their answer—that it is not required of a moral theory that it be able to convince scoundrels, no matter how intelligent. A certain seriousness in the hearer is also required.

But if this was to be their reply—and I must not put words in their mouths—it does suggest that their arguments will only find a starting-point with hearers who are already convinced that it is right to lead a principled life—for what else is it to be serious— where by "principled" we mean something much more than any notion of rationality can supply. And indeed I take it that just this *is* generally presupposed in modern moral philosophy.

One outcome of this weakness in the central conceptions of such moral philosophy is that it presents us with no way of dealing with conflicts of rules or principles. Methods of justification for individual rules or principles are overabundant: we have utilitarian justifications, contractarian justifications, universalizability justifications, intuitionist justifications, and each of these in more than one variety. But from Ross to Rawls the treatment of priority questions is notoriously weak. For it always presupposes some prior unargued position about how our values are to be organized. Here arbitrariness becomes visible.

These failures have historical roots. Analytical moral philosophers, who have often treated the history of philosophy as an optional extra for philosophers (much like dancing lessons at a private school, they lend a touch of elegance, but are scarcely essential), have often recognized their particular debts to Kant, who is clearly the ancestor of the concept of reason in Hare, or to Hume or to Mill or to whomever. What they have not recognized is that they have been systematically retreading the ground of the great eighteenth- and nineteenth-century debates and now emerge with no greater success than their predecessors. Kant's notorious failure to derive substantial moral principles from a purely formal concept of practical reason has simply been repeated by his successors; and Hume and Mill have had their ghosts too.

One feature of the eighteenth-century debate that has reappeared is the superiority of negative over positive argument. What we owe to Hume, Smith, Diderot, Kant, and Mill are good arguments *against* the positions of their rivals; each destroys the pretentions of the others, while failing to establish his own position. Similarly with recent moral philosophy—instead of myself adverting to its weaknesses, I might simply have quoted each author against some other; Hare against Rawls, Warnock against

Hare, Harman against Nagel, and so on. There is indeed a striking consensus against modern analytical moral philosophy concealed within it: every modern moral philosopher is against all modern moral philosophers except himself and his immediate allies. There is scarcely a need for any external attack.

Moral Philosophy and Modern Culture

What is striking then is the concordance between the ordinary contemporary moral consciousness and the condition of analytical moral philosophy. Precisely at those points at which the ordinary moral consciousness reveals arbitrariness and instability analytical moral philosophy discovers problems insoluble by it with any of the means available to it. It is difficult to resist the conclusion that such moral philosophy is a mirror-image of its age; and this conclusion is reinforced by attention to detail. Just as the inability of the adherents of each contemporary moral standpoint to convince the protagonists of other standpoints is reflected in the inability of moral philosophy to provide agreed rational criteria by which to judge moral argument, so a number of particular moral positions are mirrored in some moral philosopher's account. Not all, for moral philosophers are characteristically middle-class liberals, and it is unsurprising therefore that the moral stance presented in philosophical guise is normally that of such liberalism. But even that liberalism has its varieties and so the contemporary political liberals of *Time* can inspect their portraits in Rawls's theory of justice, while the contemporary economic liberals of *Newsweek* can inspect *their* portrait in Nozick's theory. There is therefore a case to be made that analytical moral philosophy is one of the many ideological masks worn by modern liberalism. But to pursue that case would be to overemphasize a merely negative polemic. Instead I want to try to gain a new perspective both on the predicament of contemporary morality and on the related predicament of contemporary moral philosophy. One way to do this is to alienate oneself from the present by adopting some external standpoint: what standpoint more external than that of Polynesia in the late eighteenth century?

In the journal of Captain James Cook's third voyage, Cook

records the first discovery by English speakers of the Polynesian word *taboo*. The English seamen had been astonished at what they took to be the lax sexual habits of the Polynesians and were even more astonished to discover the sharp contrast with the rigorous prohibition placed on such conduct as that of men and women eating together. When they enquired why men and women were prohibited from eating together, they were told that that practice was *taboo*. But when they enquired further what *taboo* meant, they could get little further information. Clearly *taboo* did not simply mean *prohibited*; for to say that something—person or practice or theory—is *taboo* is to give some particular sort of reason for its prohibition. But what sort of reason? It has not only been Cook's seamen who have had trouble with that question; from James Frazer and Edward Tylor to Franz Steiner and Mary Douglas the anthropologists have had to struggle with it. From that struggle two keys to the problem emerge. The first is the significance of the fact that Cook's seamen were unable to get any intelligible reply to their queries from their native informants. What this suggests is that the native informants themselves did not really understand the word they were using, and this suggestion is reinforced by the ease with which and the lack of social consequences when Kamehameha II abolished the taboos in Hawaii forty years later in 1819.

But how could the Polynesians come to be using a word which they themselves did not really understand? Here Steiner and Douglas are illuminating. For they both suggest that taboo rules often and perhaps characteristically have a two-stage history. In the first stage taboo rules are embedded in a context that confers intelligibility upon them. So Mary Douglas has argued that the taboo rules of Deuteronomy presuppose a cosmology and a taxonomy of a certain kind. Deprive the taboo rules of their original context and they at once are apt to appear as a set of arbitrary prohibitions, as indeed they characteristically do appear when the initial context is lost, when those background beliefs in the light of which the taboo rules had originally been understood have not only been abandoned but forgotten.

In such a situation the rules have been deprived of any status that can secure their authority and, if they do not acquire some new status quickly, both their interpretation and their justification become debatable. When the resources of a culture are too meager to carry through the task of reinterpretation, then the task of justification becomes impossible. Hence the relatively easy, although to some contemporary observers astonishing, victory of Kamehameha II over the taboos (and the creation thereby of a moral vacuum in which the banalities of the New England Protestant missionaries were received all too quickly). But had Polynesian culture enjoyed the blessings of analytical philosophy it is all too clear that the question of the meaning of *taboo* could have been resolved in a number of ways. *Taboo*, it would have been said by one party, is clearly the name of a nonnatural property; and precisely the same reasoning which led Moore to see *good* as the name of such a property and Prichard and Ross to see *obligatory* and *right* as the names of such properties would have been available to show that *taboo* is the name of such a property. Another party would doubtless have argued that "This is taboo" means roughly the same as "I disapprove of this; do so as well"; and precisely the same reasoning which led Stevenson and Ayer to see "good" as having primarily an emotive use would have been available to support the emotive theory of *taboo*. A third party would presumably have arisen, which would have argued that the grammatical form of "This is taboo" disguises a universalizable imperative prescription.

The pointlessness of this imaginary debate arises from a shared presupposition of the contending parties, namely that the set of rules whose status and justification they are investigating provides an adequately demarcated subject-matter for investigation, provides the material for an autonomous field of study. We from our standpoint in the real world know that this is not the case, that there is no way to understand the character of the taboo rules, except as a survival from some previous, more elaborate cultural background. We know also and as a consequence that any theory that makes the taboo rules of the late eighteenth century in Polynesia intelligible without reference to their history is necessarily a false theory; the only true theory can be one that exhibits their unintelligibility as they stand at that moment in time. Moreover the only adequate true theory will be one that will *both* enable us to distinguish between what it is for a set of taboo rules and practices to be in good order and what it is for a set of such rules and practices to have been fragmented and thrown into disorder *and* enable us to understand the historical transitions by which the latter state emerged from the former. Only the writing of a certain kind of history will supply what we need.

And now the question inexorably arises in the light of my earlier argument: why should we think about real analytical moral philosophers such as Moore, Ross, Prichard, Stevenson, Hare, and the rest in any way different from that in which we were thinking just now about their imaginary Polynesian counterparts? Why should we think about *good, right* and *obligatory* in any different way from that in which we think about *taboo*? The attempt to answer this question will at once raise another: why should we not treat the moral utterances of our own cultures as *survivals*? But from what then did they survive?

The answer is in surprisingly large part that the patterns of common moral utterance in our culture are the graveyard for fragments of culturally dead large-scale philosophical *systems*. In everyday moral arguments in bars and boardrooms, in newspapers and on television, in which rival conclusions about war are canvassed, we find, as I already noted, remnants of the medieval doctrine of the just war contending against cut-down, secondhand versions of utilitarianism, both being confronted in turn by amateur Machiavellianism. And in a precisely similar way debates about abortion, about death and dying, about marriage and the family, about the place of law in society and about the relationship of justice to equality, to desert, and to charity become encounters between a wide range of variously truncated concepts and theories out of our different pasts.

It is because of this that the procedures of piecemeal philosophical analysis are so inadequate. They become in practice a kind of unsystematic conceptual archaeology whose practitioners possess no means of distinguishing the different aspects of our past of which our present is so very largely composed. So it produces, piece by piece, as *what we would say* or as *the concept of x* or as *our commonsense beliefs* what are in fact survivals from large-scale philosophical and theological systems that have been deprived of their original context.

It is unsurprising as a result that the contemporary moral philosopher has so little to say to the crises of contemporary morality. For he fails to understand either himself or that morality historically; and in so failing he condemns himself to handling systematically rival positions without that context of systematic thought that was and is required even to define the nature of such rivalries, let alone to decide between the contending positions. Consider just one such juxtaposition: that of modern consequentialism to its absolutist rivals and critics.

Every moral scheme contains a set of injunctions to and prohibitions of particular types of action on the one hand ("Do not murder," "Do not bear false witness," "Honor thy father and thy mother") and a general injunction to do good and to avoid and frustrate evil on the other. But the different relationship between these two elements is one of the principal differences between rival and alternative moral schemes. For on the one hand Thomists and Kantians make what they take to be the injunctions and prohibitions of the moral law absolute and exceptionless; it follows that our duties to promote the good of others and of ourselves and to prevent harm to others and to ourselves are bounded and limited by the injunctions and prohibitions of the moral law. On no occasion whatsoever may I disobey a precept of the moral law in order to promote the general good or to avoid any degree of ruin whatsoever; and there can be no question of weighing or balancing the beneficial consequences that might be reasonably predicted to result from such a breach on a particular occasion against the importance of obeying the precept.

A utilitarian by contrast sees any injunction to or prohibition of any particular type of action as having only provisional and conditional force. Rules of conduct, wrote Mill, "point out the manner in which it will be least perilous to act, where time and means do not exist for analyzing the actual circumstances of the case," but when circumstances permit us to carry through such an analysis, any rule may be suspended or modified or replaced in the interests of promoting the greatest happiness or the least pain. Thus the precepts of morality are bounded and limited by our calculation of the general good.

Between the Kantian position and the act utilitarian position a number of others are ranged. At the utilitarian end of the spectrum a rule utilitarian may treat rules with a less conditional and provisional respect than does the act utilitarian, although he will hold that the rules themselves must be subject to an evaluation of the consequences of their being generally followed; and, since contingent circumstances change, even the rules that seem to offer the best possible reason to respect may have to be reevaluated from time to time. Consequently, the rule utilitarian can never assert of any specific type of action that it is forbidden irrespective of circumstances any more than the act utilitarian can; and this would remain true, even if David Lyon's argument that rule utilitarianism collapses into act utilitarianism were not as successful as I take it to be.

Nearer the Kantian end of the spectrum—although still abhorrent to Kant—would be any moralist who holds that in some situations all choices of action involve the doing of some evil, but that some evils are lesser than others. Such a moralist would resemble the utilitarians in holding that sometimes it is necessary to do evil, but unlike a utilitarian would still see the best possible action open to him as evil.

Nonetheless, although these intermediate positions are important, I believe that we can evaluate their claims upon our allegiance only if we first consider the conflict between those who hold that certain types of action ought to be done or not done irrespective of circumstances and consequences and those who deny this. I wish for the moment, although only for the moment, to consider these contentions in forms in which they are least entangled with the variety of philosophical contexts in which they have been at home. After all, moralists as different as Aristotle, St. Paul, and Aquinas hold the former absolutist position as stringently as do Kantians; and consequentialists, to borrow G.E.M. Anscombe's term for them, are of many varieties also. It is enough to remember the contrast between the Benthamites and the followers of G.E. Moore.

What is striking is the way in which the stauncher adherents of both views find their own position apparently obviously true and their opponents equally obviously false. So Anscombe once wrote that "if someone really thinks, *in advance*, that it is open to question whether such an action as procuring the judicial execution of the innocent should be quite excluded from consideration—I do not want to argue with him; he shows a corrupt mind." (*Modern Moral Philosophy*, Philosophy, Vol. XXXIII, No. 126, p. 17.) Whereas Jonathan Bennett thinks it equally obvious that if predicted consequences of harm are recognized as a reason for not acting in certain types of case, then no prohibition of any type of action whatsoever irrespective of consequences can be rationally defensible and to uphold together such a recognition and such a prohibition can only be the consequence of "muddle" (*Whatever the Consequences*, Analysis, 26, p. 102) or, even perhaps worse, "conservatism."

But what is it about which the rival protagonists are in fact disagreeing? There are at least, so I suspect, three major areas of disagreement involved. One centers around the concepts of causality, predictability, and intentionality and involves the relationship of consciousness to the world. Another is concerned with the concepts of law, evil, emotion, and the integrity of the self. A third focuses upon the relationship of individual identity to social identity and involves the question of the relation of ethics to politics. Let me consider each in turn briefly.

What is an action? What is the connection between, what is the distinction between an action and its effects, results or consequences? Can causal connections be established without a knowledge of law-like generalizations? Can causal relationships be established where one term of the relationship has to be characterized nonextensionally, that is, in terms of an agent's beliefs and intentions? This group of questions is conventionally allocated to the philosophy of action or to the philosophy of mind; but an answer to them—or at the very least some theories about why we do not need an answer to them—is presupposed by any account of morality. For what an agent is or can be depends upon what the answers are.

The force of this consideration can be brought out by considering the answers presupposed by some novelists. Dickens's world is one of brisk practical effects where sentiments can become deeds the moment the material in which the deeds can be embodied, money and persons, becomes available and in which harm and benefit are matters of immediate human agency. Proust's world by contrast is one in which the inaccessibility of each consciousness to others—that range of illusions that constitutes a hall of distorting mirrors—makes the character of our actions in the external world ("in what?" one is sometimes disposed to say in Proustian moments) essentially ambiguous. The irrefragable realities are pain, disillusionment, and art. In Tolstoy's world art is one of the illusions and the notion of large-scale contrivance is equally illusory: victories in war and the rise and fall of empires are not made or unmade, they happen. All that is to hand is the immediate moral deed.

It is crucial to recognize that in answering the questions or evaluating the answers of an Anscombe, a Quine, a Davidson, or a Wisdom on the philosophy of causality, action, and mind, we are deciding the case between Dickens, Tolstoy, and Proust, deciding it perhaps against all of them. What is not open to us is to leave the case undecided. In our actions, even if we choose not to acknowledge it, we have to inhabit some such world. Thus ethics requires a *systematic* connection with the philosophy of causality, mind, and action.

A second set of questions concerns law, evil, emotion, and the integrity of the self. Stoics, Thomists, and Kantians perceive the self as situated in a cosmic order in which it can receive fatal or near fatal wounds. Utilitarians perceive the self as always able to choose the most beneficial or least harmful course of action open to it, *whatever* that may involve the self in doing. No deed is morally beyond the self; there are no limits. But from this standpoint, as Bernard Williams has noted, the traditional notion of a virtue of integrity disappears; for integrity consists precisely in setting unbreakable limits to what one will do. For Stoics, Thomists, and Kantians therefore my passions must be educated by reason, lest they betray my integrity; and this requires a thesis about the relation of reason to the passions and of both to law and to breaches of law. For a central distinctive emotion in the Thomist and Kantian schemes at least has to become that of remorse, the embodiment in feeling of repentance. Whereas a Utilitarian scheme may have some room for emotions of regret, but none surely for emotions of remorse or repentance. Moreover Stoics, Thomists, and Kantians believe that they confront a timeless moral order, whatever the variations in human psychology, while for Bentham and his successors the moral order can vary only within the limits imposed by a timeless psychology. Here once again it is clear that *systematic* answers to metaphysical questions are presupposed by rival moral outlooks. And so it is also with the third group of questions.

Who am I? In what role do I act? Whom do I represent in acting? Who is answerable for what I do? If I am a German now, how can I stand in relationship to a Jew now? If my father burnt his grandparents? If my father stayed home and did nothing while his grandparents were burnt? Liberal political theory has envisaged all the political and social, familial and ethnic characteristics of a moral agent as contingent and inessential except insofar as he chose them himself. Abstract, autonomous humanity has been its subject matter. But the deeds of individuals are often corporate deeds: I am my family, my country, my party, my corporation, as it presents itself to the world. Their past is my past. Hence the question arises: how is moral identity related to political identity? Aristotle, Kant, Hegel, and Marx all give different answers. Each answer presupposes a particular view of the state and of the relationship of state and citizen. So that I cannot solve the problems of ethics without making a *systematic* connection with political theory.

The implications of my earlier thesis are now clear. Ours was once a culture in which the systematic interrelationship of these questions was recognized both by philosophers at the level of theory and in the presuppositions of everyday practice. But when we left behind us the ancient, medieval, and early modern worlds, we entered a culture largely and increasingly deprived of the vision of the whole, except at the aesthetic level. Each part of our experience is detached from the rest in quite a new way; and the activities of intellectual enquiry become divided and compartmentalized along with the rest. The intellectual division of labor allocates problems in a piecemeal and partial way; and the consequent modes of thought answer very well to the experience of everyday life.

The consequences for moral philosophy are clear; it reflects in its modes the society and the culture of which it is a part. It becomes a symptom rather than a means of diagnosis. And it is unable to solve its own problems because it has been isolated as a separate and distinct form of enquiry and so has been deprived of the systematic context that those problems require for their solution.

The Fate of the Moral Sciences

The history of how moral philosophy underwent its transition from large-scale systematic enquiry to piecemeal analysis—and therefore the explanation of why the search for the foundations of ethics is so frustrating—needs to be supplemented in at least three ways, if it is to be adequately characterized. First, of course, there are the parallel intellectual transformations within adjacent enquiries. Not only has philosophy been subdivided, but the rest of the moral sciences have been similarly reapportioned. Hence arises that peculiarly modern phenomenon, the intellectual boundary stone jealously guarded by professionals and signalled by such cries as "But that's not philosophy!" or "You are really doing sociology." Adam Smith by contrast, when he published the second part of his course at Glasgow as *The Theory of the Moral Sentiments* and the fourth part as *The Wealth of Nations*, was not aware that he was contributing to more than one discipline. So moral philosophy since the eighteenth century has become partially defined in terms of what it is not or rather what it is no longer. And consequently, the history of the changes in moral philosophy will be partially unintelligible, unless it is accompanied by a history of what used to be the moral sciences and their subsequent fate. This fate is symbolized by the fact that when Mill's translator came to translate the expression "the moral sciences," he had to invent the German word *Geisteswissenschaften*, a word taken over by Dilthey and others for their own purposes; when in this century Englishmen came to translate such German writers, they proclaimed that *Geisteswissenschaften* is a word without any English equivalent.

Second there are significant questions of genre. It is far from unimportant that up to the early nineteenth century moral philosophy is written almost exclusively in books, whereas now it is written primarily in articles. The length, and therefore the possible scope, of an argument is part of what is affected by this change; but it also reflects a change in the continuities of reading of the public to which the philosophical writer addresses himself. Hume, Smith, and Mill still presuppose a generally educated public whose minds are informed by a shared stock of reading which provides both points of reference and touchstones. They seek in part, sometimes in large part, to add to the stock and alter these points of reference and touchstones. This is a very different endeavor from the contemporary professionalized contributions to a dialogue to be shared only by professors. Philosophy becomes not only piecemeal, but occasional. (It is perhaps worth noting here that part of the destruction of the generally educated mind is the sheer multiplication of professional philosophical literature. From this point of view the increase in the number of philosophical journals—and the pressure to write that produces that increase—are almost unmitigated evils. The case for making nonpublication a prerequisite for tenure or promotion is becoming very strong.)

Finally it would be necessary to reflect upon the *ideological* functions served by recent moral philosophy's reflection of the liberal *status quo*. What is clear at the very least is that a moral philosophy which aspires to put our intuitions in order is going to be protective of those intuitions in one way, while a moral philosophy that claims to derive its tenets from an analysis of *what it is to be rational*, but that in fact has a large unadmitted component whose roots are quite other, is likely to be protective of them in another way. That recent moral philosophy should function in this protective way is scarcely surprising if I am right in identifying that philosophy as the heir of the eighteenth century; for the morality that it protects is the heir of the eighteenth century too. But the eighteenth century claimed for its liberalism epistemological foundations of a kind philosophy has since had to repudiate; *we* hold no nontrivial truths to be self-evident, *we* cannot accept Bentham's psychology or Kant's view of the powers of reason. Thus liberalism itself became foundationless; and since the morality of our age is liberal we have one more reason to expect the search for the foundations of ethics to be unrewarded.

Commentary

Ethics, Foundations, and Science: Response to Alasdair MacIntyre

Gerald Dworkin

. . . The foundations of ethics . . . those universal principles, from which all censure or approbation is ultimately derived.

Hume

Foundations of morality are like all other foundations; if you dig too much about them the superstructure will come tumbling down.

Butler

To a philosopher the only sight less cheering than MacIntyre's portrait of philosophers attacking the views of other philosophers is that of a philosopher attacking philosophy. I propose to defend moral philosophy against MacIntyre's critique. I shall focus on the work of John Rawls, both because I believe that MacIntyre's criticisms are incorrect, and because I believe that a proper understanding of Rawls's theory can throw some light on issues concerning the foundations of ethics as well as their relationship to science. It is strange that so little philosophical attention has been paid to specifying what might be meant by reference to the foundations of ethics, and I shall make some initial attempts to clarify that question.

I

MacIntyre criticizes three central features of modern moral philosophy: its reliance on intuitions, its use of the notion of

21

reason, and its inability to settle priority questions involving rival moral claims. Let us consider each of these features as they arise in Rawls's work.

The starting point for moral theory, according to Rawls, is our considered moral judgments, i.e., those moral judgments (which can be about particular actions or institutions or about principles or reasons for action) that we are most confident about and that have been formed under conditions most conducive to sound judgment. The first task of moral theory is to formulate a set of principles or rules that accounts for these judgments. MacIntyre points out that we have no reason to suppose this set is consistent and, therefore, capable of being systematically and rationally articulated but whether this is so is an empirical question and it is reasonable from a methodological standpoint to assume consistency until we find otherwise.

The methodological device Rawls uses to generate the principles of distributive justice is that of a hypothetical social contract.[1] MacIntyre asks why we should accept as correct, principles chosen by these contractors rather than, say, Nozick's views about natural rights. It is essential to recognize that it is only part of Rawls's defense that the principles chosen account for our considered judgments. If this were the whole story then we would, at most, have explained our moral judgments, not justified them. We would be doing moral psychology not moral philosophy. What is needed is what Kant called a "deduction," i.e., establishing a claim to legitimacy. This is why Rawls's own analogy to the task of the theoretical linguist is faulty.

Rawls argues for the correctness of the principles chosen in terms of the independent plausibility of the contractual scheme. It is obvious that such a scheme makes many assumptions about the nature of the choice situation. There are assumptions about the list of principles from which the contractors are to choose (a small set suggested by the history of moral theory), the formal constraints on the nature of the principles (no proper names), the rationality of the contractors (nonenvious), the information available to them (no knowledge of their social class), the procedures governing the choice (unanimity), the domain that the principles are supposed to regulate (the basic structure of the society), and others. These assumptions are in turn justified in terms of a large number of complex theoretical considerations. These include a theory of the nature of persons (autonomous individuals who assume responsibility for their fundamental projects), a theory of the function of principles of justice (to provide an ordering of conflicting claims concerning the division of the products of social cooperation), a theory about the range of application of moral principles (cases likely to arise given the circumstances that human beings are in), a theory of fair procedures (which facts it is morally relevant for the contractors to know), a theory of moral motivation (the contractors have, and view themselves as having, a sense of justice, and their desire to act on this conception normally determines their conduct), and more. The justification of a set of moral principles is an enormously complicated matter of seeing how the principles both account for considered judgments and cohere with, follow from, are made plausible by (these are quite distinct relations of support) a large body of other theories, views, and assumptions.

Let me now enumerate what I consider to be mistakes in MacIntyre's accounts of Rawls. First, it is misleading to speak of Rawls constructing "*the* concept of justice" implying a moral imperialism. Rawls distinguishes between the concept of justice (which is a purely formal notion characterized by the absence of arbitrary distinctions between persons and by rules determining a proper balance among competing claims) and conceptions of justice which consist of the substantive principles which provide the content for the concept. The disagreement between Rawls and Nozick is over conceptions of justice, not concepts. Second, Rawls does not deny that our "intuitions" may be incoherent. He starts with them, he does not end with them, and he explicitly admits that even after reaching what he calls "reflective equilibrium," different persons may "affirm opposing conceptions." Third, it is not an answer that "Rawls *might* give" (assuming consistency) to why we should accept his premises that those who do not cannot be considered rational. Rawls agrees with MacIntyre that no conception of reason is sufficient to yield moral principles with substantive content.

MacIntyre need not worry about putting words in Rawls's mouth when he suggests that Rawls's arguments assume persons "who are already convinced that it is right to lead a principled life." As I indicated above, Rawls explicitly assumes the contractors have a sense of justice. But why does MacIntyre think that this is a "weakness" that prevents moral theory from dealing with conflicts of rules or principles? What does working out priority questions have to do with assumptions about moral motivation?

Finally, I disagree with the claim that Rawls's treatment of priority questions is "arbitrary." It may not be correct but it is argued for in terms of a conception of the person as autonomous, i.e., as desiring to retain the capacity to change his system of final ends and to be active in choosing his own conception of the good. Such a person will, if rational, seek to preserve access to information and the power to shape his political and cultural environment. He ought, therefore, to accord a priority to the liberties of citizenship over more material goods (at least once a certain level of abundance has been reached). Perhaps this argument only applies to persons who conceive of themselves in a way that has been shaped by social and historical circumstances. But this fact by itself does not show that the claim of priority for liberty is arbitrary.

Let me conclude my direct commentary by noting how much of Rawls's work runs counter to the diagnosis MacIntyre gives of the state of contemporary moral philosophy. It is a *book*, not an article, and a *big* book. It is not addressed only to professional philosophers nor does it respect narrow intellectual boundaries. It is informed by and contributes to decision theory, economics, and moral psychology. It is linked in the most direct way to the history of philosophy. The debt to Kant is most obvious, but Aristotle, Marx, Rousseau, Mill, and Sidgwick all have their influence. It is not piecemeal, but systematic and comprehensive. Lest it be thought I am arguing from the isolated case, it should be noted that there are a number of philosophers who have, in recent years, written books that share many of the above features—Fried, Donagan, Nozick, Gewirth, Brandt, and Richards.

II

Does Rawls's theory, if correct, provide us with foundations for ethics? What is the relationship of such a theory to science?

An answer to either of these questions requires some specification of what is meant by the idea of ethical foundations. Philosophers have meant very different things by this obscure phrase.

Some philosophers have thought of it as a question about motivation. Why should any rational person do what is morally correct? Do we have good reasons to do what is right? Do moral principles have, by themselves, motivational force? Are there considerations that can convince all rational persons to accept certain moral principles as correct? Notice that all these questions presuppose that we know very well what is right and what is wrong; which principles are correct and which faulty. The issue is either how to convince others or get ourselves to do what we know to be right. I shall call this set of issues that of motivational foundations.

Other philosophers have worried about questions of justification. How do we tell which principles are correct? Is there a decision procedure for resolving moral problems? How do we prove that courage is a virtue? What priority rules can we justify? What are the starting points for moral reasoning? Is there a class of self-evident or a priori truths that can be used as premises to support less fundamental propositions? Let us call this set of questions that of the epistemological foundations of ethics. It is, I suppose, this set of issues that occurs to most people as foundational.

Still other philosophers have worried about the role of objectivity and truth in moral theory. Are the statements of ethics bearers of truth-values? Are values part of the world, out there, in the way that physical objects are? Do we discover values or choose them? Can we reduce moral judgments to nonmoral ones? Call this the question of ontological foundations.

With respect to each of these types of foundational issues, I want to say something about how Rawls's theory bears on them and about their relationship to science (which I understand to be any general, systematic, theoretically and empirically grounded knowledge about the natural and social world).

Rawls does not attempt to show that *any* rational person has good reason to develop or maintain a sense of justice. We cannot simply decide to alter our character at will. We always begin from where we are, and what we have reason to develop depends in large part on our existing preferences. Rawls does assume that there is psychological evidence that people raised under conditions of a just society will have a sense of justice and that all of us have, at least, the capacity to develop such a sense. He does, moreover, argue that for most persons (not all) we can give good reasons why they ought to affirm and maintain their sense of justice; why it is good *for* the person to be just. This argument relies on contingent truths of moral psychology. Unlike the argument that Nagel gives in *The Possibility of Altruism*, Rawls does not claim to show on a priori grounds that ethical requirements have motivational force for rational agents. Thus the findings of psychology or theories of biological motivation, such as reciprocal altruism or the results of game-theoretical work on the Prisoners Dilemma and coordination problems, are all relevant to questions of motivational foundations. I say relevant but not dispositive, for all such knowledge has to be mediated by philosophical investigation of concepts such as "good reason," "rationality," "prudential," and so forth.

With respect to the ontological issues, Rawls's view is that the theory is neutral with respect to the question of the objectivity of moral judgments or, at least, that an answer to these questions will be forthcoming only after we have studied in a systematic fashion various alternative moral theories. He suggests that it may be a necessary condition for the existence of objective moral truths that there be sufficient convergence among the various moral conceptions that are developed in reflective equilibrium. My own view is that intersubjective agreement is neither necessary nor sufficient for establishing objectivity. One must always know why there is agreement or lack of it. Is the agreement accidental or does it reflect essential features of human nature? Has the agreement been manipulated or is it the product of processes that we believe are related in rational ways to the securing of agreement? The argument for objectivity has to be one about the best explanation of intersubjective agreement.

If, for example, the correct explanation of such agreement is that the favored set of principles provides a solution to coordination problems that any creatures living in a complex society would face, or if the explanation is in terms of reproductive fitness à la Alexander, then we will be relying on certain objective features of the world. We would be making the claim that creatures constructed with certain features and facing certain problems in given circumstances would arrive at the following beliefs. This seems to me as much objectivity as we can get and as much as we need. Obviously, the findings of decision theory, evolutionary biology, and moral anthropology are all relevant to such a claim.

Finally we come to the issue of epistemological foundations. On a number of interpretations of this question a theory such as Rawls's suggests a negative answer. There are no self-evident moral truths that have substantive content. If "murder is wrong" is self-evident that is because we are defining murder as wrongful killing. If, on the other hand, murder is defined in terms of the deliberate killing of the innocent, then only a theory will give content to the notion of innocence. There are no incorrigible intuitions that provide a safe starting point for ethical reflection. In Neurath's metaphor we are always rebuilding the ship while we are sailing. There is no "faculty" (not even Harvard's) which perceives the truth of moral claims. No analysis of the nature of moral concepts can establish a priori the truth of ethical claims. Nor can we reduce the moral to the nonmoral. As an examination of Rawls's system shows, there are moral assumptions present in the theory from the start. At most one may be able to make partial reductions in the sense that one may be able to reduce rights to ideals or rules to virtues.

It may be that, as similar investigations of scientific and common-sense knowledge seem to show, all justification is ultimately circular. What one is looking for is as large a circle as possible.

Again, however, it is clear that if justification is going to take the kind of coherence form suggested by Rawls's theory, then scientific knowledge will be relevant. Such knowledge will enter into the argument at rather different levels. Some knowledge will be relevant to the feasibility of various moral and political principles. Thus, one way of arguing for or against a principle of positive responsibility to render aid to others is in terms of the constraints on liberty and autonomy which such principles pose, and to ask whether we can commit ourselves to such constraints and expect to act in accordance with them.

Some knowledge will be relevant to questions of theory construction. For example, some recent work in social choice theory has shown that given plausible assumptions one can prove an analogue of Rawls's difference principle. But the analogous principle violates the mathematical requirement of continuity. While Rawls does not take this as a refutation, he recognizes it as an objection to his theory and seeks to explain the anomaly.

Some knowledge will be relevant to the stability of various principles, i.e., whether they tend to generate (psychologically) their own support or to undermine it. The latter is what Marxists call the "contradictions" of a social system.

Lest it be thought that the relationship between moral philosophy and science is, in the words of Kolakowski, like the relationship between the city and the countryside—the former receiving life-giving sustenance and giving back in return garbage—it should be noticed that the interaction proceeds in both directions. Rawls's theory has stimulated work in social psychology, economics, and social choice theory.

One last point. It is not clear to me whether MacIntyre intends to suggest that whatever moral crises we face would or could be alleviated by discovering foundations for ethics. Such a hope would be as false in its way as the fear that Frege expressed when Russell pointed out a contradiction in the system Frege invented as a foundation of arithmetic. Frege wrote to Russell that "arithmetic totters." But we no more need foundations in order to count correctly than we need them in order to act correctly.

NOTES

1. For the most recent development and elaboration of Rawls's theory see his "Reply to Alexander and Musgrave," *Quarterly Journal of Economics*, November, 1974. "The Independence of Moral Theory," Proceedings and Addresses of the American Philosophical Association, vol. 48, 1974–75, pp. 5–22. "The Basic Structure as Subject," *American Philosophical Quarterly*, vol. 14, no. 2, April, 1977.

2

Moral Autonomy

Gerald Dworkin

> The will is therefore not merely subject to the law, but is so subject that it must be considered as also making the law for itself and precisely on this account as first of all subject to the law (of which it can regard itself as the author).
>
> —Kant

> [Virtue] is not a troubling oneself about a particular and isolated morality of one's own . . . the striving for a positive morality of one's own is futile, and in its very nature impossible of attainment . . . to be moral is to live in accordance with the moral tradition of one's own country.
>
> —Hegel

1. There is a philosophical view about morality which is shared by moral philosophers as divergent as Kant, Kierkegaard, Nietzsche, Royce, Hare, Popper, Sartre, and Wolff. It is a view of the moral agent as necessarily autonomous. It is this view that I wish to understand and evaluate in this essay. I speak of a view and not a thesis because the position involves not merely a conception of autonomy but connected views about the nature of moral principles, of moral epistemology, of rationality, and of responsibility.

2. I shall begin by distinguishing a number of ways of explicating the notion of moral autonomy. In the philosophical debate very different notions have been confused, and since they are

involved in claims which range from the trivially true to the profoundly false it is essential to distinguish them.

3. The most general formulation of moral autonomy is: A person is morally autonomous if and only if his moral principles are his own. The following are more specific characterizations of what it might mean for moral principles to be one's own.

1. A person is morally autonomous if and only if he is the author of his moral principles, their originator.
2. A person is morally autonomous if and only if he chooses his moral principles.
3. A person is morally autonomous if and only if the ultimate authority or source of his moral principles is his will.
4. A person is morally autonomous if and only if he decides which moral principles to accept as binding upon him.
5. A person is morally autonomous if and only if he bears the responsibility for the moral theory he accepts and the principles he applies.
6. A person is morally autonomous if and only if he refuses to accept others as moral authorities, i.e., he does not accept without independent consideration the judgment of others as to what is morally correct.

4. In this essay I am not concerned with other issues that have been discussed under the heading of autonomy. I am not concerned with the general question of what it is for an individual to act autonomously. I am not concerned with various views that have been discussed under the heading of the autonomy of morals—whether one can derive an "ought" from an "is"; or the relations, if any, between facts and values; or whether the acceptance of moral principles necessarily carries with it a motivating influence upon conduct. Clearly, there are connections between one's views on these matters and the issue of moral autonomy. I do not propose to draw them here.

5. What could it mean to say that a person's moral principles are his own? We have already identified them as "his" when we referred to them as "a person's moral principles." But how do we make that identification? In terms of considerations such as: Which moral principles occur as part of the best explanation of a person's actions? Which moral principles would the person de-

fend as correct? Which moral principles does he use as a basis for self-criticism? For the criticism of others? Which moral principles make his enthymematic moral arguments into valid arguments? There are practical problems in making this identification—the issue of rationalization, and theoretical problems (*akrasia*—are they the person's principles if he doesn't act in accordance with them?), but there is no special problem connected with autonomy. That issue concerns the notion of moral principles being his "own."

6. How could a person's moral principles not be his own? Not by being at the same time someone else's. For the fact that we share a common set of principles no more shows them not to be my own, than our sharing a taste for chocolate shows that my taste is not my own. Perhaps I borrowed your principles, or illegitimately appropriated them, or simply found them and never bothered to acknowledge their true owner. But all of these notions (as with the idea on which they trade—property) assume the notion that is to be explained. They all assume that somebody's principles are his own and that somebody else is not in the appropriate relation to his principles that the first person is.

7. With property, how one acquired it is essential. Perhaps that is what we must look for here as well. One suggestion is that we create or invent our moral principles. Sartre speaks of a young man deciding between joining the Free French or staying with his aged mother as being "obliged to invent the law for himself." Kant says the will "must be considered as also making the law for itself."

8. If this is what moral autonomy demands, then it is impossible on both empirical and conceptual grounds. On empirical grounds this view denies our *history*. We are born in a given environment with a given set of biological endowments. We mature more slowly than other animals and are deeply influenced by parents, siblings, peers, culture, class, climate, schools, accident, genes, and the accumulated history of the species. It makes no more sense to suppose we invent the moral law for ourselves than to suppose that we invent the language we speak for ourselves.

9. This is perhaps—I doubt it—a contingent difficulty. There are logical difficulties as well. For suppose one did invent a set

of principles independently of the various influences enumerated above. What would make them *moral* principles? I may act in accordance with them and take my deviation from them as a defect but that is not enough. I might be engaged in some kind of private ritual.

10. A central feature of moral principles is their social character. By this I mean, partly, that their interpretation often bears a conventional character. What my duties are as a parent, how close a relative must be to be owed respect, what duties of aid are owed to another, how one expresses regret or respect, are to some extent relative to the understandings of a given society. In addition, moral rules often function to provide solutions to a coordination problem—a situation in which what one agent chooses to do depends upon his expectations of what other agents will do—agents whose choices are in turn dependent on what the first agent will do. Such conventions depend upon the mutual convergence of patterns of behavior. The principles of morality are also social in that they have what Hart calls an internal aspect. They provide common standards which are used as the basis of criticism, and demands for obedience. All of these preclude individual invention.

11. Does this imply that moral reform is impossible? Not at all. It just implies that moral reform takes place against a background of accepted understandings about our moral relationships with one another. And *these* are not invented. Moral reforms (almost?) always take the form of attacking inconsistencies in the accepted moral framework, refusals to extend rights and privileges that are seen as legitimate already. Analogy and precedent—the weapons of the conservatives—are the engines of reform as well.

12. If I do not and cannot make the moral law for myself, at least, so it is claimed, I can always choose to accept or reject the existing moral framework. It is up to me to decide what is morally proper. This is the proper interpretation of Sartre's claim that his young man is "obliged to invent the law for himself." Nothing in the situation he faces shows him what to do. The competing claims are equally compelling. He must simply decide.

13. Choice and decision do enter here but it is crucial to see

how late in the game they enter. For Sartre (and the young man) already know they are faced with competing claims, and that these claims are of comparable moral force. That a son has obligations to his aged mother; that a citizen has a duty to defend his country against evil men; that neither of these claims is obviously more important or weighty than the other—none of these are matters of choice or decision. Indeed, the idea that they are is incompatible with the quality of tragic choice or moral dilemma that the situation poses. For if one could just choose the moral quality of one's situation, then all the young man would have to do is choose to regard his mother's welfare as morally insignificant, or choose to regard the Nazi invasion as a good thing, or choose to regard one of these evils as much more serious than the other.

14. Could someone *choose* to regard accidental injuries as having the same moral gravity as intentional ones? Utilitarians, some of whom say something like this, do so on the basis of a *theory*.

15. Still, if one cannot originate one's moral principles, and if the relevance of various factors to moral decision making is not always a matter of choice, the ultimate weighting of the moral factors is the agent's decision and his alone. A moral agent must retain autonomy, must make his own moral choices. The problem is to give this idea content in such a way that it escapes being trivial (who else could make my decisions?) or false (the denial of authority, tradition, and community).

16. How could a person's moral principles not be his own? Here is one case. It is from *Anna Karenina*.

> Stefan Arkadyevitch always read a liberal paper. It was not extreme in its views, but advocated those principles held by the majority of people. In spite of the fact that he was not really interested in science, or art, or politics, he strongly adhered to the same views on all such subjects as the majority and this paper in particular advocated, and changed them only when the majority changed. Or rather, it might be said, he did not change them at all—they changed themselves imperceptibly.

Here the beliefs are not his because they are borrowed; and they are borrowed without even being aware of their source; and, it is implied, Stefan is not capable of giving some account of their validity—not even an account which, say, stresses the likelihood of the majority being correct, or the necessity for moral consensus. All of these are important here—not just the borrowing

17. It is not sufficient for showing that my moral beliefs are not my own to show that my holding them has been casually influenced by others. Almost all our beliefs have been so influenced. Nor is it enough to show that while I have reasons that justify my beliefs, those reasons are not the causes of my beliefs. I may have acquired a belief from my father in, say, the importance of equality. But if I now have reasons which justify my belief, it is my belief. Nor is it enough to show that among the reasons I present to justify my belief are reasons that make reference to the beliefs of others.

18. If I believe Father knows best, and I do what Father tells me to do because I believe Father knows best, then Father's principles become mine as well. To deny this is to assume that what is mine must only be mine.

19. Underlying the notions of autonomy considered so far are assumptions about objectivity, the role of conscientiousness, obligation, responsibility, and the way in which we come to see that certain moral claims are correct. I shall argue that with respect to all of these issues the doctrine of autonomy in any of the interpretations (1-4) is one-sided and misleading.

20. These doctrines of autonomy conflict with views we hold about objectivity in morals. We believe that the answering of moral questions is a rational process not just in the sense that there are better and worse ways of going about it, but that it matters what answer we find. It makes sense to speak of someone as being mistaken or misled in his moral views. The idea of objectivity is tied up with that which is independent of will or choice. That a certain inference is valid, that a certain event causes another, that a certain course of conduct is illegal, that Bach is superior to Bacharach, that Gandhi was a better person than Hitler, that the manufacturer who substituted an inert substance for the active ingredient in Ipecac did an evil thing, are independent of my will or decision.

21. There is a paradox for notions of autonomy that rely on the agent's will or decision. Consider the statement that moral agents ought to be autonomous. Either that statement is an objec-

tively true statement or it is not. If it is, then there is at least one moral assertion whose claim to validity does not rest on its being accepted by a moral agent. If it is not, then no criticism can be made of a moral agent who refuses to accept it.

22. Another form of the paradox. Consider the following two claims.

1. P ought to be autonomous
2. P chooses not to be autonomous

Does P have any reason to accept (1)?

23. We can see in Kant the confusion engendered by his attempt to reconcile objectivity and autonomy. For Kant the moral law does *not* obtain its objective character by being chosen or willed by us. The categorical imperative commands us to act on that maxim which we *can* will as universal law. In a second formulation we are enjoined to act *as if* the maxim of our action were to become through our will a universal law of nature. What is essential is that one could will to act in such and such a way, not that we actually so will.

24. But when Kant faces the problem of how such an imperative can be binding on us he reverts to the notion of willing. The argument is that a categorical imperative cannot be binding because of some interest I have—because then it would be hypothetical. So, in the philosophical move than Putnam calls the "what else argument," Kant concludes that it must be binding because we have legislated it ourselves. But there are other possibilities, including the thesis that there are objective requirements of reason which provide their own form of rational motivation.

25. For Rawls, the objectivity of principles is defined in terms of their being the principles that would be chosen by free, equal, and rational beings. As such they are binding upon individuals whether or not they view them as binding. But agents are able to put themselves in the position of being choosers, to follow the arguments for the principles, and to desire that everyone (including themselves) accept such principles as binding. To the extent that they are motivated in this manner—and not, say, by mere submission to parental authority—they are morally autonomous.[1]

26. In addition, there arises at the level of the interpretation

and application of moral principles a substantive political conception of autonomy. Given the fact that real persons, even if they accepted a common moral framework, will have different and conflicting ideas of the correct interpretation of that theory, a state may be required to recognize political autonomy of its citizens. That is, it may not restrict the liberty of individuals unless it can justify such restrictions with arguments that the person himself can (given certain minimal rationality) see as correct. Such a doctrine can be invoked in defense of freedom of expression and conscience. But it is important to note that this argument applies to a specific area of moral life—the limits of state power. And even there, I have argued elsewhere, there are difficulties.[2]

27. Preoccupation with autonomy carries with it the attribution of supremacy to the concepts of integrity and conscientiousness. For if what is morally correct is what one has decided for oneself is correct, then for another to interfere with one's freedom of action based on that decision is to stifle moral personality and encourage hypocrisy. Politically this leads to the type of philosophical anarchism that Wolff espouses.[3] Socially it leads to the rejection of any use of community and peer pressure to limit the liberty of individuals. This is often defended in the name of Mill—a defense that only charity could attribute to a misreading (since it is obvious that anyone who believes this cannot have read Mill at all).

28. At the very least a defender of autonomy must distinguish between autonomy of judgment and autonomy of action. The arguments in favor of allowing people to determine for themselves what is right are more compelling than those that favor allowing people to always act in accordance with their beliefs. It is one thing to argue in defense of freedom of expression from premises concerning what individuals who wish to retain autonomy would be willing to grant the state by way of authority to limit expression. It is quite another to argue, as Wolff does, that law qua law creates no obligation to obey.

29. As for integrity—that second-order value which consists in acting in accordance with one's first-order values—it is not to be despised. There is something admirable about the person who acts on principle, even if his principles are awful. But there is

also something to be said for Huck Finn, who "knowing" that slavery was right, and believing that he was morally damned if he helped Jim to escape, was willing to sacrifice his integrity in favor of his humanitarian impulses.

30. A moral theory that stresses the supremacy of autonomy will have difficulties with the concept of obligation. As the etymology suggests, to be obliged is to be bound. And to be bound is to have one's will restricted; to have one's moral status altered so that it is no longer one's choice how one should act. The usual suggestion of the defender of autonomy is that one can, so to speak, tie oneself up. And this is the only way one becomes bound. All obligation is ultimately self-imposed, hence a product of one's decision or choice to be so limited.

> I am persuaded that moral obligations, strictly so-called, arise from freely chosen contractual commitments between or among rational agents who have entered into some continuing and organized interaction with one another.[4]

(How the notions of autonomy, individualism, Protestantism, and contract emerge (and merge) in moral, social, religious, and economic thought is a subject (still) worth historical investigation.)

31. This attempted solution cannot succeed. Tying oneself up is binding only if the knot is no longer in one's hands. For if I can, at will, release myself I am only in appearance bound. As Hume put it with respect to the obligations created by promises, on this view the will

> has no object to which it could tend but must return to itself *in infinitum*.[5]

To say that promises create obligations because they create expectations is true enough but of no help here. For that these expectations have moral weight is not itself chosen or decided by the maker of the promise.

32. Another way of looking at this. From the temporal perspective the commitments of my earlier self must bind (to some degree) my later self. It cannot always be open for the later self to renounce the commitments of the earlier self. This implies that even self-imposed obligations create a world of "otherness"—a world which is independent of my (current) will and which is not

subject to my choices and decisions. The distance between my earlier and later selves is only quantitatively different from that between myself and others.

33. In his discussion of the one state he believes has authority and is consistent with autonomy—unanimous direct democracy—Wolff fails to see this point. He argues that there is no sacrifice of autonomy because all laws are accepted by every citizen. But this is only true at a given point in time. What if the individual changes his mind about the wisdom or goodness of the law? Is he then bound to obey it?

34. Leaving the internal difficulties to the side, the claim that all obligations are self-imposed does not fit the moral facts. That I have obligations of gratitude to my aged parents, of aid to the stranger attacked by thieves, of obedience to the laws of a democratic and just state, of rectification to those treated unjustly by my ancestors or nation are matters that are independent of my voluntary commitments.

35. The defender of autonomy has a particular picture of the role of discovery in morality.

> [the moral agent] may learn from others about his moral obligations, but only in the sense that a mathematician learns from other mathematicians—namely by hearing from them arguments whose validity he recognizes even though he did not think of them himself. He does not learn in the sense that one learns from an explorer, by accepting as true his accounts of things one cannot see for oneself.[6]

This picture is inaccurate even for the mathematician. Mathematicians often accept results on the word of other mathematicians without going through the proofs for themselves. And they may do so (particularly) in fields in which they do not possess the techniques to assess the proof even if they were inclined to do so.

36. The image of the explorer is an interesting one and is analogous to the role of the seer in the moral systems of various tribal peoples. Lest one think that this view is one that only "primitives" hold, compare the role of the "practically wise" man in Aristotle.

37. For Aristotle moral virtue is a disposition to choose which is developed in the process of choosing. We do not do good acts

because we are already good (at first anyway). We do good acts, and in doing so become good. This is paradoxical. How are we to identify those acts which are good, if we are not ourselves already good? By aiming at the mean which is determined by the "proper rule." How do we identify the proper rule? It is "the rule by which a practically wise man would determine it." Thus, to be morally virtuous one must follow the example or precept of one who is practically wise.

38. Such an account, which places reliance on the exemplary individual, on imitation of goodness, on what would in a more barbarous term be called role-modeling, seems to me to be, if not the whole story, at least a significant part of it. Such a view has its own vices of excess. There is, no doubt, the morally unappetizing sight of the person who abandons all attempts to think critically about who he is imitating, who imitates out of laziness or fear or sycophancy. This excess has received its share of attention from an excessively protestant and individualistic age. I am calling attention to the opposite defect: the refusal to acknowledge the very idea of moral authority, the equation of imitation with animal characteristics (copycat; monkey see, monkey do), the identification of maturity with doing things without help, by (and for?) oneself.

39. Consider the fifth interpretation of autonomy—being responsible for the moral theory we believe correct and for the interpretation of the principles that follow from it. Leaving aside general metaphysical doubts about freedom of the will and empirical doubts about causes of our conduct which are beyond our control, this thesis seems to me correct but vacuous. One cannot evade responsibility by asserting that one was only following orders or doing what everybody does or accepting the general will. But this leaves completely open the issue of whether one ought to be autonomous in the sense of (6), i.e., being prepared to examine one's principles in a critical fashion. Whether one does so or not, one will still be (held) responsible.

It is the confusion of these two distinct notions that leads Aiken to assert that

> no man is morally responsible for actions unless they are performed for the sake of principles which he cannot in conscience disavow.[7]

This implies that all one has to do to avoid responsibility is either be completely unprincipled or accept principles without conscientious scrutiny.

40. We come now to the last interpretation of autonomy. A person is morally autonomous only if he

> cannot accept without independent consideration the judgment of others as to what he should do. If he relies on the judgment of others he must be prepared to advance independent reasons for thinking their judgment likely to be correct.[8]

41. This is the denial of any strong notion of moral authority. On this view none of the following justifications could be acceptable.

> These principles are acceptable because they are the revealed word of God.
>
> These principles are acceptable because they are part of the moral tradition to which I belong.
>
> These principles are acceptable because the elders have pronounced them acceptable.
>
> These principles are acceptable because they are those of my class or my clan or my comrades.
>
> These principles are acceptable because they are embodied in the common law or the Constitution.
>
> These principles are acceptable because they were passed on to me as part of my training as doctor, lawyer, Indian chief.
>
> These principles are acceptable because they are customary, or the ways of my father and my father's father.
>
> These principles are acceptable because they are in accord with Nature or the Tao or the course of evolution.
>
> These principles are acceptable because they are those of Gandhi or Thoreau or Socrates or Confucius or Jesus or Tolstoy.

42. The idea of there being independent reasons for thinking the judgments of an authority correct is ambiguous. There are reasons for thinking his *judgment* likely to be correct, i.e., independent reasons for believing the content of his judgment correct. Or there can be independent reasons for thinking *his* judgment to be correct, i.e., for thinking *him* likely to be right. Corresponding to these we have a weaker and stronger notion of "checking"

an authority. In one case, having checked out his authority, we no longer check his advice in the particular case (weak checking). In the other case we may take his opinion into account but still seek independent verification (strong checking).

43. It will be useful to turn for a moment to the idea of epistemological authority. Do we not frequently accept without independent consideration the judgment of others as to what we should believe or do in nonmoral matters? If I am uncertain about a statistical question, or what that pain in my leg is, or whether this appliance should be purchased, or why the thermostat is not working, or whether Aristotle believed there was a mind-body problem, or why the souffle keeps falling, or the number of words for "snow" that the Eskimo have, I consult an authority. I take his advice, I rely on his judgment, I accept what he says. I do not—unless there are special reasons for doubt—investigate the matter independently to see if he is correct.

44. There are various reasons why such a policy is rational. We lack time, knowledge, training, skill. In addition there is a necessary and useful division of labor. It is more efficient for each of us to specialize in a few areas of competence and be able to draw, when we need it, upon the resources and expertise of others. Knowledge is socially stored and there are evolutionary advantages for a species that does not require each individual member to acquire and retain all the knowledge needed for survival and reproduction. It may also be true that our reliance upon authority assumes that somewhere in the chain of authority conferral, someone has engaged in (weak or strong) checking. But that each individual do so, on every occasion, is neither necessary nor rational.

45. It is said that things are different with morality.

> In the domain of science and logic . . . situations often arise in which we properly defer to the authority of observers whom we recognize to be more competent or qualified than ourselves. And it is because of that, without qualms, we accept certain statements as objectively true even though we ourselves do not fully see why they are so. But in morals such situations can hardly arise . . . no one can be expected to conform his judgment and his will to certain allegedly objective principles which he has not in conscience made absolutely his own. Nor is this situation altered by

the fact that some men take their principles from some "authority". For that authority can make no moral claims upon anyone who does not adopt it as *his* authority.[9]

46. There is no argument here, only assertion. But consider the following bad argument for the same claim by Hare.

> It might be objected that moral questions are not peculiar in this respect—that we are free also to form our own opinions about such matters as whether the world is round. . . . but we are free to form our own moral opinions in a much stronger sense than this. For if we say that the world is flat, we can in principle be shown certain facts such that, once we have admitted them, we cannot go on saying that the world is flat without being guilty of self-contradiction or misuse of language . . . nothing of the sort can be done in morals.[10]

This is mistaken on both counts. There are no facts—which are not logically equivalent to the roundness of the earth—which preclude a person from insisting upon an alternative explanation of them. Upholders of ad hoc and silly hypotheses are guilty neither of contradiction nor misuse of language. But if one wants to say this kind of thing, then one can say it in moral matters. To admit that I ran over your child's dog deliberately, without excuse, because I dislike both the dog and your child, and to go on saying that what I did was right, is as plausibly being guilty of self-contradiction or misuse of language.

47. We have not yet discovered an argument for the view that autonomy understood as critical, self-conscious reflection on one's moral principles plays a more distinctive or greater role in moral reasoning than it does elsewhere in our theoretical or practical reasoning, e.g., in scientific theorizing. Still, this conception of autonomy as critical reflection avoids the difficulties of the earlier interpretations. It is consistent with objectivity, for critical reflection is aimed at what is correct. It need not reject the view that some of us may be better at moral reasoning than others. It is compatible with the recognition of a notion of (limited) authority, and can accept the relevance (if not the conclusiveness) of tradition in moral life.

48. It is one ideal of morality, and like other ideals it may turn imperialistic and try to exclude alternative conceptions. But, as Oakeshott observes,

this is a corruption which every disposition recognized as a virtue is apt to suffer at the hands of fanatics.[11]

49. I have argued that there is no interesting thesis about moral autonomy which follows from any conceptual thesis about the nature of morality or moral agency. It is a substantive thesis and represents a particular conception of morality—one that, among other features, places a heavy emphasis on rules and principles rather than virtues and practices. Considered purely internally there are conceptual, moral, and empirical difficulties in defining and elaborating a conception of autonomy which is coherent and provides us with an ideal worthy of pursuit.

50. It is only through a more adequate understanding of notions such as tradition, authority, commitment, and loyalty, and of the forms of human community in which these have their roots, that we shall be able to develop a conception of autonomy free from paradox and worthy of admiration.

NOTES

1. John Rawls, *A Theory of Justice* (Cambridge, Mass.: Harvard University Press, 1971), pp. 516-19.
2. Gerald Dworkin, "Non-neutral Principles," *Journal of Philosophy,* vol. 71, no. 14 (August 15, 1974).
3. Robert Paul Wolff, *In Defense of Anarchism* (New York: Harper and Row, 1970).
4. Robert Paul Wolff, *The Autonomy of Reason* (New York: Harper and Row, 1973), p. 219.
5. David Hume, *Treatise of Human Nature* (Oxford: Clarendon Press, 1888) pp. 517-18.
6. Wolff, *In Defense of Anarchism,* p. 7.
7. Henry Aiken, *Reason and Conduct* (New York: Alfred A. Knopf, 1962), p. 143.
8. Thomas Scanlon, "A Theory of Freedom of Expression," *Philosophy and Public Affairs,* 1 (Winter, 1972): 216. This is not put forward by Scanlon as a notion of *moral* autonomy. I adopt his words for my own purposes.
9. Aiken, *Reason and Conduct,* p. 143.

10. R. M. Hare, *Freedom and Reason* (Oxford: Clarendon Press, 1963), p. 2.
11. Michael Oakeshott, *On Human Conduct* (Oxford: Clarendon Press, 1975), p. 238.

The Concept of Responsibility: An Inquiry into the Foundations of an Ethics for Our Age

Hans Jonas

THE FRAGMENTARY REFLECTIONS presented here are extracted from a much larger body of work in progress, viz., an *Essay on Ethics in the Age of Technology*. Just a few words on this by way of background to what follows. The major premise of the work is: that, with the wielding of contemporary (and foreseeably still rising) technological *power*, the nature and scope of human action has decisively changed; the minor premise: that a relevant ethics must match the types and powers of action for which it is to provide the norms; the conclusion follows: that we must review, and if necessary revise, ethical theory so as to bring it into line with what it has to deal with now and for some time to come. Thus, one has to look at the actions on the one hand, and at the theory of ethics on the other hand. A first obvious finding then is: that the actions that ethics has to deal with now have an unprecedented causal reach into the future. This, together with the sheer magnitude of the effects, moves "responsibility" into the center of ethics, where it has never stood before. And that, in turn, demands an examination of this new arrival on the stage of ethical theory, i.e., an investigation into the nature of responsibility. It should not be surprising that such a task compels the philosopher to probe into the foundations of morals. In what follows, I cannot entirely avoid the inhospitable terrain of first principles and general ethical theory and even metaphysics; but most of my attention will dwell on the more concrete, and more or less familiar, phenomenon of responsibility itself, which seems to me somewhat neglected in traditional ethical discourse.

I. The Objective and the Subjective in Ethics

A theory of responsibility, as any ethical theory, must deal both with the rational ground of obligation, that is, the validating principle behind the claim to a binding "ought," and with the psychological ground of its moving the will, that is, of an agent's letting it determine his course of action. This is to say that ethics has an objective side and a subjective side, the one having to do with reason, the other with emotion. Sometimes the one, sometimes the other has been more in the center of ethical theory, and traditionally the problem of validation, i.e., the objective side, has posed the greater challenge to philosophers. But the two sides are mutually complementary and both are integral to ethics itself. Without our being, at least by disposition, responsive to the call of duty in terms of feeling, the most cogent demonstration of its right, even when compelling theoretical assent, would be powerless to make it a motivating force. Conversely, without some credentials of its right, our de facto responsiveness to appeals of this kind would remain at the mercy of fortuitous predilections (variously preconditioned themselves), and the options made by it would lack justification. This, to be sure, would still leave room for moral behavior from a naively good will whose direct self-certainty asks for no further validation—and, indeed, may not need it in those favored cases where the promptings of the heart are "naturally" in unison with the biddings of the law. A subjectivity so graced (and who will exclude the possibility of it?) could act all by itself. No similar sufficiency can ever be enjoyed by the objective side: its imperative, evident as its truth may be, cannot become operative at all unless it meets with a sensitivity to the like of it. This sheer fact of feeling, presumably a universal potential of human experience, is thus the cardinal datum of the moral life and, as such, implied in the "ought" itself. It is indeed of the very meaning of the normative principle that its call is addressed to recipients so constituted that they are by nature receptive to it (which does not, of course, already insure its being heeded). One may well say that there would be no "thou shalt" if there were no one to hear it and on his own attuned to its message, even straining toward its voice. This is the same as saying that men already *are* potentially "moral beings" by possessing that affectibility, and only thereby can also be immoral. But it is equally true that the moral sentiment itself demands its authorization from beyond itself, and this not merely in defense against challenges from without (including those from rival motives in oneself), but from an inner need of that very sentiment to be in its own eyes more than a mere impulse. Not the validity, to be sure, only the efficacy of the moral command depends on the subjective condition, which is its premise and its object at the same time, solicited, appealed to, claimed with success or in vain. In any case, the gap between abstract validation and concrete motivation must be bridged by the arc of sentiment, which alone can sway the will. The phenomenon of morality rests a priori on this correlation, even though one of its members is only a posteriori given as a fact of our existence: the subjective presence of our moral interest.

In the order of logic, the validity of obligation would have to come first and the responding sentiment second. But in the order of approach, there is advantage in beginning with the subjective side, as not only the immanent given but also as implied in the transcendent summons directed at it. We can take only the briefest of looks at the emotional aspect of morality in past ethical theory.

II. The Role of Sentiment in Past Ethical Theory

Moral philosophers have always recognized that feeling must supplement reason so that the objectively good can exert a force on our will; in other words, that morality, which is meant to have command over the emotions, requires an emotion of its own to do so. Among the great ones, it was probably Kant alone who had to wring this from his rigorism as a concession to our sensuous nature, instead of seeing it as an integral aspect of the ethical as such. Explicitly or implicitly, the insight lives in every doctrine of virtue, however differently the feeling in question may have been determined. Jewish "fear of the Lord," Platonic "eros," Aristotelian "eudaimonia," Christian "charity," Spinoza's "amor dei intellectualis," Hutcheson's "benevolence," Kant's "reverence," Kierkegaard's "interest," Nietzsche's "lust of the will" (and so on), are modes of defining this affective element in ethics. We cannot discuss them here, but we observe that the feeling of responsibility is not among them. This absence must later be explained in defense of our choice. We also observe that most, though not all, of the feelings named were of the kind inspired by and directed at an *object* of supreme worth, a "highest good," which often carried the ontological connotation (a corollary to the idea of perfection) that this must be something timeless, confronting our mortality with the lure of eternity. The aim of ethical striving is, then, to emulate this object in our own condition and also help its approximation in the state of things: the imperishable invites participation by the perishable and elicits in it the desire thereto. By contrast, the object of responsibility is emphatically the perishable qua perishable, yet, in spite of this shared condition, more unsharably an "other" to the agent than any of the transcendent objects of classical ethics; "other" not as the surpassing better but as nothing-but-itself in its own right, with no bridging of *this* otherness by a qualitative assimilation on the part of the subject. Still, this far-from-supreme object, perceived in its perishability and insecurity, must be able to move the subject to a supreme commitment, without any appetite of appropriation, or there could be no "feeling responsible" for it. But there is the fact of such a feeling, given in experience and no less real than the appetitive feelings of the *summum bonum* aspiration. Of this, we have to speak later. Here we note what is nonetheless common between the two contrasting types: that the committing force issues from the claim of an object, and the commitment is to that object, whether eternal or temporal. In both cases, something is to be brought about in the order of things.

Over against these object-inspired and object-committed ethical stances, in which the content of the aim reigns supreme, stand the objectless kinds, in which the form or spirit of the action itself is the theme of the norm, and the external object, provided by the situation, is more the occasion than the aim for the deed. Not the "what" but the "how" of acting really matters. Existentialism is the modern extreme of this ethics of subjective intention (cf. Nietzsche's "will to will," Sartre's "authentic decision," Heidegger's "resoluteness," etc.), where the worldly issue is not by itself endowed with a claim on us but receives its significance from the choice of our passionate concern. Here the self-committing freedom of the self reigns supreme. Whether this position is tenable and does not hide a surreptitious recognition of a value in the object itself for which the decision opts (for which it therefore *ought* to opt), and whether this is not the true ground for the allegedly groundless choice, need not be discussed here. What matters for ethical theory is the conceptual denial of any immanent order of rank or right among objects and, therefore, of the very idea of objectively valid obligations toward them of which they themselves could be the source.

Unique (as in so many other respects) is Kant's position in this quarrel between "material" and "formal," "objective" and "subjective," principles of moral action. While not denying that objects can affect us by their worth, he denies (for the sake of the "autonomy" of reason) that this emotive affection supplies the true motive for moral action; and while stressing the rational objectivity of a universal moral law, he concedes the necessary role of feeling in conforming to it. It was indeed among the profound insights of Kant, the more telling for coming from the champion of unadulterated autonomy of reason in moral matters, that besides reason there must also be sentiment at work so that the moral law can gain the force to affect our will. According to him, this was a sentiment evoked in us not by an object (which would make the morality heteronomous) but by the *idea* of duty, i.e., of the moral law itself; and this sentiment was "reverence"

(*Ehrfurcht*). Kant thought: reverence for the law, for the sub-limity of the unconditional "thou shalt" that issues from reason. In other words, reason itself becomes the source of an affect and its ultimate object. Not, of course, reason as a cognitive faculty, but reason as a principle of universality, to which the will is enjoined to conform; and this not through the choice of its objects, but through the form of choosing them, i.e., through the mode of determining itself with a view to possible universaliza-tion. This internal form of willing alone is the content of the "categorical imperative," whose sublime right is said to inspire us with reverence. Here is not the place to explain why this thought (which cannot be denied a sublimity of its own) must be rejected. The vacuity into which the purely formal categorical imperative leads with its criterion of noncontradictory "universalizability" of the maxim of the will has been often noted;[1] and we may add that every attempt to conceive the moral law as its own end must similarly fail.[2] We simply state the counterposition that underlies our own reflections on responsibility throughout this paper: What matters are things rather than states of my will. By engaging the latter, the former become ends. Ends may sometimes be sub-lime—by *what* they are, and even certain acts or lives may be so; but not the formal rule of the will whose observance is for any chosen end, or act, the *condition* of being a moral one, or, more precisely, of not being an immoral one. The law as such can be neither the cause nor the object of reverence; but Being (or instances of it), disclosed to a sight not blocked by selfishness or dimmed by dullness, can be both—and can with this affection of our feeling come to the aid of the, otherwise powerless, moral law which bids us to honor the intrinsic claim of Being. To be "heteronomous" in this way, i.e., to let oneself be moved by the just appeal of entities, need not be feared or disclaimed in the cause of pure principle. Yet not even "reverence" is enough, for this feeling affirmation of the perceived dignity of the object, however vivid, can remain entirely passive. Only the added *feeling of responsibility*, which binds *this* subject to this object, will make us act on its behalf. We contend that it is this feeling, more than any other, which may generate a willingness to sustain the object's claim to existence by our action. Let us then turn to this phenomenon, "responsibility," about which ethical theory has been so silent.

III. Theory of Responsibility

The first and most general condition of responsibility is causal power, i.e., that acting makes an impact on the world; the second, that such acting is under the agent's control; and third, that he can foresee its consequences to some extent. Under these necessary conditions, there can be "responsibility," but in two widely differing senses: (a) responsibility as being *accountable* "for" one's deeds, whatever they are; and (b) responsibility "for" particular objects that commits an agent to particular deeds concerning them. (Note the different referent of "for"!) The one is a formal, the other a substantive concept, and we really speak of two different things when we say that someone is responsible for what happened (which is neither praise nor blame), and that someone is a responsible person, i.e., honors his responsibilities (which is praise). Some further articulation will make the distinction clearer.

a. *Formal responsibility.* "He is responsible, because he did it." That means: the doer must answer for his deed: he is held responsible for its consequences and, where the case warrants it, can be made liable for them. So understood, "responsibility" does not itself set ends or disallow ends but is the mere formal burden on all causal acting among men, viz., that they can be called to account for it. As the mere fact of accountability independent of the agent's consent, it is thus the precondition of morality but not yet itself morality. Consenting to it, i.e., acknowledging one's accountability, is already more than the choiceless fact. To identify with one's deed, e.g., by readiness to take the consequences, has indeed some moral quality which may adorn even utter immorality. That is, owning the deed is better than dissembling it. An example is Mozart's Don Giovanni, whose defiant avowal at the end, paying the extreme price rather than repent, lends a certain grandeur to his misdeeds. But the example also shows that the affirmation of formal responsibility is not a sufficient principle of morality.

b. *Substantive responsibility.* There is, however, the vastly different concept of responsibility that concerns not the ex-post-facto account for what has been done, but the forward determination of what is to do; by whose command, therefore, I feel responsible, not in the first place for my conduct and its consequences, but for the *matter* that has a claim on my acting. For example, responsibility for the welfare of others does not merely "screen" intended actions with respect to their moral acceptability but obligates to actions not otherwise contemplated at all. Here, the "for" of being responsible is obviously distinct from that in the purely self-related sense. The "what for" lies outside me, but in the effective range of my power, in need of it or threatened by it. It confronts this power of mine with its right-to-be and, through the moral will, enlists it for itself. The matter becomes mine because the power is mine and has a causative relation to just this matter. The dependent in its immanent right becomes commanding, the power in its transcendent causality becomes committed, and committed in the double sense of being objectively responsible for what is thus entrusted to it, *and* affectively engaged through the feeling that sides with it, viz., "feeling responsible." In this feeling the abstractly binding finds its concrete tie to the subjective will. This siding of sentiment with the object originates not from the idea of responsibility in general but from the perceived right-plus-need of the object, as it affects the sensibility and puts the selfishness of power to shame. First comes the "ought-to-be" of the object, second the ought-to-do of the subject who, in virtue of his power, is called to its care. The demand of the object in the unassuredness of its existence, on the one hand, and the conscience of power in the guilt of its causality, on the other hand, conjoin in the affirmative feeling of responsibility on the part of a self that anyway and always must actively encroach on the being of things. If love is also present, then responsibility is inspirited beyond duty by the devotion of the person who learns to tremble for the fate of that which is both worthy of being loved and beloved.

This kind of "responsibility" and "feeling responsible" we have in mind, not the empty, formal one of every agent's being responsible for his acts,[3] when speaking of "responsibility for the future" as the mark of an ethics needed today. We come empirically closer to this substantive, goal-committed concept of responsibility by asking what is meant by "*ir*responsible action."

The gambler who puts his whole fortune at stake acts recklessly; when it is not his but another's, then criminally; but when a family depends on him, then irresponsibly, even with ownership indisputable, and no matter whether he loses or wins. The example tells: Only one who *has* responsibilities can act *ir*responsibly. Whether the responsibility violated is of the pervasive and enduring kind as in the example of the pater-familias, or more circumscribed, as that of a physician, a ship's captain, even as casual and passing as that of the driver giving someone a ride, there always obtains a definable, *non*reciprocal *relation* of responsibility. The well-being, the interest, the fate of others has, by circumstance or agreement, come under my care, which means that my control *over* it involves at the same time my obligation *for* it. The exercise of the power with disregard of the obligation is, then, "irresponsible," i.e., a breach of the trust-relation of responsibility. A distinct disparity of power or competence belongs to this relationship. Within its terms and while it lasts, the responsible one is superior: he is responsible *because* of that superiority, whether it anteceded or only originated with the relation of responsibility.

IV. Natural and Contractual Responsibility

In the parental example just used, we have a case of responsibility instituted by nature, which is independent of prior assent or choice, irrevocable, and not given to alteration of its terms by the participants; and, in that prime example, it encompasses its object totally. Not so a responsibility instituted "artificially" by bestowal and acceptance of a task, e.g., appointment to an office (but also that coming about by tacit agreement or the mere fact of competence): This is circumscribed in content and time by the particular task; its acceptance has in it an element of choice, from which one may later resign or be released. Also, in its inception at least, if not in its existence, there is some degree of mutuality involved. Most important is the difference that here the responsibility draws its binding force from the agreement whose creature it is, and not from the intrinsic validity of the cause. (The tax official's responsibility for collecting taxes is not predicated on the merits of the tax system but on his undertaking the office.) We have thus to distinguish between natural responsibility, where the immanent "ought-to-be" of the object claims its agent a priori and quite unilaterally, and contracted or appointed responsibility, which is conditional a posteriori upon the fact and the terms of the relationship actually entered into. In the latter case, even the requisite power, without which there can be no responsibility, is typically generated by the contract itself together with the duty; in the natural case, it is there to begin with and underlies the object's sovereign claim on it. Evidently, in moral (as distinct from legal) status, the natural is the stronger, if less defined, sort of responsibility. What is more, it is the original from which any other responsibility ultimately derives its more or less contingent validity. This is to say that if there were no responsibility "by nature" there could be none "by contract."

V. Self-chosen Responsibility of the Politician

There remains, however, a third possibility which, in a manner eminently distinctive of human freedom, transcends the difference of natural and contractual responsibility. So far we have found that a good of the first, self-validating order, if and insofar as it lies in the effective range of our power, and all the more, if in any case already impinged on by our activity, engages our responsibility without our choosing and knows no discharge from it. The (at least partly) chosen responsibility of the appointed task has, per se, no such commanding good for its immediate object and permits abdication in appropriate ways. But it also occurs that a good of the first order and dignity, that is, one endowed with a "natural" claim, but which of itself lies quite *beyond* one's present range of power, which he thus *cannot* as yet be responsible for at all and may well leave alone—that such a good is *made* the object of a freely chosen responsibility, so that the choice comes first, from the gratuitous and, as it were, presumptuous wish for just that responsibility, and only then procures for itself the power necessary for implementing it; and with it then, indeed, also the duty. This is clearly an *opus supererogationis*, but familiar enough. What is outwardly visible is the reach for power. The paradigm case is the politician, who seeks power in order to gain responsibility, and supreme power for the sake of supreme responsibility. Power, to be sure, has its own lures and rewards—prestige, glamour, the enjoyment of authority, of commanding and initiating, the inscribing of one's trace in the world, even the enjoyment of the mere consciousness of it (not to speak of the vulgar gains). The motives of the ambitious in striving for it are probably always mixed, and some vanity at least will have played its part already in the self-confidence of the initial choice. But leaving aside the most blatantly selfish tyranny, for which the "political" is merely a pretext, it will be the rule that the responsibility going with the power and made *possible* by it is co-intended in the striving for it, and by the genuine *homo politicus* intended in the first place. The real statesman will see his fame (which he may have quite at heart) precisely in that it can be said of him that he has acted for the good of those over whom he had power, i.e., *for* whom he had it. This, that "over" becomes "for," sums up the essence of responsibility.

Here we have a unique privilege of human spontaneity. Unasked, needlessly, without a prior mandate or agreement (which may later add their legitimation) does the aspirant vie for power so as to burden himself with responsibility. The object of the responsibility is the *res publica*, the common cause, which in a republic is latently everybody's cause, but actually only in the limits of the general civic duties. These do not comprise the assumption of leadership in public affairs; nobody is formally bound to compete for public office, usually not even to accept an unsought call to it. But he who feels the calling for it in himself, seeks the call and demands it as his right. Public peril in particular, meeting with the conviction to *know* the way to salvation and to be fit to *lead* it, becomes a powerful incentive for the courageous to offer himself and force his way to responsibility. Thus came Churchill's hour in May, 1940, when in a nearly hopeless situation he assumed the direction of affairs that no fainthearted one could covet. Having made the first necessary arrangements, so he tells us, he went to bed in the serene confidence that the right task had found the right man, and slept a restful sleep.

And yet he could have been wrong. If not his estimate of the situation, that of himself might have been in error. If this had later turned out to be the case, history would pronounce him guilty together with his erroneous conviction. But as little as this conviction, in all its sincerity, could serve him as an excuse, as little can the wagering on its truth in the reach for power, which might eliminate better claimants to the task, be made a straight-forward moral duty. For no general rule of ethics can make it a duty, on the mere criterion of subjective certainty, to risk com-mitting possibly fatal mistakes at others' expense. Rather must he who wagers on his own certainty take the never excludable possibility of being in error upon his own conscience. For this, there exists no general law, only the free deed, which in the unassuredness of its eventual justification (even in the mere pre-sumption of its self-confidence, which surely cannot be part of any moral prescription) is entirely its own venture. After this moment of supreme arbitrariness, the law takes over again. Hav-ing appropriated the ownerless responsibility, its holder is hence-forth owned by it and no longer by himself. The highest and most presumptuous freedom of the self leads into the most impe-rious and unrelenting bondage.

VI. The Object of Responsibility: Human Existence

Now, it is of the utmost theoretical interest to see how *this* responsibility from freest choice and the one most under the dictate of nature, that of the statesman and that of the parent, have, nonetheless, across the whole spectrum at whose opposite ends they lie, most in common and *together* can teach most about the nature of responsibility. The differences are many and ob-vious, and we must here forego their elaboration, instructive as they are. What is common to them can be summed up in the three concepts of "totality," "continuity," and "future," referring to the existence and welfare of human beings. Let us first take a look at this fundamental relatum, "human existence." It has the precarious, vulnerable and revocable character, the peculiar mode of transience, of all *life*, which makes it alone a proper object of "caring"; and, moreover, it shares with the agent subject the *humanum*, which has the first, if not the sole, claim on him. Responsibility is first and foremost of men for men. This subject-object kinship in the relation of responsibility implies that the relation, though unilateral in itself and in every single case, is yet, on principle, reversible and includes possible reciprocity. Generically, indeed, the reciprocity is always there, insofar as I, who am responsible for someone, am always, by living among men, also someone's responsibility. This follows from the non-autarky of man; and in any case, at least the primal responsibility of parental care *everybody* has first experienced on himself. In this archetypal paradigm, the reference of responsibility to the animate and to the kindred is most convincingly displayed. Thus, to repeat, only what is alive, in its constitutive indigence and fragility, *can* be an object of responsibility. But this is only the necessary, not the sufficient condition for it. Man's distinction that he alone can *have* responsibility means also that he *must* have it for others of his like—i.e., for such that are themselves potential bearers of responsibility—and that in one or another respect he, in fact, always has it. Here the mere capacity is the sufficient condition for the actuality. To be de facto responsible in some respect for someone at some time (whether acknowledging it or not) belongs so inseparably to the being of man as his a priori capacity for it—as inseparably indeed as his being a speaking creature—and is therefore to be included in his definition if one is interested in this dubious pursuit. In this sense an "ought" is concretely given with the very existence of man; the mere attribute of being a causative subject involves of itself *objective* obligation in the form of external responsibility. With this, he is not yet moral, but a member of the moral order, i.e., one who can be moral or immoral.

VII. Mankind's Existence—the First Commandment

Of man's prerogative among the claimants on human responsibility there is this to say: that it has nothing to do with a balance sheet of mankind's performance on earth, i.e., whether it has so far made itself deserving of the preference. The Socratic life or the Beethoven symphony, which one might cite for the justification of the whole, can always be countered with such a catalogue of incessant atrocities that, depending on the appraiser's disposition, the balance can turn out to be very negative indeed. Pity and outrage of the pessimist are not really refutable here; the price of the human enterprise is, in any case, enormous; man's wretchedness has at least the measure of his greatness; and on the whole, I believe, the defender of mankind, in spite of the great atoners like Saint Francis on his side, has the harder case. But such value assessments have no bearing on the ontological issue, as little as the hedonistic balance of happiness and unhappiness (which also tends to turn out negative when—and because— attempted). The dignity of man per se can only be spoken of as potential, or it is the speech of unpardonable vanity. Against all this, the *existence* of mankind comes first, whether deserved on its past record *and* its likely continuation or not. It is the ever-transcendent *possibility*, obligatory in itself, which must be kept open by the continued existence. To preserve this possibility is a cosmic responsibility—hence the duty for mankind to exist. Put epigrammatically: The possibility of there being responsibility in the world, which is bound to the existence of men, is of all objects of responsibility the first.

"Existence of a mankind" means simply: that there live men on earth; that they live well is the second commandment. The naked ontic fact of their existing at all, in which they had no say, becomes for them the ontological command: that there continue to be such.[4] The immediate execution of this command is en-trusted to the instinct of procreation, and so it can normally remain hidden behind the particular commands of human virtue, which work out its wider meaning. Only very exceptional cir-cumstances (as today's) may necessitate its becoming explicit as such. But tacitly, it always stands behind the others as their common sanctioning ground. Groundless itself (for there could be no commandment to invent such creatures in the first place), brought about with all the opaque contingency of brute fact, the ontological imperative institutes on its own authority the primor-dial "cause in the world" to which a mankind once in existence, even if initially by blind chance, is henceforth committed. It is the prior cause of all causes that can ever become the object of collective and even individual human responsibility.

VIII. Parental and Political Responsibility: Both Are "Total"

Of such causes we have singled out the two eminent ones of parental and political responsibility, and we named "totality," "continuity," and "future" as the distinctive traits by which they most fully exemplify the nature of responsibility as such. Let us run through them briefly, taking "totality" first. By this we mean that these responsibilities encompass the total being of their objects, i.e., all the aspects of them, from naked existence to highest interests. This is obvious for parental responsibility, which really, in time and in essence, is the archetype of all responsibility (and also genetically, I believe, the origin of every disposition for it, certainly its elementary school). The child as a whole and in all its possibilities, not only in its immediate needs, is its object. The bodily aspect comes first, of course, in the beginning perhaps solely; but then more and more is added, all that which falls under "education" in the broadest sense: faculties, conduct, relation, character, knowledge, which have to be stimulated and guided in their development; and together with these also, if possible, happiness. In brief: the pure being as such, and then the best being of the child is what parental care is about. But isn't this precisely what Aristotle said of the *raison d'être* of the state: that it came into being so that human life be possible, and continues in being so that the good life be possible? This then is also the object of the true statesman.

No wonder, then, that the two so divergent responsibilities interpenetrate in remarkable ways from the opposite ends of greatest singularity and greatest generality. First, in their object. Education, for instance, is private *and* public. Even in the closest sphere of the home it includes socialization toward the wider community; and this, in turn, takes a hand in the molding of its future members, the would-be citizens. Thus all developed states have a public school system and an educational policy. This is just one telling example of how parental and political responsibilities, the most private and the most public, the most intimate and the most general, overlap in virtue of the totality of their respective object.

Not only from the side of the object, but also from that of their condition in the subject do the two "total" responsibilities meet. Everybody knows what the subjective conditions are in the parental case: the consciousness of one's total authorship; the immediate appeal of the child's total need for care; and spontaneous love, first as the post-partural, "blindly" compulsive feeling of the mammal mother for the newborn as such, then increasingly, with the emergence of the person, the seeing, personal love for this subject of unique identity. In such choiceless force of immediacy, the subjective condition is as little as the objective replicable in other, less original relations, and the reproductive bond retains a status of primacy that no analogue can equal in evidence of responsibility. The statesman is not the originator of the community for which he assumes responsibility unto himself; rather is its prior existence the ground for his doing so, and from it he also derives whatever power he may concentrate in his hands. Nor is he, parent-like, the source of sustenance for the collective, but at best the guardian of its continued capacity to sustain itself. More generally, the ruler's responsibility concerns independent beings who at a pinch might manage for themselves. And "love," finally, in the genuine sense cannot be felt for a non-individual, collective, largely abstract entity. Nonetheless, to take the last point first, there does exist an emotional relation comparable to love on the part of the political individual toward the community whose destinies he wishes to guide to the best, for it is "his" in a much deeper sense than that of a mere community of interests: he is (in the normal case) descended from it and through it has become what he is; he is thus, indeed, not the father, but a "son" of his people and country (also class, etc.) and thereby in a kind of sibling-relation to all the others—present, future, even past—with whom he shares this bond. This fact engenders, as in the family, from which the symbolism is borrowed, something more than merely a recognition of duty, namely, that emotional identification with the whole, the felt "solidarity," which is analogous to the love for the individual. Even solidarity of fate can in terms of sentiment take the place of common descent. If both coincide (a radical contingency the one as much as the other), their combination is overpowering. The fact of feeling then makes the heart receptive to the duty which of itself does not ask about it, and ensouls the affirmed responsibility with its impulse. It is difficult, though not impossible, to carry responsibility for something one doesn't love, and one rather generates the love for it than do one's duty "free from inclination."

The spectacle of the total dependency of the infant, too, has a somewhat more abstract analogue in the political sphere: the general but always perceptually particularized knowledge that the issues of common welfare do not simply look after themselves but require conscious direction and decision, nearly always improvement, and sometimes salvation from disaster. It is, in brief, the insistent knowledge that the *res publica* too exists precariously. Thus, we have here again the fact of vulnerability and peril in that with which sentiment identifies and of which "one" must take care. This "one," meaning abstractly everybody, turns into the self-chosen concrete "I" of the politician who believes that he at this moment knows best what is best for "all," or is best fitted to carry out an existing consensus about it. Whether the belief is right remains forever objectively moot (for his occupying the role prevents the trying out of others), but subjectively this belief belongs inalienably to the total nature of political responsibility as it responds to the call of public necessity. But he who thus responds to public necessity is himself subject to it and rises to the challenge out of the condition of an equal among equals; in the public cause he promotes his very own cause as included in the former. This clearly sets his role off from that of parents who do not share the child's needs, but must have outgrown them to be able to minister to them. Beyond this automatically fulfilled condition (as concomitant with procreative maturity), no qualification of special ability is required, whereas the political pretender needs that distinction to legitimate his chosen role.

What, therefore, has no equivalent at all in the political sphere is the unilateral and absolute causation of existence, wherein alone, without further supplements, the obligation as well as the qualification for the parental role is grounded, and no analogous feeling unites political responsibility with the parental one. The statesman, however much of a "founder," is himself already a creature of the community whose cause he takes into his hands. Indebted he is, therefore, not to what he has made but to what has made him, to the forebears who transmitted the common-wealth down to the present, to the contemporary joint-heirs as the immediate source of his mandate, and to the continuation of the received into an indefinite future. Something of this applies also to the parental role, in qualification of the purely originative relation toward a *de novo* beginning life. But here we are already touching upon the two other characteristics of our two models of responsibility, "continuity" and "future," which almost auto-matically follow from the characteristic of "totality."

IX. The Dimension of Future in Total Responsibility

Of these, "continuity" means simply that responsibilities of that kind (unlike limited ones) have no pause as long as they last and permit of no "vacation" from their duties. More interesting is the dimension of "future" in responsibility of the total sort. In its indefinite scope, it presents something of a paradox. Children outgrow parental care, communities outlive statesmen. And yet, the pertinent responsibilities, in all of their particular, timebound tasks, somehow extend into the whole future of their charge, even though that future lies beyond their ken and control. Can the unknowable be included in my duty? Here lies the paradox. For it is the future of the whole existence, beyond the direct efficacy of the responsible agent and thus beyond his concrete calculation, which is the invisible co-object of such a respon-sibility in each of its single, defined occasions. These occasions, and the interventions they provoke, are each time about the proximate particular, and this lies more or less within the range of informed prescience. The totality that will absorb the long-range effect of the particular decision is beyond such prescience, not only because of the unknown number of unknowns in the equation of objective circumstances, but ultimately because of the *spontaneity* or freedom of the life in question—the greatest of all unknowns, which yet must be included in the total responsibility. Indeed, precisely that in the object for whose eventual self-assertion the original agent can no longer be held responsible himself, viz., the own, autonomous causality of the life under his care, is yet an ultimate object of his commitment. It can be so in one way only: respecting this transcendent horizon, the intent of the responsibility must be not so much to determine as to enable, i.e., to prepare and keep the capacity for itself in those to come intact, never foreclosing the future exercise of responsibility by them. The object's self-owned futurity is the truest futural aspect of the responsibility, which thus makes itself the guardian of the very source of that irksome unpredictability in the fruits of its labors. Its highest fulfillment, which it must be able to dare, is its abdication before the right of the never-anticipated which emerges as the outcome of its care. Its highest duty, therefore, is to see that responsibility itself is not stifled, be it from its source within, be it from constraints without. In the light of such self-transcending width, it becomes apparent that responsibility as such is nothing else but the moral complement to the ontological constitution of our *temporality*.

Where does that leave us practically? For mere mortals, the incalculability of the long-term outcome of any action might seem either to place an impossible strain on responsibility, which could paralyze action, or to provide a facile shelter in the immunity of ignorance, which could excuse recklessness. But the above considerations tell otherwise: in explaining the unknowability and deferring to its cause, they allow us to extract a practical knowledge from ignorance itself. First of all—to say the obvious—as there is no complete knowledge about the future, neither is there complete ignorance, and an agent's *concrete* moral responsibility at the time of action does extend farther than to its proximate effects. How far ahead, that depends on the nature of the "object" and on our power and prescience. In the case of the child, a definite terminus is set by the object itself: parental responsibility has maturity for its goal and terminates with it. Adulthood, if its self-assertive powers have not been impaired in advance (a vital "if" indeed), is trusted to make its own new start of coping with the—generally recurrent—conditions of individual life. Each generation stands on itself, repeating the parental precedent in its own way. The aged onlooker may have occasion to doubt if his educative record was blameless, but he has at least nurtured the chance of autonomous life to make up for his sins. "Maturity" just implies this chance, which takes over where parental responsibility ceases. That preordained threshold defines the latter's terminal goal.

No such intrinsic terminus is set to political responsibility or that for mankind as a whole by the nature of its object. The continuous life of communities has no true analogy to the ages of man, and major deeds in this field are apt to create facts never to be undone, constraining the options of all posterity. Abstractly, therefore, responsibility is here endless: power and prescience of the agent alone limit its concrete span. If the two were coextensive, there were no ethical problem in wielding the one informed by the other. But that preestablished harmony between the power actually wielded and the predictability of its long-term effects does not exist.[5] Political responsibility is plagued by the excess of the causal reach over that of prescience. The consequences of the single action enmesh with the immensity of strands in the causal fabric of the whole, which defies analysis even for the now, and exponentially so into the future. Dispatched into that interplay, the original intent may become immoderately magnified or—just as well—obliterated, and almost surely distorted; in any case, it is set adrift. This amounts to no more than saying that the course of history is unpredictable—and with it the afterlife of political decisions of the moment. Any long-range prognosis is at best an informed guess (usually proved wrong by events: almost every purpose is destined to become estranged from itself in the long run). The spectator, according to his temperament, may be thrilled or chastised by the perennial surprises of the historical drama; the actor must still wager on his guess and live with its uncertainty.

Nonetheless—remembering what we said before—even the most skeptical estimate of historical prognosis leaves at least one basic certainty, itself a prognosis: that political spontaneity will remain necessary at all times, precisely because the excessively intricate web of events will, on principle, never conform to plan. From this there follows a highly general, but by no means empty, *imperative* precisely for the statesman whose action consciously has this enormous causal thrust into the distant unknown, namely, to do nothing that will prevent the further appearance of his like; that is, not to plug up the indispensable though not calculable wellspring of spontaneity in the body politic from which future statesmen can arise—therefore, neither in the goal *nor on the road to it* to create a condition in which the potential candidates for a repetition of his own role have become lackeys or robots. In brief, *one* responsibility of the art of politics is to see that the art of politics remains possible in the future. Nobody can say that this principle, a knowledge wrested from ignorance, is trivial and not capable of intentional violation (which is one of the criteria of the non-triviality of a principle). The general principle here is that any total responsibility, with all its particular tasks and in all its single actions, is always responsible also for preserving, beyond its own termination, the *possibility* of responsible action in the future.

Contemporary civilization has lent a new edge to these considerations. If political action has always been beset by the excess of causal reach over that of prediction and so was never free of an element of gambling, today's global technology has raised the stakes immeasurably and, at the same time, has only widened the gap between the power actually wielded and the predictability of its long-range effects. To be sure, the time span of informed planning has lengthened greatly with the aid of science and its analytical tools, but the span of objective responsibility even more so with the runaway momentum of the novel things set afoot with that same aid. Novelty itself, this greatest boon, has the cost of denying to prediction the benefit of past precedent. Yet no pleading of ignorance will avail the daring innovators. Possibilities discerned by scientifically schooled imagination take the place of familiar experience in distant anticipation, which has become a moral duty. And among them is for the first time, as a realistic danger of progress, the quenching of future spontaneity in a world of behavioral automata. The point is that the changed scale and content of human action have put the whole human enterprise at its mercy.[6]

Reflecting on all this—on the magnitude of our novel powers and the novelty of their products, their impact on the human condition everywhere, and the dynamism they let loose into an indefinite future—we see that *responsibility* with a never known burden has moved into the center of political morality. This is why we make the present effort to clarify the phenomenon of responsibility as such. Here we also have an answer to the question, raised at the beginning, why "responsibility," for which we claim this central place, lacks that prominence and has largely been ignored in traditional ethical theory. Both the fact and the explanation are interesting.

X. Why "Responsibility" Was Not Central in Former Ethical Theory

The fact is that the *concept* of responsibility nowhere plays a conspicuous role in the moral systems of the past nor in the philosophical theories of ethics. Accordingly, the *feeling* of responsibility appears nowhere as the affective moment in the formation of the moral will: quite different feelings, as I have indicated, like love, reverence, etc., have been assigned this office. What is the explanation? Responsibility, so we learned, is a function of power and knowledge, with their mutual relation not a simple one. Both were formerly so limited that, of the future, most had to be left to fate and the constancy of the natural order, and all attention focused on doing right what had to be done now. But right action is best assured by right being: therefore, ethics concerned itself mainly with "virtue," which just represents the best possible being of man and little looks beyond its performance to the thereafter. To be sure, rulers looked to the permanence of the dynasty, and republics to that of the common-wealth. But what was to be done to this end consisted essentially in strengthening the institutional and social orderings (including their ideological supports) that would assure such permanence, and moreover in the right education of the heir (in a monarchy) or of the coming citizens (in a republic). What is being prepared is always the next generation, and later ones are seen as its repetition—generations that can live in the same house with the same furnishings. The house must be well built to begin with, and to its preservation is also directed the concept of virtue. Wherever the classical philosophers, to whom we owe the science of the state, reflected on the relative goodness of constitutions, a decisive criterion was durability, i.e., stability, and to this end, a right balance of freedom and discipline seemed the proper means. The best constitution is that which is most apt to last, and virtue, in addition to good laws, is the best guarantee of lasting. Therefore, the good constitution must through itself promote the virtue of the citizens. Justice, in particular, belongs to the conditions of stability and is accordingly emphasized, but equally for its being a form of personal excellence. (Never is the shaking of the whole edifice recommended for the sake of absolute justice: it is a virtue, that is, a form of conduct, not an ideal of the objective order of things.) The generally held rule is: what is good for man as a personal and public being now will be so in the future; therefore, the best pre-shaping of the future lies in the goodness of the present state which, by its internal properties, promises to continue itself. For the rest, one was conscious of the uncertainty of human affairs, of the role of chance and luck, which one could not anticipate, but against which one could arm with a good constitution of the souls and a sound constitution of the political body.

The premise for this reckoning with the essentially same that is threatened only by inscrutable fate is, of course, the *absence of that dynamism* which dominates all of modern existence and consciousness. Things human were seen not otherwise in flux than those of nature, i.e., like everything in the world of becoming; this flux has no special definite direction, unless toward decay, and against that the existing order must be secured by good laws (just as the cosmos secures its existence by the preservative laws of its cyclical order). It is understandable, therefore, that for those before us, whose present did not throw such a long shadow ahead into the future as does ours, but mainly counted for itself, "responsibility for the coming" was not a natural norm of action: it would have had no object comparable to ours and be considered hubris rather than virtue.

XI. Eternity versus Time

But the explanation can go deeper than to lack of power (control of fate and nature), limited precognition, and absent dynamism, all of them negative traits. If the human condition, compounded of the nature of man and the nature of the environment, is essentially always the same, and if, on the other hand, the flux of becoming wherein it is immersed is essentially irrational and not a creative or directional or otherwise transcending process, then the true goal toward which man should live cannot be seen in the "horizontal," in the prolongation of the temporal, but must be seen in the "vertical," i.e., in the eternal, which overarches temporality and is equally "there" for every now. This is best exemplified by Plato, still the mightiest countervoice to the ontology and ethic of modernity. The object of eros is the good-in-itself, which is not of this world, i.e., the world of becoming and time. The eros is striving relatively for the better, absolutely for perfect being. A measure of perfection is "to be forever." Toward this goal, eros already labors blindly in animal procreation, obtaining a token of eternity in the survival of the species. The "ever again," "always the same," is the first approximation to true being. The seeing eros of man surpasses this in more direct approximations; the eros of the wise aims at it most directly. The drive is upward, not forward, toward being, not into becoming. This direction of the ethical quest is based on a definite ontology. So is ours, but the ontology has changed. Ours is not that of eternity, but of time. No longer is immutability the measure of perfection; almost the opposite is true. Abandoned to "sovereign becoming" (Nietzsche), condemned to it after abrogating transcendent being, we must seek the essential in transience itself. It is in this context that responsibility can become dominant in morality. The Platonic eros, directed at eternity, at the non-temporal, is not responsible for its object. For this "is" and never "becomes." What time cannot affect and to which nothing can happen is an object not of responsibility, but of emulation. Only for the changeable and perishable can one be responsible, for what is threatened by corruption, for the mortal in its mortality. If this alone is left and at the same time our power over it has grown so enormous, then the consequences for morality are immeasurable but still unclear, and this is what occupies us. The Platonic position was clear: he wanted not that the eternal turn temporal, but that by means of the eros the temporal turn eternal ("as far as is possible for it"). This thirst for eternity is ultimately the meaning of eros, much as it is aroused by temporal images. Our concern about the preservation of the species, to the contrary, is thirst for temporality in its ever new, always unprecedented productions, which no knowledge of essence can predict. Such a thirst imposes its own novel duties; the striving for ultimate perfection, for the intrinsically definitive, is not among them.

The turning-around of the millennial "platonic" position is tellingly exhibited in the quasi-eschatological philosophies of history from the eighteenth century on, precisely because they still retain, in the idea of progress, a residue of the ideal of perfection. Kant, Hegel, and Marx, for example, with all their profound differences, have this in common: that the axis of approximation to the absolute has been pivoted from the vertical down to the horizontal, the ordinate has become the abscissa, the goal, e.g., the highest good, the absolute spirit, the classless society, lies in the time-series that stretches before the subject indefinitely into the future, and is to be progressively approximated through the cumulative activity of many subjects along the series.

We today are beyond even that stage. Threatened by catastrophe from the very progress of history itself, we surely can no longer trust in an immanent "reason in history"; and to speak of a self-realizing "meaning" of the drift of events would be sheer frivolity. This relegates all former conceptions to obsolescence and charges responsibility with tasks by whose measure even the great question which has agitated minds for so long—whether a socialist or individualist society, an authoritarian or free one, would be better for man—changes to the second-grade question of which would be better suited to deal with the coming situations—a question of expediency, perhaps even of survival, but no longer of "Weltanschauung."

XII. Parent-Child Relation: the Archetype of Responsibility

To conclude these very incomplete reflections on a theory of responsibility we return once more to the timeless archetype of all responsibility, the parental for the child. Archetype it is in the genetic and typological respect, but also in the epistemological, because of its immediate evidence. What has it to tell us?

1. The elemental "ought" in the "is" of the newborn. The concept of responsibility implies that of an ought—first of an ought-to-be of something, then of an ought-to-do of someone in response to the first. The intrinsic right of the object is prior to the duty of the subject. Only an immanent claim can objectively ground for someone else an obligation to transitive causality. The objectivity must really stem from the object. Thus all proofs of validity for moral prescriptions are ultimately reduced to obtaining evidence of an "ontological" ought. If the chances for this were not better than those of the famous "ontological proof" for the existence of God, the theory of ethics would be in a bad way, as indeed it is today. For the crux of present theory is just the alleged chasm between "is" and "ought." It denies that from any "is" as such, in either its given or possible being, something like an "ought" can issue. Premised here is the concept of a naked "is," present, past, or future. Needed, therefore, is an *ontic* paradigm in which the plain factual "is" evidently coincides with an "ought"—which does not, therefore, admit for itself the concept of a "mere is" at all. Is there such a paradigm? Yes, we answer: that which was the beginning of each of us, when we could not know it yet, but ever again offers itself to the eye when we can look and know. For when asked: show us a single instance (one is enough to break the ontological dogma) where that coincidence of "is" and "ought" occurs, we can point at the most familiar sight: the newborn, whose mere breathing uncontradictably addresses an ought to the world around, namely, to take care of him. Look and you know. I say: "uncontradictably," not "irresistibly": for of course the force of this, as of any, "ought" can be resisted, its call can meet with deafness or can be drowned by other calls and pressures, like sacrifice of the first-born, Spartan child-exposure, bare self-preservation—this fact takes nothing away from the claim being incontestable as such and immediately evident. Nor do I say "an entreaty" to the world ("please take care of me"), for the infant cannot entreat as yet; and anyway, an entreaty, be it ever so moving, does not oblige. Thus no mention also is made of sympathy, pity or whichever of the emotions may come into play on our part, and not even of love. I mean strictly just this: that here the plain being of a *de facto* existent immanently and evidently contains an ought for others, and would do so even if nature would not succor this ought with powerful instincts or assume its job alone.

"But why 'evident'?" the theoretical rigorist may ask: What is really and objectively "there" is a conglomeration of cells, which are conglomerations of molecules with their physico-chemical transactions, which as such *plus the conditions of their continuation* can be known; but that there *ought* to be such a continuation and, therefore, somebody ought to do something for it, that does not belong to the finding and can in no manner be seen in it. Indeed not. But is it the infant who is seen here? He does not enter at all into the mathematical physicist's view, which purposely confines itself to an exceedingly filtered residue of his otherwise screened-off reality. And naturally, even the brightest visibility still requires the use of the visual faculty for which it is meant. Look, and you will see.

2. What the evidence of the newborn teaches about the nature of responsibility. It only remains to explicate *what* is seen here: which traits, besides the unquestionable immediacy itself, distinguish this evidence from all other manifestations of an ought in reality and make it not only empirically the first and most intuitive, but also in content the most perfect paradigm, literally the prototype, of an object of responsibility. We shall find that its distinction lies in the unique relation between possession and non-possession of being displayed by beginning life, which demands from its cause to continue what it has begun.

The newborn unites in himself the self-accrediting force of being-already-there and the demanding impotence of being-not-yet; the unconditional end-in-itself of everything alive and the still-have-to-come of the faculties for securing this end. This need-to-become is an in-between, a suspension of helpless being over not-being, which must be bridged by another causality. The radical insufficiency of the begotten as such carries with it the mandate to the begetters to avert its sinking back into nothing and to tend its further becoming. The undertaking thereto was implicit in the generating. Its observance (even by others) becomes an ineluctable duty toward a being now existing in its authentic right and in the total dependence on such observance. The immanent ought-to-be of the suckling, which his every breath proclaims, turns thus into the transitive ought-to-do of others who alone can help the claim continually to its right and make possible the gradual coming true of the teleological promise which it carries in itself from the first. They must do this continually, so that the breathing continue and with it also the claim renew itself continually, until the fulfillment of the immanent-teleological promise of eventual self-sufficiency releases them from the duty. Their power over the object of responsibility is here not only that of commission but also that of omission, which alone would be lethal. They are thus responsible totally, and this is more than the common human obligation toward the plight of fellow humans, whose basis is something other than responsibility. In its most original and massive sense, responsibility follows from being the cause of existence; and all those share in it who endorse the fiat of procreation by not revoking it in their own case, viz., by permitting themselves to live—thus, the coexisting family of man.

With every newborn child humanity begins anew, and in that sense also the responsibility for the continuation of mankind is involved. But this is much too abstract for the prime phenomenon of utter concreteness we are considering here. Under that abstract responsibility there may have been, let us assume, the duty to produce "a child," but none possibly to produce *this* one, as the "this" was entirely beyond anticipation. But precisely *this* in its wholly contingent uniqueness is that to which responsibility is now committed—the only case where the "cause" one serves has nothing to do with appraisal of worthiness, nothing with comparison, and nothing with a contract. An element of impersonal guilt is inherent in the causing of existence (the most radical of all causalities of a subject) and permeates all personal responsibility toward the unconsulted object. The guilt is shared by all, because the act of the progenitors was generic and not thought up by them (perhaps not even known); and the later accusation by children and children's children for neglected responsibility, the most comprehensive and practically most futile of all accusations, can apply to everyone living today. So also the thanks.

Thus the "ought" manifest in the infant enjoys indubitable evidence, concreteness, and urgency. Utmost facticity of "this-ness," utmost right thereto, and utmost fragility of being meet here together. In him it is paradigmatically visible that the locus of responsibility is the being that is immersed in becoming, surrendered to mortality, threatened by corruptibility. Not *sub specie aeternitatis*, rather *sub specie temporis* must responsibility look at things; and it can lose its all in the flash of an instant. In the case of continually critical vulnerability of being, as given in our paradigm, responsibility becomes a continuum of such instants.

How this archetype of all responsibility sheds light on other, more public occasions for it, including the most pressing ones of the present state of things, and how its lessons on the essence of responsibility can benefit ethical theory, that is a subject for further arduous thought.

NOTES

1. For a most powerful critique, see Max Scheler, *Der Formalismus in der Ethik und die materiale Wertethik* (Halle, 1916).
2. Kant himself, of course, has rescued the mere formality of the categorical imperative by a "material" principle of conduct (ostensibly inferred from it, but, in fact, added to it): respect for the dignity of persons as "ends in themselves." To this, the charge of vacuity does not apply!
3. The same word for two so different meanings is no mere equivocation. Their logical connection is that the substantive meaning anticipates the full force of the formal meaning to fall on the agent in the future for what he did or failed to do under the substantive mandate.
4. Compare what I have said about the "ontological imperative" in "Responsibility Today: The Ethics of an Endangered Future," *Social Research* 43.1 (Spring 1976), p. 94.
5. Strictly speaking, of course, this holds for the education of children too, but there as we indicated—with the perennial "new beginning" afforded by the resources of personal spontaneity—antecedent deed has not the same finality of "results."
6. See "Responsibility Today . . .", p. 89-93, for a discussion of the discrepancy, in modern technology, between the tremendous time-reach of our actions and the much shorter reach of our foresight

concerning their outcome, and how to deal with it morally, i.e., responsibly. See also H. Jonas, *Philosophical Essays: From Ancient Creed to Technological Man* (Englewood Cliffs, N.J.: Prentice-Hall, 1974), p. 10, 18.

From System to Story:
An Alternative Pattern
for Rationality in Ethics

David Burrell
Stanley Hauerwas

I. Narrative, Ethics, and Theology

IN THE INTEREST of securing a rational foundation for morality, contemporary ethical theory has ignored or rejected the significance of narrative for ethical reflection. It is our contention that this has been a profound mistake, resulting in a distorted account of moral experience. Furthermore, the attempt to portray practical reason as independent of narrative contexts has made it difficult to assess the value which convictions characteristic of Christians or Jews might have for moral existence. As a result, we have lost sight of the ways these traditions might help us deal with the moral issues raised by modern science and medicine.[1]

To substantiate this thesis we will develop a negative and positive argument. Negatively, we will characterize the standard account of ethical rationality and the anomalies that such an account occasions. This aspect of our argument will hold no surprises for anyone acquainted with recent ethical theory. Most of the criticisms we will develop have already been made by others. However, we hope to show that these criticisms cannot be met within the standard account and at least suggest why narra-

75

tive might be significant for an adequate analysis of moral existence. In developing this negative argument we will use
"narrative" and "character" without trying to analyze them fully.

Positively, we will analyze the concept of narrative and show
how it provides a pattern for moral rationality. We will argue that
the standard account of moral rationality has been wrong to
associate the narrative aspects of our experience with the subjective or arbitrary. In contrast we will suggest that narrative constitutes the form that does justice to the kind of objectivity proper
to practical reason. In order to show how it is possible to
discriminate between the truth of stories we will pay particular
attention to the way this was done by a master of narrative, St.
Augustine. Building on his story, we will suggest how the veracity of stories can be tested.

Our argument involves two independent but interrelated theses.
First, we will try to establish the significance of narrative for
ethical reflection. By the phrase, "the significance of narrative,"
we mean to call attention to three points:[2] (1) that character and
moral notions only take on meaning in a narrative; (2) that
narrative and explanation stand in an intimate relationship, and,
therefore, moral disagreements involve rival histories of explanation; (3) that the standard account of moral objectivity is the
obverse of existentialist ethics, since the latter assumes that the
failure to secure moral objectivity implies that all moral judgments must be subjective or arbitrary. By showing the way
narrative can function as a form of rationality, we hope to
demonstrate that these do not represent the only alternatives.

Secondly, we will try to show how the convictions displayed
in the Christian story have moral significance. We will call
particular attention to the manner in which story teaches us to
know and do what is right under finite conditions. For at least
one indication of the moral truthfulness of a particular narrative is
the way it enables us to recognize the limits of our engagements
and yet continue to pursue them.

II. The Standard Account of Moral Rationality

At least partly under the inspiration of the scientific ideal of
objectivity,[3] contemporary ethical theory has tried to secure for

moral judgments an objectivity that would free such judgments from the subjective beliefs, wants, and stories of the agents who make them. Just as science tries to insure objectivity by adhering to an explicitly disinterested method, so ethical theory tries to show that moral judgments, insofar as they can be considered true, must be the result of an impersonal rationality. Thus moral judgments, whatever else they may involve, must at least be non-egoistic in the sense that they involve no special pleading colored by the agent's own history, community identification, or other particular point of view in order to establish their truthfulness.

Thus the hallmark of contemporary ethical theory, whether in a Kantian or utilitarian mode, has been to free moral behavior from the arbitrary and contingent nature of the agent's beliefs, dispositions, and character. Just as science strives to free the experiment from the experimenter, so, ethically, if we are to avoid un-checked subjectivism or relativism, it is thought that the moral life must be freed from the peculiarities of agents caught in the limits of their particular histories. Ethical rationality assumes it must take the form of science if it is to have any claim to being objective.[4]

There is an interesting parallel to this development in modern medical theory. Eric Cassell has located a tension between the explanation of a disease proper to science and the diagnosis a clinician makes for a particular patient.[5] The latter is well de-scribed by Tolstoy in *War and Peace*,

> Doctors came to see Natasha, both separately and in consultation. They said a great deal in French, in German, and in Latin. They criticised one another, and prescribed the most diverse remedies for all the diseases they were familiar with. But it never occurred to one of them to make the simple reflection that they could not understand the disease from which Natasha was suffering, as no single disease can be fully understood in a living person; for every living person has his complaints unknown to medicine—not a disease of the lungs, of the kidneys, of the skin, of the heart, and so on, as described in medical books, but a disease that consists of one out of the innumerable combinations of ailments of those organs.[6]

The scientific form of rationality is represented by B. F. Skinner's commentary on this quote. Skinner suggests that

Tolstoy was justified, during his day, in calling every sickness a unique event, but uniqueness no longer stands in the way of the development of the science of medicine since we can now supply the necessary general principles of explanation. Thus happily, according to Skinner, "the intuitive wisdom of the old-style diagnostician has been largely replaced by the analytic procedures of the clinic, just as a scientific analysis of behavior will eventually replace the personal interpretation of unique instances."[7]

Even if we were competent to do so, it would not be relevant to our argument to try to determine whether Tolstoy or Skinner, or some combination of their theories, describes the kind of explanation most appropriate to medical diagnosis (though our hunch lies with Tolstoy). Rather, it is our contention that the tendency of modern ethical theory to find a functional equivalent to Skinner's "scientific analysis" has distorted the nature of practical reason. Ethical objectivity cannot be secured by retreating from narrative, but only by being anchored in those narratives that best direct us toward the good.

Many thinkers have tried to free the objectivity of moral reason from narrative by arguing that there are basic moral principles, procedures, or points of view to which a person is logically or conceptually committed when engaged in moral action or judgment. This logical feature has been associated with such titles as the categorical imperative, the ideal observer, universalizability, or, more recently, the original position. Each of these in its own way assumes that reasons, if they are to be morally justified, must take the form of judgments that can and must be made from anyone's point of view.[8] All of the views assume that "objectivity" will be attained in the moral life only by freeing moral judgments from the "subjective" story of the agent.

This tradition has been criticized for the formal nature of its account of moral rationality, i.e., it seems to secure the objectivity of moral judgment exactly by emptying the moral life of all substantive content. Such criticism fails to appreciate, however, that these accounts of moral rationality are attempts to secure a "thin" theory of the moral life in order to provide an account of moral duty that is not subject to any community or tradition. Such theories are not meant to tell us how to be good in relation to some ideal, but rather to insure that what we owe to others as strangers, not as friends or sharers in a tradition, is non-arbitrary.

What I am morally obligated to do is not what derives from being a father, or a son, or an American, or a teacher, or a doctor, or a Christian, but what follows from my being a person constituted by reason. To be sure all these other roles or relations may involve behavior that is morally good, but such behavior cannot be required except as it can be based upon or construed as appropriate to rationality itself. This is usually done by translating such role-dependent obligations as relations of promise-keeping that can be universalized. (Of course, what cannot be given are any moral reasons why I should become a husband, father, teacher, doctor, or Christian in the first place.)

It is our contention, however, that the standard account of moral rationality distorts the nature of the moral life: (1) by placing an unwarranted emphasis on particular decisions or quandaries; (2) by failing to account for the significance of moral notions and how they work to provide us with skills of perception; (3) by separating the agent from his interests. We will briefly spell out each of these criticisms and suggest how each stems in part from the way standard accounts avoid acknowledging the narrative character of moral existence.

II:1. Decisions, Character, and Narrative

In his article, "Quandary Ethics," Edmund Pincoffs has called attention to the way contemporary ethics concentrates on problems—situations in which it is hard to know what to do—as paradigmatic concerns for moral analysis.[9] On such a model, ethics becomes a decision procedure for resolving conflict-of-choice situations. This model assumes that no one faces an ethical issue until they find themselves in a quandary—should I or should I not have an abortion, etc. Thus the moral life appears to be concerned primarily with "hard decisions."

This picture of the moral life is not accidental, given the standard account of moral rationality. For the assumption that most of our moral concerns are "problems" suggests that ethics can be construed as a rational science that evaluates alternative "solutions." Moral decisions should be based on rationally derived principles that are not relative to any one set of convictions.

Ethics becomes a branch of decision theory. Like many of the so-called policy sciences, ethics becomes committed to those descriptions of the moral life that will prove relevant to its mode of analysis, that is, one which sees the moral life consisting of dilemmas open to rational "solutions."

By concentrating on "decisions" about "problems," this kind of ethical analysis gives the impression that judgments can be justified apart from the agent who finds himself or herself in the situation. What matters is not that David Burrell or Stanley Hauerwas confronts a certain quandary, but that anyone may or can confront X or Y. The intentions or reasons proper to a particular agent tend to become irrelevant. Thus, in considering the question of abortion, questions like: Why did the pregnancy occur? What kind of community do you live in? What do you believe about the place of children?—may be psychologically interesting but cannot be allowed to enter into the justification of the decision. For such matters are bound to vary from one agent to another. The "personal" can only be morally significant to the extent that it can be translated into the "impersonal."

(Although it is not central to our case, one of the implications of the standard account of rationality is its conservative force. Ethical choice is always making do within the societal framework we inherit, because it is only within such a framework that we are able to have a problem at all. But often the precise problem at issue cannot arise or be articulated given the limits of our society or culture. We suspect that this ineptness betrays a commitment of contemporary ethical theory to political liberalism: one can concentrate on the justification of moral decisions because one accepts the surrounding social order with its moral categories. In this sense modern ethical theory is functionally like modern pluralist democratic theory—it can afford to be concerned with incremental social change, to celebrate "issue" politics, because it assumes the underlying social structures are just.)[10]

By restricting rationality to choices between alternative courses of action, moreover, the various normative theories formed in accordance with the standard account have difficulty explaining the moral necessity to choose between lesser evils.[11] Since rational choice is also our moral duty, it must also be a good duty.

Otherwise one would be obliged rationally to do what is morally a lesser evil. There is no place for moral tragedy; whatever is morally obligatory must be good, even though the consequences may be less than happy. We may subjectively regret what we had to do, but it cannot be a moral regret. The fact that modern deontological and teleological theories assume that the lesser evil cannot be a moral duty witnesses to their common commitment to the standard view of moral rationality.

The problem of the lesser evil usually refers to tragic choices externally imposed, e.g., the necessity of killing civilians in order to destroy an arms factory. Yet the language of "necessity" is often misleading, for part of the "necessity" is the character of the actors, whether they be individuals or nations. Because moral philosophy, under the influence of the standard account, has thought it impossible to discuss what kind of character we should have—that, after all, is the result of the accident of birth and psychological conditioning—it has been assumed that moral deliberation must accept the limits of the decision required by his or her character. At best, "character" can be discussed in terms of "moral education"; but since the "moral" in education is determined by the standard account, it does not get us very far in addressing what kind of people we ought to be.

As a result, the standard account simply ignores the fact that most of the convictions that charge us morally are like the air we breathe—we never notice them, and do not do so precisely because they form us not to describe the world in certain ways and not to make certain matters subject to decision. Thus we assume that it is wrong to kill children without good reason. Or, even more strongly, we assume that it is our duty to provide children (and others who cannot protect themselves) with care that we do not need to give to the adult. These are not matters that we need to articulate or decide upon; their force lies rather in their not being subject to decision. And morally we must have the kind of character that keeps us from subjecting them to decision.

(What makes "medical ethics" so difficult is the penchant of medical care to force decisions that seem to call into question aspects of our life that we assumed not to be matters of decision, e.g., should we provide medical care for children who are born with major disabilities such as meningomyelocele.[12] In this respect the current interest in "medical ethics" does not simply represent a response to issues arising in modern medicine, but also reflects the penchant of the standard account to respond to dilemmas.)

Another way to make this point is to indicate that the standard account, by concentrating on decision, fails to deal adequately with the formation of a moral self, i.e., the virtues and character we think it important for moral agents to acquire. But the kind of decisions we confront, indeed the very way we describe a situation, is a function of the kind of character we have. And character is not acquired through decisions, though it may be confirmed and qualified there, but rather through the beliefs and dispositions we have acquired.

From the perspective of the standard account, beliefs and dispositions cannot be subject to rational deliberation and formation.[13] Positions based on the standard account do not claim that our dispositions, or our character, are irrelevant to how we act morally. But these aspects of our self are rational only as they enter into a moral decision. It is our contention, however, that it is rather character, inasmuch as it is displayed by a narrative, that provides the context necessary to pose the terms of a decision, or to determine whether a decision should be made at all.[14]

We cannot account for our moral life solely by the decisions we make; we also need the narratives that form us to have one kind of character rather than another. These narratives are not arbitrarily acquired, although they will embody many factors we might consider "contingent." As our stories, however, they will determine what kind of moral considerations—that is, what reasons—will count at all. Hence these narratives must be included in any account of moral rationality that does not unwarrantedly exclude large aspects of our moral existence—i.e., moral character.[15]

The standard account cannot help but view a narrative account as a retreat from moral objectivity. For if the individual agent's intentions and motives—in short, the narrative embodied in his or her character—are to have systematic significance for moral judgment, then it seems that we will have to give preference to the agent's interpretation of what he has done. So the dreaded first person singular, which the standard account was meant to purge from moral argument, would be reintroduced. To recall the force of "I," however, does not imply that we would propose "because I want to" as a moral reason. The fact is that the first person singular is seldom the assertion of the solitary "I," but rather the narrative of that "I." It is exactly the category of narrative that helps us to see that we are not forced to choose between some universal standpoint and the subjectivistic appeals to our own experience. For our experiences always come in the form of narratives that can be checked against themselves as well as others' experiences. I cannot make my behavior mean anything I want it to mean, for I have learned to understand my life from the stories I have learned from others.

The language the agent uses to describe his behavior, to himself and to others, is not uniquely his—it is *ours*, just as the notions we use have meanings that can be checked for appropriate or inappropriate use. But what allows us to check the truthfulness of these accounts of our behavior are the narratives from which our moral notions derive their paradigms. An agent cannot make his behavior mean anything he wants, since at the very least it must make sense within his own story, as well as be compatible with the narrative embodied in the language he uses. All our notions are narrative-dependent, including the notion of rationality.

II:2. Moral Notions, Language, and Narrative

We can show how our very notion of rationality depends on narrative by noting how the standard account tends to ignore the significance and meaning of moral notions. The standard account pictures our world as a *given* about which we need to make decisions. So terms like "murder," "stealing," "abortion," although admitted to be evaluative, are nonetheless regarded as descriptive. However, as Julius Kovesi has persuasively argued, our moral notions are not descriptive in the sense that yellow is, but rather describe only as we have purposes for such descriptions.[16] Moral notions, in other words, like many of our non-moral notions (though we are not nearly so sure as is the standard account how this distinction should be made), do not merely describe our activity; they also form it. Marx's claim, that the point of philosophy should be not to analyze the world but to change it, is not only a directive to ethicists but also an astute observation about the way our grammar displays the moral direction of our lives. The notions that form our moral perceptions involve skills that require narratives, that is, accounts of their institutional contexts and purposes, which we must know if we are to know how to employ them correctly. In other words, these notions resemble skills of perception which we must learn how to use properly.

The standard account's attempt to separate our moral notions from their narrative context by trying to ground them in, or derive their meaning from, rationality in itself has made it difficult to account for two reasons why moral controversies are so irresolvable. The standard account, for example, encourages us to assume that the pro- and anti-abortion advocates mean the same thing by the word "abortion." It is assumed, therefore, that the moral disagreement between these two sides must involve a basic moral principle, such as "all life is sacred," or be a matter of fact, such as whether the fetus is considered a human life. But this kind of analysis fails to see that the issue is not one of principle or fact, but one of perception determined by a history of interpretation.

Pro- and anti-abortion advocates do not communicate on the notion "abortion," since each group holds a different story about the purpose of the notion. At least as far as "abortion" is concerned, they live in conceptually different worlds. This fact does not prohibit discussion, but if abortion takes place, it cannot begin with the simple question of whether it is right or wrong. It is rather more like an argument between a member of the PLO and an Israeli about whether an attack on a village is unjustified terrorism. They both know the same "facts" but the issue turns on the story each holds, and within which those "facts" are known.

The advocates of the standard account try to train us to ignore the dependence of the meaning and use of notions on their narrative contexts, by providing a normative theory for the derivation and justification of basic moral notions. But to be narrative-dependent is not the same as being theory-dependent, at least in the way that a utilitarian or deontological position would have us think. What makes abortion right or wrong is not its capacity to work for or against the greatest good of the greatest number in a certain subclass. What sets the context for one's moral judgment is rather the stories we hold about the place of children in our lives, or the connection one deems ought or ought not to hold between sexuality and procreation, or some other such account. Deontological or utilitarian theories that try to free moral notions from their dependence on examples and the narratives that display them, prove to be too monochromatic to account for the variety of our notions and the histories on which they are dependent.

There can be no normative theory of the moral life that is sufficient to capture the rich texture of the many moral notions we inherit. What we actually possess are various and sometimes conflicting stories that provide us with the skills to use certain moral notions. What we need to develop is the reflective capacity to analyze those stories, so that we better understand how they function. It is not theory-building that develops such a capacity so much as close attention to the ways our distinctive communities tell their stories. Furthermore, an analysis of this sort carries us to the point of assessing the worth these moral notions have for directing our life-projects and shaping our stories.

The standard account's project to supply a theory of basic moral principles from which all other principles and actions can be justified or derived represents an attempt to make the moral life take on the characteristics of a system. But it is profoundly misleading to think that a rational explanation needs to be given for holding rational beliefs,[17] for to attempt to provide such an account assumes that rationality itself does not depend on narrative. What must be faced, however, is that our lives are not and cannot be subject to such an account, for the consistency necessary for governing our lives is more a matter of integrity than one of principle. The narratives that provide the pattern of integrity cannot be based on principle, nor are they engaging ways of talking about principles. Rather such narratives are the ones that allow us to determine how our behavior "fits" within our ongoing pattern.[18] To be sure, fittingness cannot have the necessitating form desired by those who want the moral life to have the "firmness" of some sciences, but it can exhibit the rationality of a good story.

II:3. Rationality, Alienation, and the Self

The standard account also has the distressing effect of making alienation the central moral virtue. We are moral exactly to the extent that we learn to view our desires, interests, and passions as if they could belong to anyone. The moral point of view, whether it is construed in a deontological or teleological manner, requires that we view our own projects and life as if we were outside observers. This can perhaps be seen most vividly in utilitarianism (and interestingly in Rawls's account of the original position) since the utilitarian invites us to assume that perspective toward our projects which will produce the best consequences for anyone's life plan. Thus, the standard account obligates us to regard our life as would an observer.

Paradoxically, what makes our projects valuable to us (as Bernard Williams has argued) is that they are ours. As soon as we take the perspective of the standard account, we accept the odd position of viewing our stories as if they were anyone's, or at least capable of being lived out by anyone. Thus, we are required to alienate ourselves from the projects that interest us in being anything at all.

The alienation involved in the standard account manifests itself in the different ways the self is understood by modern ethical theory. The self is often pictured as consisting of reason and desire, with the primary function of reason being to control desire. It is further assumed that desire or passion can give no clues to the nature of the good, for the good can only be determined in accordance with "reason." Thus, the standard account places us in the odd position of excluding pleasure as an integral aspect of doing the good. The good cannot be the satisfaction of desire, since the morality of reason requires a sharp distinction between universal rules of conduct and the "contingent" appetites of individuals.

Not only are we taught to view our desires in contrast to our reason, but the standard account also separates our present from our past. Morally, the self represents a collection of discontinuous decisions bound together only in the measure they approximate the moral point of view. Our moral capacity thus depends exactly on our ability to view our past in discontinuity with our present. The past is a limitation, since it can only prevent us from embodying more fully the new opportunities always guaranteed by the moral point of view. Thus, our moral potentiality depends on our being able to alienate ourselves from our past in order to grasp the timelessness of the rationality offered by the standard account.[19]

(In theological terms the alienation of the self is a necessary consequence of sinful pretensions. When the self tries to be more than it was meant to be, it becomes alienated from itself and all its relations are disordered. The view of rationality offered by the standard account is pretentious exactly as it encourages us to try to free ourselves from history. In effect it offers us the possibility of being like God. Ironically enough, however, this is not the God of the Jews and the Christians since, as we shall see, that God does not will himself to be free from history.)

In fairness, the alienation recommended by the standard account is motivated by the interest of securing moral truthfulness. But it mistakenly assumes that truthfulness is possible only if we judge ourselves and others from the position of complete (or as complete as possible) disinterest. Even if it were possible to assume such a stance, however, it would not provide us with the conditions for truthfulness. For morally there is no neutral story that insures the truthfulness of our particular stories. Moreover, any ethical theory that is sufficiently abstract and universal to claim neutrality would not be able to form character. For it would have deprived itself of the notions and convictions that are the necessary conditions for character. Far from assuring truthfulness, a species of rationality that prizes objectivity to the neglect of particular stories distorts moral reasoning by the way it omits the stories of character formation. If truthfulness (and the selflessness characteristic of moral behavior) is to be found, it will have to occur in and through the stories that we find tie the contingencies of our life together.

It is not our intention to call into question the significance of disinterestedness for the moral life, but rather to deny that recent accounts of "universality" or the "moral point of view" provide adequate basis for such disinterest. For genuine disinterest reflects

a non-interest in the self occasioned by the lure of a greater good
or a more beautiful object than we can create or will into
existence.[20] In this sense we are not able to choose to conform to
the moral point of view, for it is a gift. But as a gift it depends
on our self being formed by a narrative that provides the conditions for developing the disinterest required for moral behavior.

II:4. The Standard Account's Story

None of the criticisms above constitute a decisive objection to
the standard account, but taken together they indicate that the
standard account is seriously inadequate as a description of our
moral existence. How then are we to account for the continued
dominance of the standard account for contemporary ethical theory? If our analysis has been right, the explanation should be
found in the narrative that provides an apparent cogency for the
standard account in spite of its internal and external difficulties.[21]

It is difficult, however, to identify any one narrative that sets
the context for the standard account, for it is not one but many
narratives that sustain its plausibility. The form of some of these
stories is of recent origin, but we suspect that the basic story
underlying the standard account is of more ancient lineage—
namely, humankind's quest for certainty in a world of contingency.

It seems inappropriate to attribute such a grand story to the
standard account, since one of its attractions is its humility: it
does not pretend to address matters of the human condition, for it
is only a method. As a method it does not promise truth, only
clarity.

Yet the process of acculturating ourselves and others in the use
of this method requires a systematic disparaging of narrative. By
teaching us to prefer a "principle" or "rational" description (just
as science prefers a statistical description) to a narrative description, the standard account not only fails to account for the
significance of narrative but also sets obstacles to any therapy
designed to bring that tendency to light. It thus fails to provide us
with the critical skills to know the limits of the narrative which
currently has us in its grasp.

The reason for this lack of critical perspective lies in the narrative that was born during the Enlightenment. The plot was given in capsule by Auguste Comte: first came religion in the form of stories, then philosophy in the form of metaphysical analysis, and then science with its exact methods.[22] The story he tells in outline is set within another elaborated by Hegel, to show us how each of these ages supplanted the other as a refinement in the progressive development of reason. Therefore, stories are pre-scientific, according to the story legitimizing the age that calls itself scientific. Yet if one overlooks that budding contradiction, or fails to spell it out because everyone knows that stories are out of favor anyway, then the subterfuge has worked and the way out been blocked off.

Henceforth, any careful or respectable analysis, especially if it is moral in intent, will strike directly for the problem, leaving the rest for journalists who titillate or novelists who entertain. Serious folk, intent on improving the human condition, will have no time for that (except, maybe, after hours) for they must focus all available talent and resources on solving the problems in front of them. We all recognize the crude polarities acting here, and know how effectively they function as blinders. It is sufficient for our interests to call attention only to the capacity stories hold for eliciting critical awareness, and how an awareness of story enhances that approach known as scientific by awakening it to its presuppositions. Hence, we have argued for a renewed awareness of stories as an analytic tool, and one especially adapted to our moral existence, since stories are designed to effect critical awareness as well as describe a state of affairs.

By calling attention to the narrative context of the standard account, we are not proposing a wholesale rejection of that account or of the theories formed under its inspiration. In fact, the efforts expended on developing contrasting ethical theories (like utilitarianism or formalism) have become part of our legacy, and offer a useful way to introduce one to ethical reasoning. Furthermore, the manner of proceeding that we associate with the standard account embodies concerns that any substantive moral narrative must respect: a high regard for public discourse, the demand that we be able to offer reasons for acting, at once cogent and appropriate, and a way to develop critical skills of discrimination and judgment. Finally, any morality depends on a capacity to generate and to articulate moral principles which can set boundaries for proper behavior and guide our conduct.

Our emphasis on narrative need not militate against any of these distinctive concerns. Our difficulty rather lies with the way the standard account attempts to express and to ground these concerns in a narrative-free manner of accounting. We are given the impression that moral principles offer actual grounds for conduct, while in fact they present abstractions whose significance continues to depend on original narrative contexts. Abstractions play useful roles in reasoning, but a continual failure to identify them as abstractions becomes systematically misleading: a concern for rationality thereby degenerates into a form of rationalism.

Our criticism of the standard account has focused on the anomalies that result from that rationalism. We have tried to show how the hegemony of the standard account in ethics has in fact ignored or distorted significant aspects of moral experience. We do not wish to gainsay the importance of rationality for ethics; only expose a pretentious form of rationalism. Though the point can be made in different ways, it is no accident that the stories that form the lives of Jews and of Christians make them peculiarly sensitive to any account that demands that human existence fit a rational framework. The legitimate human concern for rationality is framed by a range of powers of quite another order. It is this larger contingent context which narrative is designed to order in the only manner available to us.

In this way, we offer a substantive explication of narrative as a constructive alternative to the standard account. Our penchant has been to rely upon the standard account as though it were the only lifeboat in a sea of subjective reactions and reductive explanations. To question it would be tantamount to exposing the leaks in the only bark remaining to us. In harkening to the narrative context for action, we are trying to direct attention to an alternative boat available to us. This one cannot provide the security promised by the other, but in return it contains instructions designed to equip us with the skills required to negotiate the dangers of the open sea.

III. Stories and Reasons for Acting

Ethics deals explicitly with reasons for acting. The trick lies in turning reasons into a form proper to acting. The normal form for reasoning requires propositions to be linked so as to display how the conclusion follows quite naturally. The very skills that allow us to form statements lead us to draw other statements from them as conclusions. The same Aristotle who perfected this art, however, also reminded us that practical syllogisms must conclude in an action rather than another proposition.[23] As syllogisms, they will display the form proper to reasoning, yet they must do so in a way that issues in action.

This difference reflects the fact that practical wisdom cannot claim to be a science, since it must deal with particular courses of action (rather than recurrent patterns); nor can it call itself an art, since "action and making are different kinds of thing." The alternative Aristotle settles for is "a true and reasoned . . . capacity to act with regard to the things that are good or bad for man" (*N. Ethics* 6.4, 1140b5). We have suggested that stories in fact help us all to develop that capacity as a reasoned capacity. This section will focus on the narrative form as a form of rationality; the following section will show how discriminating among stories develops skills for judging truly what is "good or bad for man." Using Aristotle's discriminations as a point of reference is meant to indicate that our thesis could be regarded as a development of his—in fact, we would be pleased to find it judged to be so.

III:1. Narrative Form as Rational Discourse

There are many kinds of stories, and little agreement on how to separate them into kinds. We distinguish short stories from novels, while acknowledging the short novel as well. We recognize that some stories offer with a particular lucidity patterns of plots that recur in countless other stories. We call these more archetypal stories myths, and often use them as a shorthand for referring to a typical tangle or dilemma that persons find themselves facing—whether in a story or in real life. That feature common to all stories, which gives them their peculiar aptitude for illuminating real life situations, is their narrative structure.

Experts will want to anatomize narrative as well, of course, but for our purposes let it be the connected description of action and of suffering which moves to a point. The point need not be detachable from the narrative itself; in fact, we think a story better that does not issue in a determinate *moral*. The "point" we call attention to here has to do with that form of connectedness that characterizes a novel. It is not the mere material connection of happenings to one individual, but the connected unfolding that we call *plot*. Difficult as this is to characterize—independently of displaying it in a good story!—we can nonetheless identify it as a connection among elements (actions, events, situations) which is neither one of logical consequence nor one of mere sequence. The connection seems rather designed to move our understanding of a situation forward by developing or unfolding it. We have described this movement as gathering to a point. Like implication, it seeks to make explicit what would otherwise remain implicit; unlike implication, the rules of development are not those of logic but stem from some more mysterious source.

The rules of development are not logical rules because narrative connects contingent events. The intelligibility which plot affords is not a necessary one, because the events connected do not exhibit recurrent patterns. Narrative is not required to be explanatory, then, in the sense in which a scientific theory must show necessary connections among occurrences. What we demand of a narrative is that it display how occurrences are actions. Intentional behavior is purposeful but not necessary. We are not possessed of the theoretical capacities to predict what will happen on the basis of what has occurred. Thus, a narrative moves us on to answer the question that dogs us: what happened next? It cannot answer that question by arbitrary statement, for our inquiring minds are already involved in the process. Yet the question is a genuine one precisely because we lack the capacity for sure prediction.

It is the intentional nature of human action that evokes a narrative account. We act for an end, yet our actions affect a field of forces in ways that may be characteristic yet remain unpredictable. So we can ask: What would follow from our hiring Jones?—as though certain events might be deduced from his coming on board. Yet we also know that whatever follows will not do so deductively, but rather as a plot unfolds. Nevertheless, we are right in inquiring into what might *follow from* our hiring him, since we must act responsibly. By structuring a plausible response to the question—and what happened next?—narrative offers just the intelligibility we need for acting properly.

III:2. What the Narrative Unfolds

But what makes a narrative plausible? The field of a story is actions (either deeds or dreams) or their opposite, sufferings. In either case, whatever action or passion is seen to unfold is something we call "character." *Character*, of course, is not a theoretical notion, but merely the name we give to the cumulative source of human actions. Stories themselves attempt to probe that source and discover its inner structure by trying to display how human actions and passions connect with one another to develop a character. As we follow the story, we gain some insight into recurrent connecting patterns, and also some ability to assess them. We learn to recognize different configurations and to rank some characters better than others.

Gradually, then, the characters (or ways of unifying actions) that we can recognize offer patterns for predicting recurring ways of acting. Expectations are set up, and the way an individual or others deal with those expectations shows us some of the capacities of the human spirit. In this way, character can assume the role of an analytic tool even though it is not itself an explanatory notion. Character is neither explanatory in origin nor in use, for it cannot be formulated prior to nor independently of the narrative that develops it. Yet it can play an illuminating or analytic role by calling attention to what is going on in a narrative as the plot unfolds: a character is being developed. Moreover, this character, as it develops, serves as a relative baseline for further developing itself or other characters, as we measure subsequent actions and responses against those anticipated by the character already developed. In this way, character plays an analytic role by offering a baseline for further development. That the baseline itself will shift represents one more way of distinguishing narrative development from logical implication.

We may consider the set of expectations associated with a developing character as a "language"—a systematic set of connections between actions that offers a setting or syntax for subsequent responses. Since character cannot be presented independently of the story or stories that develop it, however, the connection between a syntactical system and use, or the way in which a language embodies a form of life, becomes crystal clear. By attending to character, stories will display this fact to us without any need for philosophical reminders.

Similarly, we will see how actions, like expressions, accomplish what they do as part of a traditional repertoire. What a narrative must do is to set out the antecedent actions in such a way as to clarify how the resulting pattern becomes a tradition. In this way, we will see why certain actions prove effective and others fail, much as some expressions succeed in saying what they mean while others cannot. Some forms of story, like the three-generational Victorian novel, are expressly designed to display how a grammar for actions develops, by adopting a deliberately historical, even explicitly generational, structure. Lawrence's *Rainbow*, for example, shows how the shaping habits of speech and personal interaction are altered over three generations in response to industrial development. As he skillfully displays this alteration in grammar over against a traditional syntax, we can grasp something of the capacities latent in us as human beings. In articulating the characters, Lawrence succeeds in making explicit some reaches of the human spirit as yet unexplored.

Stories, then, certainly offer more than entertainment. What they do offer, however, cannot be formulated independently of our appreciating the story, so seeking entertainment is less distracting than looking for a moral. The reason lies with the narrative structure, whose plot cannot be abstracted without banality, yet whose unity does depend on its having a point. Hence it is appropriate to speak of a plot, to call attention to the ordering peculiar to narrative. It is that ordering, that capacity to unfold or develop character, and thus offer insight into the human condition, which recommends narrative as a form of rationality especially appropriate to ethics.

III:3. How a Narrative Unfolds

If a narrative becomes plausible as it succeeds in displaying a believable character, we may still ask how *that* achievement offers us an intelligibility appropriate to discriminating among courses of action. Using Aristotle's language, how can stories assist in the formation of a practical wisdom? How can stories themselves develop a capacity for judging among alternatives, and further: how does discriminating among stories make that capacity even keener? Since reading stories for more than mere entertainment is usually described as "appreciating" them, some skills for assessing among them are already implied in one's appreciating any single story.

We often find ourselves quite unable, however, to specify the grounds for preferring one story to another. Critics, of course, develop a language for doing this, trying to formulate our normally inchoate criteria. Yet these criteria themselves are notoriously ambiguous. They must be rendered in utterly analogous terms, like "unity," "wholeness," "consistency," "integrity," etc. We cannot hope to grasp the criteria without a paradigmatic instance, yet how present an exemplary instance without telling a story?[24] Criticism thus can only conceive itself as disciplining our native capacity to appreciate a good story.

A complete account of the way narrative functions, then, would be a narrative recounting how one came to judge certain stories as better than others. Since this narrative would have to be autobiographical, in the perceived character of its author we would have a vantage for judgment beyond the intrinsic merit of the narrative itself. If stories are designed to display how one might create and relate to a world and so offer us a paradigm for adopting a similar posture, this autobiographical story would have to show how a person's current manner of relating himself to the world itself represents a posture towards alternative stances. The narrative will have to recount why, and do so in the fashion proper to narrative: that one stance comes after another, preferably by improving upon its predecessor.[25]

Augustine's *Confessions* offer just such an account by showing how Augustine's many relationships, all patterned on available stories, were gradually relativized to one overriding and ordering relationship with the God revealing himself in Jesus. Augustine's life story is the story of that process of ordering.

III:4. Augustine's *Confessions*: A Narrative Assessment of Life Stories

Writing ten years after the decisive moment in the garden, Augustine sees that event as culminating a quest shaped by two questions: How to account for evil, and how to conceive of God? That quest was also dogged by demands much more immediate than questions, of course. These needs were symbolically ordered in the experience recounted in Book 9, and monitored sense by sense, passion by passion, in Book 10. What interests us here, however, is the step-like manner in which Augustine describes himself relating to the shaping questions: How explain evil? How conceive divinity?

The pear-tree story allows him to telegraph to the reader how he was able to discriminate one question from the other early on, even though the skills developed to respond to one would help him meet the other. For his own action, reflected upon, allowed him to glimpse an evil deed as wanton or pointless (2.4-10). From the perspective displayed by the *Confessions*, he formulates clearly an intimation that guided his earlier quest: what makes an action evil is not so much a reason as the lack of one. So we would be misled to attribute evil to the creator who orders all things, since ordering and giving reasons belong together.

By separating in this way the query into the source of evil from the attempt to conceive divinity, Augustine took a categorial step. That is, he was learning how to slip from the grip in which Manichean teaching held him, as he came to realize that nothing could properly explain the presence of evil in the world. Nothing, that is, short of a quality of human freedom that allowed us to act for no reason at all. Since explanations offer reasons, and evil turns on the lack of reasons, some form other than a causal explanation must be called for. The only form that can exhibit an action without pretending to explain it is the very one he adopted for the book itself: narrative. So Augustine took his first decisive step toward responding to the shaping questions by eschewing the pretense of explanation in favor of a reflective story.

Categorial discriminations are not usually made all at once, of course. If we are set to turn up an explanation, we will ordinarily keep trying to find a satisfactory one. We cannot give up the enterprise of looking for an explanation unless our very horizon shifts. (It is just such a horizon-shift or paradigmatic change that we identify as a categorial discrimination.) Yet horizons form the stable background for inquiry, so normally we cannot allow them to shift. In Augustine's case, as in many, it only occurred to him to seek elsewhere after repeated attempts at explaining proved fruitless. Furthermore, the specific way in which the Manichean scheme failed to explain the presence of evil also suggested why seeking an explanation was itself a fruitless tack.

To be sure, the Manichean accounts to which Augustine alludes strike us as altogether too crude to qualify as explanations. In fact, it sounds odd to identify his rejection of Manichean teachings with the explicit adoption of a story form, since it is their schemes which sound to us like "stories." The confusion is understandable enough, of course; it is the very one this essay addresses: stories are fanciful, while explanations are what offer intelligibility. Yet fanciful as they appear to us, the Manichean schemes are explanatory in form. They postulate causes for behavior in the form of diverse combinations of "particles" of light or darkness. The nature of the particles is less relevant, of course, than the explanatory pretense.

What first struck Augustine was the scheme's inability to explain diverse kinds of behavior coherently (5.10, 7.1-6). What he came to realize, however, was that *any* explanatory scheme would, in principle, undermine a person's ability to repent because it would remove whatever capacity we might have for assuming responsibility for our own actions (6.5, 7.12-13, 8.10). This capacity to assume responsibility would not always suffice to accomplish what we (or at least a part of us) desire (8.8-9); but such a capacity is logically necessary if we are to claim our actions as our own—and so receive praise or blame for them. If our contrary actions could be explained by contrary substances within us, then we would not be able to own them. And if we cannot own our actions, then we have no self to speak of. So the incoherence of the explanations offered led Augustine to see how the very quest for explanation itself failed to cohere with the larger life project belonging to every person.

As the narrative of Augustine's own life project displays, this deliberate shift away from the explanatory modes of the Manichees or the astrologers led to adopting a form which would also help him better to conceive divinity. If evil is senseless, we cannot attribute it to the one who creates with order and reason. If we commit evil deeds, we must be able to own up to them—to confess them—if we want to open ourselves to a change of heart. And the more we examine that self who can act responsibly—in accomplishing deeds or in judging among opinions—the more we come into possession of a language for articulating divinity. It was a language of inwardness, as practiced by the Platonists of his day (7.10). It assumed a scheme of powers of the soul, but made its point by transcendental argument: if we are to make the discriminations we do, we must do so by virtue of an innate light or power (7.17). This way of articulating the power by which we act responsibly, then, becomes the model for expressing divinity. The path which led away from seeking an explanation for evil offers some promise for responding to the second question as well.

Augustine must take one more step, however, lest he forfeit the larger lesson of his struggle with the Manichees, and simply substitute a Platonist explanatory scheme for theirs.[26] They appeal to formal facts by way of transcendental argument. His life, however, was framed by facts of another kind: of rights and wrongs dealt to others (6.15); of an order to which he now aspired to conform, but which he found himself unable to accomplish (8.11). What he misses in the Platonists' books is "the mien of the true love of God. They make no mention of the tears of confession" (7.21). He can read there "of the Word, God . . ., but not read in them that 'the Word was made flesh and came to dwell among us' (John 1:14)" (7.9). While they speak persuasively of the conditions for acting and judging aright, they do not tell us how to do what we find ourselves unable to do: to set our hearts aright.

The key to that feat Augustine finds not in the books of the Platonists, but in the gospels. Or better, he finds it in allowing the stories of the gospels to shape his story. The moment of permission, as he records it, is preceded by stories of others allowing the same to happen to them—recounting how they did it and what allowing it to happen did to them. The effect of these stories is to insinuate a shift in grammar tantamount to the shift from explanation to narrative, although quite in line with that earlier shift. Since we think of stories as relating accomplishments, Augustine must use these stories together with his own to show us another way of conceiving them.

It is not a new way, for it consciously imitates the biblical manner of displaying God's great deeds in behalf of his people. Without ceasing to be the story of Israel, the tales of the Bible present the story of God. Similarly, without ceasing to be autobiography, Augustine's *Confessions* offer an account of God's way with him. The language of will and of struggle is replaced by that of the heart: "as I came to the end of the sentence, it was as though the light of confidence flooded into my heart and all the darkness of doubt was dispelled" (8.12). Yet the transformation is not a piece of magic; the narrative testifies to that. And his narrative will give final testimony to the transformation of that moment in the measure that it conforms to the life story of the "Word made flesh." So the answer to his shaping questions is finally received rather than formulated, and that reception is displayed in the narrative we have analyzed.

IV. Truthfulness as Veracity and Faithfulness

The second step which Augustine relates is not a categorial one. It no longer has to do with finding the proper form for rendering a life project intelligible. The narrative Augustine tells shows us how he was moved to accept the gospel story by allowing it to shape his own. In more conventional terms, this second step moves beyond philosophical therapy to a judgment of truth. That is why recognizable arguments surround the first step, but not this one. Assent involves more subtle movements than clarification does, notably, assent of this sort, which is not assent *to* evidence but an assent *of* faith. Yet we will grasp its peculiar warrants better if we see how it moves along the same lines as the categorial discrimination.

Accepting a story as normative, by allowing it to shape one's own story, in effect reinforces the categorial preference for story over explanation as a vehicle of understanding. Augustine adumbrates the way one step leads into the other towards the beginning of Book 6:

> From now on I began to prefer the Catholic teaching. The Church demanded that certain things should be believed even though they could not be proved. . . . I thought that the Church was entirely honest in this and far less pretentious than the Manichees, who laughed at people who took things on faith, made rash promises of scientific knowledge, and then put forward a whole system of preposterous inventions which they expected their followers to believe on trust because they could not be proved (6.5).

The chapter continues in a similar vein, echoing many contemporary critiques of modern rationalist pretensions.

IV:1. Criteria for Judging among Stories

The studied preference for story over explanation, then, moves one into a neighborhood more amenable to what thirteenth-century theologians called an "assent of faith," and in doing so, helps us develop a set of criteria for judging among stories. Books 8-9-10 of the *Confessions* record the ways in which this capacity for discriminating among stories is developed. It is less a matter of weighing arguments than of displaying how adopting different stories will lead us to become different sorts of persons. The test of each story is the sort of person it shapes. When examples of diverse types are offered to us for our acceptance, the choices we make display, in turn, our own grasp of the *humanum*. Aristotle presumed we could not fail to recognize a just man, but also knew he would come in different guises (*N. Ethics* I, 1-7).

The criteria for judging among stories, then, will most probably not pass an impartial inspection. For the powers of recognition cannot be divorced from one's own capacity to recognize the good for humankind. This observation need not amount to a counsel of despair, however. It is simply a reminder that on matters of judgment we consult more readily with some persons than others, because we recognize them to be in a better position to weigh matters sensibly. Any account of that "position" would have to be autobiographical, of course. But it is not an account we count on; it is simply our recognition of the person's integrity.

Should we want to characterize the story that gives such coherence to a person's life, however, it would doubtless prove helpful to contrast it with alternatives. The task is a difficult one, either for oneself or for another, for we cannot always identify the paths we have taken; Augustine continued to be engaged in mapping out the paths he was actually traversing at the very time of composing the *Confessions—vide* Book 10. Yet we can certainly formulate a list of working criteria, provided we realize that any such list cannot pretend to completeness or achieve unambiguous expression.

Any story which we adopt, or allow to adopt us, will have to display:

(1) power to release us from destructive alternatives
(2) ways of seeing through current distortions
(3) room to keep us from having to resort to violence
(4) a sense for the tragic: how meaning transcends power.

It is inaccurate, of course, to list these criteria as features that a story must display. They envisage rather the effect that stories might be expected to have on those who allow them to shape their lives. The fact that stories are meant to be read, however, forces one to speak of them as relational facts. So we cannot help regarding a story as something that (when well constructed) will help us develop certain skills of perception and understanding. This perspective corresponds exactly to the primary function of narratives by contrast with explanatory schemes: to relate us to the world, including our plans for modifying it. Those plans have consequences of their own, but their shape as well as their execution depends on the expectations we entertain for planning.

Such expectations become a part of the plans themselves, but they can be articulated independently and when they are, they take the form of stories, notably of heros. Thus the process of industrialization becomes the story of tycoons, as the technology we know embodies a myth of man's dominating and transforming the earth. Not that industrial processes are themselves stories, or technological expertise a myth. In fact, we are witnessing today many attempts to turn those processes and that expertise to different ends by yoking them to a different outlook. Stories of these experiments suggest new ways of using some of the skills we have developed, and illustrate the role of narrative in helping us formulate and practice new perspectives.[27]

Stories, then, help us, as we hold them, to relate to our world and our destiny: the origins and goal of our lives, as they embody in narrative form specific ways of acting out that relatedness. In allowing ourselves to adopt and be adopted by a particular story, we are, in fact, assuming a set of practices that will shape the ways we relate to our world and destiny. Lest this sound too instrumental, we should remind ourselves that the world is not simply waiting to be seen, but that language and institutions train us to regard it in certain ways.[28] The criteria listed above assume this fact; let us consider them in greater detail.

IV:2. Testing the Criteria

Stories that (1) empower us to free ourselves from destructive alternatives can also (2) offer ways to see through current distortions. To judge an alternative course to be destructive, of course, requires some experience of its effects on those who practice the skills it embodies. It is the precise role of narrative to offer us a way of experiencing those effects without experimenting with our own lives as well. The verisimilitude of the story, along with its assessable literary structure, will allow us to ascertain whether we can trust it as a vehicle of insight, or whether we are being misled. In the absence of narratives, recommendations for adopting a set of practices can only present themselves as a form of propaganda and be judged accordingly.[29] Only narrative can allow us to take the measure of a scheme for human improvement—granting that we possess the usual skills for discriminating among narratives as well.

For we can learn how to see a current ideology as a distortion by watching what it can do to people who let it shape their story. The seduction of Manichean doctrine for Augustine and his contemporaries lay precisely in its offering itself as a *story* for humankind—much as current problem-solving techniques will invariably also be packaged as a set of practices leading to personal fulfillment. Therefore, Augustine's subsequent discrimination between explanation and story first required an accurate identification of Manichean teaching as explanatory pretense in the guise of a story.

The last two criteria also go together: (3) providing room to keep us from having to resort to violence, and (4) offering a sense for the tragic: how meaning transcends power. We can watch these criteria operate if we contrast the story characteristic to Christians and Jews with one of the prevailing presumptions of contemporary culture: that we can count on technique to offer eventual relief from the human condition. This conviction is reflected in the penchant of consequential ethical theories not only to equate doing one's duty with the greatest good for all, but also to presume that meeting our obligations will provide the satisfaction we seek. Surely, current medical practice is confirmed by the conviction that harnessing more human energies into preventing and curing disease will increasingly free our lives from tragic dilemmas.[30] Indeed, science as a moral enterprise has provided what Ernest Becker has called an anthropodicy, as it holds out the possibility that our increased knowledge serves human progress toward the creation of a new human ideal—namely, to create a mankind free of suffering.[31]

But this particular ethos has belied the fact that medicine, at least as characterized by its moral commitment to the individual patient, is a tragic profession. To attend to one in distress often means many others cannot be helped. To save a child born retarded may well destroy the child's family and cause unnecessary burdens on society. But the doctor is pledged to care for each patient because medicine does not aim at some ideal moral good, but to care for the needs of the patient whom the doctor finds before him. Because we do not know how to regard medicine as a tragic profession, we tend of course to confuse caring with curing. The story that accompanies technology—of setting nature aright—results in the clinical anomalies to which we are subjecting others and ourselves in order to avoid the limits of our existence.[32]

The practice of medicine under the conditions of finitude offers an intense paradigm of the moral life. The moral task is to learn to continue to do the right, to care for this immediate patient, even when we have no assurance that it will be the successful thing to do. To live morally, in other words, we need a substantive story that will sustain moral activity in a finite and limited world. Classically, the name we give to such stories is tragedy. When a culture loses touch with the tragic, as ours clearly has done, we must describe our failures in acceptable terms. Yet to do so *ipso facto* traps us in self-deceiving accounts of what we have done.[33] Thus, our stories quickly acquire the characteristics of a policy, especially as they are reinforced by our need to find self-justifying reasons for our new-found necessities.

This tactic becomes especially troublesome as the policy itself assumes the form of a central story that gives our individual and collective lives coherence. This story then becomes indispensable to us, as it provides us with a place to be. Phrases like "current medical practice," "standard hospital policy," or even "professional ethics," embody exemplary stories that guide the way we use the means at hand to care for patients. Since we fail to regard them as stories, however, but must see them as a set of principles, the establishment must set itself to secure them against competing views. If the disadvantaged regard this as a form of institutional violence, they are certainly correct.

Such violence need not take the form of physical coercion, of course. But we can detect it in descriptions that countenance coercion. For example, an abortion at times may be a morally necessary, but sorrowful, occurrence. But our desire for righteousness quickly invites us to turn what is morally unavoidable into a self-deceiving policy, e.g., the fetus, after all, is just another piece of flesh. It takes no mean skill, certainly, to know how to hold onto a description that acknowledges significant life, while remaining open to judging that it may have to be destroyed. Yet medical practice and human integrity cannot settle for less. Situations like these suggest, however, that we do not lie because we are evil, but because we wish to be good or preserve what good we already embody.[34]

We do not wish to claim that the stories with which Christians and Jews identify are the only stories that offer skills for truthfulness in the moral life. We only want to identify them as ways to countenance a posture of locating and doing the good which must be done, even if it does not lead to human progress. Rather than encourage us to assume that the moral life can be freed from the tragedies that come from living in a limited and sinful world, these stories demand that we be faithful to God as we believe he has been faithful to us through his covenant with Israel and (for Christians) in the cross of Christ.[35]

IV:3. A Canonical Story

Religious faith, on this account, comes to accepting a certain set of stories as canonical. We come to regard them not only as meeting the criteria sketched above (along with others we may develop) but find them offering ways of clarifying and expanding our sense of the criteria themselves. In short, we discover our human self more effectively through these stories, and so use them in judging the adequacy of alternative schemes for humankind.

In this formal sense, one is tempted to wonder whether everyone does not accept a set of stories as canonical. To identify those stories would be to discover the shape one's basic convictions take. To be unable to do so would either mark a factual incapacity or an utterly fragmented self. Current discussion of "polytheism" leads one to ask whether indiscriminate pluralism represents a real psychic possibility for a contemporary person.[36] In our terms, arguing against the need for a canonical story amounts to questioning, "Why be good?" Just as we do not require ethics to answer that question, so we need not demand a perspicuously canonical story. But we can point to the endemic tendency of men and women to allow certain stories to assume that role, just as ethicists remind us of the assessments we do, in fact, count on to live our lives.[37]

NOTES

1. For example, James Gustafson ends his recent Marquette Lecture, "The Contributions of Theology to Medical Ethics," by saying: "For most persons involved in medical care and practice, the contribution of theology is likely to be of minimal importance, for the moral principles and values needed can be justified without reference to God, and the attitudes that religious beliefs ground can be grounded in other ways. From the standpoint of immediate practicality, the contribution of theology is not great, either in its extent

or in its importance." (p. 94) While we have no wish to challenge this as a descriptive statement of what pertains today, we think we can show that even though "moral principles can be justified without reference to God," how they are accounted for still makes a difference for the meaning of the principle and how it works to form institutions and ways of life that may have practical importance. To be sure, Christians may have common moral convictions with non-Christians, but it seems unwise to separate a moral conviction from the story that forms its context of interpretation. Moreover, a stance such as Gustafson's would seem to assume that medicine as it is currently formed is the way it ought to be. In this respect, we at least want to leave open the possibility of a more reformist, if not radical, stance.

2. We wish to thank Professor MacIntyre for helping us clarify these issues. As will be obvious to anyone acquainted with his work we are deeply influenced by his argument that the "conflict over how morality is to be defined is itself a moral conflict. Different and rival definitions cannot be defended apart from defending different and rival sets of moral principles." ("How to Identify Ethical Principles," unpublished paper prepared for the National Commission for the Protection of Human Subjects of Biomedical and Behavioral Research, p. 8.)

3. The search for ethical objectivity, of course, is also a response to the social and political diversity of our day. Thus the search for a "foundation" for ethics involves the attempt to secure rational agreement short of violence. The attraction of the ideal of science for ethicists may be partly because science appears to be the last form of universal culture we have left. Of course this strategy comes to grief on the diversity of activity and disciplines that constitute what we generally call science. For example see Ernest Becker's reflection on this in his *The Structure of Evil* (New York: Braziller, 1968).

4. We do not mean to claim the actual practice of science involves this sense of objectivity. Indeed we are very sympathetic with Toulmin's analysis of science not as a tight and coherent logical system, but "as a conceptual aggregate, or 'population,' within which there are—at most—localized pockets of logical systematicity." *Human Understanding* (Princeton: Princeton University Press, 1972), p. 128. It is exactly his stress on necessity of understanding the history of the development of a discipline in order to understand its sense of "rationality" that we feel must be recovered in science as well as, though with different significance,

in ethics. As he suggests, "In science as much as in ethics the historical and cultural diversity of our concepts gives rise to intractable problems, only so long as we continue to think of 'rationality' as a character of particular systems of propositions or concepts, rather than in terms of the procedures by which men change from one set of concepts and beliefs to another" (p. 478). Rather what must be seen is that rationality "is an attribute, not of logical or conceptual systems as such, but of the human activities or enterprises of which particular sets of concepts are the temporary cross-sections" (p. 133).

5. Eric Cassell, "Preliminary Exploration of Thinking in Medicine," *Ethics in Science and Medicine*, 2, 1 (1975), pp. 1-12. MacIntyre and Gorovitz's "Toward a Theory of Medical Error" also obviously bears on this issue. See *Science, Ethics and Medicine*, ed. by H. Tristram Engelhardt, Jr. and Daniel Callahan (Hastings-on-Hudson: The Hastings Center, 1976).

6. Quoted by B. F. Skinner in *Science and Human Behavior* (New York: MacMillan, 1953), pp. 18-19. Eric Cassell's, "Illness and Disease," *Hastings Center Report*, 6, 2 (April, 1976), pp. 27-37 is extremely interesting in this respect. It is his contention that we as yet have failed to appreciate the obvious fact that doctors do not treat diseases but patients who have diseases.

7. Ibid., p. 19. In the light of Skinner's claim it is interesting to reflect on John Wisdom's observation in *Paradox and Discovery* (New York: Philosophical Library, 1965). "It is, I believe, extremely difficult to breed lions. But there was at one time at the Dublin zoo a keeper by the name of Mr. Flood who bred many lion cubs without losing one. Asked the secret of his success, Mr. Flood replied, 'Understanding lions'. Asked in what consists the understanding of lions, he replied, 'Every lion is different'. It is not to be thought that Mr. Flood, in seeking to understand an individual lion, did not bring to bear his great experience with other lions. Only he remained free to see each lion for itself." (p. 138.) We are indebted to Professor Ed Erde for the Tolstoy and Wisdom quotes.

8. We are aware that this judgment would need to be qualified if each of these positions were considered in detail. Yet we think that this does characterize a tendency that these positions share. For each position is attempting to establish what Frankena calls the "institution of morality,"—that is to show that morality is an institution that stands on its own, separate from other human activities such as politics, religion, etiquette. (We suspect that connected with this attempt to establish the independence of ethics is the desire to give

ethics a disciplinary character like that of the sciences. For an excellent discussion of ethics as a "quasi-discipline" see Toulmin, *Human Understanding*, pp. 406-411.) The language of obligation tends to become central for these interpretations of the moral life as they trade on our feeling that we ought to do our duty irrespective of how it effects or relates to our other interests and activities. Obligation and rationality are thus interpreted in interdependent terms as it is assumed that an ethics of obligation can provide the standpoint needed to establish the independence of moral discourse from all the relativities of interests, institutions, and commitments save one—the interests of being rational. Thus the moral life, at least as it involves only those obligations that we owe one another apart from any special relationships, needs no further grounding apart from our common rationality. It should be obvious that our criticisms of this approach have much in common with such thinkers as Foot, MacIntyre, Toulmin, and Hampshire. For a critique of the emphasis on obligation to the exclusion of virtue in contemporary accounts of the moral life, see Hauerwas, "Obligation and Virtue Once More," *Journal of Religious Ethics* 3, 1 (Spring, 1975), 27-44, and the following response and critique by Frankena.

9. *Mind*, 80 (1971), 552-71. For similar criticism see Hauerwas, *Vision and Virtue: Essays in Christian Ethical Reflection* (Notre Dame: Fides, 1974).

10. To our mind one of the most disastrous aspects of the standard account of rationality is the resulting divorce of ethical reflection from political theory. It may be objected that the work of Rawls and Nozick are impressive counters to such a claim. However, it is interesting to note that the political theory they generate exists on a high level of abstraction from the actual workings of the modern state. It is only when ethicists turn their attention to C. B. Mac-Pherson's challenge to the liberal democratic assumptions that Rawls and Nozick presuppose that they will address questions that are basic, for liberal political theory and the objectivist's account of moral rationality share the assumption that morally and politically we are strangers to one another. Thus, any common life can only be built on our willingness to qualify our self-interest in order to increase our long-term satisfaction. From this perspective the standard account can be viewed as an attempt to secure a basis for rational politics for a society that shares no interests beyond each individual increasing his chance for survival. It is our hunch that historically the disputes and disagreements in ethical theory, such as that between Rawls and Hare, will appear as scholastic debates

within a liberal framework. For the disputants agree far more than they disagree. For MacPherson's critique of these assumptions see his *Democratic Theory* (Oxford: Clarendon Press, 1973). For a radical critique of liberal democracy, both in terms of the liberal understanding of rationality and the self similar to our own, see Roberto Unger's *Knowledge and Politics* (New York: Free Press, 1975).

11. For a critique of this assumption see Michael Walzer, "Political Action: The Problem of Dirty Hands," *Philosophy and Public Affairs*, 2, 2 (Winter, 1973), 160-80. He is responding to Hare's "Rules of War and Moral Reasoning," *Philosophy and Public Affairs*, 1, 2 (Winter, 1972), 161-81. Hare argued that though one might wrongly think he was faced with a moral dilemma this could not be the case if a course of action suggested itself that was moral. See also John Ladd's very useful discussion of this issue in his "Are Science and Ethics Compatible?" *Science, Ethics and Medicine*, edited by Engelhardt and Callahan (Hastings-on-Hudson: Hastings Center Publication, 1976). This is also the issue that lies behind the theory of double effect in Roman Catholic moral theology although it is seldom explicitly discussed in these terms. For example, see Richard McCormick's *Ambiguity in Moral Choice* (Marquette Theology Lectures: Marquette University, 1973). (See Hauerwas, "Natural Law, Tragedy, and Theological Ethics," *American Journal of Jurisprudence* 20 (1975), 1-19 for a different perspective.)

For a fascinating study of the problem of moral evil in terms of the economic category of scarcity see Vivian Walsh, *Scarcity and Evil* (Englewood Cliffs: Prentice-Hall, 1961). Ms. Walsh argues that we are often mistaken to try to ascribe responsibility for actions that are the result of scarcity even when the scarcity is not the result of the "external" limits but in the person doing the action. What we often must do is the lesser good because of our own limits, but we must learn to know it is a lesser good without implying that we are morally blameworthy. Even though we are sympathetic with Ms. Walsh's analysis we think the concept of character provides a way to suggest what is an inappropriate "scarcity" for anyone to lack in their character given the form of their engagements. Albert Speer lacked political sense that became morally blameworthy because of his political involvement, but that does not mean that morally there is no way to indicate that his character should have provided him with the skills to know what kind of politics he was involved with. In classical terms the concept of character gives the means to assess in what ways we are blameworthy or praiseworthy for that which we have omitted as well as for what we have "done."

12. For a discussion of these issues see Hauerwas, "The Demands and Limits of Care: Ethical Reflections on the Moral Dilemma of Neonatal Intensive Care," *American Journal of the Medical Sciences*, 269, 2 (March-April, 1975), 222-36; and Hauerwas, "Meningomyelocele: To Treat or Not to Treat: An Ethical Analysis of the Dispute between Drs. Freeman and Lorber" (forthcoming).

13. It is not just Prichard that argues in this way but, as Henry Veatch suggests, Kant is the primary inspiration behind those that would make interest, desires, and beliefs in principle unjustifiable. This, of course, relates to the matter discussed in footnote 4 as Kant wanted to provide a basis for morality not dependent on any theological or anthropological assumption—except that of man's rational capacity. That is why Kant's principle of universalizability, which has so often been misinterpreted, applies only to men as rational beings and not just to all human beings. As Veatch points out in this latter case, "the maxim of one's action would be based on a regard simply for certain desires and likings characteristic of human nature—albeit desires that all human beings happen to share in. But any mere desire or inclination or liking or sentiment of approbation, even if it be shared by the entire human race, would still not be universalizable in the relevant sense, simply because it was something characteristic of and peculiar to human kind, and hence not truly universal." "Justification of Moral Principles," *Review of Metaphysics*, XXIX, 2 (December, 1975) p. 225.

14. For example witness this exchange between Lucy and Linus as Lucy walks by while Linus is preparing a snowball for launching.
    Lucy: "Life is full of Choices.
         You may choose, if you so wish, to throw that snowball at me.
         You may also choose, if you so wish, not to throw that snowball at me.
         Now, if you choose to throw that snowball at me I will pound you right into the ground.
         If you choose not to throw that snowball at me, your head will be spared."
    Linus: (Throwing the snowball to the ground) "Life is full of choices, but you never get any."

15. For a more extended analysis of the concept of character see

Hauerwas, *Character and the Christian Life: A Study in Theologi-cal Ethics* (San Antonio: Trinity University Press, 1975).

16. Julius Kovesi, *Moral Notions* (New York: Humanities Press, 1967); and Hauerwas, *Vision and Virtue*, pp. 11-29. For a detailed account of the historical development of meaning of words, see Raymond Williams, *Keywords* (New York: Oxford, 1976).

17. For example R. S. Downie and Elizabeth Telfer attempt to argue that "the ordinary rules and judgments of social morality presuppose respect for persons as their ultimate ground . . . (and) that the area of private or self-referring morality also presupposes respect for persons as its ultimate ground." *Respect for Persons* (New York: Schocken, 1970), p. 9. They interpret respect for persons in a Kantian fashion of respecting the claim another rational capacity— that is, capable of self-determining and rule-governing behavior— can demand. It never seems to occur to them that the "ordinary rules of social morality" or "self-referring morality" may not need an "ultimate ground." Moreover, they have a good deal of trouble explaining why we owe respect to children or "idiots" on such grounds. They simply assert that there "are sufficient resemblances between them and persons" to justify extending respect to them. (p. 35.) (For a different perspective on this issue see Hauerwas, "The Retarded and the Criteria for the Human," *Linacre Quarterly*, 40 (November, 1973), 217-22.) It is Downie and Telfer's contention that "respect for persons" is the basis of such Christian notions as agape. It is certainly true that much of what a "respect for persons" ethic represents has been assumed by Christian morality, but we think that it is misleading to assume that the story that informs the latter can be translated into the former. One of the places to see this is where each construes the relationship between obligation and supererogation. The Christian ethic of charity necessarily makes obligatory what a follower of "respect for persons" can see only as supererogation. For an analysis of agape in terms of equal regard see Gene Outka, *Agape: An Ethical Analysis* (New Haven: Yale University Press, 1972).

18. For an account of the moral life that makes "fittingness" central see H. R. Niebuhr, *The Responsible Self* (New York: Harper and Row, 1963).

19. It would take us too far afield to explore this point further, but surely it is Kant that stands behind this understanding of the self. It is impossible to document this, but it is at least worthwhile calling attention to two passages from *Religion Within the Limits of Reason*

Alone, translated by Theodore Green (New York: Harper, 1960). "In the search for the rational origins of evil action, every such action must be regarded as though the individual had fallen into it directly from a state of innocence. For whatever his previous deportment may have been, whatever natural causes may have been influencing him, and whatever these causes were to be found within or outside him, his action is yet free and determined by none of these causes; hence it can and must always be judged as an original use of his will. . . . Hence we cannot inquire into the temporal origins of this deed, but solely into its rational origin, if we are thereby to determine and, whereby possible, to elucidate the propensity, if it exists, i.e., the general subjective ground of the adoption of transgression into our maxim." (p. 36.) In case it is objected that Kant is only dealing with moral evil, consider "To reconcile the concept of freedom with the idea of God as a *necessary* Being raises no difficulty at all: for freedom consists not in the contingency of the act, i.e., not in indeterminism, but rather in absolute spontaneity. Such spontaneity is endangered only by predeterminism, where the determining ground of the act is in *antecedent time*, with the result that, the act being now no longer in my power but in the hands of nature, I am irresistibly determined; but since in God no temporal sequence is thinkable, this difficulty vanishes." (p. 45.) It is, of course, the possibility of the moral law that Kant thinks gives men the possibility to be like God—timeless. It is not a far distance from Kant to the existentialist in this respect.

20. For this point and much else that is involved in this paper see Iris Murdoch, *The Sovereignty of the Good Over Other Concepts* (Cambridge: Cambridge University Press, 1967).

21. We have not based our criticism of the standard account on the debates between those that share its presuppositions. It is, of course, true that as yet no single theory of the standard account has proved to be persuasive to those that share its presuppositions. We still find Kant's theory the single most satisfying statement of the program implied by the standard account.

22. Ernest Becker, however, argues that Comte has been misunderstood, as his purpose was not to free science from morality but to call attention to what kind of moral activity science involved. Thus, Becker suggests, "Comte's Positivism, in sum, solved the problem of science and morals by using science to support a man-based morality. With all the force at his command he showed that life is a moral problem, and science only a tool whose unity would serve the larger unity of life. Like de Maistre and de Bonald, and

like Carlyle in England, he looked approvingly on the Middle Ages. But he did not pine nostalgically for their institutions; he saw the Middle Ages as possessing what man needed most, and has since lost: a critical, unitary world view by which to judge right and wrong, good and bad, by which to subordinate personal desire to social interest. But instead of basing this knowledge on theological fiat, man could now settle it firmly on science. In this way, the Enlightenment could achieve what the Middle Ages almost possessed; but it could do this on a much sounder footing than could ever have been possible during the earlier time, namely, it could achieve the subordination of politics to morality on a scientific rather than on a theological basis. Social order and social harmony would be a call of the new day, and human progress could then be progress in social feeling, community, and love—all of it based on the superordinate science of man in society, serving man, elevating humanity." (*The Structure of Evil*, p. 50.)

In this respect consider Simone Weil's observation that "The criticism of religion is always, as Marx said, the condition for all progress; but what Marx and the Marxists have not clearly seen is that, in our day, everything that is most retrograde in the spirit of religion has taken refuge, above all, in science itself. A science like ours, essentially closed to the layman, and therefore to scientists themselves, because each is a layman outside his narrow specialism, is the proper theology of an ever increasingly bureaucratic society."

23. Cf. G. E. M. Anscombe, "Thought and Action in Aristotle," in R. Bambrough (ed.), *New Essays on Plato and Aristotle* (New York: Humanities Press, 1965), pp. 151-52. See also Hauerwas, *Character and the Christian Life*, Ch. 2.

24. For an account of the way analogous terms can be used once they are effectively linked to a paradigmatic instance, cf. Burrell, *Analogy and Philosophical Language* (New Haven and London: Yale University Press, 1973).

25. It may, of course, happen that one cannot sustain a particular relationship and "fails." Again, the way he deals with that becomes a story. Stories often seem better the more they overturn conventional assessments and challenge settled attitudes.

26. Peter Brown shows how this choice represented an existential decision as well. The *Platonici* formed an identifiable group of noble humanists, and as such offered a viable alternative to Christianity. While they were not formed into a church, their common aspirations could well be imagined to constitute a community of like-

minded persons—*Augustine of Hippo* (Berkeley: University of California Press, 1967).

27. This is the point of Peter Winch's oft-cited analysis: "Understanding a Primitive Society," reprinted in Bryan R. Wilson (ed.), *Rationality* (New York: Oxford University Press, 1970). More constructively, it forms the focus of alternative endeavors like *Creative Simplicity* (Minneapolis, Minn. 55410).

28. For further elaboration of this, see Iris Murdoch, *The Sovereignty of the Good Over Other Concepts*.

29. Cf. James Cameron's efforts to offer perspective to current writing on the "sexual revolution," in *The New York Review of Books*, 23 (May 13, 1976), 19-28.

30. MacIntyre's argument in "Towards a Theory of Medical Error," that medicine must necessarily deal with explanations of individuals, only makes this claim more poignant. For the attempt to claim that the only errors in medicine were those characteristic of a science of universals was necessary if medicine was to make good its claim to be the means to free mankind of the limits of disease. To recognize that medical explanation and prediction are subject to the same limits as explanation and prediction of individuals will require a radical reorientation of the story that morally supports and directs medical care.

31. Becker, *The Structure of Evil*, p. 18. "The central problem posed by the Newtonian revolution was not long in making itself felt. This was the momentous new problem; it is still ours today—I mean of course the problem of a new theodicy. If the new nature was so regular and beautiful, then why was there evil in the human world? Man needs a new theodicy, but this time he could not put the burden on God. Man had to settle for a new limited explanation, an anthropodicy which would cover only those evils that allow for human remedy." Science naturally presented itself as the "remedy."

32. It is tempting to try to make, as many have, the ethic of "respect for persons" sufficient as a moral basis for medical care. (Cf. Paul Ramsey's *The Patient as Person*.) But if, as we suggest, medicine is necessarily involved in tragic choices, a more substantive story than that is needed to sustain and give direction to medical care. Without such a story we will be tempted to make technology serve as a substitute, since it allows us to delay further decisions of life and death that we must make in one or another arena. For a critique of the way "person" is being used as a regulative moral notion in medical ethics see Hauerwas, "Must a Patient Be a 'Person' To Be

a Patient, or My Uncle Charlie is Not Much of a Person But He Is Still my Uncle Charlie," *Connecticut Medicine*, 39, 12 (December, 1975), 815-17.

33. For an analysis of the concept of self-deception see Burrell and Hauerwas, "Self-Deception and Autobiography: Theological and Ethical Reflections on Speer's *Inside the Third Reich*," *Journal of Religious Ethics*, 2, 1 (1974), 99-117.

34. Jules Henry's analysis of the phenomenon of "sham" is perhaps the most graphic depiction of this. He says, "Children in our culture cannot avoid sham, for adults cannot escape depression, hostility and so on. Since sham consists in one person's withholding information, while implying that the other person should act as if he had it all; since sham consists also in giving false information while expecting the other person to act as if the information were true; since sham consists in deriving advantage from withholding or giving information—and since, on the whole, our culture is sham-wise, it might seem that the main problem for the mental health of children is to familiarize them with the edges of sham. Yet, if we were to do that, they would be 'shot' for Albee is right. Our main problem then is to tell them the world lies but they should act as if it told the truth. But this too is impossible, for if one acted as if all sham were truth he might not be shot, but he certainly would lose all his money and marry the wrong person though he would have lots of friends. What then is the main problem; or rather, what does mankind do? People do not like children who lack innocence, for they hold the mirror up to adults. If children could not be deceived they would threaten adults beyond toleration, they would never be orderly in elementary school and they clearly could not be taught the rot-gut dished out to them as truth. Personally I do not know what to do; and I anticipate a geometric increase in madness, for sham is at the basis of schizophrenia and murder itself." *On Sham, Vulnerability, and Other Forms of Self-Destruction* (New York: Vintage Books, 1973), pp. 123-4. See also his *Pathways to Madness* (New York: Vintage Books, 1971), pp. 99-187.

35. For a fuller development of the issues in this last section see Hauerwas, "Natural Law, Tragedy, and Theological Ethics," *American Journal of Jurisprudence*, 20 (1975), 1-19. Moreover for a perspective similar to this see Ernest Becker, *The Denial of Death* (New York: Free Press, 1975). In a broad sense Becker suggests man's situation is tragic because, "Man has a symbolic identity that brings him sharply out of nature. He is a symbolic self, a creature with a name, a life history. He is a creator with a mind that soars

to speculate about atoms and infinity, who can place himself imaginatively at a point in space and contemplate bemusedly his own planet . . . . Yet at the same time man is a worm and food for worms. This is the paradox: He is out of nature and hopeless in it; he is dual, up in the stars and yet housed in a heart-pumping, breath-grasping body that once belonged to a fish. Man literally is split in two: he has awareness of his own splendid uniqueness in that he sticks out of nature with a towering majesty, and yet he goes back into the ground a few feet in order blindly to rot and disappear forever. It is a terrifying dilemma to be in and to have to live with." (p. 26.)

36. In his *Revisioning Psychology* (New York, 1975), Ch. 1, James Hillman questions whether psychic integration has not been conceived in too "monotheistic" a manner. His discussion is flawed by failing to see how an analogical "reference to one" offers a feasible way of mediating between an ideal which is too confining and a *laissez faire* program which jettisons ideals altogether.

37. A special note of gratitude to Larry McCullough of Texas A & M Medical School for his careful reading of our argument. Many of his suggestions would have clarified our argument had we been able to incorporate them more organically into our text.

II

Religion and the
Foundations of Ethics

5

Can Medicine Dispense with a Theological Perspective on Human Nature?

Alasdair MacIntyre

I

"The offices of T-4 prepared a questionnaire which was sent to all mental hospitals and psychiatric clinics in Germany. On the basis of the completed questionnaire . . . a committee of three experts, chosen from among the doctors connected with T-4, made a decision. If this long-distance diagnosis was unfavorable, the patient was sent to an 'observation station' . . . unless there was a contrary diagnosis by the director of the 'observation station,' he was transferred to a euthanasia establishment proper . . . when doctors were placed at the head of these establishments, more efficient methods were introduced. . . . The method they devised was asphyxiation by carbon monoxide gas. . . . Patients were generally rendered somnolent by being given morphine, scopolamine injections or narcotic tablets before being taken, in groups of ten, to the gas chamber. . . . Families were advised of the patient's death by form letters which stated that the patient had succumbed to 'heart failure' or 'pneumonia.' "[1]

Poliakov is describing the euthanasia program introduced in Germany by government decree on September 1, 1939. Two features of the episode deserve to be noticed. The first is that, as Poliakov shows, the euthanasia program for the mentally feeble and the insane was an important prelude to the extermination program for the Jews. The second is that there was no difficulty at all in recruiting distinguished and able members of the German medical profession first to the euthanasia program and then to the extermination program. It is no part of my intention to suggest that Germans have a peculiarly horrifying lack of moral capacity or that physicians are peculiarly corruptible; quite the opposite. It is, in fact, precisely because the German medical profession in pre-Nazi Germany honored the Hippocratic Oath with apparently the same degree of sincerity, conviction, and moral capacity with which it is honored by our own medical men that the ready participation of such professors of psychiatry as Heyde, Nietzsche, and Pfannmüller in the euthanasia program, and of such professors of medicine as Clauberg and Kremer at Auschwitz and Ravensbruck, puts us too to the question.

Discussions of medical ethics usually focus upon what has now become problematic for physicians and surgeons. I want to attend instead to what is still taken for granted, namely, the unconditional and absolute character of certain of the doctor's obligations to his patients. The German example shows how fragile commitment to this absolute and unconditional character may be; it is all the more important, therefore, to enquire what grounds we have for such commitment. If we omit from view all the areas about which there is now argument and debate—voluntary euthanasia, abortion, continuation of life by extraordinary means—there remains that large and central area of medical practice in which the doctor is required to treat the life of the patient as an object of unconditional regard and concern—it seems natural to say that he is required to treat the life of the patient as sacred. This kind of requirement is, of course, central to *all* morality: the same unconditional character is embodied in the student's obligation not to cheat in an examination, the patriot soldier's (as contrasted with the mercenary's) obligation to accept death rather than dishonor, the obligation on us all not to engage in malicious gossip—and, most strikingly, the simple obligation upon all of us to give up our lives rather than allow certain evils of Auschwitz and Ravensbruck. Any account of morality which does not allow for the fact that my death may be required of me at any moment is thereby an inadequate account.

When someone says truly, "I ought to do so-and-so," he or she is not, of course, always acknowledging such a requirement. What discriminates the occasions on which such an obligation or requirement is acknowledged from those in which it is not? Kant believed that the two occasions could be distinguished by a reference to what he took to be the logical form of the sentence uttered. Only a categorical sentence, one containing no explicit or implied "if " clause, could express such a requirement. But on this Kant is clearly wrong. For although he was right to exclude such "if " clauses as "if I want to be happy" or "if I want to reach Boston within the hour" from such utterances, there may be other "if " clauses that are not only compatible with the expression of such an obligation or requirement, but that may throw light on its nature. They seem to fall into two classes.

The first class refers to the consequences for the agent him- or herself. "I ought to do so-and-so, if I am not to incur guilt," where guilt is to be contrasted with both regret and shame. If I merely regret doing something, then my concern is only for myself; if I feel shame, then my concern is for how I may be regarded by others. But if I acknowledge guilt, I understand myself to be in the wrong, to be a person whom others ought to view in a radically different light from previously, an outlaw from the moral order. (It may be that in using the words "regret," "shame," and "guilt" to mark these distinctions I am not using them in a way entirely consistent with ordinary usage, but I doubt if ordinary usage is itself internally consistent on these topics.) Thus guilt presupposes a moral order with which I can be at one or at variance.

Closely connected with this presupposition is the way in which an acknowledgment of guilt entails an admission of liability to repair in any way possible the wrong that has been done, to compensate, to make the world as nearly as possible what it was before I did evil. "I acknowledge my guilt, but I admit no obligation to make reparation," is, if "guilt" is being used as I am using it, self-contradictory. The discussion of guilt, shame, and regret has been of course clouded by the modern tendency to view them primarily as states of feeling. But although there are indeed feelings of guilt, shame, and regret, these may be appropriate or inappropriate, and they are appropriate only where an agent truthfully can acknowledge guilt or shame or regret, where the acknowledgment is of a concern or an obligation and not of a feeling. Thus the feeling states are secondary phenomena.

The second class of "if" clauses, which may occur in the expression of an absolute obligation or requirement of morality, refers to the consequences for the moral order which will be violated if the obligation or requirement in question is not upheld. They are of the form "if evil is not to enter the world." The concept of evil involved is the concept of that which is absolutely prohibited. No reason of any kind can justify or excuse the doing of evil. This, however, does not settle the question whether it may not on occasion be necessary to do evil in order, for example, to prevent a greater evil. But even if this is ever right, the moral agent who made this choice would not thereby be excused from the charge of having done evil. He would still need to acknowledge guilt, to receive forgiveness, to be reconciled. For the moral order is not necessarily a coherent one; demands may be made upon us such that we cannot meet them all and yet all are required of us, absolutely and unconditionally.

II

The accounts of this absolute and unconditional character given by moral philosophers all seem to encounter the following dilemma: *either* they distort and misrepresent it *or* they render it unintelligible. Teleological moralists characteristically end up by distorting and misrepresenting. For they begin with a notion of moral rules as specifying how we are to behave if we are to achieve certain ends, perhaps *the* end for man, the *summum bonum*. If I break such rules I shall fail to achieve some human good and will thereby be frustrated and impoverished. Virtues are dispositions, the cultivation of which will enable men to achieve the good, and defects in virtue are marks of a failure to achieve it. This is a scheme embodied in one way in Aristotle's moral theory, in another in J.S. Mill's.

There are two closely connected inadequacies in any account

which remains within the limits imposed by such a teleological scheme. The first is that it suggests that moral failure is like, say, educational failure. I set myself to get a degree in medieval literature, but I find Italian difficult and I give up temporarily or permanently. I am the poorer for not being able to read Dante in the original, and I am forced to recognize that my knowledge and taste are less adequate than they might be. But it would be parodying morality to suggest that my temporary or permanent failure to become truthful is a failure of the same kind as my failure to learn Italian; what is wrong with a grossly untruthful person is not that he has a less rich and achieved personality than a truthful man. The appropriate attitude to my own educational failure is regret, perhaps deep regret; the appropriate attitude to my own acts of untruthfulness is guilt.

Secondly what was wrong with the German professors and physicians at Auschwitz was not that they were not good enough, that they had not progressed far enough towards the *summum bonum*. It was that they were positively evil. Aristotelians characteristically treat indulgence in vices as failure to be virtuous; utilitarians characteristically treat goodness and badness as defined by one continuous scale so that "the bad" is simply "the less good." Evil is nothing other for both than an absence or deprivation of good. But the cruelties of the camps cannot be characterized as failures to be kind or sensitive. What the Nazis set up was a systematic inversion of the moral order in which virtues appeared as vices. "The new measures are so convincing," wrote Dr. F. Hölzel of the German euthanasia program in 1940, "that I had hoped to be able to discard all personal considerations. But it is one thing to approve state measures with conviction, and another to carry them out yourself down to the last consequences. . . . If this leads you to put the children's home in other hands, it would mean a painful loss for me. However, I prefer to see clearly and to recognize that I am too gentle for this work. . . . Heil Hitler!"[2]

An evil person is not just someone who has not yet approached the good closely enough; he or she is someone engaged in an attempt to disrupt the whole moral order by setting him- or herself and others to move in the opposite direction, in a positive cultivation of wickedness. It is complicity with positive evil that requires guilt and repentance, and for which regret is clearly inadequate.

Yet, those moral philosophers who have understood the inadequacies of teleological ethics—thinkers as various as Kant, Bradley, and Prichard—have tended to present the unconditional and absolute character of the central requirements of morality in a way which makes it difficult to understand their precise character. For Kant, the requirements of morality are requirements of practical reason; this makes it easy to understand why Kant tries to use a criterion of *consistent* universalizability to discriminate genuine categorical imperatives from false pretenders to that status, but very hard to understand the connection that he makes with the conception of *law* and of the respect required by law. For since "moral principles are not based on properties of human nature,"[3] since all positive knowledge is irrelevant, we cannot build up our conception of the moral law by any analogy with positive law, whether human or divine. Hence the concept of a moral *law* derives its absolute and unconditional character from elsewhere; indeed the movement in Kant's own thought is from the requirements of the moral law to those of positive law and not *vice versa*.

When later philosophers discarded Kant's theory, but retained his notion of the special character of moral duties, the character of this absolute and unconditional requirement of morality became even less intelligible. In Prichard's writing, for example, the claim is that there is a distinctive sense of the word "ought" which expresses the distinctive demand that morality makes of us. What is this demand? Prichard speaks of a feeling of imperativeness, but he only characterizes this imperativeness as that which morality makes us feel. Indeed it is clear that Prichard believes that we all know perfectly well what "ought" means in its distinctive moral sense and that it cannot be further explicated without circularity. Why is this so unsatisfactory?

Elsewhere,[4] I have compared the "ought" discussed by Prichard with "taboo" as used in the late eighteenth century in the Pacific Islands. Captain Cook and his sailors were told that men and women could not eat together, because it was *taboo*. But when they enquired what that meant, they could learn nothing except that it was an absolute and unconditional requirement which could not be further explained. We do not take *taboo* seriously; why then should we take seriously Kant's or Prichard's *ought*?

The dilemma, which I suggested earlier, can now be framed more clearly. Either we try to place the absolute requirement of morality in a teleological framework or we do not. If we do so place it, however, we find ourselves dictating and misrepresenting its character, as Aristotle and J. S. Mill do; if we do not, we find ourselves unable to discriminate this requirement from irrational demands for absolute obedience of a superstitious or neurotic kind. The relevance of this dilemma to contemporary discussions of medical ethics is clear. At the one extreme we have the warm partisans of voluntary euthanasia or of a pregnant woman's unlimited right to an abortion, at least within the first three months of pregnancy; at the other, those equally warmly opposed. The latter party see the first as having moved the obligations of the physicians on to shifting ground. If each particular case can be decided on its merits, no matter by whom, we lose the notion of an unconditional requirement on all human beings to abide by some general rule; and once we have abandoned that we shall have lost our hold on the central concept of morality. Hence, their fear, which appears so unreasonable to their opponents, that, if certain types of practice are permitted, in time anything will be permitted. Their opponents, in turn, see those opposed to liberal permissiveness in areas such as abortion and euthanasia as the victims of a superstitious fetishism, who are able to give no further *rational* ground for their moral appeal.

To understand that these contending groups reincarnate in their controversy a continuing dilemma of moral philosophy may make us a little more sympathetic to their stances. But it also suggests that to secure a reasonable consensus in medical ethics may require a solution to the problem posed by this dilemma. Where should we begin to look for such a solution? It is worth noticing at this point that Kant himself felt the pressure of some of the considerations which I have been arguing. I therefore turn from the Kant of the *Fundamental Principles* to the Kant of the second *Critique* and of *Religion Within the Bounds of Reason Alone* to consider Kant's own solution.

III

In Book II of the second *Critique*, Kant argues that if I seriously consider what is involved in the requirements of morality, I shall find that they commit me to a belief not only in freedom, but also in God and in immortality. Modern moral philosophers have, therefore, often wanted to detach Book I from Book II, following Heine in seeing the introduction of theological notions as essentially arbitrary. It appears to me that the introduction of these notions is much less arbitrary than is commonly supposed, because in understanding Kant's arguments a key step is passed over. Kant argues that it is a requirement of practical reason to pursue the *summum bonum*; that the *summum bonum* consists not merely of moral perfection, but of moral perfection crowned with happiness; that practical reason cannot require the impossible; and that the affixing of happiness to a completed virtue is possible only beyond this present world and by divine power. It is possible to quarrel with any of the first three stages in this argument. Some existentialist writers have suggested that precisely the impossible is required of us—hence the applicability of the myth of Sisyphus; and the very conception of a *summum bonum* has been put in question radically enough to make both the first and second steps doubtful. But most critics have not given sufficient emphasis to what is the key concept here, that of a moral progress.

Kant's conception of moral progress is inseparable from his conception of the radical evil in human nature. Men are not merely frail and so desirous of satisfying certain inclinations that they often act with mixed motives; their depravity lies in their deliberately preferring other maxims to those of morality. It is the universality of this depravity in the human species which leads Kant to speak of it as natural to man. And since Kant speaks of nature as that which is to be contrasted with the realm of freedom, the realm in which the maxims of the categorical imperative find their application, we may treat Kant's account of radical evil as in some sense empirical. Certainly he finds it easy to cite examples of moral evil; whereas he allows that we cannot be certain that there is even one actual case in which the maxims of the categorical imperative have been obeyed simply for the motive of duty. But if Kant's thesis is empirical we have not far to look for evidence.

Not one of the subjects in Milgram's famous experiments[5] refused to continue intensifying what they took to be electrical shocks administered to the body of a subject in a learning experiment before the level labelled *Intense Shock* (300 volts). Most went beyond this; and more than half to the limit. Milgram's sample of postal clerks, high school teachers, salesmen, engineers, and workers suggests what seemed also to emerge from denazification proceedings: that there was nothing psychologically extraordinary in the vast majority of concentration camp guards or S.S. men. The capacity for positive evil is indeed normally both restrained and disguised by social and institutional practice; it seems clear that what enabled Milgram's subjects to behave as they did was a definition of the social situation—that of a scientific experiment—that legitimated behavior not normally permitted; just as a definition of a situation as *a war* legitimates forms of behavior that individuals do not normally permit themselves. But this first crude sketch of a possible sociological explanation for such changes in behavior does nothing to displace the moral question: why and how to create social structures which do not distract agents from the unconditional requirements at the heart of morality.

How does the presence of radical evil in the world connect with the notion of moral progress? Underlying Kant's account of morality, concealed from view almost altogether in the *Fundamental Principles*, obtruding in the second *Critique*, and manifesting itself much more clearly not only in *Religion Within the Bounds of Reason Alone* but also and especially in the writings on history, is a crucial metaphor, that of the life of the individual and also of that of the human race as a journey toward a goal. This journey has two aspects. There is the progress toward creating the external conditions for the achievement of moral perfection by individuals: "with advancing civilization reason grows pragmatically in its capacity to realize ideas of law. But at the same time the culpability for the transgression also grows."[6] Within the framework of law and civility the individual progresses toward moral perfection, a progress "directed to a goal infinitely remote." It follows that the significance of a particular moral action does not lie solely in its conformity to the moral law; it marks a stage in that journey the carrying through of which confers significance on the individual's life. Thus a link does exist between the acts of duty and the *summum bonum* conceived as the goal of the individual's journey. Radical evil provides the obstacles both to the progress of the race and that of the individual. Without radical evil there would be no progress, no journey, for there would be nothing to overcome; without the *summum bonum* there would be no goal to reach by overcoming the obstacles.

Kant's moral philosophy thus has kinship to a whole family of narrative portrayals of human life, of which the Grail legends are prime examples. Human life is a quest in which a variety of dangers and harms may befall me; unless I am prepared to sacrifice my life on occasion I cannot achieve that which I seek. To fail to sacrifice my life, necessarily will be to fail as a man. The themes are originally perhaps Pythagorean and Orphic; they reappear in Plato's myths as well as in his attitude to the death of Socrates and they are crucial to Jewish and to Christian theology. In both Platonic and Judeo-Christian versions it turns out to be the case that *only* if I am prepared to—in some versions only if I do—sacrifice my life can I achieve the goal. Only if I place my own physical survival lower on the scale of values than other goods, can my self be perfected. Teleology has thus been restored but in a form very alien to either Aristotle's thought or Mill's. It is no wonder that Kant finds in Greek ethics no adequate conceptual scheme for the representation of morality, but views Christianity as providing just such a scheme.

So the basic thesis of Book II of the second *Critique* and of *Religion Within the Bounds of Reason Alone* can now be restated. Our moral experience presupposes the form of a progress toward a goal never to be achieved in this present world; but this in turn presupposes that the moral agent has a more than earthly identity, and that there is a power in the universe able to sustain our progress toward the goal in and after the earthly life. Morality thus does presuppose our own life after death and the existence of a power that we may call divine. Since the whole point of this power's activity, as belief in it is presupposed by us, is to bring about moral perfection and the *summum bonum*, we cannot, if we see rightly, see our duty as in any way different from the precepts of such a power. We must see our duties as divine commands.

This brief and compressed outline of Kant's account of the presuppositions of pure practical reason, highly inadequate although it is, suggests that the connection between Kant's conception of morality and his theological commitments is a great deal more plausible than is usually supposed. To put the matter crudely, it is beginning to seem that if you take Kant's account of morality seriously then you may find that *either* your position has to move steadily toward that of Prichard *or* it has to retain something uncomfortably like Kant's philosophy of religion. Most modern commentators on Kant have thought it deeply implausible that belief in the unconditional character of the absolute and unconditional requirements of morality should commit the agent to belief in God; but once it is seen that the choice is between God and Prichard, God may appear the less daunting prospect.

IV

Yet theologians will be ill-advised to seize upon this conclusion too eagerly. Every deductive argument is reversible. If I discover that my well-established belief that *p* logically presupposes a previously unaccepted and taken to be unacceptable belief that *q*, instead of accepting a commitment to *q* as well as to *p*, I may decide that the rational course is to reject *p* as well as *q*. The argument may move in either direction and I must find sure reasons for moving in one rather than the other. Moreover, we may be reminded at this point of the parallels between the concept of *moral obligation* as specified by Prichard and the concept of *taboo* as encountered by Captain Cook. That concept presupposed a more complex background of beliefs, but to recover that connection would not make belief in *taboos* more warrantable. We should merely understand how both background beliefs and the concept of *taboo* had to be rejected together. Perhaps in a parallel way belief in the absolute and unconditional character of certain moral requirements is discredited by its presupposing belief in something akin to Kant's philosophy of religion, rather than the latter made more credible by this presupposition.

What might lead toward this conclusion is the *arbitrariness* which the premises of all theological argument now seem to possess to those who do not already accept them. This sense of arbitrariness does not derive from the reading of skeptics, such as Voltaire and Russell, so much as from reading widely in contemporary theology. For the theologian in a secularized world finds himself in the following difficulty: *either* he is able to present his position in terms which are intelligible within that secularized world *or* he is not. If he is so able, then he may find himself in one of two difficulties. For either his assertions will conflict with some of the body of secular beliefs or they will not. The former possibility is less often realized these days than formerly; theologians no longer usually claim that certain features of the natural world require explanation in terms of the divine. But the latter possibility is all too real. A Bultmann decodes Christianity and what is left is—Heidegger's philosophy; a van Buren decodes it and what is left is. . . . To decode turns out to be to destroy.

It is the theologians who have resisted all decoding who preserve Christianity; and they do so by insisting that the secular world must accept Christianity on its terms and not on the terms of a secularized universe. It is no accident that Karl Barth is the greatest of modern theologians and that he characterizes the problem for the man who confronts Christianity as: "He has to speak about something of which no man can speak."[8] Or to put matters less dramatically, he has first to believe in order to be able to come to terms with belief—part of the message of Barth's book on Anselm. The theological universe depends on epistemological circularities. To this the rejoinder may be—it was the rejoinder of Raphael Demos, for example[9]—that the natural sciences also involve epistemological circularities, that the interpretations of the theologian raise no more grounds for unbelief than do the problems of induction. The force of this rejoinder ought not to be underrated, but it does not meet what is in fact the central difficulty.

The difficulty is that we all, including contemporary theologians, inhabit an intellectual universe in which the natural sciences are at home and theology is not. The believer has not only to make theological claims about the existence and nature of God, but he also has to make special epistemological claims about the character of his theological claims, if he wants to be heard. The unbeliever equally has to decide what grounds he might have for giving credibility of any kind to the theologian's interpretations. For both parties, the question of what would settle the argument has characteristically become unclear in a way in which it was not unclear either for medieval theologians or for eighteenth-century materialists. Hence the interesting irrelevance of unbelievers who focus their attack on the theses of the Middle Ages or the Reformation and of theologians who believe as though what they had to rebut was the atheism of the eighteenth or nineteenth centuries. Yet just because the argument between theologians and unbelievers is in this peculiarly contemporary state of unclarity, we may be brought back to something very like Kant's own position. For Kant's account of the limits of theoretical reason clearly excluded the possibility of finding good reasons for theological beliefs by means of theoretical enquiry. In other words, the *only* ground, according to Kant, for theological belief arises from the way in which morality presupposes a belief in God and in immortality. But this seems to be the outcome of the present argument too. Hence we may seem to be free not merely to reject theology, but to have no reason not to accept *both* such a dismissal *and* a concomitant dismissal of any absolute and unconditional requirement in morality. But is this really so? Do the absolute and unconditional requirements of morality and theological presuppositions of a Kantian kind really stand or fall together?

It is certainly worth noting that, as a matter of sociological fact, theological beliefs may not prove supportive of this central part of morality. Or they may assist in seeing as sacred and absolute obligations which are, on occasion, subversive of morality. There is no doubt that German Lutheranism did at least as much (to put matters charitably) to hallow the German officers' oath of allegiance to the Führer, and the German people's definition of their situation as one in which obedience to authority was paramount, as it did to underpin the resistance of the Confessional Church. Heydrich had a Lutheran upbringing; Himmler, Goebbels and Hoess came from strict Catholic families. Such considerations make the question of the last paragraph the more urgent.

V

I argued earlier that Kant's moral philosophy does have more of a teleological framework than is usually recognized, and I suggested that his teleology is less distorting to moral experience than Aristotle's or Mill's. I now need to amplify this point. I shall begin by considering two other defects in Aristotelian ethics.

The first is the dreadful banality of the true end for man when its content is finally made known. All those remarkable virtues are to be practiced, all that judgment and prudence is to be exercised so that we may become—upper middle class Athenian gentlemen devoted to metaphysical enquiry. What matters here is not just the unintendedly comic character of Aristotle's conclusion; any attempt to specify the true end for man by describing some state of affairs, the achievement of which will constitute that end, is bound to fail in a parallel way. That is why descriptions of heaven or of earthly Utopias, such as the communist society that Marx envisaged at the end of history, are seldom, if ever, convincing.

A closely related defect in Aristotle's view is that he is forced to take an entirely negative attitude to suffering and death. Hence his revulsion at the *Republic*'s description of the wholly good man suffering from calumny and torture and finally put to death. For Aristotle, as for utilitarianism, my death, if it comes too soon, simply frustrates the moral quest. For I will be deprived by death or suffering of achieving that state of affairs that constitutes *eudaimonia* or *the-greatest-possible-happiness-for-me-and-for-others* or whatever. It is then paradoxical that at the heart of morality there should be an absolute and unconditional requirement which may demand of me that I give up my life to prevent certain evils. For those who obey this demand are likely to be the very people who are frustrated thereby in the moral quest.

This is, of course, far more than an objection to Aristotle or Mill. It is a problem about the character of morality, not about the particular doctrines of any moral philosopher. On the one hand it seems difficult to make sense of morality except within some teleological framework; yet, on the other hand, at the heart of morality there lies this absolute demand so incompatible with most and perhaps all teleological theories of any power. Prichard, faced with this fact, separated moral obligation entirely from the exercise of virtues. The right and the good lose all connection. And this too seems thoroughly implausible.

What I want to suggest is that the mistake at the heart of most teleological doctrines lies in understanding the true end for man as a state of affairs. Christian teleology, as in Augustine or Aquinas, begins to approach nearer to the truth with its recognition that in this life we are always *in via*. But it retains the notion of a state of affairs in some other world as constituting man's true end; and it bequeaths this notion to Kant. Yet perhaps this too both can and ought to be expelled from our moral teleology. Perhaps we are *in via* in a more radical sense than even Christianity supposes. Consider the following possibility: that a crucial part of moral progress consists in learning how to transform our notion of moral progress, that the meaning of a particular life does not lie in attaining any particular state of affairs but in the agent's having traversed a course which is part of a larger moral history in which death and suffering are not merely negative deprivations. Indeed, it is at those moments at which risking death is morally required that an individual life is most clearly seen to have significance in the context of a larger history.

What kind of history could this be? The *Orestes* and the *Antigone* provide one type of example; the story of Abraham another; Livy a third; Guiccardini a fourth; the Marxist tradition a fifth. Such histories present human life as enacted dramatic narrative. The death of Iphigenia, the demand upon Abraham to take Isaac's life, the stand of the Horatii, the struggle of the Paris commune show that a conception central to such narratives is that of *sacrifice*, a notion totally alien to Aristotle or to Mill. If sacrifice is to be an intelligible notion, the individual has to be understood as a participant in the larger history of a group or an institution: the house of Atreus, the people of Israel, the city of Rome, the revolutionary proletariat. The enacted narrative of the individual's life derives its point from its place in the enacted narrative of the group or the institution. And this, in turn, may derive its significance from some more extended narrative. The most basic moral question for each agent is, therefore: of what histories am I a part?

How is such a question to be answered? Any acceptable answer must meet at least three requirements. First, only *true* stories are acceptable. Hence for us the interpretation of our historical existence cannot be mythological. The question of the criteria of truth for extended historical narratives is notoriously complex, and there may well be periods in which the conflicting claims of rival historical interpretations cannot be put to a finally decisive test. Secondly, the history of which I am a part must belong to some identifiable genre. The narrative that constitutes my life[10]—and not merely the reward of my life—may be tragic, comic, or of many other kinds. But as a narrative it must have some generic shape. The implicit assumption of many of our contemporaries is that the genre to which their lives belong is that to which Beckett's *End Game* also belongs.

Thirdly, any acceptable answer must do justice to the facts of moral complexity and more especially to the tragic character of human existence. This tragic character is inseparable from the relationship of the absolute and unconditional requirements of morality to guilt and evil. It puts the vulnerability and the failures of moral agents at the center of the moral picture. But it insists also upon giving a significance to that vulnerability and that failure of a kind that is implicitly denied in much contemporary writing about morality, both philosophical and practical. It is also worth noting that in a tragic perspective the activities of praising and blaming, of passing moral judgments, so central to so much contemporary moralizing, themselves become ambiguous activities about which we ought to practice a certain asceticism. For the individual who knows himself to be part of a moral history whose outcome is as yet unsettled may be less likely to claim prematurely that title of universal moral legislator that Kant bestowed on all rational agents and which has had such great effects on the character of moral activity.

At the heart of the difference in outlooks between, on the one hand, that perspective according to which the individual only has his moral identity as part of a larger history and, on the other hand, the prevailing moral views of our own culture, lie the individualist assumptions which have dominated both our social life and our moral philosophy since the early years of the bourgeois age. It was his reliance on such individualist assumptions which was responsible for the defects in Kant's treatment of the relationship between moral obligation and teleology. For Kant makes the significance of history depend on the moral progress of individuals rather than *vice versa*. Hence, death must be for him merely a negative boundary, and individual immortality is required for the only significant events that can take place after any individual's death. Hence, also, God is required as a power to give that moral form to the events in the after-life of individuals that Kant sees as lacking in the events of their mortal life. Kant's thesis that moral obligation necessarily presupposes teleology turns out to be correct; his thesis that teleology necessarily presupposes theology turns out to be incorrect. Hence the incredibility of Christian theology need not endanger belief in moral obligation after all.

VI

But what kind of teleology does the absolute character of moral obligation require? One apt immediate comment on my examples of moral histories would be that they are an exceptionally heterogeneous and various collection. Clearly, the moral structure of Greek tragic drama differs radically from that of early Hebrew narrative and so do both from the histories of ancient Rome or of renascence Italy. Yet these very different histories themselves stand in an important historical and moral relationship to each other; there is a larger moral history of which all these histories are themselves a part—and it is this that we inherit, or fail to inherit.

Kant's moral philosophy is itself yet another episode in this larger history and a peculiarly significant one. For in the seventeenth, eighteenth, and early nineteenth centuries, two rival currents of thought coexist uneasily in our predecessor culture. Both express reactions to the destruction of the classical or theistic view of the world; both inherit fragments from that view. The classical and theistic view of the world from its place in a cosmic order; the destruction of belief in that order seemed to some thinkers to reveal that human society was nothing but a set of isolated individuals. The task of philosophy was to show how, out of the experiences of such individuals, justified belief in an objective world could be constructed. Kant's genius was to show the impossibility of fulfilling this program either by rationalist or by empiricist methods. Rational belief in persons or objects cannot find its only basis in individual experiences; rational belief in moral precepts cannot find its only basis in individual feelings or goals. But Kant's great negative demonstrations of these truths were accompanied, in the name of individualist autonomy, by a divorce of morality from any social and historical context and a treatment of the social and historical as part of the realm of value-free fact. From which arises his difficulty in making absolute and unconditional obligation intelligible.

Yet counter to this development of thought, which moves from rationalists and empiricists through Kant to neoKantianism and empiricism, was the development of a quite different type of reaction to the loss of the classical and theistic world view. Its founder is Vico and it has later representatives in thinkers as different as Herder and Hegel. One of the most important theses shared by these thinkers is that individualism itself is most illuminatingly to be viewed as an episode in an enacted dramatic narrative, and that the moral history of individualism is, in fact, one in which the quest for individual autonomy is continuously frustrated. But if this is so, then the dilemmas within which the controversialists over absolute obligation in the realm of medical ethics have been imprisoned may be the outcome of viewing the problems of absolute obligation within an individualist framework. We could hope to escape those dilemmas, not by any attempt to find a theological solution—although as long as the problems remain in their present state there will be a recurrent temptation to seek such solutions—but only by a renewed criticism of the individualist framework and of the social institutions that sustain it and are sustained by it. More fruitful work in medical ethics requires new initiatives in general moral and political theory and in the philosophy of history.

NOTES

1. Leon Poliakov, *Harvest of Hate* (Philadelphia: Jewish Publication Society, 1954), pp. 185-6.
2. Ibid., pp. 186-7.
3. T. K. Abbott, *Kant's Critique of Practical Reason and other works on the theory of ethics* (London: Longmans, Green, 1873), p. 27.
4. Alasdair MacIntyre, *Against the Self-Images of the Age: Essays in Ideology and Philosophy* (London: Duckworth, 1971), p. 166.
5. Stanley Milgram, *Obedience to Authority* (New York: Harper & Row, 1974).
6. Immanuel Kant, *Perpetual Peace*, Appendix I. Professor Ramsey appears to think that Kant's moral philosophy is incompatible with any belief in moral progress in time and history. He can only do so by ignoring what Kant actually wrote about this and especially *An Old Question Raised Again: Is The Human Race Constantly Progressing?* (Both works cited in Lewis White Beck, ed., *On History*, [Indianapolis: Bobbs Merrill, 1963]).
7. Abbott, *Kant's Critique*, p. 220.
8. Karl Barth, *Römerbrief*, 2d ed. (Munich, 1922), p. 128.
9. S. Hook, ed., *Religious Experience and Truth* (New York: Collier, 1961).
10. Alasdair MacIntyre, *Epistemology and Dramatic Narrative* in *After Virtue* (forthcoming).

Commentary

Kant's Moral Theology
or A Religious Ethics?

Paul Ramsey

I

THE FIRST TITLE GIVEN US for this conference was "Does Medical Ethics Need a Basis in Theological Ethics?" or ". . . Theological Ethics as a Foundation?" Whether under that head or under Alasdair MacIntyre's more limited title, I want first to indicate what a proper theologian should never attempt to demonstrate about the bearing of religion or theology on sorts of human activity other than the religious (or in particular on medical practice).

My sweeping disavowal, which brackets all of my following discussion, can best be expressed in three favorite quotations of mine which with increasing clarity and exactitude express the initial point I wish to make.

The first are the words of Paul Weiss in an article entitled "The True, the Good and the Jew,"[1] where he wrote: "It is desirable that religious men endorse and encourage the ethical life, but they have lost their religion when they forget that ethics must play a subordinate role. Ethics should, from the perspective of religion, stand to religion as the lower to the higher, the easier to the harder, the negative to the positive, commands to avoid to commands to do."

The second is Soren Kierkegaard's assertion[2] that "in our age

139

speculative philosophy has arrogated to itself such authority that it has almost tempted God to feel uncertain of Himself, like a king who awaits anxiously to learn whether the Constitutional Assembly will make him an absolute or a limited monarch."

Best of all is the view of true religion obliquely voiced by C. S. Lewis's Screwtape, an archdemon, giving advice to his nephew Wormwood on how most shrewdly to tempt mankind into the service of "our Father below."

> . . . We do want, and want very much [wrote Screwtape] to make men treat Christianity as a means; preferably as a means to their own advantage, but, failing that, as a means to anything—even social justice. . . . For the Enemy [God] will not be used as a convenience. Men or nations who think they can revive the Faith in order to make a good society might just as well think they can use the stairs of Heaven as a short cut to the nearest chemist's shop. Fortunately it is easy to coax humans around this little corner.

I introduce Screwtape's advice into our present concern about the foundations of ethics not simply because of its pertinent medical reference to short cuts to the nearest chemist's shop. Its appropriateness is rather to be found in Screwtape's further enforcement of Wormwood's mission on earth in the service of "our Father below." He continues:

> Only today I have found a passage in a Christian writer where he recommends his own version of Christianity on the ground that "only such a faith can outlast the death of old cultures and the birth of new civilizations." [Then directly to Wormwood:] You see the little rift?[3]

The internal quotation is from one of Reinhold Niebuhr's early books entitled *Does Civilization Need Religion?* Which brings us back to our topic, Does Medical Ethics Need Religious Backing? Or foundation and warrant in theological perspectives?

If this brief introduction means anything, it means that as a theological ethicist I approach grappling with MacIntyre's essay with a certain divine nonchalance about the outcome. If Christian ethics exerted a shaping influence to date on our extant medical ethics (which no doubt it did), it was not because Christianity or Christian theological ethics took that to be one among its primary tasks. The same must be said about shoring up the shaking foundations of medical ethics today. To a religious man or to an authentically religious age it will seem self-evident that religion as a vocation, or rather as *the* vocation, of humankind should not be used as a convenience for anything else or anything less. If anyone needs religion in order to sleep soundly at night, or to endure the journey of life between drugstores, or as an engine behind extremely worthwhile social causes, or as enabling power to support already-known moral principles needing help, or to save civilization, or to undergird a physician's absolute loyalty to his patient—that is his problem. In any such situation, an authentically religious man will rightly suspect he is being asked to lend the dwindling allurements of religious platitudes to support worthwhile but weak or threatened earthly causes. A theological ethicist will know he is being asked to justify faith in God in terms of some other *plus ultra*. He has, properly, little interest in the success or defeat of Kant's enterprise, to which MacIntyre narrowed the question. I shall not join in treating God as a fool, not even to secure foundation for medical ethics. That explains my title.

II

"Medical ethics" can mean a number of things. So also does "theological perspective." These are the obvious variables. The Jehovah's Witness medical ethics in regard to blood transfusion certainly cannot dispense with a particular theological perspective. Medical practice can dispense with both, while leaving room for the right of a believing Witness to refuse treatment. On the other hand, the medical ethics produced by utilitarianism, cost/benefit analysis, or a teleological outlook that at no time finds good reason for preferring a righteous death to survival certainly needs no background justification in theological perspectives. Indeed, medical ethics in general may need certain theological perspectives in order to withstand the coming triumph of these viewpoints. Jewish medical ethics and Christian medical ethics in some of their features seem *prima facie* to require distinctive theological outlooks. The ethics and the theology were twin-born; they may also be Siamese, so bound together that they are destined to perish together.

There is, however, a third variable, namely, how justifying reasons found in theological perspectives are alleged to sustain or warrant the cardinal principles of a particular religious ethics or unconditional obligation. Kant's view is only one among many ways of relating unconditional moral requirements to a religious philosophy or outlook.

I propose, therefore, in this paper, first, to make a few comments on MacIntyre's chapter. These remarks concern points I judge worthy of note or needing further debate or clarification, and questions that remain at the end of his post-Kantian[4] critique of Kant. Then I shall simply set down a view of theological ethics that gives authorizing reasons for unconditional imperatives alongside of Kant's (and alongside the position MacIntyre develops by retaining a version of Kant's unconditional imperative and his view of radical evil enfolded into a philosophy of history that only by stipulation or as a consequence of future intellectual labors can, it is hoped, provide authorizing ground for such obligations).

1. MacIntyre clearly identifies the chief canon of medical ethics he means to espouse, namely, "the unconditional and absolute character of the doctor's obligations to his patients." If the doctor is required to treat the life of the patient as an object of unconditional regard and concern, MacIntyre observes that "it seems natural to say that he is required to treat the life of the patient as sacred." That canon of medical ethics is only a special case of the moral point of view in general. It rests upon "the simple obligation upon all of us to give up our lives rather than allow certain evils to occur; . . . any account of morality which does not allow for the fact that my death may be required of me at any moment is thereby an inadequate account."

Even here it is worth noting that MacIntyre speaks only of "certain" of a doctor's obligations to his patient. In any ethics, of course, only certain obligations are unconditional; others may not be. In this instance, however, MacIntyre stipulates that "we *omit* from view *all* the areas about which there is *now* argument and debate—voluntary euthanasia, abortion," etc. (italics added).

Then there "remains" a core of medical ethics that requires treating the life of the patient as an object of unconditional concern. The admission of cultural conditioning, the "now" looming historicism which triumphs in the end of the paper (along with collectivism over individualism in our approach to ethics) makes it a fair question to ask what future times may deem fit issues to omit. Peeling off the layers of a physician's obligation to his patient may, as in *Peer Gynt*, disclose that the onion has no core. This is only to say that if we reject the authorization Kant proposed for an unconditional obligation, along with more adequate accounts of a theological perspective, we need clear and crucial justifications to put in their place.

2. Clearly MacIntyre peels off very little. It is important for us "to enquire what grounds we have for such a commitment," I should say, not only because the German example shows how fragile medical commitment is, but also because of the absoluteness of the moral demand itself. MacIntyre's medical ethics seems on its face to be a prime example of an ethics needing theological justification, one that cannot dispense with any backing that anyone have good reason to believe forthcoming from theological perspective. For this cause also, the author pursues the question assiduously. For my part, I must say that MacIntyre is brilliant in criticizing what he rejects; obscure and futuristic when he tries himself to state the context of, or authorization for, unconditional obligation which he affirms to replace that of Kant or any other theological perspective.

3. MacIntyre's anti-theological feet are showing when he draws up the security of the warm blanket of the *facticity* of the modern world view around his neck. He speaks of "*arbitrariness* which the premises of all theological argument now seem to possess to those who do not readily accept them." That reads to me rather like a definition of *felt* arbitrariness. He basically assumes that we "inhabit an intellectual universe in which the natural sciences are at home and theology is not." He believes it is "certainly worth noting that *as a matter of sociological fact* theological beliefs may *not* prove supportive" of a central core of unconditional morality (italics added). MacIntyre suggests that we are equally free to reject theological justifications or to "accept a

concomitant dismissal of any absolute and unconditional requirement in morality." He states, *factually*, that "most modern com-
mentaries on Kant have thought it deeply implausible that belief
in the unconditional character of the absolute and unconditional
requirements of morality should commit the agent to belief in
God . . ." That argument he expresses in p's and q's—as is the
custom among philosophers. "Every deductive argument is reversible," he writes. "If I discover that my well established belief
that p logically presupposes a previously unacceptable . . . belief
that q, instead of accepting a commitment to q as well as to p, I
may decide that the rational course is to reject p as well as q."

Concerning that, it must simply be said that MacIntyre has no
intention of abandoning p. He does not weaken the moral imperative. Therefore his statement that "*theologians* will be ill advised
to seize upon this conclusion too eagerly" (italics added) is a
statement binding him to establish p firmly on some other foundation than q. His warning to theologians that they not cite
theological perspectives as authorizing grounds for unconditional
obligation (for fear that their contemporaries are more likely to
abandon such an understanding of certain of their moral obligations) sounds like a threat or special pleading, and, moreover,
one MacIntyre is not entitled to use in good faith, since he
himself does not believe it permissible to abandon that moral
point of view (p).

The foregoing quotations from MacIntyre, however, do focus
our attention on "burden of proof" arguments. I do not suppose
that MacIntyre meant to count noses to settle intellectual questions, i.e., the number of persons now moldering in their graves
who believed the medieval religious world view against the number of moderns, living or dead, who believe the contrary. If not,
then what?

The claimed rational situation is as follows. Suppose someone
fifty years ago put forth the claim that parallel lines meet. He
would have borne the burden to show that was the case. A
properly operative "conservative" principle on the part of adherents of euclidean geometry rightly placed on him the burden of
proof. So it must be to a similar and proper conservative principle to which MacIntyre must appeal when he generally believes

that in our time and place theology has the task of making itself credible, and concludes that it fails.[5]

If MacIntyre's is not a nose-count argument, but more like the Quine/Ullian "conservative" principle, we still must ask: How should one in a secular age attempt to counter the burden-of-proof argument? One way to proceed is to contend that the original *casting* of the burden of proof on a religious view as against the secular view was a mistake.

Here for brevity's sake I simply appeal to my distinguished former colleague Walter T. Stace.[6] Concerning the world history of the seventeenth-century scientific revolution, Stace asserts that "no single discovery was made, no idea was put forward which, from the point of view of logic, should have had the slightest effect in the way of destroying belief in God. And yet the scientific revolution actually did have such an effect." That revolution produced a devastating effect upon the central beliefs of religion only because of "non-logical transitions due to suggestion and association."[7] ". . . The scientific picture of the world has penetrated the marrow of our minds. It has become an unconscious background of all human thinking." ". . . A view of the world as having no purpose, is not a logical transition. . . . Nevertheless the modern mind has made the illogical jump." The burden of proof placed on a religious perspective was simply a mistake.

That can, I think, be said while not forgetting that the *sort* of religious perspective Stace made room for was quite unlike the explanations and justification procedures for unconditional morality that are at home in Judaism or Christianity.

Moreover, there are sociological facts that are sufficient explanations of MacIntyre's sociological facts to which appeal may be made to explain the mistaken *casting* of the burden of proof upon a religious outlook in the modern age. One need not appeal only to erroneous extrapolations from "the world history of the seventeenth-century scientific revolution," as Stace does. That may have been only a ripple upon the modern mind in comparison to what C. S. Lewis believed was the most significant division in western history—"that which divides the present from, say, the age of Jane Austen and Scott"—namely, the machine and industrial civilization.[8] That presents a vast and overwhelming problem for, say, Christian apologetics; but it *ought* not to determine the "premises" upon which an intellectual builds his theological or philosophical edifice.

4. MacIntyre takes from Kant a notion of moral progress. (Below, I question this interpretation of Kant.) He affirms that "the significance of a particular moral action does not lie solely in its conformity to the moral law; it marks a stage in that journey the carrying through of which confers significance on the individual's life." Radical evil makes that journey significant; the *summum bonum* sets for Kant the goal. But MacIntyre objects to the notion of "moral perfection *crowned* with happiness" (italics added). He rejects Kant's "*affixing* of happiness to a completed virtue . . . possible only beyond this present world and by divine power" (italics added). Below we shall look at the account of moral progress MacIntyre endorses instead of Kant's.

Here my comment is directed to MacIntyre's understanding of Christian theological ethics which, he says, bequeathed to Kant the *addendum* of happiness to virtue, yet (MacIntyre acknowledges) held a more radical notion of *homo viator*.

MacIntyre's point is that Kant appealed to a "state of affairs," beyond all family resemblance to states of affairs we know, which would support our doing our duty to death. This is also his view of a defect in the Christian world view. He calls for a more radical understanding of *homo viator* than either the Christian or the Kantian expectation of a future, confirmatory "state of affairs" allows. Therefore, MacIntyre objects not only to some teleological doctrines because they mistake "the true end for man to be a state of affairs." This is also his objection to the Kantian appeal to the *summum bonum* and to ordinary Christian appeals to an ultimate congruence of duty with blessednesss. He wants to construe our moral lives to be always *in via*, radicalizing both Kantianism and Christianity.

While MacIntyre is correct when he says that the mistake at the heart of some religious teachings lies in understanding the true end of man as a state of affairs, he could go further than he has in disassociating Christian theology from such a view. That in this life we are always *in via* is a truth he takes from Christian theology. He then is left with a journey having no goal; mankind's moral history having no eventuality in a state of affairs.

But the goal need not be a state of affairs, or Kant's addendum of the *summum bonum* to a virtuous life. I grant, of course, not only that in popular Christian beliefs heaven is portrayed as a place where rewards are given to faithful persons.[9] I grant also that this is a prominent element in the portrayal of great theologians and religious literature such as the *Revelation of St. John* (all addressed, MacIntyre is correct, to sustaining the "patient endurance" of humankind *in via*). Still, a deeper comprehension of Christian theology will show, I think, that its great representatives have not been as trivial as Kant. Of course, I grant "the dreadful banality of the true end for man when its content is finally made known"—if that end is a state of affairs simply added to the Way thereto. However, the blessedness of heaven is *not* in happiness added, but simply and only the perfection of virtue, the completion of holiness, the achievement and gift of perfect love to God and love for one another in God. *That's* the happiness of it; no additional state of affairs needed. So here we have a journey with a goal whose goal is part of the journey. The Way participates in the End, and the End is the Way.

It is true that Christian theology spoke more often of the good than of obligation. So Augustine spoke of the enjoyment of God (fruition) and of the enjoyment of one another (fruition) in God as the supreme good or end of humankind. But that is also the good here and now.

5. In the end MacIntyre's position is a teleology without end. ". . . A crucial part of moral progress," he writes, "consists in learning how to transform our notion of moral progress." By that he means learning that an individual's moral progress is not located on the way toward an individual goal but rather "the agent's having traversed a course which is part of a larger moral history in which death and suffering are not merely negative deprivations. Indeed, it is at those moments at which risking death is morally required that an individual life is most clearly seen to have significance in the context of a larger history."

So a man may die for his country, but his country does not die for him. So also a physician may refuse to train Green Beret aidmen in medical arts, because he locates his life within a different moral history for which he is willing to suffer imprisonment rather than participate in evil-doing. Thus, in general, an individual's life "derives its point from its place in the enacted narrative of the group or institution." Those enacted narratives, in turn, derive significance from "some more extended narrative." Presumably, that more extended narrative is the moral history of mankind. But I do not know that this is MacIntyre's position, since at this point his paper ends with a summons.

One characteristic of an account of that larger moral history, of which all these histories are a part, seems clear. It must be a moral history "whose outcome is as yet unsettled." It must be a Way without End, which we inherit or fail to inherit. As likely as not that will mean making moral progress by, slowly over the decades, eroding certain unconditional moral obligations as we learn how to transform our notion of moral progress. For this reason, in an earlier version of my response, I said that MacIntyre must have a Cartesian "seeing eye" by which he perceives clearly and distinctly the validity of a physician's unconditional concern for the life of his patient. That must be a self-justifying claim. At least MacIntyre has not given us the authorizing context. He has called for one.

I am left with the feeling Soren Kierkegaard expressed about Lessing's conclusion, that if God held all truth [the extended history in which unconditional moral obligation finds authorizing reasons] in his right hand, and in his left the lifelong pursuit of it, he would choose the left hand.[10] Kierkegaard's comment[11] was: "When Lessing wrote these words the System was presumably not finished; alas! and now Lessing is dead." Likewise, MacIntyre sets out on the path of replacing superstitious fetishisms by rational ground for their moral appeal. In his case, however, it is stipulated that the outcome of our most encompassing narrative moral history remain unsettled.

By Jove, I do believe the watered-down Kantianism of R. M. Hare is to be preferred. Hare writes that the world must be believed to be such that the moral life is not pointless or futile.[12] He could have added (as Aquinas said at the end of each of his "five ways" of proving the existence of God): "and that men call God." Hare says something that seems reasonable and necessary to affirm, but casts it not in terms of "future states." He says not how; but yet there is an appeal beyond self-justifying moral grounds to the ultimate nature of the universe in which we live that prevents stringent moral requirements from being illusions or nonsense or arbitrarily terminal or threatened by erosion over the course of time. Indeed, I hold that all references to future "states of affairs" are only imaged or imaginative overflows from assertions about the present relation of reality to our moral obligations.

Alas! however, MacIntyre is still alive to rebut me.

6. We noted above that, when MacIntyre issued his warning to theologians, he stated that "every deductive argument is reversible." One can simply withhold his commitment to an unconditional obligation if belief in God or the *summum bonum* follows as a conclusion. I had not thought it proper to characterize Kant's method as "deductive." Instead, Kant's critical philosophy instates a "presuppositional" method. The question of the First Critique, for example, was: What are the *conditions of the possibility* of scientific knowledge? Empiricism (induction) and rationalism (deduction) had failed to explain how knowledge of universal laws of the physical universe is possible. Kant took scientific knowledge to be possible and argued that any *necessary* presuppositions of that knowledge had to be equally valid.

The same holds for reason in its practical employment (moral reasoning). Having established (he believed) that moral reason legislates an unconditional obligation, Kant then asks: What are the *necessary* presuppositions and postulates of the categorical imperative? Not just any presuppositions or postulates that can be thought of or used in support of duty, but necessary conditions. Moral reasoning, as it were, must move on to religious reasoning, or else deny the undeniable. Kant's move is not reversible. His is *not* a hypothetical syllogism "*If p*, then *q*," where one is rationally free to deny the consequence *q* and then go back and call *p* into question. There is no "if-ness" about *p* in the first place. Moreover, "then *q*" refers to a class of assertions (by necessary presupposition) about the ultimate (noumenal) nature of the self, the world, and God that nothing observable in the phenomenal world could prove or refute. Indeed, antinomies or contradiction within reason in its pure or objective employment point to these unities as "ideals of pure reason" that are nevertheless unknowable to pure reason itself. So the way is open for the move from moral reason to the necessary presuppositions and postulates of religious reason. One must deny and then refute Kant's argument; it is not, I believe, simply reversible.

Parenthetically, we may ask why MacIntyre concentrates on God, immortality, and the *summum bonum*, and says nothing about freedom. The self's freedom is no less a necessary presupposition and postulate of moral reason (unconditional obligation). Kant's "I ought, therefore I can" is not a deductive argument (despite the "therefore" in that shorthand expression). Nor is it a hypothetical syllogism ("If I categorically ought, then I am free") which could be disconfirmed by scientific knowledge about the phenomenal self or the phenomenal world. Someone who has a distaste for human freedom (q), or who believes science rules it out, is not rationally at liberty to go back and deny p (unconditional obligation) since, according to Kant, that has already been firmly established by moral reason.

7. I have argued that Kant took from his upbringing in Lutheran pietism an inadequate notion of the *summum bonum* as a state of affairs "affixed" to a virtuous life. The blessedness of heaven, I said, lies essentially in the completion or perfection of the good or righteous wills of persons on the way there. What is the good now is the good then.

Still, Kant's understanding that happiness is only "added to" the good will reflects a paradox at the heart of Christian eschatology and ethics from the New Testament onward, namely, that blessedness is given only to those who love God for his own sake and love one another in God, with no motive arising from hope for happiness or any other reward. "Blessed are they who are persecuted for righteousness' sake [who do their duty for duty's sake, a physician's unconditional care for the preciousness of his patient's life, our simple obligation to give up our lives rather than allow certain evils to occur], for they *shall be* comforted" collapses into impurity of will if that comfort is in any measure the objective of our moral wills and actions. Indeed, the latter comes close to being Kant's definition of the radical evil in the human will, as it is also Luther's heavenly-oriented mercenary spirit for which there is no hope of reward.

In addition to Kant's answers to the question, What can we know? and to the question, What ought we to do?, the *summum bonum* provides the answer to his third question, What may we hope? Still that hope is not a goal to be morally willed; it is not pursued. Whoever seeks a life of happiness congruent with virtue shall lose it.

MacIntyre's rejection of Kant's "added" state of affairs, strangely enough, brings him closer to the narrative account of our moral histories contained in Christian and other religious outlooks (which he wishes to radicalize still further), and at the same time propels him further away from the Christian *homo viator* than Kant was. MacIntyre's radicalization of our human moral pilgrimage does more violence to (at least) the Christian story than Kant did. I also believe that he gives an inaccurate account of Kant's views, or at least that his rendition of Kant's meaning is a free, modern translation in which the original sense has been lost.

So we read that for Kant "it is a requirement of practical reason *to pursue* [italics added] the *summum bonum*," to seek moral perfection *crowned with happiness*. Heretofore, I have supposed that Kant taught that while we can pursue our neighbor's happiness but not his virtue, only moral perfection is the objective of our own moral wills, not our happiness. Again we read, in MacIntyre's rendition, that "the significance of a particular moral action does not lie solely in its conformity to the moral law; it marks a stage in that journey the carrying through of which confers significance on the individual's life." The latter expression, however eloquent a rendition, is obscure until we are told in the next sentence that "thus a link does exist between the acts of duty and the *summum bonum* conceived of as *the goal of the individual's journey*" (italics added).

How can this be? How can this be Kant? In the same paragraph Kant is quoted to the effect that "with advancing civilization reason grows pragmatically in its capacity to realize ideas of law. But at the same time the culpability for the transgression also grows." That would seem to be a stand-off, admitting no temporal moral progress at all. Still, MacIntyre assures us that within "the framework of law and civility the individual progresses toward moral perfection—a progress 'directed toward a goal infinitely remote.'" The latter internal quotation, I suppose, is from Kant. But MacIntyre transfers to the empirical, phenomenal world, and flattens out temporally, Kant's meaning of "infinitely remote" in order to ascribe to Kant or to derive from him some notion of historical moral progress. The same has to be said about MacIntyre's rendering of Kant as believing that "the life of the individual and also of that of the human race [is] a journey towards a goal."

How can this be? How can this be Kant? The word "journey" entails temporality, and we all know that, for Kant, time was a form of perception of the phenomenal world, not the world in which moral reason dwells.

Quite decisive is MacIntyre's admission that, while Kant's account of radical evil is in some sense empirical and abundant examples of moral evil can be accumulated from the moral history of humankind, "we cannot be certain that there is even one actual case in which the maxims of the categorical imperative have been obeyed simply from the motive of duty." If there is no actual case in the observable historical world or its institutions of which we can truthfully say that a moral agent obeyed the unconditional imperative simply from the motive of duty, how is it possible for anyone to appraise moral action by anything other than its interior conformity to the moral law? How could any moral agent locate any moral action, his own or another's, along the stages of a journey or a narrative history, or esteem any moral action because of its place in historical moral progress? How can anyone or how can social institutions learn in time how to apportion happiness to virtue if we can never detect a genuine moral act, if there is no way to infer from phenomenal actions to noumenal dispositions?

I draw two conclusions from the foregoing, one concerning Kant, the other concerning *tendencies* inherent in MacIntyre's position to which he certainly does not subscribe.

For Kant, there is no such thing as moral progress in temporal history. Moral progress conferring significance on an individual's life takes place only in the noumenal world. In that ultimately real world, a moral agent who acts in accord with his unconditional obligation can be described as someone who is now being righteous (he does his duty for duty's sake) and as someone who is now being made happy (by a scientifically unknowable "causality" not his own that "affixes" the *summum bonum* to his righteous moral will). Moreover, MacIntyre's charge that Kant is too individualistic is untrue. In the noumenal world, where alone moral progress is possible, the individual is a member of a "kingdom of ends."

MacIntyre, however, has transposed Kant's "link" between acts of duty and the *summum bonum* to the temporal, observable, phenomenal world. He has made the *summum bonum* something to be instituted and pursued by human moral agents.

There in the phenomenal world the pursuit of "moral perfection crowned by happiness" can only mean the pursuit of happiness—since there is no phenomenally evident case of moral obedience to the unconditional moral imperative simply from the motive of duty. If that is too strong a claim, let me suggest simply that, in aiming at the *summum bonum* in human history, one of its ingredients (happiness) is bound to prove more and more evidently able to be pursued than the other (unconditional obligation) in social history and institutions. This is especially the case if the "kingdom of ends" is shifted to the historical plane. MacIntyre's restoration of teleology may at first yield the perfection of the self by placing one's own physical survival lower on the scale of values than other goods. I venture to suggest *contra* MacIntyre that—if those are historical goods and goals—the yield is apt to be placing the preciousness of someone else's life also lower in some scale of values. The reader of this "debate" should at least be troubled by these possible consequences, since MacIntyre nowhere gives us the grounds or warrants for the unconditional obligation to which he subscribes, and his chapter ends in a summons.

I must, therefore, say that MacIntyre's reiterated allegiance to an unconditional moral obligation—as things now stand—is rhetoric only, or seeks its ground in a philosophy of history that, in any present moment, is not yet finished. This being the case, his summons that "a crucial part of moral progress consists in learning how to transform our notion of moral progress" seems apt to lead to peeling off more layers of the onion of unconditional moral obligation in pursuit of the temporally overriding happiness-aspect of the *summum bonum*. This is the more likely consequence of MacIntyre's location of moral progress in historical time where Kant located it not.

III

In this section I shall undertake to exhibit the religious perspective common and uncommon to Judaism and Christianity. My purpose is to show the appeals, warrants, outlooks that the Judeo-Christian tradition understands to be needed in explanation and justification of, say, a doctor's unconditional obligation to his patient. This will be to say more about that story, or extended narrative account, in which individual moral histories are set; the story of God's dealings with humankind that may require suffering or even martyrdom of us rather than complicity in evil-doing.

The view I mean to explain and espouse contains the source of its own moral norms within the religious dimension itself. God is worthy of worship because of who he is and his actions among men, and not because he incorporates in his commands the judgments men are capable of making without knowledge and acknowledgment of him. I do not deny the importance of the relation of Jewish and Christian ethics to natural morality. Indeed, for a complete ethics a Jew or Christian also needs judgments based on man's sense of justice or injustice. That, however, is not the concern of this paper. Instead, I want to explore the strictly theological ethics of Christianity (and of Judaism, so far as I may partially understand it[13]); and to show how religion is ethics and ethics is religion, without waiting for the addition of a natural or rational morality (however necessary the latter may also be). Such a view does not make morality *depend* on or *derive* from religion, or religion *depend* on or *derive* from morality. Neither is secondary to the other. Instead, the two are not at all separate things. The question simply does not arise whether God is worthy of honor and worship because his will and purposes are good, or his claims upon us and his purposes for us are right because he is good, in terms of antecedent or autonomous human conceptions of "goodness." The latter may, I have said, be also *needed* in a religious ethics.

The covenantal religious and the covenantal moral categories of the Bible are a way of saying that men "faith" in all their doing, and in all their doing, they and their communities "faith." The will of God constitutes the meaning, the cardinal content of morality; he is not simply the sanction of a morality that may be fashioned and fashionable apart from his righteousness. Nor is he there simply to "affix" happiness to virtue. Such is the common heritage of our three western religions, Judaism, Catholicism, and Protestantism.

My thesis is that the Jewish people and the Christian community in all ages are standing "metaethical" communities of discourse about substantive moral matters; they propose to shape and fashion how that discourse should proceed. This may be the way to understand Karl Barth's "Dogmatics as Ethics, Ethics as Dogmatics,"[14] a program he executes everywhere in his systematic theology. There is no theological statement that is not at the same time an ethical claim, no ethical statement that does not indicate its theological reason. The metaethics function of religious faith and community, I suggest, is the way to understand statements like those of Emil Brunner: "What God does and wills is good; all that opposes the will of God is bad" and "The Good is that which God does; the goodness of man can be no other than letting himself be placed within the activity of God."[15] Suchlike theological ethical statements are first to be understood as meta-ethical *definitions* of the good.

In order to explain this thesis I shall make use of what Professor William K. Frankena has written about metaethics. Since "performative language analysis" is a proper and the most profound way to understand the covenantal *normative* ethics of the Bible, I shall also draw upon that school of thought. My use of these philosophical positions requires no "decoding"; quite the contrary. Only for brevity's sake need these philosophers be invoked at all. In what follows, I hope simply to enable the reader to follow Wittgenstein's counsel to "look and see" the use to which religious ethical concepts are put.

In trying to understand theology (and behind every theological formulation, the faith-ing of religious men) to function as a metaethics, we need to learn from what Frankena has written concerning a "*normative* metaethics" in distinction from a simply descriptive, elucidatory or reportive type of metaethics.[16] The latter analyzes the meaning that "right," "good," and other ethical terms have in ordinary moral discourse, how they function in *the* or in *an* extant moral language. Reportive metaethics attempts "to lay bare what we actually mean when we judge that something is good or right."[17] But behind every descriptive or elucidatory metaethics, Frankena contends, there is a *normative* metaethics, i.e., a proposal for how ethical terms *should* be used. This may be hidden from view, because the *normative* metaethics behind a number of elucidatory analyses of moral discourse is a *conservative* one, i.e., a proposal that moral terms should continue to be used in the way and with the meaning described as being the case. It is only when someone or some community of men come forward with a *revisionary* proposal, a reforming normative metaethics, that the distinction between normative and descriptive metaethics becomes quite evident.

There are a plurality of universes of moral discourse. Within each of these a descriptive account can attempt to lay bare what "we" actually mean when "we" judge that something is good and right. Such descriptions of the meaning of ethical terms have already the force of a *normative* metaethical statement, i.e., that we ought readily to conclude that what "we" mean "men" mean (or should mean) when they judge that something is good and right. Among normative metaethical communities, for example, is one that would *reduce* the meaning of ethical terms to non-moral meanings, whether by shouting silence in a loud metaethical voice, or by recommending that the terms continue to be used but henceforth only with the meaning some science gives to them. ("An 'onlook which rejects onlooks,' " Evans writes, "is perhaps what some people have called 'the scientific attitude.' "[18]) Most contemporary philosophers do not subscribe to such a normative metaethics.

Also among the plurality of universes of moral discourse are the world's living religious communities. Philosophers do not seem to be able to take the language of these communities with utmost seriousness, even though they generally have concluded that there is more than one meaning for a term, and that one must simply listen to hear what is meant. At the center of every congregation of church and synagogue, men and women are continually giving themselves, renewing and enforcing, from the faith that has brought them together, the meanings that are appropriately to be used in making moral appraisals.

A report that the world's living religious communities are among extant *normative* metaethical proposals may be simply to report mankind's ethical division at its deepest level. Nevertheless, a religious community that is living from the past through the present into the future is surely engaged continually in recommending or conveying its view of what should be the meaning of the terms of future moral discourse.

Its reasons for doing so are at bottom religious or theological reasons, or else it has slipped from being religion. There is nothing wrong with offering theological considerations as good reasons for moral meanings. Frankena can be called to testify to that, in his contention that a good reason in support of a normative metaethics may be either a good *moral* reason or a good reason of some other sort. ". . . An inquiry into the meaning and logic of moral discourse may be normative without being moral. Normative judgements and proposals [in metaethics] are not necessarily moral."[19] The judgment, for example, that we should in normative metaethics presume that revisions are not to be advocated unless necessary (which goes to support our continuing to use ethical terms with the meaning they currently have among some groups of human beings) may not itself be a *moral* reason. Likewise, a "people of God," a people in the service of God, proposes to understand the righteousness by which it judges performances among men according to the measure of the righteousness it believes God displayed in his word-deeds intervening in times past in men's deeds and moral talk. Such a community of moral discourse is, formally, like any other under the sun, in this case plainly giving non-moral, i.e., religious, warrants for its "first order" moral meanings.

Frankena formulates the place in normative metaethics that Christian theological ethics, faithful to its task, must occupy. There are statements at the heart of any theological ethics that refer for the meaning of "good" or "right" to "the will of God" or to "how God brought us up out of the house of bondage" or "how God first loved us." These religious acknowledgments or faith commitments refer the "correlative performative force" of man's obligation to a "divine performance." "[A] human utterance concerning this divine performative is a self-involving acknowledgment which has correlative performative force."[20] A believing community affirms that it is placed under obligation by the actions of another (as in gift-giving). Performative language analysis in ethics need not be limited to *human* word-deeds (which is the usual understanding of this school of thought).

Such statements are usually objected to in ordinary language analysis on the ground that one cannot derive an Ought from an Is. This reply takes classically the form of "the open question" argument. That is to say, the rejoinder in the case of any alleged theological ultimate will be, "But is 'the will of God' or that divine performative action *good*?" Frankena contends, and I think rightly, that the objector can only riposte a *like* normative meta-ethical statement; he can say "surely this is not a desirable use of words,"[21] or the meaning that should be assigned the terms "good" or "right" or "obligatory." It is perfectly proper for a normative metaethics (e.g., Jewish or Christian theological ethics) to appeal to reasons that are not themselves intrinsically moral. One appeals rather to God's word-deeds in the extended narrative moral history of our lives.

Good reasons in Jewish or Christian normative metaethics cannot without circularity themselves fall within the system of Jewish or Christian normative ethics (e.g., forgiveness is good). Nor can such good reasons be drawn from *another* normative metaethics with its *prescriptions* as to what moral terms must mean and how be used. That would simply show the dissolution of church or synagogue. There is no need for Jew or Christian— either in normative ethics or in normative metaethics—to be "frightened out of our wits by the relativists, subjectivists, and sceptics,"[22] or by MacIntyre's appeal to an as yet uncompleted moral history of mankind, when they are only explaining the reasons they affirm to be good ones in support of a certain use of moral terms, and appealing to the religious foundations in which they believe unconditional moral obligations to be grounded. Frankena concludes (in language that itself shows, verbally at least, the influence of Christianity functioning as a standing meta-ethical community by going beyond laying bare the meaning of ordinary morality and undertaking to affect what men shall mean by "good," etc.): ". . . Perhaps we may now roll away the stone from before the tomb in which naturalism [and also what is called 'supernaturalism'] has lain ever since that day when the earth trembled under the naturalistic fallacy and the rocks were rent by the open question."[23] Those objections to Jewish or

Christian theological ethics (even in the mind of a philosopher who himself does not undertake its task) fall before the simple realization that "No metaethical Ought can logically be derived from any metaethical Is alone."[24] It is perfectly proper for the synagogue or the Christian church throughout history to have proposed the meanings it intends to assign to certain primary ethical terms, and to have tried to influence men to come and do likewise, on grounds not all of which are already intrinsically moral, i.e., falling within the Judeo-Christian system of ethics or borrowed from some other.

So much is at stake in saying that Our Father in heaven is the Name from whom the meaning of all performatives (like all fatherhood) in heaven or in earth is taken. This I suppose can be more simply stated by saying that Jewish and Christian ethics makes ultimate appeal to a divine performance, making prototypical use of something that is also said in the analysis of human performatives, namely, that it is not only one's own committing action that creates an obligation; one can also be put under obligation by another's conduct rather than by one's own,[25] as when a beggar asks us for help or in claims upon our hospitality or in the so-called "Good Samaritan" principle in our law. This does not mean that God is good because he is a father; but the claim is that from the measure of his steadfastness we know something of the meaning to assign to "good" fatherhood. It does not mean that God's performative actions are to be acknowledged because they have a moral quality gathered from men's committals, but rather that from the nature of his self-involvement with us in our history we know something of the self-involvement men should display in their elected and their nonelected covenants of life with life. If, as Helen Oppenheimer writes, "to marry, to become a parent, to make friends, is to put oneself morally into a distinct situation," then ". . . *a fortiori*, to be made God's children by adoption and grace can be understood as a change of status capable of transforming one's elementary categories."[26]

It is not at all necessary to prove first by a general or autonomous ethical investigation the correctness of such normative ethical statements as that we should be thankful to all who benefit us or that we should forgive others because others have forgiven us;

or that one should obey God's ordinances because it is "right" to do so or that God's will is "good" according to tests for this that have arisen in some other community of moral discourse, or according to an elucidatory metaethics that describes the meanings and logic and what men mean by good in some other "ordinary language." This is not necessary even though there are good reasons for some or many of these statements in a good many systems of normative ethics. It is not necessary because all these are statements of *normative* Christian metaethics (and, I venture to say, normative Jewish metaethics as well). Those statements express what Jews and Christians mean and are resolved to mean by the right and the good among men. Synagogue and church propose to inculcate an entire "symbolic form," "type of discourse," or "realm of meaning."[27]

Whether this means a *revisionist* or a *conservative* normative metaethics can scarcely be decided. It is conservative in the sense that there are these standing metaethical communities whose moral discourse can simply be elucidated or described in these terms, plus the recommendation that these moral meanings and this logic of ethics continue to be fostered and used. It is *revisionist* in the sense that, amid the pluralism of discourse today about ethics, these understandings of the elements of ethics would cut athwart many an all-too-ordinary language or rival normative metaethics—so much so that the Christian language and logic of ethics is hardly understandable today to a good many notable intelligences, including some who are by denomination "Jewish" or "Christian."

In any case, Jews and Christians mean or should mean in ethics to say that there are correlative performative understandings of moral acts, relations, and situations that arise from their faith-commitment or acknowledgment of God's performance and his mandates. This they mean to say in some sense also of all men and their good always. This they express when they say, "I look on all men as brothers whom God made to be one," or "I look on each man as a brother for whom Christ died."[28] In these primary "norms," which are controlling, certainly, in a Christian ethical system, there is appeal to the performative force of God's "verdictives"; and then there follows for the Christian ethicist the task of living the meaning of this in all his rational reflection, and of elaborating and deepening every one of its requirements.

This, I suppose, is not far from Frankena's meaning when he speaks of adopting an "appropriate mode of expressing oneself when one is taking a cognitive point of view and meaning to be rational within it"; or when he writes that in making a normative ethical judgment, we mean to suggest "that there are good reasons for a certain action or attitude, and we usually have in mind more or less clearly a certain type of reason, that is, we are taking a certain point of view and claiming that one who is rational from that point of view would or would not have that attitude or perform that action."[29] If one *begins* in Christian normative ethics with some such statement as "Look on all men as brothers for whom Christ died," or "Be grateful to the Lord who made us his covenant people," and if all moral reasoning is then reasoning from these "premises," then the ultimate warrant for moral norms must be an appeal to what the Lord of heaven and earth is believed to have been doing and to be doing in enacting and establishing his covenant with us and all mankind, in all the estates and orders and relations of life to which we have been called. These performative actions, the final authorizing reasons for normative ethics, are celebrated in the action and worship of synagogue and church through all ages. This is what makes a religious community a standing normative metaethical community. Within the larger setting of these narrative histories, it is proposed to show our children's children (if not our children) what should be the meaning of "righteousness" and "faithfulness" among men.

Church and synagogue are communities of adoration, re- membrance, celebration, worship, and praise. These communities engage in faith-ing whenever by common liturgical action or procession they say forth their faith by doing; or when by song, recital, confession, reading, or preaching they, by saying, do. These acts-speech and speech-acts are understood to be human performatives in response to a divine performative. Each of these faith-acts and faith-statements of a congregation is at the same time a way of talking about ethical talk, a way of conveying and fostering what the community means to mean by righteousness.

Doubtless, religious folk also belong to other communities of moral discourse; this does not concern us here. Insofar as they have religion in exercise, however, they are also saying how they want to say the ethical thing, how they want the ethical thing to be said in their midst, in society generally, and in the future, how they want their moral behavior and that of other men finally to be judged. They nurture meanings in the ethical terms they use. They transmit from generation to generation "second order" instruction in what *should be* the "first order" meaning, out of faith in and love to God, of the terms used in ethical deliberations and moral decisions and actions.

If the question is how one should treat a wanderer, the answer terminates not in the proposition that wanderers should be cared for for their manhood's sake, but in: "A wandering Aramean was my father, yet the Lord called him" and made something of us. If the question is how to treat strangers, righteousness takes its measure from, "You know the heart of a stranger, since you were strangers and sojourners in the land of Egypt; and the Lord your God acted rightly by you when he brought you up by a mighty hand, and so rightwised your dealings with every stranger." In *giving* that meaning to "righteousness," Judaism in its normative metaethics does not need to go further and reduce its religious reasons to generally valid ethical statements, like: Be grateful for gifts of rescue. "Hear, O Israel, the Lord thy God is one God, extending his steadfast love (*hesed*) to thousands of generations, and thou shalt love the lord your God with all your heart, soul, mind and strength" is sufficient in itself to convey the meaning of fidelity to every covenant.

"Love one another *as I have loved you*," "Have this mind in you which was also in Christ Jesus . . ." and "God shows his love for us in that while we were yet sinners, helpless, his unreconciled enemies, Christ died for us" may be outlandish proposals for the meaning of "charity" and its primacy in moral discourse; but there is no formal reason requiring anyone to give up using the term in that way or trace it home to another moral meaning having greater currency. If the question is "Why look on each man as a brother for whom Christ died?" the answer need not be "Because that is 'good.'" The answer can perfectly well be, "Because he *is* a man for whom Christ died and that's the rock-bottom meaning we mean and shall continue to mean by 'righteousness' and 'fidelity' to the 'good' for him" (whatever source there may be for getting to know needed additional and the more specific meaning these claims have).

In this way Jewish and Christian ethics makes ultimate appeal to a divine performance as the ground for and the source of the core-content of men's correlative obligations to one another. The theology of the Exodus is at the same time an Exodus morality. A Christocentric theology is at the same time a Christo-*nomos* and a Christo-*didacti* in ethics. Jewish or Christian ethics would no more propose to establish themselves upon the foundation of men's general moral insights or judgments, than Jewish theology propose to prove the God of Abraham, Isaac and Jacob or Christian theology propose to prove Jesus Christ worthy of lordship because he measures up to men's general knowledge of God. In either case, if that were so, men should simply resort at once to that other knowledge of God and to that other lead given to morality. The Judeo-Christian knowledge *into God* and the knowledge *into ethics* in these religions would, by such a procedure, be simply bypassed or rendered dubious in ostensible certification of them.

The vitality of church-community has a great deal to do with what we in our generation and the generations to come shall mean by righteousness, justice, and injustice. What Christians owe to Christians and to all men, because they look upon men as brothers for whom Christ died, has also some degree of influence upon what men acknowledge to be the claims of mankind upon them. (The same can be said of every "high" or universal religion.) The actions of church and synagogue as communities of adoration, celebration, worship, and praise constitute a wellspring of ethical terms and judgment having the highest significance for human actions and relations. Where they have not made themselves a convenience—an engine behind other communities of moral discourse—synagogue and church are normative metaethical communities existing through time. From faith's apprehension of the chief end of man, its pursuit of the highest and universal vocation of man, its narrative account of the moral history our lives inherit or fail to inherit, and its vision of reality flow substantive moral claims. Any "faith-ing" serves to intervene in any talk about the normative ethical terms men should be using in every substantive moral deliberation.

In our pluralistic society there are, of course, many communities having moral significance. But this simply means that every man must decide the community of moral discourse to which he belongs, and whose continuation into the future he seeks. Each of us has to decide how he wants the ethical thing to be said in our society, by what standards of righteousness or faithfulness he is willing for his own action and those of other men to be judged. In faith-communities of all sorts is laid bare what men finally mean when they judge something to be good or right. We form our consciences and shape our behavior in accord with some community of ultimate reference in terms of which we understand what we should mean by the right and the good. This establishes a community of moral discourse in which these meanings are enlivened and renewed and transmitted to future generations of mankind. By a person's answering religious performances to the verdicts or performances of the God confessed, his status, role in life, basic moral standards undergo significant alteration.

To repeat the foregoing in another way. N. Fotion argues[30] that a speaker may include in the content portion of a language act the form and character of his speech to follow. Then that was a Master Speech Act, like: Come, let us reason together; hereby other language acts are given a certain ordering. Variations in the content portion of a spoken formula can control important aspects of the use of language to which we are thereafter committed. There are Master Speech Acts that do a job for subordinate speech acts. Something is said that applies to a whole conversation, discussion, book—or a realm of moral discourse—that follows. Master Speech Acts generate, control, or have jurisdiction over new and subsequent speech acts. They do not simply *report* what the following speech acts are or will be; they *express* forcefully what the following speech acts *should* be. A Master Speech Act is therefore indivisibly connected with those speech acts over which it has jurisdiction; the reasoning-together announced is not a separate or another thing from reasoning-together in execution. Subsequent speech acts are "in" or "out" of character according to the meaning set by the content portion of the Master Speech Act.

Fotion's analysis can be extended from performative language to actions that speak. That is the meaning of "liturgy." In liturgy, the synagogue or church by saying do, and by doing say. Not only can a *speaker* control the character of his subsequent language acts. Also a speech-*actor*, by master acts of non-verbal religious acknowledgment, exercises command over his subordinate (moral) performative word-deeds. Faith-acts or religious acknowledgments of divine performances are Master Speech Acts, whether of a religious individual or a religious community. The "content portion" of the verbal or non-verbal "faith-ing" of men and of communities varies. It varies according to the divine performance or according to the nature and character of the god confessed. Subsequent acts are "in" or "out" of character with that.

Whoever *acknowledges* with Abraham Lincoln, "Four score and seven years ago *our fathers* brought forth on this continent a new nation conceived in liberty and dedicated to the proposition . . .," thereby dedicates himself to future performatives of like character. (He derives, if some say so, an "ought" from an "is.") Likewise—if men may be obligated by the action of another—whoever says with the prophet Hosea, "When Israel was a child [when *we* were children], then I [the Lord, *our* God] loved him, and called my son out of Egypt. . . . I taught Ephraim also to walk, taking them by their arms. . . . I drew them with cords of a man, with bands of love . . ." (11:1, 3a, 4a), whoever acknowledges and adheres to this divine performance, whoever "faiths" in this way, dedicates himself to future performatives of like character (thereby deriving, if some say so, an "ought" from an "is").

One might argue, of course, that statements of the religious warrants are not value-free, that the "content portion" of statements about a divine performance or the divine nature, or in the narrative account of our histories are not value-free; and that consequent statements of men's correlative beliefs are not simple statements of (theological) fact. One can search for a prescription in there somewhere. Thus one might avoid saying that religious ethics derives ought-statements from is-statements strictly construed. It is more correct, however, and more forthcoming, simply to deny that the supernaturalistic fallacy is a fallacy.

It is better, in explanation of religious ethics, forthrightly to appeal beyond all human righteousness to a divine performance in which the righteousness of God was revealed "from faith to faith" for us men and for our salvation—and for men's judgments and appraisals, too. Only then will one find himself discussing theological ethics or even the *possibility* of a religious ethics, and not something else.

IV

One final word about the account of religious ethics outlined above. In a religious ethics, the "justifying reasons" are at the same time the "exciting reasons" (Francis Hucheson).[31] MacIntyre may doubt my view that his unconditional moral obligation, no less than Kant's, needs theological authorization. In any case, I think it cannot be denied that neither view of obligation is explicable historically, culturally, or in point of origin without reference to some sort of "divine command" account of the moral life or a theological perspective upon human beings as created in the "image of God." The source of an unconditional obligation, tested by suffering and giving up one's life rather than to do or to allow evil to be done, is to be found in the web of authorizing and exciting reasons that once were the fabric of our civilization. In numerous works of philosophical ethics today after "the moral point of view" has been fully set forth, there is yet another chapter called for, one usually entitled "Why Be Moral?" Given the univocity of the authorizing and the exciting reasons in religious ethics, no such chapter is needed.

As philosophy bakes no bread, it also rarely produces a cultural movement capable of shaping moral practice to the standard of stern moral laws. The Presocratic philosophers were often the founders of a quasi-cult. This Justice Blackmun noted when he called the Hippocratic Oath a "Pythagorean manifesto,"[32] in its condemnation of abortion uncharacteristic of Greco-Roman medicine, which Christianity happened to take up and use to influence Western civilization (no mention made of the fact that pre-Christian morality also condemned neither the exposure of infants nor sports spectaculars in which gladiators killed one another).

There are, of course, other philosophies which, like the great religions, have shaped the moral thinking and behavior of masses of mankind. The chief example in modern times is utilitarianism (which MacIntyre regards as quite incapable of producing an authentic moral point of view) and Marxism (which I doubt can be credited with sustaining MacIntyre's belief that the moral history of mankind—and within that history, the moral history of individual agents—is more important than its medical or economic history).

MacIntyre may have to follow Voltaire's advice to get himself crucified and found a religious movement in order to halt the onward march of utilitarianism as a dominant influence upon medical and moral practice (however philosophically discredited that position may be). So also, Hans Jonas's ontology of purposive being's absolute obligation to protect purposive being into the future, against all the pre-mortem threats of modern technology, reflects along every vein and sinew the Biblical outlook of a Fackenheim who says that—for all the problematic of believing in God after the Holocaust—we Jews ought not to give Hitler a posthumous victory. So across the Holocaust the generations pick up again the story of God's dealings with them.

There seems to me to be good authorizing and exciting reasons for going beyond what MacIntyre and Jonas regard as the terminus in philosophical justification. That, I suggest, seems to be a sufficient terminal justification only because of precedent religious or cultural movements. And I am certain that, if MacIntyre and Jonas are concerned that their views influence a professional practice, they have good reason to appeal to an existing movement which is the bearer of such absolute moral claims, or they must set about creating their own cults in the hope that they will grow to have general influence in contemporary cultures. One thing that will not do the job is MacIntyre's appeal to a philosophy of history yet to be completed.

168   PAUL RAMSEY

NOTES

1. *Commentary*, 2, no. 4 (October 1946), p. 316.
2. Soren Kierkegaard, *The Concept of Dread* (Princeton, N.J.: Princeton University Press, 1944), p. 134n.
3. C. S. Lewis, *The Screwtape Letters* (New York: The Macmillan Co., 1944), pp. 119-20.
4. I use this term because it is more neutral than "Hegelian" or "Marxist" or "historicist."
5. See W. V. Quine and J. S. Ullian, *The Web of Belief* (New York: Random House, 1970), p. 43ff, for an account of the conservative principle: an hypothesis proposed for our belief "may have to conflict with some of our previous beliefs; but the fewer the better."
6. *Religion and the Modern Mind* (New York: Lippincott, 1960), pp. 90, 94, 107, 109.
7. For example, "the terrible gulfs of time which have elapsed since God made himself manifest in the world chill our minds and numb our hearts. This train of thought, of course, is not logic. But logic has little to do with human thinking" (p. 98).
8. C. S. Lewis, "De Descriptione Temorum." Inaugural Lecture at Cambridge. Walter Hopper, ed., *Selected Literary Essays* (Cambridge University Press, 1969), p. 7.
9. Paradoxically, in Christian eschatology, e.g., in Luther, rewards are given only to the pure in heart, i.e., only to those who serve God for his own sake with no motive arising from hope for reward. Moral progress is not measured by approximation to a future state of affairs.
10. Lessing, *Werke* (Maltzahn's ed.) X, p. 53.
11. Soren Kierkegaard, *Concluding Scientific Postscript* (Princeton, N.J.: Princeton University Press, 1941), p. 97.
12. R. M. Hare, "The Simple Believer," in Gene Outka and John P. Reeder, Jr., eds., *Religion and Morality* (Garden City, N.Y.: Doubleday Anchor Book, 1973), pp. 393-427.
13. I believe I am not mistaken in what I affirm about Jewish ethics. My account, however, is clearly inadequate in what I omit: the role of law and the tradition of rabbinical interpretation.
14. Karl Barth, *Church Dogmatics*, I/2 (Edinburgh: T & T Clark, 1956), p. 782-96.
15. Emil Brunner, *The Divine Imperative* (London: The Lutterworth Press, 1932), pp. 53, 55.
16. William K. Frankena, "On Saying the Ethical Thing," Presidential

address delivered before the Sixty-Fourth Annual Meeting of the Western Division of the American Philosophical Association in Minneapolis, Minnesota, May 5-7, 1966. *Proceedings and Addresses of the American Philosophical Association*, 1965-6 (Yellow Springs, Ohio: The Antioch Press, 1966), 39, pp. 21-42.

17. Ibid., p. 22.
18. Donald Evans, *The Language of Self-Involvement* (London: SCM Press, 1963), p. 254.
19. Frankena, "On Saying the Ethical Thing," p. 23.
20. Evans, *The Language of Self-Involvement*, p. 77. The reader's attention should be directed to the fact that, in the text above, this point and this point alone is used in elucidating the nature of a religious ethics. Here I am not concerned with other aspects of the performative language school of ethics as developed by Austin and Evans.
21. Frankena, "On Saying the Ethical Thing," p. 25.
22. Ibid., p. 32.
23. Ibid., p. 33.
24. Ibid., p. 25.
25. John Lemmon: "Moral Dilemmas," in Ian T. Ramsey, ed., *Christian Ethics and Contemporary Philosophy* (New York and London: The Macmillan Co., 1966), p. 264.
26. Helen Oppenheimer, "Moral Choice and Divine Authority," in Ian T. Ramsey, ed., *op. cit.*, p. 231.
27. See Frankena, "On Saying the Ethical Thing," p. 26.
28. See Evans, *The Language of Self-Involvement*, p. 129; and the entire section on "Onlooks," pp. 124ff.
29. Frankena, "On Saying the Ethical Thing," pp. 37, 39. As for the claim that, among the rivalry of *normative* metaethics, the Christian outlook and consequent ethical onlook may in some sense be true for all men, the reader might ponder Frankena's remark on p. 41: "At any rate, so long as the case against the absolutist claim is not better established than it is, we may still make that claim; it may take some temerity, but it is not unreasonable. As for me and my house, therefore, we will continue to serve the Lord—or, as others may prefer to say, the Ideal Observer."
30. N. Fotion, "Master Speech Acts" (unpublished paper).
31. In L. A. Selby-Biggs, *British Moralists* (Oxford: Clarendon Press, 1897,) I, pp. 403ff.
32. *Roe* v. *Wade*, 410 U.S. 113 (1973).

Commentary

A Rejoinder to a Rejoinder

Alasdair MacIntyre

I

I CAN DISCOVER ONLY ONE POINT OF AGREEMENT between myself and Professor Paul Ramsey. Of course it is true that, as a matter of history, belief in the unconditional requirements of morality was originally rooted in a religious view of the world—provided, for example, we recognize Sophocles as a religious writer, just as much as the author of Deuteronomy. But Ramsey's contention that belief in morality's unconditional demands requires (both for logical warrant and that it may have practical effect) some kind of theological belief is much less precise than Kant's. Ramsey says (p. 161) "that the ultimate warrant for moral norms must be an appeal to what the Lord of heaven and earth is believed to have been doing and to be doing in enacting and establishing his covenant with us and with all mankind. . . ." A little earlier he puts the word "premises" into quotes, thus casting some doubt on what exactly he means by using the word "warrant." Either, I take it, the beliefs that he cites function as premises in an argument, thus providing a putative warrant, or they do not. If Ramsey's claim is not that such beliefs function as premises, then his use of such expressions as "warrant" and "premises" is still not clear enough to discuss; if his claim is that they do so function, then his argument encounters an obvious difficulty.

171

For how do we derive any norms detailed enough to guide us in medical ethics, say, from *any* account of what the Lord of heaven and earth was or is doing? The biblical accounts of what the Lord of heaven and earth did and does belong to the premodern world in which most of our contemporary issues just did not arise; and the Lord of heaven and earth carefully refrained from giving guidance on any issues except those engaging those contemporary with the biblical revelation. How then to extrapolate? I know how the Catholic church extrapolates; I know how John Calvin extrapolated. But Ramsey gives us no clue at all as to where he stands. Rome and Geneva spoke and speak clearly enough for it to be possible to disbelieve what they say; but Princeton does not as yet provide anything clear enough even to disbelieve.

Let me put the challenge in this way. Let Ramsey provide one decisive position on a question disputed in contemporary medical ethics; let him provide one belief about the Lord of heaven and earth; and then let him show us how the former is derived from the latter. Until he does this, what he is asserting will remain quite unclear.

Two final points in this initial section: Ramsey claims that the theological beliefs that he cites function as "a normative metaethics" (p. 157), citing Frankena in support. But no one, including Frankena, has as yet made clear to me the meaning of that barbarous neologism "metaethics." The notion of a metalanguage has a clear and precise meaning in the context of formal logic; outside that context it seems at best a metaphor and a metaphor which still needs to be shown to be appropriate. A similar comment needs to be made on the use of the expression "performative." However Ramsey may be using this expression, he is not using it as J. L. Austin used it. A little explanation might be in order.

II

My own argument began with some reflections on the impact of Nazism on medical ethics. At first sight, of course, any Christian position will seem in stark contrast with the Nazi view.

Yet it may help to identify a central weakness in Ramsey's argument if, for a moment, I stress the similarities.

Let me summarize what was involved in the doctrine of *Ein Volk, Ein Reich, Ein Führer*. It was that ethics was subordinate to the spirit of the German nation; that the norms of ethical practice should be derived from what the Lord of Germany was believed to have been doing and be doing. The German people were to be conceived as a community of faith. We thus have two rival communities of faith, each invoking the name of a different Lord—the Nazi and the Christian. How are we to decide between these claims? Why are we to prefer Jehovah to Hitler (remembering that the existence of the latter—until 1945—is perhaps more soundly established than that of the former)?

A central part of the answer is surely that Christianity passes a number of ethical tests that Nazism fails. Yet this argument presupposes just what Ramsey denies, namely, that ethics cannot be subordinated to religion, but does indeed provide an independent criterion by which religions are to be judged. Yet one ought to note that in this Ramsey, although he may have Kierkegaard on his side (the most dubious of allies, I should have thought), is at odds with much Christian and even more Jewish theology. Catholic Christianity has classically been commended by apologists because its revelation is congruent with our natural knowledge of the good for men. One strand in Judaism, at once metaphysically daring and historically accurate, goes further; God is held to moral account in the light of the Torah.

The question then is posed to Ramsey: when faith meets faith, how are we to judge between them, if not in the light of an ethics that is not subordinated to the very religion it is required to judge?

III

Ramsey is right in his view that I hold that we do not as yet know how to provide the kind of warrant that ethics needs. But this is not because, as his quotation from Lessing is gratuitously used to suggest, I prefer to be in such a state. I find it painful. The only state I would find more painful would be one in which I claimed to possess a form of justification, but could not in fact make good my claim. But Ramsey apparently has a superior alternative which, at the very least, involves taking the claims of the Christian community seriously. Only—he nowhere tells us what it is. Ramsey regrets that I am still alive to refute him; alas, I cannot, for I still do not know on what rational ground, if any, he stands.

Theology and Ethics:
An Interpretation of the
Agenda

James M. Gustafson

"THAT THE CONTEMPORARY THEOLOGICAL SCENE has become chaotic is evident to everyone who attempts to work in theology. There appears to be no consensus on what the task of theology is or how theology is to be pursued. Some see it as the 'science of religion'; others as exposition of the Christian faith; still others as prophetic pronouncement on the conditions of, for example, contemporary American culture (or Western cultural [sic] generally). There are those who are attempting to develop a 'non-sectarian' theology which will not be restricted in meaningfulness to any of the great historic religious traditions; others are attempting to exploit theological insights for developing a more profound understanding of human nature; yet others still see theology as primarily a work of the church attempting to come to better understanding of itself."[1]

Gordon Kaufman's statement is accurate. Whether theology has become more chaotic than some other disciplines is not a matter to be judged here; surely the absence of consensus occurs in some other classic humanistic studies and in some social scientific studies as well. To prepare a paper for nontheologians in the face of this description presents an almost insuperable obstacle; if there is confusion within the discipline it is necessary to locate one's own efforts within some clear margins to make them intelligible to readers who are not very interested in, not to

175

mention impressed by, contemporary theology. Even intelligibly to account for all of one's assumptions, not to mention defending them is a much larger assignment than can be accomplished in a paper.[2]

Assumptions

Just as individual philosophers have distinctive ways of organizing and defending their views, so do theologians. Just as philosophers share certain common grounds, at least within general "schools" of philosophy, so do theologians. I shall begin by stating and briefly expounding eight assumptions that I make. The first six, I believe, are generally shared by theologians in the Christian tradition. All of them, with appropriate qualifications, can be used in Jewish theology as well. The last two are not so widely shared.

1. To work as a Christian theologian is to work within a historic tradition which is grounded in the rich and diverse collection of texts that form the Bible. Rich and diverse must be emphasized, for not only does the Bible contain a variety of types of literature, but also these texts were given their present form over extended periods of time and are related to the historical experiences and individual concerns of their authors.

2. The historical character of the Bible is accepted. By "historical character" I wish to suggest the following. The texts were written under particular historical conditions, and thus to understand them requires that they be related to those conditions insofar as scholarship makes this possible. The subject matter of the texts is frequently historical events or historical persons; little or no "speculative reasoning" in the classic Thomistic sense can be found in the Bible. Even within the biblical books the significance of certain historical events and persons is used to interpret the significance of contemporary events and persons, and also to suggest the significance of the future.

For the theologian this means that from its beginning his enterprise has been grounded in historical and social experience and for many theologians (not only modern ones) it means that efforts to ossify particular interpretations of biblical persons and events violates both the actuality and the value of this historical character of the Bible.

3. The tradition of thought and life of the community of Christians obviously continues to have historical character, and thus provides rich and diverse resources. For example, Augustine's theology developed in relation to events in his life, events in Roman history, events in the life of the Catholic Church, and in relation to religious and philosophical ideas that prevailed in his time. Certain events and persons in the history of the community become more decisive than others in formulating the significance of the religion, both intellectually and in practical activities. Contemporary theology, as part of the tradition, is shaped and reshaped in relation to knowledge and concepts from philosophy and other fields, and in relation to political and other events.

4. Every effort to formulate a coherent theological perspective must be selective from the richness and diversity of the Bible and the tradition, in relation to the events and ideas of the time and place in which the theologian and the community are living and thinking. This "historical" character of theological work is assumed and accepted. When the religious communities are in unusual flux, as Kaufman's statement suggests they are today, the criteria to be used to evaluate theological perspectives and statements are less clear.

5. There is a "faith" aspect to all genuine *theo*logy. (I stress *theo*logy since much of the activity of theologians today simply uses religious symbols to disclose some dimensions of human experience while remaining agnostic about whether there is any meaningful reference to a deity.) This faith aspect is not, in my conception of theology, a blind acceptance of ecclesiastical or doctrinal authority. Rather it is a confidence, sometimes painfully weak, in an ultimate power that has brought the "worlds" into being, sustains them, and determines their destinies. It is a confidence, sometimes an even weaker one and sometimes a confidence that is lost, in the goodness of this power. I call it a "faith aspect" because its claims are never fully demonstrable in rationalistic or scientific terms. It is a faith aspect for which reasons can be given, but such confirmation as it has is also affective. The evidences that are drawn upon to explain and

defend it are taken from the experience of communities and individuals recorded in the documents of the tradition and confirmed in contemporary life.

6. Traditional and contemporary theologians are correct when they affirm the mystery of God, not only for epistemological reasons, but also on experiential grounds. The awe experienced in religious life stems not only from the limitations of our knowledge of the ultimate power, but also from our sense of dependence on powers we did not create, the determination (acknowledgedly a very strong term) of the worlds by powers and events humans cannot fully control. Two comments on this assumption are required. First, theological statements are never literal, they are always tentative. Second, theological statements are abstractions from more primary religious language.

7. Theological language has primarily a practical function (which is not to deny it has other functions); it provides the symbols and concepts that interpret life in the world (not merely individual human life) so as to sustain and give direction to a way of human life. I stress the "primarily," for there are apologetic functions of theology, functions of elucidation of its plausibility, and so forth, directed to persons both within and outside the religious community.

8. Theology provides a way of construing the world. I follow, here, with a slight emendation, a construction by Julian N. Hartt. Hartt indicates that to construe, in a religious context, "is more than a linguistic-intellectual activity." His more substantive affirmation is: *"it means an intention to relate all things in ways appropriate to their belonging to God."* [3] My alteration would be: "an intention to relate to all things in ways appropriate to their *relations* to God," though I share with Hartt in that part of the classic theological tradition that stresses the sovereignty of the ultimate power at least in the sense that the destiny of the worlds is not in control of a biological species recently evolved on one planet. The formulation, "an intention to relate to all things in ways appropriate to their relations to God," clearly includes an ethical imperative, and within the necessary modesty of theological knowledge, a grounding of right relations and proper ends of human conduct. The moral question for humans within the context of a theological construing of the world becomes "What is

God, the ultimate power, enabling and requiring humans to be and to do?" The affirmation that we are to relate to *all things* in ways appropriate to their relations to God is very significant; it extends the scope of activity and of ends beyond the confinements of the "moral" as this is often articulated by theologians and philosophers alike; it provides a basis for some critical judgment of the anthropocentrism that has characterized western religion and ethics. (In the theologies based on the Bible the "doctrine of creation" is the backing for such a view; Christian theologians have, since early times, in their speculative theologies appealed to New Testament texts that stress that "all things" are created in and through Christ [as the second person of the Trinity] for a Christological authorization of this point.)

These eight assumptions are quite general in character; no single precise way to develop the relations of theology and ethics is necessitated by them. Certain ways, however, in which theology and ethics have been related are excluded by them. One is the use of the Bible as verbally inspired in such a way that the theology and the morality present in it have a dogmatic authority. The ethical teachings of the Bible in this literalistic view have the authority of a literal inspiration, as do the theological teachings; the task of theological ethics is then to apply these teachings to present occasions. Protestant fundamentalism and certain Jewish orthodox views of the revelation of Torah cannot be developed from my assumptions.

A second excluded way of relating theology and ethics is that of a purely rational philosophical theology which establishes the metaphysical principles grounded in the being of God from which ethical principles are derived by deduction or by inference. While the assumptions do not exclude the use of reason and common human experience in the authorization and development of theology and ethics, the Bible and the historic tradition carry weight as a source for understanding the relations of all things to God.

The assumptions do permit a *development* of both theological and ethical thought. The historical character of both the Bible and the tradition is stressed, and the recognition is made that religious communities as historical entities change and develop as they relate their traditional sources to contemporary events and knowledge. To indicate the possibilities for development does not mean that there are no presumptions in favor of the tradition, nor does it indicate that there is no significant continuity in theological and ethical thought. Thus, while development is permitted, attention to the tradition is required. My assumptions are the ground for a direction of theological ethical thought that is too "relativistic" for many religious persons and thinkers, and too "conservative" or "traditionalistic" for others.

The last two assumptions are the basis for the development of the rest of this chapter.

Construing of the World Theologically

Particular historical communities can be identified in part by the ways in which they construe the world. Particular individuals who have relatively coherent life plans and outlooks on the world are likely to have tacit if not articulated centers of meaning and value from which they construe the world. Theology involves construing the world from a position of believing in and beliefs about the ultimate power.[4]

In this section I shall focus on "construing the world" in order to illustrate the aspects of ethical thought that are affected by a theological viewpoint. In the next section I shall indicate what is involved in relating to all things in ways appropriate to their relations to God.

What are the sources of a theological perspective and construing of the world? My conviction, only asserted and not defended here, is that all the sources are grounded in the experience of human beings as they reflect upon and articulate the significance of historical events, the natural world, and individual occasions in the light of their (affective and also conceptualized) sense of the reality of an ultimate power. The presence of the Deity is always a mediated presence; it is mediated through the experiences of humans in their relations to the natural world, to other individuals, and to historical events. Without a sense of the presence of the Deity in these experiences they cannot yield a theological perspective. (It can be noted that here I am rejecting those views of theology and of religion that call any concern that is "ultimate," any symbols that represent a hierarchy of significance, any attitude of reverence, or any dominant interest, theological or religious. Such things do function to construe the world, and in this sense they function like a theology functions.)

There is a variety of forms of expression of the reflections on human experiences in the light of the sense of the presence of the Deity. The theologically significant forms of discourse even within the Bible are many; most of them are in primary religious language. For example, one has the mythic accounts of the creation in the book of Genesis; one way to interpret these is as efforts to express the significance of the origins of the world and of human life in the world in the light of the presence of an ultimate power. Historical narratives are the basis of interpreting the significance of historical and political events under the conviction of the presence of Yahweh; the exodus narratives and even the accounts of it given in the books of Kings and Chronicles are of this sort. The poetic discourse not only of the Psalms, but also of the Song of Deborah, early hymns as in Paul's letter to the Philippians, and others, express the religious significance of human experiences. Prophetic discourse, a kind of literature of moral and religious indictment, has a distinctively evocative way of bringing human conditions under the light of beliefs about God. There are symbols, what some New Testament scholars (following literary critics such as Wheelwright) call tensive symbols, such as the kingdom of God. Metaphors, analogies, and parables abound, pointing, often cryptically, to the religious significance of natural, social, and interpersonal events. And, particularly in the Christian scriptures, there are concepts such as sin and righteousness which have been shaped to express somewhat more precisely those meanings of human experience in relation to God that are expressed in other linguistic patterns in other places.

The point of stating this partial list is to indicate that in the Bible (and one could also indicate similar things in the postbiblical tradition) there are many literary devices by which the world is construed theologically; also many aspects of human experience—experience of the natural world as well as history—are construed theologically.

For the purposes of this chapter I shall indicate three aspects of the "moral world" that have been, and continue to be construed theologically. To these shall be added a more inclusive theme. The circumstances in which action takes place, the agents and their acts, and the ends and consequences of action can all be construed theologically. Finally, the meaning and significance of the whole, of all things related to each other, is construed theologically. Such is the audacity of theology, responding as theologians must do to the conviction that the ultimate power is related to the whole, to all things in their interrelatedness. I shall develop each of these with a selected illustration; I am not prepared to defend the adequacy of the theology of each illustration I use, but I am prepared to defend the intention they illustrate as part of the theological task.

First, the circumstances of action. Contemporary liberation theologians present rather vivid examples of how historical circumstances are construed theologically in such a way that religious and moral significance is disclosed. Characteristic of most, but not all, of this literature is the isolation of the exodus of the Hebrew people from bondage in Egypt as a paradigmatic event, an event that discloses the divine intentionality for humanity. The Hebrew people were oppressed in Egypt; Yahweh, their God, not only desired their liberation, but was present in the historical events that led them out of the house of bondage. Exodus takes on a symbolic significance; it discloses not only what the God of the biblical tradition desires for humans, but also how he "acts" in and through historical events to achieve his intention. The observation is made that the circumstances of large portions of humanity in our present time are those of oppression. The sequence of events symbolized by exodus is used to interpret the plight of present humanity, the purposes of God for humanity under these conditions of oppression, and the direction of the course of events that reasonably follows from this interpretation of the circumstances, namely, movements for liberation. Put in the current religious vernacular, where there is oppression God wills liberation; where there are movements for liberation, there is the presence of God; persons who conscientiously desire to act consonant with the will of God under these circumstances are engaged in the political and other struggles for liberation. The general point is that circumstances are construed by the use of a historical religious symbol in such a way that their theological and moral significance is disclosed; a course of action seems to follow reasonably from this construal of the circumstances.[5]

Second, moral agents and their acts are construed theologically. Reinhold Niebuhr's theology and the ways in which he used it in his ethical writings provide a good illustration of this. Niebuhr, particularly in *The Nature and Destiny of Man,* formulated a theological interpretation of the human condition that is deeply informed by the theologies of Paul, Augustine, the sixteenth-century reformers, and Kierkegaard.[6] Briefly summarized, humans have "spirits," which is a way to indicate that they have capacities for "free self-determination."[7] To have this freedom is to be anxious, and out of this anxiety persons act in such ways as to refuse to acknowledge their finitude, their creatureliness. Presumably, if they were rightly related to the Creator they would properly acknowledge their limits, and if they shared in the Christian "myth" they would have a ground of confidence that the destiny of the worlds is finally to be in the control of an almighty power who will fulfill it in accord with his redemptive and loving purposes. The persistent character of the human condition, however, is that in our loyalties and in our actions we wrongly use our freedom. This is the case even for those who share Niebuhr's religious views. Human beings seek to overcome their anxiety by fixing upon objects of confidence and loyalty that provide security, but essentially a false security. They develop false senses of confidence about their own motives and about their own moral capacities. Their sin is their wrong use of freedom. This is not only a moral indictment; it is also a religious indictment, for while lack of trust in God is "inevitable" it is not "necessary."[8]

Niebuhr's doctrine of sin is not the whole of his theology, but it is an important aspect of it. A theological concept, sin, for which he finds backing in the biblical accounts, in traditional theological reflections, and in general human experience, becomes a basis for construing moral agents and their acts. His intention is to disclose some things about humans, universally, or at least almost without exception, which have to be taken into account in the assessment of their conduct both as individuals and in social collectivities. The theological construing of human agents provides not only an interpretation of the significance of their actions (even, for example, the most altruistic actions are corrupted by the desire to secure the agents' own sense of righteousness), but in his case also an explanation of their actions. Given this theological account of human agents, certain attitudes follow, certain ways of critically assessing particular agents and their actions follow. To say the least, an attitude of a wariness is grounded; a self-criticism and a suspicion of others is supported pertaining to their moral claims and their moral intentions. Human agency is theologically construed so that one aspect of it is brought to rather vivid consciousness. Practically, during the years of Niebuhr's development, this view functioned to disclose the moral pretensions of "liberal" Christians and of nonreligious thinkers and leaders.

The ends and consequences of action are construed theologically. The *telos* of human action has been construed theologically throughout the tradition, and particular consequences of human activity have been assessed in relation to whether they contribute to, or deflect from the fulfillment of that *telos*. Systematic developments of this task have absorbed constructions by philosophers or philosophical theologians who are not primarily identified with the religious tradition. The theology and ethics of Thomas Aquinas present themselves as obvious candidates to illustrate this point. The grand, cosmic pattern is clear: all things come from God and return to God. The neo-Platonic sources for this have always been evident. Human action, and human life more inclusively, are part of the "all things" that are oriented toward God. The "supernatural" end of human life is communion with God, friendship with God, the vision of God. The natural end of human life is the fulfillment of its natural goodness. The dependence on Aristotle for the development of the "morphology" of the human has always been clear and acknowledged. While there is no unbroken continuity between the fulfillment of the natural end and the supernatural end (the grace of Christ which is in part dependent on the assent of faith is required), human actions and their consequences are judged to contribute to or deter from the fulfillment of the supernatural end. Actions, including moral actions, that are in accord with human nature contribute to the fulfillment of the natural good, and since the natural end is directed toward the supernatural end they also contribute to the fulfillment of the supernatural end. The ends of life, both "supernatural" and "natural" are construed theologically. Even the natural is construed theologically in such a way that assessments of the consequences of human action can be made in the light of judgments of what constitutes the flourishing of human nature, the fulfillment of the human both temporally and eternally. The development of the ethics of natural law occurs within this interpretation of the ends of human life; the consequences of human action are judged, to be sure, by moral norms, but these moral norms have theological backing; they are part of a theological ethical construing of life.

Finally, many theologians have been concerned to construe "the whole" theologically. Already we have noted this in the *exitus et reditus* pattern of Thomistic theology (Augustinian and other theologies also share in it). That such attempts are audacious is very clear; that there is legitimacy to them in the theological enterprise, especially for theologians who are disposed to strong views about the sovereignty of the Deity, is also clear. My illustration of a construing of "the whole" is Jonathan Edwards' *Dissertation Concerning the End for which God Created the World,* which like his more widely known *Dissertation Concerning True Virtue,* was published after his death.[9] The essay is vintage Edwards, and in a sense vintage eighteenth-century Christian theology. It consists of three parts: an introduction which carefully explains his use of terms (a virtue in Edwards not always present in the history of theology), a chapter "Wherein is considered, what reason teaches concerning this affair," and a chapter "Wherein it is inquired, what is to be learned from Holy Scriptures, concerning God's last end in the creation of the world." My judgment is that the first chapter determines the second, that his speculative philosophical argument provides the principles by which he selects his biblical materials and interprets them. (Indeed, one section of the second chapter is largely the stating of proof-texts with exposition of them in terms of the first chapter.)[10] A critical Pauline text indicates the flavor of the enterprise, "For from him and through him and to him are all things. To him be glory forever" (Rom. 11:36, RSV). The most succinct summary sentence is as follows: "Therefore . . . we may suppose, *that a disposition in God, as an original property of his nature, to an emanation of his own infinite fullness, was what excited him to create the world; and so, that the emanation itself was aimed at him as the last end of creation.*"[11] God makes himself his own end. The creation in generally neo-Platonic terms is an emanation of the fullness of the being of God; there is a properly proportionate relation of all things to each other in the creation; the interests of all creatures (who participate in this emanation) is God's own interest; their value is their value to God; and ultimately God's end is his own glorification. It is not important here to elaborate the argument, or to review Edwards' own answers to objections to his argument. My intention is only to illustrate briefly that a theologian attempts to construe the significance of the "whole" and how he does it. Classic doctrines of divine providence, with all their variations, are a part of this purpose. Given certain views about the nature of the Deity it is reasonable for theologians to construe in meaningful (granted speculative) terms the significance of the "whole."

In this section I have attempted to indicate what is involved in a theological construing of the world, and particularly the "moral world." As was indicated in the first paragraph, theologians are not the only persons engaged in such an enterprise. The conditions *sine qua non* for a theological construing of the world are "believing in" and "beliefs about" the reality of an ultimate power. Not all persons who call themselves theologians in our time would agree with the necessity of these conditions; any story, for example, that provides an orientation of the agent or the community toward the world is judged by some to be at least religious, if not theological. One can be a thoroughgoing Feuerbachian and still claim to be a theologian (not merely as a scholar working in theological texts, but also as a constructive theologian) in our present times. The root objection to this on my part is that while the traditional claim adhered to here creates its grave difficulties, any other approach surrenders what has made theology a distinctive field and endeavor.

Relating to All Things Appropriate to Their Relations to God

That persons do construe the world theologically, I take it, is indisputable. That it is a reasonable thing to do, even when claims to plausibility and not to truth in a traditional narrow sense are made, is questionable from many perspectives, and not merely contemporary ones, but historical ones as well. To assume that anyone cares about such an enterprise outside of the communities of those who are disposed to believe in the reality of an ultimate power and those who judge it to be false and pernicious enough to require elimination is in error. (My observation is that much of the concern by contemporary theologians for "method," while important to the clarification of theological work, is largely an effort to justify its legitimacy to a population that does not take it seriously enough even to care whether it is legitimate. At the same time participants in religious communities are getting little critical and sophisticated interpretation and understanding of the faith that lies within them from theologians.)

That the intellectual agenda required to make a case for relating to all things appropriate to their relations to God is too vast to be developed thoroughly here, not to mention defending how the agenda might be fulfilled, must be admitted. I indicated in my seventh assumption that theological language has primarily a practical function; it provides a way of construing the world that sustains and gives direction to a way of life. A religious perspective is self-involving; it includes a basic intentionality of the "will" as well as "linguistic-intellectual activity." Religion is a matter of the affections in a rich Edwardsian use of that term as well as a matter of the "intellect."[12] To make a case for relating all things appropriate to their relations to God requires that the readers entertain at least hypothetically the possibility that there is an ultimate power related to all things, and that persons can have a sufficient conviction of this reality to orient their individual and communal lives toward and by it.

I propose here only an outline of the task of theological ethics, that is, of the choices that are involved in the intention to relate to all things in ways appropriate to their relations to God. I shall indicate what I believe to be the most crucial problems, and therefore the critical judgments that the theologian must make. I shall also indicate the significance and the limits of this enterprise for moral life.[13]

The most obvious problematic area is to discern with some certitude how all things are related to God. Speculative philosophical theologians such as the "process theologians" and "transcendental Thomists" and Tillichians among contemporary theologians are better able than I to develop theories about the relations of all things to God. Clearly there are significant differences between these three groups, and one can add the followers of Teilhard de Chardin, theologians who choose to remain silent on these philosophical-theological issues, and others to the options that are discussed. In addition to the problems of how all things are related to God is the problem of *what* one judges the divine ends and purposes to be, and on what basis one comes to such a judgment.

As regards the matter of the theories of the relations of all things to God, I take it that there are two important ways of thinking. One, which is clearly dominant in the biblical tradition and which continues in theologies through the centuries that are strongly oriented by the Bible, is to use analogies of the person and of roles (or perhaps they are only metaphors) to speak of how God is related to all things, and particularly to persons. The second, which involves a judgment that personal terms are too misleading, is to use more abstract language such as "the ground of being," or "being."

From the biblical tradition I select two sorts of language that have been used. One, which is based strongly in the Torah tradition, is the language of God as a power and authority who determines the course of events, and who exercises his moral authority through commands. The analogy (or metaphor) is drawn, I believe, for social experiences of a certain sort; human societies were organized under the authority of a leader, part of whose role it was to issue commands. Yahweh was judged to have this sort of "social role." The relations of the people to Yahweh are those of subjects to an authority, and the proper language for understanding their actions is that of obedience or disobedience to his commands. To be sure, on other grounds, namely, his covenant with his people (also a social analogy or metaphor), they were persuaded that his intentions were for their benefit, but the condition for receiving the benefits was obedience to his commands. The development of moral and religious rules took place in the context of believing in and beliefs about Yahweh; he had the power to determine the consequences of the historical course of events of his people, and he had the power and authority to issue (as a result of his covenant with them) commands.

The second sort of language from the biblical tradition that has been used is that of "God acting." Some such notion is present in the idea of covenant and the idea that the consequences of obedience or disobedience to the commands were "in the hands" of God the determiner of the historical destiny of his people. What I wish to indicate here is that the notion of "God acting" has been developed somewhat independently of the notion of commands, and that it is drawn from reflections upon the nature of human action. God is understood to be an "agent" just as persons are agents. Like persons he is understood to have intentions which are fulfilled or not in part through human action and in history. Like persons, he has a volitional capacity, not only in the sense of stating what is desirable, but also in the sense of exercising power in such ways that his actions can be fulfilled. "Knowledge" of his intentions is gained through his "revelation" of himself. Many different views of how God reveals himself, of course, have been used to back this kind of assertion. My own view, acknowledgedly weak from the perspectives of those more orthodox than I, is that interpretations of God's intentions are developed and discerned through events of human history and human experience, as communities who live in the sense of the presence of an ultimate power reflect on these events and experiences in the light of that sense.

The ongoing task of theology becomes one of seeking to interpret God's action in all events and relations in which humans participate—interpersonal, political and historical, and natural. One biblical tradition in which this is done is that of the eighth-century prophets, the literature of moral indictments based not only on infractions of the law (which the prophets assume that the people know and believe themselves obligated to obey), but also on the conviction that God is speaking by the voice of the prophet (a very personal metaphor) to the people through the consequences of the historical and personal events in which they participate.

Whereas the dominant moral language of the commander-subject pattern is obedience and disobedience, in modern times the dominant language of the language of God acting is appropriate responsiveness to the action (intentions and activities) of God in the events in which humans are participants. God is related to all things as the ultimate agent whose intentions and purposes are to be discerned in all events. (Whether God is an omnipotent agent who absolutely determines each event in detail, or a limited agent, is, like the view of revelation, a matter on which there is dispute, though "hard determinists" are hard to come by in recent theology.) As some recent Protestant theologians have stated the matter, the morally appropriate response in a religious context requires that persons discern God's action, or discern the intention of God's activity in the circumstances in which human action is required. The processes recommended for doing this vary from complex procedures of interpretation to an almost purely intuitive sense on the part of members of the religious community. Human actions are to "respond" to God's action, or are to "endorse" God's action, or to be "consonant with" God's action, and so forth.

(I wish to indicate that even within the biblical, more social and personal language, the language a theologian chooses to use for the analogy or the metaphor predisposes him or her to a particular way of describing moral experience, and in turn to particular ways of prescribing how moral actions should be guided and judged.)

The second way of thinking about the relations of all things to God, as indicated above, attempts to use more abstract language such as "ground of being" partly because theologians judge the use of personal terms to be excessively anthropocentric and misleading. For some theologians the effort stands quite independent from the historic distinctiveness of the Christian religious tradition. It is a matter of ontology and metaphysics, and the adequacy of a delineated position is to be judged by evidences and argumentation appropriate to those fields. The philosophical theological argument is not deemed by some theologians to be stating explicitly what is implicit in the religious tradition; what the historic religious traditions add is an account of the human condition in relation to the Deity whose nature is expounded philosophically. Others believe that in their more abstract language they are expounding a philosophical theology that, if it is not implicit in the historic religious language, is at least a rational interpretation that is coherent with the more primary religious language. The philosophical theology is an exposition of the faith, or apologetically an interpretation of the meaning of the faith in language that presumably has wider public accessibility. In this approach the anticipated result is not so much rational "proofs" for the existence of the Deity and the ways in which the Deity is related to all things, so much as an illumination or expository analysis of the primary religious language in language that is less personal and less determined by religious historical particularity.

One example of this which shows its importance to ethics can be drawn from the Thomistic interpretation of law. In this work, as in many others in the Christian tradition, the concept of participation plays a crucial role. Put briefly, the pattern is that the moral law of nature participates in the mind of God; it participates in the divine intentionality of and for all things. While it is argued on exegetical grounds that there is a biblical acknowledgment of a natural moral law (using the first two chapters of Paul's letter to the Romans, and the concept of man being made in the image and likeness of God and the "high Christologies" of the New Testament as principal bases), there is no *theory* of natural law developed in the biblical texts. The more speculative doctrine of the natural law is to be defended on purely philosophical grounds, including the concept of the participation of the natural in the divine purpose, but it is also an exposition of what is implicit in (a stronger claim) or of what is authorized by (a weaker claim) certain biblical themes, texts, and concepts. One consequence of this view is that the biblical moral teachings are deemed to be expressions of this natural moral law, for like it they are also expressions of the divine intentionality in which human life participates. The historical biblical teachings are justifiable on the basis of the more speculative philosophical theology and ethics (with three principal exceptions in Thomas's writings: the command to Abraham to slay Isaac, the "suicide" of Samson, and Hosea's marriage to Gomer).

The advantage that is presumably gained by such an enterprise (and many other examples of the same intention on the part of theologians could be given) is that the relations between God and the moral, between theology and ethics, are established on rational principles on which all rational persons might agree, and thus the historical particularity of the biblical tradition is not an obstacle to making universal claims for the moral principles and moral values that are stated. An example of this is the claim that Roman Catholics make, a correct one in principle, that their teaching on abortion is not a Catholic or Christian teaching, but is based upon human reason, on the natural moral law.

I have attempted to indicate that there have been two general ways used to delineate how God is related to all things, and particularly to persons. The first was using the more personal and social role language of the biblical tradition, and the second the more abstract and impersonal language of various metaphysical theories. The second large issue, alluded to previously but not lifted out clearly, is how the theologian can claim knowledge about God's relations to all things. "Revelation," conceptualized in a variety of ways and with various justifications of the ways in which it is conceptualized, is one claim. The other general claim is that reason exercised in relation to human experience, or in relation to human knowledge of the natural world, is a basis for knowing how God is related to all things. That there are mixed claims is also the case: what one finds in the biblical and ongoing tradition is itself a process of human reflection on the nature and purposes of the ultimate power (a weak view of revelation), or there is a basic coherence between speculative thinking about the nature of ultimate reality and what is known through the particular historic tradition in which that reality has revealed itself. I shall illustrate how a strong doctrine of revelation works.

The modern classic of this approach is the work of Karl Barth. Faced with what were to Barth insuperable obstacles for claiming natural knowledge of God, and yet deeply convinced of the reality and presence of God (who is a God for man), he opts for the fundamental principle that knowledge of God can come only through God's revealing of himself. God, who is free, chose freely to reveal himself through the history of the Jewish people, and ultimately through the person and events of Jesus. With joyous confidence and with brilliance, Barth then can expound the theological themes he finds central to the biblical tradition. The fundamental knowledge of God that he discerns is that God is gracious, that he intends the good of man. While there is a historic particularity to the locus of the revelation of God, what is revealed there is of universal significance; the sovereign power who is gracious intends the salvation, the fulfillment of all humans. Indeed, the prime reality is that all humans *de jure* do participate in the goodness of the divine reality and the divine intention.

Without appropriate attention to how this is worked out in relation to ethics in the pattern of the relation of the divine reality and intention to the proper human response to it, one point nonetheless needs to be made clear. One moral consequence of this view of God's revelation is that the primary command is "Thou *mayest* . . . " and not "Thou shalt not . . . " This does not rule out certain almost absolute prohibitions of conduct in certain circumstances, but it does ground a basic affirmation of the goodness of the creation, and a basic openness (a word Barth uses) to new possibilities of human well-being in the world. Not only is the way of construing the world grounded in his exceedingly strong view of revelation, but what he finds revealed (a gracious God) grounds an orientation toward life in the world.[14]

That Barth's confidence in revelation in the Bible is excessive to many other theologians is indeed clear. That theologians, such as myself, who choose not to accept his certitude, but nonetheless do not relinquish a claim of some biblical authorization for their work, must find some "mixed" view is also clear. Indeed, both classic Catholic theology and all "liberal theology" since the Enlightenment have been engaged in establishing some reliable knowledge of God drawn from biblical sources and from common human experience and reason. No matter how much "knowledge" is justified, *what* is claimed to be known is crucial to how a theologian or a community construes the world both religiously and morally.

What is claimed about God and his intentionality is patently related to the sources used. Both the more philosophically developed aspects of the tradition and those that are developed more biblically offer various delineations of the significant characteristics of the ultimate power and its purposes. Different delineations become the bases for different inferences of a generally moral sort. Different degrees of certitude claimed for what is known also affect what moral inferences can be drawn from theological statements. I shall illustrate these matters from current discussions in Roman Catholic theology and ethics.

The neo-Thomist manuals of moral theology that dominated the latter part of the nineteenth century and the first six decades of the present century are not known for carefully relating the moral prescriptions to basic theological principles, though it is clear that they assumed certain principles that were articulated in the neo-Thomist theological tracts. Put oversimply, the theological principle that governed the moral theologians was that of a divine law in which the natural law participates. What was crucial was the opinion that the Deity had an almost absolutely fixed, immutable and eternal moral law from which prescriptions could be deduced or inferred and applied to changing historical and natural conditions with the greatest of certitude. The point made in polemical writings against these manuals is that God's moral order was "static," and that it was assumed to be known with certitude. Certain polemical attacks on it distinguish between the "classical" tradition and the modern "historical" ways of thinking.

The point of significance for our discussion is that for many reasons both Roman Catholic theology and moral theology began to reconceptualize the knowledge of God, and that the new concepts are correlated with changes in both the procedures of moral theology and in some of the particular moral judgments that are made. (One significant factor was the increasing use of the more personal language and the more historically oriented ways of thinking that have dominated most of Protestant theology in recent decades.) As against the "neo-Thomists," who construed the relation of all things to God in terms of the requirement that all things conform to God's law conceived in "static" terms, the revisionists have conceptualized God as (in part) creating the conditions of possibility for some novelty in human life and in the relations of humans to each other in society and in relation to the natural world. When the Deity is conceptualized more as a "dynamic" presence than as a "static" order, there is a basis for some significant changes in ethical thought. The way is opened for continuing revision of the moral tradition and even for discovery of new possibilities of human action that might sustain human well-being. When the Deity is conceived in more "personal" terms, and correlatively humans are conceived more "personally" (in contrast to "physically"), the considerations that have to be taken into account in the domain of the ethical become increased in number and complexity. I forego here the opportunity to develop this with a more specific illustration, but the controversy over *Humanae Vitae* by Pope Paul VI provides material by which this can readily be done. Not only is there a change in what is believed about God, but correlated with certain changes is a qualification of the traditional certitude about the wrongness and rightness of certain human actions. The relations of all things to God are conceptualized differently, in part because God is thought about differently; how the world is then construed is different and a difference in both procedures of ethical reflection and of particular judgments in some cases reasonably follows.[15]

I have by no means indicated all the crucial points at which judgments are made by theologians both about how the ultimate power is known and what is claimed to be known about the ultimate power. Also I have not indicated at all how different judgments about humans and their capacities affect the development of theological ethics. I have attempted only to indicate something of what is required if one is to fulfill a project based on the last two assumptions stated in the early part of this chapter.

Finally, what contributions theology makes to ethics clearly depend upon the choices and specifications of theological points by particular religious communities or individual theologians.[16]

NOTES

1. Gordon D. Kaufman, *An Essay on Theological Method* (Missoula, Mont.: Scholars Press, 1975) p. ix.

2. I have given my own views about theological ethics in Gustafson, *Can Ethics Be Christian?* (Chicago: University of Chicago Press, 1975).

3. Julian N. Hartt, "Encounter and Inference in Our Awareness of God," in *The God Experience*, ed. Joseph P. Whalen, S.J. (New York: Newman Press, 1971), p. 52. This theme is elaborated in Hartt, *Theological Method and Imagination* (New York: Seabury Press, 1976).

4. I cannot undertake here to discuss the crucial matter of whether and how such believing and beliefs might be justified. My own views are most fully expressed in *Can Ethics Be Christian?*, pp. 82–116.

5. I have critically assessed this use of historical analogies, in ibid., pp. 117–44.

6. Reinhold Niebuhr, *The Nature and Destiny of Man*, 2 vols. (New York: Charles Scribners Sons, 1941, 1943).

7. Ibid., vol. 1, p. 16.

8. Ibid., vol. 1, p. 251–60.

9. Jonathan Edwards, *The Works of Jonathan Edwards*, 2 vols. (Edinburgh: Banner of Truth Trust, 1974; reprint of 1834 ed.), vol. I, pp. 95–121, 122–42.

10. This judgment is not concurred in by Paul Ramsey, who is editing these texts for the Yale edition of *The Works of Jonathan Edwards*. Oral communication, January, 1978.

11. Edwards, *Works*, vol. I, p. 100, col. 1.

12. See Jonathan Edwards, *Religious Affections* (New Haven: Yale University Press, 1959), pp. 93–124.

13. I have developed this with more specific relation to medical ethics in *The Contributions of Theology to Medical Ethics* (Milwaukee: Marquette University Press, 1975).

14. For Barth's views on some medical moral problems, see Karl Barth, *Church Dogmatics* III:4 (Edinburgh: T. and T. Clark, 1961), pp. 397 ff.

15. For further development see Gustafson, *Protestant and Roman Catholic Ethics* (Chicago: University of Chicago Press, 1978), pp. 80–94.

16. See, Gustafson, *Contributions of Theology*, for further development.

Commentary

Response to James M. Gustafson

Hans Jonas

A DIFFICULTY IN COMMENTING on Gustafson's chapter lies in its more interpretative than positional stance, which allows few clues as to where the author himself stands—what he wishes to be identified with in the theological spectrum he so skillfully and impartially spreads out before us. The choice to interpret the agenda rather than enact it for us is, of course, entirely legitimate, but it leaves the commentator somewhat short on issues to come to grips with. Conceivably, the choice itself, perhaps less than free, might be a matter for comment if it could be taken to reflect the troubled state of theology in our time: its loss of self-confidence and its infection by the prevailing scepticism, historicism, cultural relativism, and so on. Some of Gustafson's own stated "assumptions" seem to point in that direction. However that may be (and such a reading of his reticence may be quite mistaken), the nontheologian and secularist would for argument's sake have welcomed something more assertive to envy and feel challenged by, something more positive to salute and get his teeth into. Especially, the philosopher wishes for a hard line in his counterpart across the fence, to bring him face to face with the—either conflicting or complementing—*excess* of faith and revelation over reason and what its stringent charter lets it do. The charter of creedal theology, after all, is allowed to be different at the outset of the encounter. Admittedly, it is easy for the outsider to be hypothetically radical in behalf of a cause he has not to live with afterward. But the itch is irresistible, and this

197

is not the first time that I feel driven—I don't know whether by the whisperings of a theologian manqué in myself or from the philosopher's need to confront a challenge at its strongest—to put myself in the theologian's place and by proxy to attempt to draw some lines of what "we others" could expect from him in answer to the riddles we share, if he but dares to use the powers of his mandate. The impudence of thus appropriating his part is excused only by my deep respect for his very mandate, whose voice indeed I deem indispensable in the concert of men's groping for ultimate directions. It is in this spirit that I offer running comments on a number of points in Gustafson's chapter and then don his garb for an experiment of my own, along the way also occasionally trying to focus the discourse somewhat more than he has done on the particular issues to which this Institute is dedicated.

I take note of the *eight assumptions* stated on pp. 176-179. *Assumptions 1–4* deal with the *historicity* of the theological endeavor: the historical character of the Bible itself, of the Christian tradition grounded in it and successively reinterpreting its message in the light of changing times, and the historical character of any present theological work in relation to the conditions of our own time. My only comment here is that I would have expected a Christian theologian to insert a word on the transhistorical status of Jesus Christ the Savior, or at least on the very peculiar "historical" character of the "Christ event" in its claimed redemptional significance for all subsequent time. However, this is no concern of mine.

Assumption 5 states the "'faith' aspect" belonging to all genuine theology. Most fundamentally put, that aspect is "a confidence . . . in an ultimate power" as the creative, sustaining, and determining cause of the world, and (less certain) in the goodness of this power. "Power" is an impersonal term, "goodness" has at least personal connotations. In most of Gustafson's discourse, the term "ultimate power" (for God) notably dominates. It is a matter of faith because not rationally demonstrable, though rationally defensible.

Accordingly (*assumption 6*), we must acknowledge the "mystery" of God, with the consequence that theological statements are never literal and always tentative.

Assumption 7 holds that theological language has primarily a practical function, i.e., to sustain and give direction to a way of life. With this I would take serious issue (as a reduction of theology to homiletics) were it not corrected by *assumption 8*, the most important, which states that "theology provides a way of *construing the world*" (p. 178), which is surely a theoretical undertaking, even if on fideistic premises. The construing is guided by "an intention to relate to all things in ways appropriate to their relations to God," and this indeed has its practical, ethical implications as "a grounding of right relations and proper ends of human conduct." The expression "to *all* things" places a potential qualification on the "anthropocentrism" of Western religion and ethics. Here we come close to the particular interest of our circle and to Gustafson's declared topic, "Theology and Ethics." With this I shall now deal in keeping with the paper itself, which is henceforth devoted to developing the implications of assumption 8.

The major theme (p. 178 ff.) is "construing the world theologically" and how it affects ethical thought. Of the *sources* for such a construing, Gustafson says that it is human *experience* reflecting on historical events, on the natural world, and on individual occasions "in the light of a sense of the reality of an ultimate power" (p. 180). I take it that this "sense" is itself an experience, viz., "of the presence of the Deity in these experiences" (p. 180), and furthermore—though Gustafson does not clearly say so—that it means a presence not only in my experiencing but also, or primarily, in the objects thereof, the events and facts I reflect upon. But in either case—whether it is my reflective experience or its objects that I invest with a sense of divine presence—the question arises whether this is to be understood in terms of the general presence of an ultimate power in all things, or in terms of a special presence in particular things, events or experiences (a difference analogous to that between *providentia generalis* and *providentia specialis* in classical Christian theology). In the first case, that of an equal ubiquity, the "sense" in question may amount to no more than the subsumption of the particular under the universal rule of God's immanence in the world—a kind of Spinozist view which does not differentiate between a more or less of such a presence and surely cannot think of his absence from anything. Considered as sources for construing the world theologically, the nondifferentiating and the differentiating views, i.e., that of a constant omnipresence and that of chosen revelations of the divine, will produce quite different theologies, nay religions, e.g., pantheism and theism, with possibly quite different *ethical* conclusions ("sin," e.g., has no place in the pantheistic variety). Knowing Gustafson to be a Christian, I guess his to be the second of the two options. But then, "presence" is too calm, too intransitive a term. The exodus narrative, e.g., which Gustafson adduces as an example of how a historical event can be interpreted "under the conviction of the presence of Yahweh," speaks to Jews of more than a "presence." When on Passover night we chant from the Bible, "With a strong hand and outstretched arm" he led us out of Egypt, we have not mysterious presence but manifest action in mind. The distinction would be a quibble if it would not carry over into the subsequent deliberations of Gustafson under the heading of the *circumstances* of human action that can be construed theologically (pp. 182-183). There, the exodus story is used as a paradigmatic event that discloses a divine intention for humanity, and thus, since the circumstances were those of oppression, and oppression exists for large portions of humanity today, its theological construing has vast contemporary applications. Namely, "where there is oppression God wills liberation; where there are movements for liberation, there is the presence of God" (p. 182). As a moving expression of this transference from the Bible to the Now, I am reminded of the famous Negro spiritual, "When Israel was in Egyptland/ Let my people go/ Oppressed so hard they could not stand/ Let my people go." Morally and emotionally compelling by any humanist standards. But immediately we must ask: go *where*? if we do not wish to let the "theology" of that appeal simply blend into the general, secular sympathy today with liberation movements of all kinds. And here, the difference between the intransitive presence of an endorsing principle and the transitive thrust of an ulterior divine purpose can be quite consequential ethically. For instance, the plausible conclusion "where there are movements for liberation, there is the presence of God" may become a non sequitur when the premise is made to read thus: Where there is oppression, God wills liberation—*on condition* of a "covenant," i.e., on the condition that the liberated will henceforth serve him, i.e., that liberation is charged with a new obligation, is indeed a new appropriation and willed by God on that condition only. From the premise thus enlarged, it follows by no means that liberation movements per se have the automatic blessing of God (which his "presence" in them must mean)—not, e.g., if their aim or result is a rampage of licence, self-gratification, or cruelty. In the language of the scriptural archetypes: Mount Sinai, not the Golden Calf, was the divine interest in the liberation. In that archetype, by the way, a liberation movement was conspicuous by its absence: Moses was resented by his oppressed brethren, they had almost to be forced into the unwelcome freedom; and the terrible price of it for the next 3,000 years almost justifies that initial shrinking from it. I bring all this up merely to indicate that a "theological construing," especially for drawing ethical conclusions, must beware of simplistic uses of the powerful symbols of the sources, and that in the Jewish-Christian context it must go beyond sensed presence to articulate divine will, command, and action. (Note that I distinguish between loosely homiletic and strictly theological use of a biblical passage.)

As circumstances, so can *ends and consequences* of action be construed theologically, namely in relation to whether they contribute to or deflect from the fulfillment of a *divine goal* (p. 184). To the alternative of contributing or deflecting one must, I think, add obstructing, defacing, even destroying divine ends, i.e., positive counteraction to them. Now, for becoming relevant to human conduct, those ends must be known. *Discernible* divine purpose clearly would provide a norm for ethics. On its utter unknowability, let us remember, Descartes specifically based his exclusion of *causae finales,* i.e. of teleology, from a science of nature. But to the theologian it may be knowable, albeit nonscientifically, or (with Gustafson) "construable," either from the clues of nature (including man's) in the context of a "natural theology," or from the pronouncements of revelation in the context of a fideistic theology. The one would be more philosophical, the other more "theological" in the strict sense. A classic combination of the two is Thomas Aquinas's theology and ethics. If, as in that case, not only particular divine ends are disclosed in creation but an overall end of the whole, then we get those grand theological construings of the world with which, as underpinnings of an ethics, Gustafson deals on pp. 178 ff. It is here where I wish to comment somewhat more thoroughly.

Obviously, to construe "the whole" theologically, something like a cosmic teleology must be conceived. But then, it makes a great difference whether it is conceived in Aristotelian terms (as Aquinas did) or, let us say, in Whiteheadian terms. In the first case, the creation is complete in itself, a hierarchy of generic ends to be reactualized from individual to individual in their genera; in the Whiteheadian case, it is an unfinished business of ever-new ends, with creative novelty itself the overall end of creation as a whole. Surely, the ethical implications of the two views are vastly different, as man's task in "fulfillment" of the divine intent might look quite different in their light. In the Aristotelian case, it would be not to go beyond but to stay within the created order, not to complete the incomplete works of God but to preserve the *integrity* of his creation—in man himself: the integrity of the "image of God"; in the world: the plenitude of earthly life; in sum, biblically: the works of the fifth and sixth days. Being the notorious and increasingly dangerous violator of both, not to spoil them rather than to improve on them would be man's prime duty toward God. The created order (*ordo creationis*), especially where it is vulnerable—and it is that within the reach of human freedom—would set the norm: to guard it against distortion, but also from frustration; that is, not only refrain from causing the one, but also remove obstacles to its fulfilling itself. This cherishing of the given is, in goal-setting, a relatively humble ethical scheme, though in execution anything but easy, considering the terrible power—man's own—with which it has to cope (let alone any native "sinfulness"). What the more ambitious teleology of endless creative novelty, with which Whiteheadian process philosophy invests the universe, enjoins in the way of ethical norms for humans is not so clear, and our Christian theologian's comment on its compatibility with his faith would interest me.[1] But of Teilhard de Chardin's "point Omega," toward which the universe moves as its final consummation (to take another example of philosophical or speculative theology), I can say with confidence that such placing of the true end of things at the distant cosmic *future*, making their original creation a mere incipient stage for a perfection that is yet to come as the terminus of a gradually transforming ascent—thus robbing any *present* along the way of its "immediacy to God," is entirely un-Jewish; and my guess is: also un-Christian. *Historical* (as distinct from cosmic) eschatology, understood in some terms of immanent "gradualism" ("progress"), is a more complex question in the Jewish-Christian context, on which I will touch later.

Having at last cited by name the tradition in which Gustafson's effort stands—viz., the Judaeo-Christian tradition—and with it the common ground on which he and I can meet, I shall now make true my threat to don the theologian's robe for a while and tell how I would go about "construing the whole theologically" if I were a theologian. The basis for my attempt must needs be confined to the biblical source we two have in common, the Old Testament alone.

First, one word more about the "ultimate power," belief in and beliefs about whose reality Gustafson rightly calls "the conditions *sine qua non* for a theological construing of the world" (p. 186). Surely with his consent, I enlarge the *sine qua non* thus: for a biblicist theology, beliefs about this "power" must include, beyond its "ultimacy," that it is in some sense "spiritual," therefore also a seat of "interest" or "concern," and not indifferent. Else, some basic force of physics which theory may one day identify as the unitary root of all the diverse forces of nature (the search for such a unified force theory is on) would qualify for the title "ultimate power," the power that, from the big bang on, drives and rules the career of the universe. In the *religious* concept of an ultimate power, mentality and interest are necessary ingredients; and the interest is affirmative of the world and discriminating of what goes on in it, according to *Jewish* religion. Taking this from now on as a basis, I find two statements in the Bible which can serve as the cornerstones for the whole edifice of a theology that leads to an ethics for man, without the help of a speculative or philosophical *theologia naturalis*. Both are from the first chapter of Genesis, the creation story: one the very first sentence of the Bible, "In the beginning God created the heavens and the earth," the other, "And God created man in his own image" (Gen. 1:27). The first conditions the relation of all things, the second the special relation of man to God; or ethically turned: the first sets a norm for man's relation to all things, i.e., the universe, the second for his relation to himself and his fellowmen. Let me, very briefly, develop at least the beginnings of theologico-ethical inferences from those two fundamental sentences.[2]

"God created heaven and earth" and then everything in them, including the multitude of life. Two related statements contribute to the meaning of this createdness of the world: the repeated one on each day's work, "And God saw that it was good," culminating in the final, "And God saw everything that he had made, and behold it was very good"; the other, "On the seventh day, God finished his work and rested from all his work which he had done" (Gen. 2:2). What have they to tell us about our relation to the world? Surely, the world's being willed by God and judged good in its creator's eyes endows it with a claim to affirmation by man. For this affirmation, the being created, i.e., willed, by God would suffice alone. But the being "good" adds to the extrinsic title an intrinsic property of its being: that such as it is, this is neither an absurd nor an indifferent universe, neutral as to value, but harbors value, and man with his value-feeling is not lost in it in cosmic solitude and arbitrary subjectivity. In this spirit, the Psalmist could aver that "The heavens tell the glory of God." And even the God of Job—by no means pure loving-kindness— could rest his case on the wonders of his creation. Belittling them as meaningless sports of mere necessity and chance would be impious under that comprehensive divine sanction of the created order. Toward the macrocosm, about which we can do little, this amounts in its ethical aspect mostly to a matter of *attitude* (such as arrogant or despairing "existentialism"); but toward the microcosm of life inhabiting this creation it also involves human *action*. Its existence in all its feeling kinds (i.e., animal species) receives a more emphatic endorsement by the creator than all the rest. While on everything else (including plants) he puts each time the summary seal that "it is good," it is at the first creation of *nefesh chaiah*, i.e., animated beings, that "he blessed them" and empowers them to be fruitful and multiply and fill the waters, etc. Stressed is the multitude of *kinds,* and although the blessing is given to their own power of filling their respective habitats, it binds man in relation to them as he is given shortly thereafter *dominion* over them. This dominion, given and thus legitimized, surely means exploitation, but also trusteeship. Exploitation without dominion is, by the universal law of life's feeding on life, the rule in interspecies relations and involves individual annihilation habitually, but not, on the whole, wiping out of kinds. Exploitation coupled with dominion poses precisely that danger, and as man's dominion has lately grown immeasurably, and with his own numbers also his needs and demands (not to speak of the gratuitous greeds of his civilization), the protective blessing of life's manifoldness at its creation is exceedingly topical today as a point of theological ethics. For the first time, one creature has become, through his power and freedom, responsible for all the others. And though perhaps not every extinction of species can be avoided in the impact of dominant man on his environment (as it surely was not avoided in past evolution), he is by the doctrine of creation clearly enjoined from wantonly impoverishing the diversity of life on this earth, which on the creator's testimony is a good in itself. Let me observe here that it is very difficult, if not impossible, from the premises of a purely secular ethics to derive something like a respect for extrahuman life, or obligations toward nature in general. What it can argue is the *unwisdom* of wanton destruction with its eventual, quite natural retribution on man's own life; or, more humanistically, the aesthetic loss suffered with the reduction of nature's magnificent wealth of forms, and thus the immorality of our robbing later generations of beauty and objects of wonder by leaving them a poorer estate. Since every secular ethics, rationalistic or other, individualist or collectivist, eudaemonistic or idealist, is necessarily *anthropocentric,* binding the title of "end-in-itself" to personhood, it cannot offer more than such cost-benefit considerations with regard to nonhuman things. A theological ethics, serious about the teaching of creation, can offer more: the element of reverence, the claim of all life to the dignity of end-in-itself, the divine will for its generic abundance, the stewardship of man for its continued presence. I need not spell out how this bears on concerns of ours.

Let me now pass to the second of the two Genesis pronouncements, the other cornerstone for a theological construing of ethics: the creation of man. Even in the sparse language of the Bible, it is clothed in emphatic, repetitive solemnity. "Let us make man in our image, after our likeness"; "So God created man in his own image, in the image of God he created him." His uniqueness is proclaimed but left mysterious. I will not try to plumb the depths of the "image" predicate. That it signifies an awesome charge is evident. In its name, humans could be exhorted "Be ye holy, *because* I am holy, the Lord, your God." This is a command, not a description, and the "because" expresses the logic of the "likeness": that it is a capacity, not a possession, and that the capacity sets our duty. While in all other cases, the "goodness" of creation rests securely in the creature and its acting by nature, in man it rests in the endowment with and for a *potentiality* which has been delivered into his hands. While all other life is innocent, he can be guilty of betraying the image. How he can do so is illustrated by what, to my knowledge, is the only later reference in the Bible to the image title of man, with the only direct practical conclusion ever explicitly drawn from it. It occurs in the so-called Noachitic law, given to Noah after the flood for all mankind until the Torah of Moses. It reads: "Of every man's brother I will require the life of man. Whosoever sheds the blood of man, by man shall his blood be shed; *for God made man in his own image*" (Gen. 9:5–6). God's argument here for capital punishment from precisely the sacredness of human life in his eyes ought surely to get a hearing in the contemporary debate, in which a nontheological, secular understanding of some such "sacredness" is often invoked to opposite effect. The measure of the sacredness, here absolute, is made the measure of the atonement, equally absolute, for the destruction of its bearer.

But as to "natural goodness" by creation, the theologian will hardly find in the Bible that the "image" distinction assures it to man as a presence that needs only be freed from the obstruction of circumstances, external and internal, to shine forth in its native purity. Much modern political ideology, as also of education, psychotherapy, and so on, is predicated on precisely this assumption. Conditions are the problem: improve them, and ethics will take care of itself. Listen to Bert Brecht in his *Threepenny Opera* (my translation):

"Who would not like to be a kind, good soul?/ Give to the poor one's own—why not? I ask./ When all are good, *His* kingdom is not far./ Who in His light would not with pleasure bask?/ Be a good person? Sure, who wouldn't rather be!/ But it so happens that on this our earth/ People are coarse and means are scarce./ To live in peace with all—who might not love that much?/ Alas! The circumstances aren't such." (*"Doch die Verhältnisse, sie sind nicht so"*: a refrain.)

Some truth in there, for sure, and at certain moments perhaps *the* truth that needs saying. But still a half-truth, as also in the more succinct and most quoted line from the same play (also a refrain) "First comes the feed, and then morality" (*"Erst kommt das Fressen und dann die Moral"*). Indeed, those denied the first may be excused from the second (especially by the luckier ones), but supplying the one does not of itself bring on the other, no more than liberation brings with it the use that liberty is for. Yet, even if these are no more than *opportunities* for meeting the real challenge of the image of God, helping to provide them and other necessary preconditions is itself a first duty toward that image. Especially to foster—beyond the palliatives of charity—freedom from oppression is bidden theologically, because it is better to serve God than men; and oppressing fellow humans is condemned as committing an insult to the mortal image of God, equally imparted to all. On all counts, religious and secular, oppression has to be done away with, and physical deprivation as much as possible. But the theologian will not fall prey to the progressivist illusion that such removals of obstacles, degradations, and privations will usher in a Golden Age. All modern utopianism—political, social, economic, technological, even psychological—is prone to that optimistic expectation. The theologians of the past, conversant with the fact of sin and the pitfalls of human freedom, knew better, or worse. "The inclination of man's heart is evil from his youth," said God after the flood, vowing to himself not to desolate the earth again because of man. Yet it was he who had created him in his own image! The seeming paradox points to the riddle that is man, which Pascal so eloquently dwelt on: poised between the infinite and the finite, between angel and beast, greatness and wretchedness, good and evil, partaking of both sides of these contraries. He can rise highest and fall lowest. The evil of the heart—of which indolence is one—will be different on a full stomach than an empty, with a commodious life than a pinched one, in security than in insecurity; but it will still be there to contend with. Neither Scripture nor experience tells otherwise. There is not the least ground for thinking that the image of God will ever be safe, certainly not by virtue of circumstances, be they the best that man can devise. They still should be striven after in a nonutopian, sober spirit. A theological ethics, therefore, when it comes to changing the world, i.e., the circumstances of men's life, will be neither pessimistic nor optimistic, but realistic. That gives ample scope to working for improvements, as justice, reason, and decency command, with no excessive expectations and at no excessive price, which any secular chiliasm is willing to pay at the cost of those living in the shadow of its supposed advent.

As always in ethical matters, the negative directives of the image attribute are easier to define than the positive—the bewareing easier than the fulfilling. The most pervasive *positive* inference from it is that every person is an end in himself and must be treated as such. This, as we know, is the supreme principle of Kant's ethics, but not really derivable from his rational premises, nor (I tend to believe) from *any* purely secular basis. From the doctrine of creation it follows naturally, and we do no injustice to Kant when we say that through his own, ostensibly immanent reasoning, there speaks the theological tradition to which he was heir.

However, with knowing *that* man is an end in himself, we do not know yet *what* that end may be, i.e., how the fulfilled image may look. But even with uncertainty about the positive "what," we can be certain about *negative* inferences from the "that," so Kant's own inference never to use persons as mere means. An even more elementary command of the image attribute, not mentioned by Kant, follows straight and uniquely from the fiat of its creation: that man must not be allowed to disappear from the earth. His presence in the world, if willed by the creator and dignified by his image, is for its collective repository not a choice but a duty. Therefore, nothing must be permitted that might endanger the continuation of that presence in the future. Speaking for a moment in my ordinary, nontheological persona: I have tried hard for myself to establish this simple, elementary, and today so important commitment on pure philosophical grounds (persuasive at least, if not compelling), and am by no means sure that I have succeeded. An axiom perhaps to feeling (who would not shudder at the thought of mankind forfeiting its future?), to reason it is a proposition hard to validate, perhaps altogether beyond its scope. Generally, ethics has something to say only about how men should behave to one another, but not that there ought to be men in the first place. Metaphysics must be called in for that—philosophically precarious at best and always dubious in its purported findings. Religion, to the contrary, leaves no doubt about it. What to instinct and emotion is merely repellent—a vanishing of man by our fault—becomes a sacrilege in the theological view.[3]

And so it is with other assaults on the created image, e.g., tampering with the genetic makeup of man. Surely, a theological ethics out of our tradition can here be categorical. I hasten to add that on this point a secular ethics is not helpless either and can speak with considerable authority when it bases itself on evident moral truths. I have found these to converge, though by quite different arguments, with what a theological ethics would have to conclude from *its* grounding verities, namely that in terms of biological endowment for its realization (and culpable stultification) the "image of God" was complete with its creation, as God indicated by resting from his finished work; that therefore a numinous sacrosanctity adheres to its given form and hallows its integrity; that consequently no "genetic engineering" on *man* may go beyond remedial help to alteration by "creative" design.

But here I had better stop playing the theologian's part. Not being a theologian, I have been indulging in a hypothetical and necessarily dilettantic game. For nothing of it do I claim theological validity, not even in the name of Judaism. The Christian theologian's "construing" from *his* sources will anyway look different, certainly more complex. Compared with Christianity, Judaism is quite unsophisticated at its roots; and so my hypothetical task, quite apart from the layman's oversimplifications, was simple compared to what Gustafson has to come up with when carrying out his own construing, for which he has articulated to us the underlying assumptions. To goad him and other theologians into just this is my sole purpose. But I did want to indicate, from the other side of the fence, immodestly perhaps, what *kind* of thing we expect or would like to hear from them. So I close with an entreaty from the rationally confined to the more amply authorized: Use your surplus and give us the real article! The sceptical hedgings we will supply, but first we want the full blast from your strongest guns. For we well know that immanent reason, as it has come to be disciplined and clipped, has not the last word on ultimate questions of our being and at some point must borrow from sources of light beyond itself, or at least consider their witness. Religion is one such source, even for those not within its dogmatic fold.

NOTES

1. His own illustration of "construing the whole theologically" by Jonathan Edwards' *Dissertation Concerning the End for which God Created the World* (p. 191) does not tell me, for God's "infinite fulness" at which the world, having emanated from it, also finally aims, does not readily define ethical norms.

2. I attempted this first in an address to the Central Conference of American Rabbis in 1967, entitled "Contemporary Problems in Ethics from a Jewish Perspective"; now included in my *Philosophical Essays* (Englewood Cliffs, N.J.: Prentice-Hall, 1974), pp. 168-82.

3. Secular ethics, to be sure, can avoid the *metaphysical* issue ("ought there to be men on earth?") by adducing the straightforward *moral* issue of the sufferings and premature deaths of the actual future individuals living at the time of the species' demise, violent or lingering: The prohibition to any generation to cause this for a future one is ethically plain by the common norms of interhuman conduct, which do include the unborn as a class sure to be born in their time. Obviously, the observance of this moral veto alone, from generation to generation, in effect (coincidentally) takes care of the metaphysical issue too, as if it were answered affirmatively without ever having been raised. But that the issue itself, with its own injunction, is nevertheless not otiose can be seen if we imagine a unanimous decision of all humans living at a particular time to stop reproducing and ensure this by universal sterilization: the never-born are not wronged, the living not subjected to suffering; any pain incurred by living and dying childless personally and with no posterity of the species is self-chosen in exchange for some preferred

gain; the latter also exculpates applying the collective decision to the children of the moment though they could not participate in it, i.e., relieving them prophylactically of the curse of their reproductive rights—in their own best interest by the lights of the decision itself. Formal ethical rules seem to be satisfied, the former veto not to apply. Yet we forcibly feel that all such balancing of the sums of temporary happiness and unhappiness, of the observing and overriding of rights, etc., even with a good showing on the credit side, does not touch on the permissibility of putting *this* up for decision at all. Therefore, the metaphysical issue of mankind's "eternal" commitment is not an idle one, even pragmatically. E.g., its affirmative answer would make off-spring a collective duty (its measure set by circumstances, and with every allowance for individual abstentions normally comprised in the statistical picture). That group mores and impulse habitually take care of this transcendent duty, sometimes even excessively, does not render the principle trivial. For man stands out from nature and even with this most natural of functions comes under more-than-natural sanctions, positive and negative.

Rejoinder to Hans Jonas

James M. Gustafson

MY CHAPTER HAS BEEN correctly perceived by Hans Jonas, and by Richard Beauchamp and Ronald Green in oral criticism, to be more interpretive or descriptive than "positional." One reason for this, though it may not be adequate, is that on a previous occasion in this group I offered a draft of a more "positional" paper and was sharply challenged to make clear its assumptions. My perception, perhaps an inaccurate one, was that it was necessary to interpret to this group *what* theological ethics is about prior to *doing* theological ethics. (Moral philosophers have for decades been telling us *what* ethics is about without being "positional" about morality. Maybe I have learned too well from them.) Perhaps I am too cautious, but theologians have good reasons to be cautious after several centuries of having theology charged with excessive certitude.

In other publications I have been more "positional," and particularly relevant to this symposium, in my Père Marquette lecture, *The Contributions of Theology to Medical Ethics*, cited in note 13. Part of the argument in that lecture is quite in tune with part of Jonas's own hypothetical (they ring, however, with greater authenticity than a purely mental exercise) theological proposals. It is dangerous to promise future work, but I do intend in the next phase of my career to develop a position more fully. I have spent more than a quarter of a century working in a critical analytical way through contemporary and historical Christian ethical literature, to a lesser extent through Jewish materials, and through philosophical and other relevant literature. The paper to which Jonas profoundly and eloquently responds is, indeed, only a short version of what has become to me a very complex agenda—so complex as to create in me persistent anxiety and sometimes despair. Candidly, it is easier for me to preach (an activity I take seriously, intellectually and rhetorically) my position than to defend it on all of its many exposed fronts. That admission may indicate other issues of theological ethics. To whom is the work addressed? What is its proper rhetorical form? How does one engage simultaneously in "language about" *and* "language of"? That admission may also indicate my most authentic "calling." But explanations become excuses, and I turn to some aspects of Jonas's substantial response.

First, with reference to the "transhistorical status of Jesus Christ." To be a Christian theologian is to find some such status to be the case—affectively and intellectually. "Some such" begs hundreds of questions; "just what" has been discussed for almost two thousand years. In *Christ and the Moral Life*, 1968, and some publications subsequent to that I have discussed the issues involved and stated my own view. The absence of more explicit references in this paper, however, stems in part from the conviction which I share with my teacher, H. Richard Niebuhr, that Christ "points beyond himself," that his significance is in what we come to know and articulate about "the Father," that is, about God. I interpret Christ's significance as a source (revelation) of insight into the reality of God more in continuity with the insights of what Christians call the Old Testament than do many theologians. Thus in writing about *theology* and ethics I do not find it necessary always to invoke the name of Christ. The "redemptional significance" of the "Christ event" for me is not so much the event as what it indicates about the Deity. What it indicates about "the Father" is what has "transhistorical" significance.

Second, the dominance of the language of "ultimate power" over the language of "goodness." Jonas's perception is accurate. Surely the Jewish and the Christian claim is that ultimate power and ultimate goodness coinhere, and I affirm that. I can only indicate here, and not give adequate defense, why the language of power dominates. Goodness for whom? Goodness for what? I have been charged with having a "high" God, and with using "chilling" rhetoric in speaking of God, and not without evidence to support the charge. For too many religious persons in the Christian tradition the coinherence of power and goodness has led to the aspiration that what humans perceive to be their "good" is what the ultimate power desires, and on this basis religion has come to have only utility value, in the crassest sense of the term. Not only Job's experience, Jeremiah's experience, the experience of the Jewish people, but also *my* experience cries out against utilitarian religion. If the ultimate power is also goodness, that goodness must not be primarily for my interests or even a generally human perception of what is in the interests of a species recently evolved, but be the good of the "whole." And not the "whole" now, but "for all time." The power of God I confront daily in the limits of human self-sufficiency and (obversely) in the ultimate dependence and interdependence of human life. The goodness of the power is often not perceptible; humans surely err if they believe that their interests (perceptions of their well-being) will be met because the ultimate power is good. I mean "human" not only in individual and social reference, but even in reference to species! To affirm that God is a God "for man" tempts all too many persons to assume that what they desire "for men" is what the goodness of the ultimate power wills. No "special providence" is guaranteed, though one is grateful to the ultimate power for every manifestation of human well-being, "he" being the condition of the possibility of each. We all know the classic issues opened by these remarks—the problem of evil, the problem of omnipotence of divine goodness, eschatology, and so on.

Third, the "practical function" of theology. Jonas, happily, finds that "practical" does not mean mere homiletics, but the practice of life. I hope he agrees that homiletics is a legitimate form of rhetoric in discerning how life ought to be lived. Like "practical," "homiletics" also is a word cheapened by religious persons themselves.

Fifth, "the presence of the Deity in these experiences." I do mean the presence of the Deity *in* the objects of experience and in the events reflected upon. Philosophical-theological explanation of this I cannot undertake here, and am not as skilled in undertaking anywhere as are others. (Ah, the many fronts that have to be defended in theological ethics, the complexity of its agenda!)

Sixth, Jonas suggests that the language of "presence" sounds too passive. Anyone who has deeply imbibed the biblical narratives must concur in Jonas's observation that in the Bible God is seen to be an active participant and not merely a passive presence. The force of this becomes even clearer when the biblically based religious traditions are set in contrast with, for example, the Upanishads. The biblical traditions generally conceive ultimate reality to be a power with a moral will, and will not only in the sense of a "desire," but also in the sense of agency. I think it is quite appropriate to explore the extent to which the analogy of human agency provides an adequate way to indicate principal features of human experience of the Deity. If I infer properly from Jonas's remarks, he suggests that the language of presence, not qualified by the adjective "active" leaves us with the shades of Spinoza, or, in more fervent piety, with mysticism.

But surely much of ethics in the Christian tradition, and perhaps also in Judaism and Islam, has erred on the side of excessive certitude about what this active presence *is* doing or *requires* persons to do. The theologies of active presence provide the possibility of moral fanaticism, for self-righteousness, and for authoritarian moral claims. I have written elsewhere that the practical moral question in theological ethics is "What is God enabling and requiring us to be and to do?" The answer is not arrived at by emotive intuition, or by rationalistic calculation: indeed, given our finitude the answer is always tentative even when sought with overwhelming sophistication. Thus for me one significance of "presence" is to suggest what Christian theologians who inform my work indicate by the dimension of inscrutability in the ways of God. I agree with Jonas that in the biblically grounded traditions an articulation of a divine will or action is required. But every such articulation is conditioned by human finitude. "My ways are higher than your ways," Isaiah has God tell the people; "we see through a glass darkly," the Apostle Paul warns us. We cannot clearly say "what God is doing" in and through recombinant DNA research, though we might get some clues about what humans ought to be doing with the results of such research in light of our perceptions and articulations of what the purposes of the ultimate power are for humanity.

Seventh, I agree with Jonas that a cosmic theology is required to explicate the agenda I have proposed, and clearly it makes a difference whether that is developed in an Aristotelian or a Whiteheadian way. I am not skilled in the art of cosmological speculation, but am persuaded that the language of an active presence which is the condition of possibility of development in nature and history, as well as development in the human understanding of nature and history, requires a cosmology that accounts for what the Whiteheadian cosmology does. Since I am convinced that cosmologies are based on inferences drawn from what is ultimately human experience of "the world," one of their tests is adequacy to our experience (including knowledge) of the world. It is interesting to observe that one reason why Roman Catholic theological ethics is undergoing revision in our time is that certain received "scholastic" forms of the Aristotelian view are judged to be too "static" in the light of contemporary experience and knowledge of "the world." For me, as for Roman Catholics, to argue for greater "openness," however, does not imply that there are no persistent continuities on which to ground "almost absolute" principles and values.

Eighth, I wholly concur in Jonas's exposition of the significance of the biblical affirmation, "God created heaven and earth," and I have expounded my views in *The Contributions of Theology to Medical Ethics* in a way that is similar to his own exposition. I suggested there that when the Psalmist states that man is only a little lower than the angels we ought to see that not as praise for human dominion, but as a charge to moral accountability, based on the evolved capacities of our species, as stewards of creation.

Finally, I am not as sure of Jonas's explication of the *imago Dei* theme in Genesis. I was privileged to hear him expound this orally in his lecture to the Central Conference of American Rabbis, the lecture cited in his response here. He develops it to support the idea that man is an end in himself and thus attacks rigorously all actions which make human beings instruments for nonhumane ends. There are good theological and ethical reasons for this exposition, and it occurs to me that the Jonathan Edwards essay I cited would be one way to support this view. If God's own glory is the proper end of creation, and man is made in God's image, man's own glory is the proper end of man.

"Glory," of course, has unfortunate connotations to some readers. Less offensive would be that God is the end of his creation; man in God's image is also his own end.

I confess that I am not sure how we ought to interpret the *imago Dei* theme. The circularity of any interpretation seems inevitable. Since any conception of God is made by analogy or inference from our perceptions of man and the world, to in turn say that man is created in God's image gives theological authority to those human perceptions. My own preference (and it is no more than that at this time) is to use human agency as the analogy, while properly acknowledging the analogical character of "God language." As the Deity is conceived to be an active purposive presence in nature and history, so is man. I believe this is coherent with what I have said above in favor of a non-Aristotelian view of theological ethics (or at least it requires a significant revision of an Aristotelian view). Or, in relation to Psalm 8, to be a little lower than the angels is to be an accountable agent or steward in the whole of creation.

And therein lies the problem. Can we have Jonas's perceptive exposition of "God created the heavens and the earth" while also holding to his exposition of the *imago Dei* which seems to make man the chief end in creation? I have more abstractly indicated in the Père Marquette Lecture what I believe is implied in "God created the heavens and the earth," namely, that the ultimate power wills the well-being of the *whole* of the creation. This creates the possibility of a moral danger from Jonas's point of view; I acknowledge the danger. There may be occasions when the human is not an end in itself, but must serve the end of the whole. The difference may not be irreconcilable at some levels of general principles; man treated as an end may be judged to be consistent with the well-being of the whole of creation. I, however, have not been persuaded of this. I believe we will in the next decades again be engaged in an ancient inquiry. What is man's place in the universe? What are the ends of man? Will it not be necessary tragically to deny the well-being of some human beings for the sake of the good of the creation (not merely society—as we do deny that in morally justified wars).

I have heard Hans Jonas articulate the tragic character of the morally serious life. I have always resonated with such a view.

Pain, suffering—denial of the rights and goods including life itself to some for the sake of others and the "whole"—these are necessary and inevitable aspects of moral life. What the ultimate power and good enables and requires us to be and to do, though discerned imperfectly, may be costly to at least the apparent goods we judge to be the proper ends of at least some persons.

Jonas closes with a challenge I have heard from others in the Foundations of Ethics group. "Use your surplus. . . . The sceptical hedgings we will supply. . . ." It is too late in the history of theological thought for an academic theologian not to supply his or her own sceptical hedgings. Like Jonas, I believe religion is *a* source of light; if I did not I would be a sociologist or a philosopher, or be satisfied to do "religious studies." Maybe "the full blast from [one's] strongest guns" comes only when one is preaching and not when one is writing a theological paper for nontheological critics.

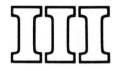

Science, Ethics, and Values

7

The Moral Psychology of Science

Stephen Toulmin

"The Reason is, and ought to be, The Slave of the Passions"
—David Hume

I

In recent years, one significant component of earlier philosophical discussion—what used to be called "moral psychology"—has fallen into unjustified neglect. Yet, to the extent that *motives* are of crucial importance to ethics, the philosophical analysis of talk about "motivation" can play a helpful part in showing how values achieve practical expression in actual conduct; and this remains true even where, on the face of it, the activities in question are as "purely intellectual" as those of the natural sciences. So, in the present chapter, I shall be raising questions about the *personal engagement* in sciences of scientists as human individuals.

We have lived too long (I shall argue) with the image of the basic scientist as the solitary embodiment of the pure reason— "voyaging through strange seas of thought, alone," like some isolated hadron moving at high velocity through field-free space—and of the life of science as committed to a passionless

223

objectivity. So, a myth has developed about the enterprise of natural science that too often deceives both its advocates and its critics. Supporters of science are tempted to take pride in its supposedly disinterested, dispassionate, and "value-free" character, in which they see the cutting edge of the objectivity that is its chief source of intellectual power.[1] Natural science is successful (on this view) just because its inquiries are purely "cognitive" and so undistorted by the affective preoccupations of individual scientists. Meanwhile, the opponents of science see in this purported objectivity the mark of its chief failing. Natural science ends by impoverishing our knowledge of the world (they retort) just because it shuts its eyes to all those affective channels through which alone real understanding might eventually be achieved.[2] I shall argue here that both these views are mistaken in their shared misconceptions about the "objectivity" of scientific work. Instead, we can hope to understand the values of science aright only if we first get our ideas about the motivation of scientific inquiry—and the moral significance of that motivation—back in proportion. Affect without cognition may be aimless; but cognition without affect is powerless, if not actually blind. The task is, therefore, not to *deny* the affective components in the life of science, but to understand them.

True, we have already begun to nibble away at the edges of the old image. For example, Frank Manuel's *Portrait of Isaac Newton* depicts the man who was for so long the totem figure of "rational" modern science as having worked under the impulsion of quite unexpected ambitions and confused self-perceptions.[3] Still, discrediting Newton's embodiment of the scientific ideal has not wholly reinforced the determination to "try harder." So, it is time to look again at the assumptions underlying the traditional ideal, in particular, at the notions that rationality itself can be a kind of motivation, and that activities pursued in a strictly "rational" spirit are to that extent "passionless."

If we accept these notions uncritically, we risk serious category confusions, which may lead to a needless undervaluing of the emotional (or affective) components in the life and work of science. This, in turn, may tempt us to play down both the individual moral choices involved when we commit ourselves to such a life, and also the moral accountability of the scientific community generally. By contrast, if we can develop a more satisfactory account of scientific motivation, this should bring with it a number of dividends. It should allow us to describe the collective scientific enterprise in more acceptable terms; to circumvent those implicit claims to moral immunity that have been—alternatively—both a major charm of the scientific life to those who pursue it, and a source of irritation to those who are only onlookers; and finally—not least—to begin extricating ourselves from the wreckage of those older dichotomies (cognitive/ affective, rational/emotional, thought/feeling, etc.) that still obstruct the road toward an adequate understanding of those human enterprises in which feeling powers thought, and emotion makes rationality effective.

II

How far, then, can rationality itself serve as a "motive" for scientific work? The chief products of science certainly include a great many *arguments*; indeed, the very success of a science might even be measured by the number and quality of the new arguments being generated within it at the time in question. Consequently, scientists pay a lot of attention to the merits of scientific arguments: the relevance of new evidence, the power of novel concepts, the soundness of proposed inferences, and the weight these all give to the resulting conclusions. As a result, the working currency of a science is largely comprised in the intellectual power, weight, or force of its arguments.

This intellectual power, weight, or force has two distinct aspects. For practical purposes, working scientists often treat the merits and shortcomings of scientific arguments as something *inherent* or *intrinsic*. Either the available evidence really is sufficient to support some conclusion, or it is insufficient, or its significance is marginal; either some new concept really does have powerful implications, or it does nothing much to help us, or its merits are as yet unclear; either sound inferences do really force some conclusion on us, or they fail to do so, or judgment needs to be suspended. . . . In each case, all competent and informed scientists will presumably reach the same positions, given only a knowledgeable and accurate scrutiny of the arguments in debate. For what *has* intellectual weight (i.e., intrinsic intellectual merit) deserves to *carry* weight (i.e., to be persuasive); and a scientific apprenticeship will presumably give the experienced scientist an ability to recognize intrinsic merits when he sees them.

All the same: leaving aside all questions about "deserts," we should be clear that the intrinsic merits of an argument alone do not ensure its actual capacity to move a reader or hearer. The power, weight, or force of an argument (or its elements) is not in itself a "motive." Only those who are *open to* the argument in question will be influenced by it: in order to be persuaded, they must be ready to change their minds in response to an argument of this particular kind. To consider whether some argument has the actual power to persuade a hearer or reader is thus quite a different matter from considering whether it has "intrinsic" intellectual power. It is to raise the question of "power," "weight," or "force" on a different level and in a different sense.

Indeed, it is even to treat the notion of an "argument" itself on a different level and in a different sense. If regarded as a network of propositions whose interrelations can be judged in intellectual terms, an "argument" has merits that can be discussed without reference to the number or character of the human beings who would acknowledge those merits. If regarded as a clash of opinions which we may participate in, be carried away by, and win or lose (by contrast), an "argument" has merits that are directly related to its persuasiveness. It is of little use for the defense attorney or scientific presenter, political speechwriter or business adviser, to have "powerful" propositional arguments at his disposal, if his actual oral arguments are so feeble that they leave everyone unmoved.[4]

With this initial distinction in mind—between *arguments* (power, weight, force, etc.) as concerned with the intellectual relations between propositions, and *arguments* (power, weight, force, etc.) as concerned with the actual persuasiveness of those interconnected statements—we can at once make two further points. In the first place, (1) an argument is operative within the scientific enterprise only if it actually *weighs with* some actual scientist; only if "the" reasons it provides for accepting certain conclusions engage the concerns of some actual scientist, and so can become "his" reasons for subscribing to those conclusions. This does not always happen at once. For some thirty years, the arguments that Gregor Mendel had formulated about "inheritable factors" as the key to genetic transmission left other botanists and zoologists unmoved. Precisely because of this fact, we now see Mendel's effective contribution to biology as dating only from the restatement of those arguments by Bateson, Correns, Tschermak and de Vries around the year 1900. (Were Mendel's arguments really *powerful* before 1900, then? This question is ambiguous. How we answer it will depend both on how we interpret the term "powerful," and also on how seriously we take the theoretical debate about heredity that went on during the 1860s, when Mendel first put forward his theories.)[5]

In the second place, (2) although we can sometimes focus on the intrinsic merits of scientific arguments in isolation from all individual scientists, this fact does not entail that the actual enterprise of science is purely "cognitive," and so strictly rational, affectless, and value-free. By focusing our attention in this way, we too easily turn away from all questions about how the scientists involved, whether individually or collectively, *in fact came* to take the intellectual steps they did; instead, we end by asking only what steps it was *appropriate and proper* to take, given all the available considerations. Maybe they were, in fact, moved by undiluted curiosity, maybe by conformism or a desire to shock, maybe by a mixture of motives: it all depends on how far they were ready to be moved by the intrinsic merits of those particular novel arguments. And this, in turn, all depends on their having been both psychically disposed, and also intellectually prepared, to accept them.

To say that an individual scientist is *psychically* disposed to accept an argument is to say, among other things, that he is personally free to move that way—or, indeed, to move at all, rather than clinging to earlier opinions despite new arguments. To say that he is *intellectually* prepared to do so is to say, furthermore, that the move represents a straightforward and manageable change from his earlier position.

So the power, weight, and force of scientific concepts, arguments, and evidence are operative within the enterprise of science—can show their power by appearing compelling to scientists, and so "weighing" with them—only when they are capable of engaging the specific concerns of the scientists involved. In a phrase, the intrinsic merits of scientific arguments are manifested in the activities of actual scientists only when their *disciplinary relevance* enables them to do so. The "intrinsic power" of novel scientific arguments is matched by an equal "effective power"—their proper intellectual merits are translated into an operative capacity to persuade—only if they are directly relevant to the currently accepted concepts, theories, and problems of the science concerned.

III

This, however, is only a preliminary conclusion, and we need to pursue the point further. If scientists are to accept the arguments they do, it is not only necessary that they have the *particular* interests required; it is necessary also—and *a fortiori*—to recruit their *general* scientific interests. And it is here that the direct route into the individual moral psychology of science is customarily blocked off. Having reached this point, we are invited to assume that any particular scientist's commitment, whether to science in general, or to some specific line of inquiry, is a direct response to the intrinsic charms of intellectual worth. The "virtues" which Alasdair MacIntyre sees lying at the heart of the collective enterprises of science are presumed to have a self-evident attraction for particular scientists.[6] The fact that "good science" is capable of engaging the interests of individual human beings at all is taken as self-explanatory.

Yet, surely we need only make this assumption explicit to see how dubious it is. A taste for natural science or pure mathematics or legal theory is no more universal than a taste for classical music or pop art or modern dance; and the divergences of taste, even among committed scientists, are as great as those between (say) lovers of Vivaldi and devotees of Stockhausen. Once we are of a mind to give it our trained attention, the cogency of a mathematical proof or the elegance of a physiological experiment may constitute a "reason" for being moved by it; but however powerful that intrinsic "reason," it is not an automatic "motive" for accepting the resulting theorem or experimental result. For that, we also need to have appropriate "springs of action": we must, for instance, be susceptible to the formal fascination of mathematics, intrigued by the art of experimental demonstration, preoccupied with these specific physiological issues, or otherwise motivated to focus our attentions on the matter in hand.

Even after acknowledging the claims of disciplinary relevance, therefore, we are only making a first beginning on the individual psychology of scientific inquiry. Granted the significance of the professional collectivity in defining the virtues of any science and determining the effectiveness of its arguments, we must also consider how individual scientists come to join that collectivity in the first place. Since the inclination to take up the work of science is not a universal human characteristic, the decision to do so presumably involves a mobilization of impulses, inclinations, ambitions and/or affects, which might alternatively have been channeled in quite other directions. Curiosity and competitiveness, spontaneous joy and the wish to please, internal censorship and delight in play, grandiosity and openness. . . . all the components normally involved in the development of an individual's general personality, character, and mode of life can presumably find expression in the particular activities of his intellectual life; and indeed, without the intervention of some such "springs of action," his professional work would scarcely have got started. In short, the natural sciences exist at all only because there is something in the work of science *for* the individual scientists involved.

What sort of thing will that "something" be? In answering that question, we shall have to pay close attention, on the one hand, to the motives that inform *any* kind of fruitful and effective human collaboration. Collective institutions and enterprises of all kinds—churches and universities, guilds and brotherhoods—develop their own patterns of expectations and standards of achievements; and in this way they come to define their own characteristic "virtues." So, we come to know what it means, in general terms, to be a "devoted" priest or teacher, master craftsman, or whatever. On the other hand (we must recognize) the virtues characteristic of any collective enterprise must be capable of "running with the grain" of the individual persons involved. The activity of being a professional minister or physician, research scientist, or whatever must bring its own real psychic rewards to individual practitioners, if the collective enterprise itself is to survive.

What kinds of psychic rewards are in question? Once again, at this point, we risk an ambiguity. (The "virtues" of a scientific enterprise can be as equivocal as the "powers" of a scientific argument.) For those who are *already* committed to the life of science, the only indispensable "virtue" is embodied in *the doing of science* itself. All fully committed scientists, that is, derive satisfaction from the conscientious and effective pursuit of their scientific work. (There's a tautology for you!) To say no more than that, however, leaves untouched several deeper questions: (1) how the work of science *comes to have* charms for those who do eventually commit themselves to it; (2) why those charms are apparent only to some and invisible to many others; and (3) what other, ancillary considerations may work together (synergize) with this central "virtue" to retain and reinforce the interest of one or another particular scientist.

Once we start looking at particular individuals, indeed, we may even come to doubt whether the intrinsic merit of science as such—either the essential "virtue" of a scientific enterprise, or the inherent "rationality" of intellectual work itself—either *must be,* or ever *in fact is,* wholly its own reward. There are so many routes by which other more familiar impulses, passions, affects and the rest can be recruited, and so many other more familiar rewards to be gained from participation in this work, that the assumption of any specific and essential "motive" as the only spring of action "proper to" science can be called into question as multiplying entities *praeter necessitatem.*

Run through the individuals of our acquaintance who are committed to some given branch of science, asking in each case what deeper concerns feed into that individual's involvement in the science; we may not have to dig very far before we bring these to light, and we shall often end by giving different answers about each person. Just now and then scientists have made their extra-scientific motives explicit, as when Jacques Loeb explained how he had moved from philosophy into physiology in the hope of pursuing the problem of free will more effectively.[7] But the existence of such idiosyncratic motives can frequently be inferred only from circumstantial evidence: from the individual scientist's extracurricular activities, from the topics he chooses for commencement addresses in later life, from the style of his work or his writing, and so on. (One biologist's scientific interests may reflect his theological commitments, since in his eyes the marvels of evolution still testify to the Wisdom of the Creator; another may value evolution, rather, as an ally in discrediting the belief in a Divine Creator; a third may find in evolutionary biology a psychic support for our ethical beliefs; and so on.)

Without our assuming any single impulse specific to scientific work as such, we can thus recognize that many more general springs of action are capable of being mobilized in ways which give sufficient motivation to one individual or another to pursue the work (even, at times, the drudgery) of his particular science, and so to be open to the intrinsic power of its ideas and arguments. The mere existence of a sound argument, accordingly, no more guarantees a motive to accept its results than the mere existence of a duty guarantees a motive to perform it. Despite all of Kant's counsels of perfection, the Reason is no more completely dependent for its scientific fruitfulness on evoking a pure emotion of "respect for rational principles as such" than Duty is wholly dependent for its moral effectiveness on mobilizing an unadulterated feeling of "respect for the moral law."

Some individual scientists, mathematicians, and other scholars, of course, may finally achieve the status of "intellectual saints," having dissociated their intellectual activities from any last dilution by ulterior motives and come to pursue truth itself out of a "pure will." Even so, this "pure will" still presumably mobilizes and channels affective inclinations directed earlier toward more worldly goals. As we find it embodied in actual human beings, that is to say, the pure love of truth is a somewhat sophisticated and far from self-explanatory product of the individual's personal development. In that sense, the very existence of science depends on every active scientist having had a prior affective investment *of some kind* in the work of science; and in this respect we can go along accordingly with David Hume's view that "Reason" is capable of being efficacious only if it is, among other things, a "Slave of the Passions."

IV

Confronted with this demand for a developmental psychology of science that does justice to the affective springs of scientific interest and inquiry, some people will respond by questioning whether anything useful can be said about these springs of a truly *general* kind. No doubt, we can collect anecdotal life histories about particular individuals who in due course became scientists, and ask what specific motives drew them into scientific work. (Of all the descendants of Charles Darwin and T.H. Huxley in their generations, for instance, why did Julian Huxley and Richard Keynes follow their ancestor into biology, while John Maynard Keynes became an economist, Geoffrey Keynes a surgeon and literary critic, and Aldous Huxley a novelist?) But is there a good reason to suppose that we can establish any definite regularities— to say nothing of universal laws—governing the psychological paths by which some talented young people find their ways into science, rather than into other alternative vocations or professions?

This doubt is one that we must respect. The whole field of individual psychology is exposed to a standing temptation to overgeneralize; and it should be a sufficient objection to any psychological theory, if it leaves no scope for individual variation and idiosyncrasy. However, the need to respect the proper demands of individuality does not wholly eliminate the need for general theories or theoretical investigations. To the contrary, even if we acknowledge the importance of collecting detailed life histories about the psychic development of particular scientists, the problem, *in what terms* these life histories should be stated if they are to be fully illuminating, will still need to be faced. And, at this point, we can indicate just why the developmental affective psychology of science is a crucial problem for traditional theory. For it is precisely the continuing inclination of psychologists to discuss "cognition" and "affect" in isolation from one another that is the most serious obstacle to a fruitful attack on this problem.

Thus, on the one hand, developmental psychologists in the tradition of Piaget write about the sequence of tasks and achievements that a child masters in the course of "growing up," without paying any close attention to the specific impulses and/or emotions that serve as the child's "motivation" for attacking those tasks. (Somehow, it seems to Piaget that a detailed scrutiny of that sequence of tasks itself will reveal in due course sufficient *implicit motives* to account for the child's passage from each "stage" in its cognitive development to the next.)[8] Meanwhile, the classical psychoanalytic approach focuses on emotional conflicts in a child's life of kinds that can lead to functional disablement in later life, without considering directly why some functions and abilities may prove intrinsically more satisfying to the growing child than others. (Yet an understanding of the ways in which psychic development can go off the rails, emotionally speaking, leaves entirely unanswered all questions about *what it is* for a child to develop in emotionally healthy ways.) Only in the last few years has any serious sign appeared of ideas that may help to bridge this gap in the vocabulary of psychological theory.[9]

The starting point of the present paper was, thus, the observation that "reasons" and "motives" are not themselves two kinds of motives; on the contrary, other "springs of action" are needed if we are to pay attention to, be moved by, accept the conclusions of, or act in accordance with even the best of "reasons" or "arguments." As a result, we must be skeptical about all attempts to classify the activities of individual agents according to the supposed "rationality" or "nonrationality" of their *motives*. Such dichotomies as "cognition versus affect," "intellect versus emotion," and "reason versus passion," too easily become invitations to fall back into the initial elementary confusion of reasons with motives. Rational enterprises are not, as such, required to be free from passions of all kinds: they are simply enterprises within which we are expected to discount and set aside all *fruitless and irrelevant* passions.

On one natural interpretation of the term, indeed, a wholly "passion-free" enterprise could never even get started—hence, the force of the tag from Hume with which I began. (At the very least, an effective natural scientist must "have a bent for," and be "drawn toward," scientific inquiries.) Nor is it helpful to suppose that there are any purely "cognitive" activities, from which all elements of "affect" and/or "volition" have been banished. Once again, the question is not *whether or not* our affects/ emotions/impulses and other springs of action are mobilized in the course of "cognitively structured" activities; rather, it is *how* these springs of action are recruited and put to work toward specific "cognitive" ends. Nor, for that matter, can we usefully depict the life of the intellect as being, in itself, intrinsically "unemotional." Where (we might ask) would such human activities as science and mathematics be without the joy of discovery, the anxiety of suspense, or the disheartenment of frustration?

The insistence on treating the "rational" and the "emotional" as essentially opposed often serves, in practice, as a rhetorical device for insuring that public, collective interests and considerations are given priority over private, personal ones. The term "rational" is then used simply as a label for collectively relevant (intersubjective) considerations, "emotional" for personally relevant (subjective) ones. Even without any dependence on the dubious contrast between "internal" feelings and "external" reasons, private or personal interests are presumed—on this view—to weigh with an agent by way of his emotions, whereas public or collective interests supposedly operate on him by way of his intellect. Yet, this way of presenting the matter misrepresents the contrast between the two kinds of interests. Public, collective interests may provide an agent with "good reasons" to act as he does; but he will be moved to act in conformity with them only if they also engage his personal concerns, and so mobilize his springs of action. Correspondingly, whatever considerations ultimately channel his conduct, and/or its justification—whether the resulting action is self-seeking or self-sacrificing—the agent may act either deliberately or impulsively, either coolly or in the heat of the moment. The vigor of his emotions, or the character of his affective involvement, thus has no direct bearing on the personal or collective nature of the interests served by his conduct. Collective interests can be pursued with passion, personal interests with calm deliberation.

Instead of purging our rational enterprises of affective content, we have in fact an alternative course open to us. William Gass has written perceptively about the ontogeny of artistic creation and aesthetic sensibility, and his line of thought can be extended for our purposes.[10] As they enter into the psychic development of individual human beings, Gass argues, art and aesthetic response typically involve a "stylization" of play and desire. However "formal" their aims and merits, works of art are sophisticated expressions of the same basic impulses and wishes that earlier led the child into less strictly organized activities; while the viewer or listener's aesthetic response to a work of art likewise recruits feelings and inclinations that operated during childhood in less focused directions. The philosophical problem about art, as a result, is neither to demonstrate that artistic and aesthetic impulses are absolutely unique, nor to equate—and so "reduce"— them to other, less exalted drives. Rather, it is to show how the progressive differentiation and "stylization" of their products or outcomes transforms the child's early impulses toward play and delight into their distinctive adult forms.

If art and aesthetics reflect the stylization of native impulses— e.g., play and desire—natural science similarly represents the channeling and directing of other equally native impulses: exploration, curiosity, or whatever. With science as with art, to focus attention on "ontogeny" is not to deny the special character of science, nor to equate, still less "reduce," scientific activity to infantile curiosity or childhood exploration. The "rationality" of natural science, too, can thus be seen as residing less in the specific motives of its practitioners than in the form and structure of its end products. The passions that move scientists to pursue their research in adult life will have moved them earlier, as children, to explore the world (or their own ideas) in less formally structured ways. When they eventually commit themselves to the life of the intellect, the demands of rationality simply transform and channel the directions in which those same "passions" operate: i.e., determine the outcome of activities whose motives and substance remain the same passions that have been with them since childhood. (More exactly, the demands of rationality begin to determine the manner in which those later outcomes are to be *publicly criticized and justified*.)

If anything is unique about science, it is thus the character of its collective procedures and results. There is no additional virtue in assuming that all those who become scientists are activated by a single specific motive directed solely at science. On the contrary, the central question in the psychology of science is how— given its abstract concepts, its demanding procedures, and its rigorous standards of criticism—the rational enterprise of science is able to engage and mobilize preexisting affective energies available in the personal development of its participants; and, in particular, to what special, typical vicissitudes this process of development may be exposed along the way.

V

Finally, then, supposing that we reopen these questions about the individual psychology of science, why should this make any difference to our ideas about the *ethics* of scientific work? (Why do I label the resulting insights as contributions to *moral* psychology?) This question, too, needs to be addressed on the collective, as well as on the personal level. We must ask both how the collective choices of scientific institutions and professional groups are to be judged from a moral point of view, and also how the individual scientist's commitment to science is to be subjected to moral scrutiny.

The road into the psychology of science has been blocked off (I argued) because, by polite convention, only one motive for doing science has been accepted as professionally respectable: viz., an unworldly love of truth and/or rationality for its own sake. There is, of course, a strong element of pious fraud to this convention. Yet, once we have accepted it, we become powerless to prevent the moral neutralization of the scientific enterprise. To the extent that the choices made by scientists in the course of their work are indeed made under this one comprehensive motive—as being so many alternative expressions of the scientist's "passion for rationality"—it might perhaps be legitimate to abstract the *intellectual content* of those choices wholly from their *moral context,* and judge them solely and exclusively in terms of disciplinary criteria and requirements. And this is something that many professional scientists are quite happy to see done.

Whatever helps to make the intellectual priorities of scientific inquiry a matter for criticism by disciplinary standards alone helps also to reinforce the professional autonomy of science, and so protects the collective scientific enterprise from interference by "outsiders." But this kind of autonomy can be achieved and maintained only at a certain *political* price. It may be professionally desirable to encourage single-minded concentration on the techniques and problems of a single scientific field among the younger apprentices to the professional guild of science. But it is no more practicable today to shield the collective affairs of the scientific community entirely from outside criticism, including *ethical* criticism, than it is to protect (say) the professional institutions of law and medicine against the demand for public scrutiny and accountability. (It might throw dazzling light on the human brain if neurophysiologists decided to study "the influence on higher mental functioning of psychoactive agents administered in the form of airborne droplets," as being a ready and effective method of investigating the biochemical keys to various neural pathways; but that scientific decision will look very different if it is judged in the context of, say, a program of work on nerve gases sponsored by the East German Department of Defense.)

Similarly, on the individual plane, once we set aside the phantasmagoria of "rationality for rationality's sake," which merely isolates our motives for intellectual work from all other intelligible motives, moral issues arise once again about any particular scientist's involvement in his work. Suppose, for instance, that a scientist is entirely candid about the charms that his work has for him. He will, no doubt, say a good deal about how he was first drawn to the concerns of science, particularly *his* science—how his early childhood curiosity became initially engaged with wildlife, and in due course focused in on (say) flying beetles; or how he came to value the delayed gratifications of professional fame and craftsmanlike self-satisfaction as substitutes for earlier and more direct rewards, such as parental approval. But this universal, commonplace scenario is unlikely to tell the whole story, and he may also acknowledge other, more mixed and even questionable motives. For instance, by devoting his personal energies to prestigious, but highly abstract inquiries, he has been able to avoid emotionally demanding situations in which he would have had to deal with complex and conflicting personal demands directed at him by others. And the impulse to avoid such external demands may prove, in turn, on closer self-examination, to spring less from proper pride than from fear of failure. In all honesty, therefore, he may finally conclude that his own commitment to the life of science has, on a certain level, been psychically self-serving, and even "inauthentic." His devotion to (say) entomology, while sincere enough in itself, has been strengthened and reinforced by other, more personal psychic rewards.[11]

So, when we ask ourselves what there is *in* Science *for* scientists, it is not enough to answer—whether ingenuously or disingenuously—"Why, Truth and Rationality, of course." Rather, we should accept this question in all its richness and acknowledge the full psychic and moral complexities of the motives that can lead us, as private persons, to find individual satisfaction as a result of committing our professional lives to (say) topology, or physical cosmology, or psychopharmacology. In particular, it is an intriguing question of psychodynamics, how talented scientists learn to distance themselves from their own ideas, in the interest of scientific criticism, and reconcile themselves to the apparent sacrifice of any personal "psychic interests" in their own brainchildren.

Is this process facilitated (for instance) by early apprenticeship to a charismatic teacher, whose standards the student "internalizes," so recruiting all the forces of conscience, paternal-filial attachment, and/or the "superego"? Must this process be reinforced by the collective institutions of professional life, and so by a sense that any falling away from the "rational ideals" of science will be an infraction against the scientific collectivity, as well as against the individual's conscience? Or is it normally strengthened, in addition, by an admixture of narcissistic grandiosity, i.e., by the individual scientist's tendency to impose unrealistic standards of achievement on his own performances, as a defense against the fears aroused by his own human fallibility? Will there thus, from a personal point of view, be a common element of perfectionism and overscrupulosity in this insistence of exemplifying in one's own person the undiluted devotion to truth and rationality conventionally claimed for the collective scientific enterprise?[12] These questions by themselves hint at the complex issues of personality development and moral judgment that need to be addressed in this field; and the scanty material currently available by way of evidence leaves us in no position to do more than speculate about possible answers.

VI

For the purposes of moral psychology, the key term in our discussion is perhaps "vicissitudes." To the extent that the affective development of future scientists displays any typical episodes, leading to the development of recognizable "psychopathologies," the nature of scientific motivation becomes a deeper and more genuinely *ethical* issue. Thus, Gerald Holton recently raised questions about the ethical concerns of young scientists, along lines hinted at above.[13] Faced with emotional conflicts (he suggests) many talented young people today display a certain psychic frailty: a commitment to the somewhat abstract inquiries of natural science can then give them a psychic "defense" against the pain of having to deal publicly with complex ethical issues. The single-valued nature of the traditional scientific life thus shields them from the emotional difficulties of other more worldly pursuits, and in this way they acquire a vested *personal* interest in the claim that the natural sciences are "value-free."

This hypothesis can easily be misunderstood. In suggesting that ethical frailty or psychic defensiveness plays a part in the recruitment of some scientists, Holton is not of course putting forward any universal generalization; still less is he implying—like Theodore Roszak and other recent romantic critics of science—that a wholehearted commitment to modern science is in itself the mark of ethical insensitivity. (On the contrary, his evidence suggests that it is, if anything, the mark of ethical *hyper*sensitivity.) So it may be helpful to compare Holton's thesis, at this point, with another claim that many people have also found perplexing: viz., Freud's thesis that Art is a sublimation of Sex—i.e., that artistic creation and sexual life are alternate adult expressions of the same "libidinal" energies, affects, and/or impulses, which are present in us all from infancy.

If Freud is right, the question may always be raised about any individual painter or writer or musician,

> How completely have the artistic and sexual aspects of libidinal expression become differentiated in the course of his development? How far does his commitment to the artist's work rest on a single-minded devotion to the demands of the art, as such; and how far is it still colored by an admixture of artistically irrelevant motives, whether sexual or others?

(To pose Freud's question in these terms is not to imply that single-minded purity of commitment, uncolored by other motives, is even desirable, to say nothing of indispensable. In Art as much as in Science, mixed motives may well be the order of the day.) If Holton is right, parallel questions may always be raised about any individual scientist:

> How far is his commitment to science personally disinterested, and directed solely at the specific virtues of the particular scientific discipline in question? And how completely is the charm that science's abstract inquiries have for him free from any suspicion (say) of an admixture with moral frailty or other scientifically irrelevant motives?

This may seem at first glance a topic for individual psychology alone, but the issues involved cannot be wholly detached from their collective context. For the established virtues of any collective enterprise must (as I remarked earlier) "run with the grain of" the personalities of the particular individuals who make up the collective. So, the professional standards of the community of science may, in certain respects, reflect not just the methodological needs imposed on scientific work by the problematics of scientific disciplines, but also the common personal needs and failings typical of "scientists" as human individuals. And this observation may serve, in conclusion, to throw some light on the deeper roots of the analogy that John Ziman has drawn, between the professional life of twentieth-century science and the life of the medieval orders.[14]

It is not just that the scientific life is in many respects a twentieth-century successor to the medieval monastic life. To go further, the "monastic orders" of modern science have largely become orders of *contemplatives,* whose devotion to Truth excludes other more worldly obligations. Now, one recurring question in the literature of monasticism is an ethical question: viz., how an order of pure contemplatives can remain in a state of grace. It is not that the rigorous separation of contemplatives from the world exposes them to an increased temptation toward worldly pleasures. Quite the contrary: the contemplative mode of life erects barriers between them and the world, which too easily acquire a charm of their own and become an excuse for moral irresponsibility.

The professional isolation of the modern scientific life may well give rise to similar problems. The disinterested pursuit of scientific truth does not enhance the attraction of scientists toward other more worldly ends. Rather, the "purity" of the scientific life has its own powerful attractions, which easily seem to justify a turning away from ethical issues. So, once we are launched into an examination of the moral psychology of science, in both its individual and collective aspects, we may find that the *vita scientifica* involves ethical difficulties and complexities no less acute than those traditionally associated with the *vita monastica,* which was its prototype and forerunner.

NOTES

1. The image of "scientific objectivity" of the *cutting edge* of discovery is used by writers whose views of science may differ quite substantially in other respects, although the general tone of their arguments is inclined to be positivistic. For a useful historical treatment, see Charles C. Gillispie, *The Edge of Objectivity* (Princeton, N.J.: Princeton University Press, 1960).
2. This is the burden of the argument in, e.g., Theodore Roszak's book, *Where the Wasteland Ends* (Garden City: Doubleday, 1972). See also my discussion of the antiscience movement in the CIBA Symposium, *Civilization and Science* (Amsterdam and New York: Associated Scientific Publishers, 1972).
3. Frank Manuel, *A Portrait of Isaac Newton* (Cambridge, Mass.: Harvard University Press, 1968), assembles a remarkable body of

argument about Newton's deeper motivation: specifically about the Divine "calling" he felt to decipher the cosmic handiwork.

4. For a fuller discussion of this point see my book, *Knowing and Acting* (New York: Macmillan, 1975), esp. Part II.
5. The immediate fate of Mendel's ideas has been frequently discussed in recent years. For a useful analysis, see E.B. Gasking, "Why Was Mendel's Work Ignored?", *Journal of the History of Ideas,* vol. 20, pp. 60-84, 1959.
6. See Alasdair MacIntyre, "Objectivity in Morality and Objectivity in Science," in this volume.
7. Jacques Loeb, *The Mechanistic Conception of Life* (Chicago: University of Chicago Press, 1912; reprinted, Cambridge, Mass.: Harvard University Press, 1964).
8. For a fuller discussion, see T. Mischel, Academic Press, ed., *Cognitive Psychology and Epistemology* (New York: 1969); and C.F. Feldman and S.E. Toulmin "Logic and the Theory of Mind," *Nebraska Symposium on Motivation, 1975* (Lincoln, Neb.: University of Nebraska Press, 1977).
9. On this topic, I have personally learned a great deal from discussions at the Center for Psychosocial Studies, Chicago, and at the Chicago Psychoanalytic Institute.
10. See William Gass, *Fiction and the Figures of Life* (New York: Knopf, 1970).
11. Compare Lionel Trilling's interesting series of essays, *Sincerity and Authenticity* (Cambridge, Mass.: Harvard University Press, 1972).
12. For relevant discussions of narcissism, grandiosity, infallibility and associated phenomena in the development of emotional life, see H. Kohut, *The Analysis of the Self* (New York: International Universities Press, 1971) and *The Restoration of the Self* (New York: International Universities Press, 1977).
13. See Gerald Holton, "Scientific Optimism and Societal Concerns," *Hastings Center Report,* vol. 5, no. 6, December 1975, pp. 39-47.
14. John Ziman, *Public Knowledge* (Cambridge, Eng.: Cambridge University Press, 1978).

8

The Poverty of Scientism and the Promise of Structuralist Ethics

Gunther S. Stent

THE IDEOLOGY OF SCIENTISM, the belief that the methods and insights of science are applicable to the entire sphere of human activity, aims to validate moral acts on scientific grounds. Indeed, this perspective sees scientific knowledge as the only kind of authentic knowledge. From this viewpoint, the only rational alternative would be an ethical nihilism under which everything is permitted, since the traditional theological grounding of ethics is seen as a morass of irrational superstitions belonging to a pre-scientific age.[1] This perception is widespread, and underlies the broad popular appeal of scientism, despite its more or less general rejection by contemporary philosophers and the often-repeated exposure of its potentially dangerous political consequences as a rational basis for the totalitarian state.[2] Thus acceptance of scientistic beliefs is usually the unstated but implicit ethical premise held by the opposing sides in current debates—"establishment" versus "science-for-the-people," "progress" versus "ecology" and "zero-population-growth."

In considering the scientistic approach to ethics it is useful to distinguish two different types of scientism—hard-core and soft-core. Believers in hard-core scientism take the view that moral norms and values can, or even must, be justified on scientific grounds. Believers in soft-core scientism may acknowledge that valid moral values can be justified on nonscientific grounds, but they still insist on the primacy of science as a guide to moral action.

Hard-core Scientism

Biology is the branch of science which obviously seems most relevant for hard-core scientism. For example, lessons gained from the study of evolution, such as the idea that survival of the species is an authentic value, are thought to have ethical relevance; hence "fitness" in the Darwinian sense is an objectively "good" quality. Herbert Spencer was one of the main nineteenth-century apostles of this particular version of hard-core scientism, which still has many adherents today. Thus, Spencer thought that the "good" can be identified with the concept of "more highly evolved," or simply with progress *tout court*.[3]

Another biological discipline often cited as a source of authentic moral values is ethology which concerns animal behavior. Here, moral goodness is assigned to those righteous features of human behavior, such as altruism, mother-love, or male supremacy, for which parallels, or sometimes merely similarities, can be found in the animal world, and for whose functional adaptiveness in nature credible explanations can be offered. Moreover, moral badness is assigned to features of human behavior, such as cannibalism or killing fellow members of one's species, which animals are alleged to avoid in the wild and exhibit only under the sociopathological conditions of captivity.[4] Although the ethological approach to ethics is most often used for trivial, a posteriori rationalizations of values generally held anyway and traditionally justified on other, nonscientistic grounds,[5] a not quite so trivial reversal of that procedure has surfaced recently. Here the ethological sanction of conventional morals is stood on its head; and traditionally negatively valued aspects of human behavior, such as aggression[6] or homosexuality,[7] are declared to be either morally neutral, or even to have positive value, on the grounds that animals also exhibit them in nature for apparently adaptive reasons.

On first sight, the diverse versions of hard-core scientism all appear to represent a logical short-circuit. For the authority of science and the claim for the authenticity of its knowledge depends critically on the very belief that scientific statements, being based on impersonal observations and measurements, are objective and value-free. But it is obviously logically invalid to derive conclusions that predicate values from value-free premises. Thus, in the case of the evolutionistic moral codes based on species survival or higher complexity, no moral value judgment can logically follow from the objective observations that live specimens of *Homo sapiens* exist or that *Homo* is more complex than the frog *Rana*. Moral values can be derived from these observations only if they are combined with nonobjective, nonscientific, value-laden premises, such as "human survival is good" or "biological complexity is good." It seems likely that the logical error of the evolutionistic moral code has its roots in the semantically troublesome "fitness" concept of Darwinian natural selection theory. Whereas in ordinary English discourse "fitness" connotes value, in the context of evolutionary theory, particularly under the mathematical formalisms of neo-Darwinian population genetics, "fitness" is supposed to be a value-free algebraic parameter that refers to the contribution made by a particular hereditary trait to the differential reproduction rate of the organism which manifests it. But even within the purely descriptive scientific domain, the "fitness" concept is troublesome, as evidenced by the current dispute among students of molecular evolution concerning the role that natural selection, as opposed to random genetic drift, is likely to have played in organic evolution.[8] Moreover, the attempt to derive value from ethological insights appears as merely a bizarre extension to the lower orders of Rousseau's romantic notion of the noble savage, or a scientistic yearning for the Good Old, pre-Fall Days in Eden.

On second sight, however, the derivation of value from scientific statements may not be logically invalid after all, but for reasons that can give little comfort to the adherents of hard-core scientism. For it is held by some contemporary philosophers[9] that the kind of impersonal and objective science on behalf of which authority is claimed is only an ideal and does not, in fact, exist. Since scientists are human beings rather than Martians, since they and the phenomena they observe necessarily interact, and since they use language to communicate their results, it follows that scientific statements, particularly in biology,[10] are rarely free of terms which imply functions, roles, and values. For instance, it is entirely possible that, protestations of neo-Darwinian population geneticists notwithstanding, the concept of "fitness" cannot be purged of all value content without losing its explanatory power for evolutionary processes. In other words, many scientific statements may be what Patrick Heelan has called "manifest images."[11] Although in this case hard-core scientism would not fail on logical grounds, the idol of the uniquely authentic scientific knowledge that inspires scientism in the first place would turn out to stand on feet of clay.

Soft-core Scientism

Since adherents of soft-core scientism do not claim to justify moral norms or values on scientific grounds, they escape the logical dilemma of the hard-core. But the more restricted claim of soft-core scientism for the primacy of science as a guide to moral action also fails, if not on logical, then on empirical or practical grounds. First, quite apart from the fact that this milder version of scientism usually neglects the subjective realm of the affects, it turns out that its adherents seem to have trouble bearing constantly in mind the admittedly nonscientific basis of the moral code.

I offer here one concrete example of this difficulty, based on a recent personal experience at a conference on "Biology and the Future of Man," held at the Sorbonne.[12] I was one of several biologists who took part in a panel discussion ostensibly devoted to defining the stage in embryonal development at which human life can be said to begin. Although this topic seemed to concern a purely technical question, it turned out to be supercharged with moral content, for the French parliament was then considering a bill to legalize abortion; in view of the extensive coverage given to the conference by the news media, it was obvious that our discussion was meant to influence the outcome of the debate in the *Assemblée Nationale*.

One of my fellow panelists was the cytogeneticist, Jerome Lejeune, a leader of the French "right-to-life" movement opposing the abortion bill. Lejeune maintained that human life begins at the moment of fertilization of the ovum by the sperm, since it is at that moment that the future person acquires a genetic individuality. Hence, abortion at any time is murder and must not be sanctioned by law in a civilized state. Most of the other panelists took the view that human life really begins only at some later developmental stage, prior to which there cannot exist any moral obstacles to artificial termination of pregnancy. Some thought life begins at the stage at which the heart muscles begin to beat rhythmically; others favored the stage at which electrical signals can first be detected in the brain; and still others thought life really begins only with parturition.

Although from the political point of view the debate was evidently effective, in that the abortion bill was eventually passed, from a philosophical point of view the discussion was quite futile. Neither Lejeune's genetic nor his opponents' physiological arguments addressed the underlying moral issue, namely, the generally accepted proscription of the taking of human life. Both Lejeune and his adversaries based their arguments on biological knowledge gained from the study of animal development, without considering that there are no moral restrictions against killing the nonhuman subjects of such studies. That is, the panelists did not seem to recognize that whereas it may be possible to have a strictly value-free scientific discussion on the subject of the most meaningful or heuristically useful definition of the beginning of the profane life of a vertebrate, mammalian, or even primate embryo, it is quite another matter to define the beginning of the sacred life of a human embryo. Any such discussion must begin with a consideration of why human life is morally protected in the first place and must confront the deep problem of the special status we confer on fellow humans, as compared to other denizens of the living world. This lack of recognition of the true nature of the problem under discussion was particularly vexing because the panel was seated in the Great Amphitheater of the Sorbonne, facing a statue of René Descartes. After all, three centuries earlier, Descartes had not only laid the philosophical foundations for physiology by advancing the fruitful notion that the human body is a machine, but he had also taken pains to point out that since moral principles do not apply to machines, man, to whom moral principles do apply, must be more than an automaton in human shape. And what makes man more than a machine is that he has a soul. Hence, when asking within a moral context when human life begins, the panelists— Cartesians one and all—should have been trying to focus on that moment when the embryo acquires a soul, or, in modern parlance, becomes a person. And that problem cannot be settled on genetic or physiological grounds.

A second, more serious deficiency of soft-core scientism is that it embraces the dubious empirical proposition that the realization of moral aims is necessarily impeded by acts that are motivated by objectively false beliefs. Indeed, a more extreme version of this proposition makes the demonstrably false claim that to escape doom a society must not base its organization on scientific falsehoods. This claim is itself false because one can point to many societies of the past which operated in a reasonably successful and stable manner while making value judgements based on witchcraft, astrology, prophecy, and other practices that we now know to be scientifically unsound. The reason why objectively false beliefs can promote the realization of moral aims is that social relations are complex, multi-causal, and highly nonlinear phenomena and that any aim must be seen as an optimization rather than maximization of value parameters. This fact is generally recognized by cultural anthropologists since Bronislaw Malinowski[13] pointed out that the function of myths and rites is to strengthen the traditions that help to maintain a social way of life. Thus, although the false belief of the Hopi Indians that they can bring about rain by dancing may have been harmful for their agriculture, the rain dance itself provided for a communal cohesion whose benefits may have outweighed the potential gains in crop yield which abandonment of that false belief might have produced.

These considerations are relevant for the current hubbub in the United States and Britain about research on the hereditary basis of intelligence, whose totalitarian miasma can be traced to this feature of soft-core scientism. The opposing sides in this dispute both appear to accept the validity of the proposition that if there *were* a significant variation in the genetic contribution to intelligence between individuals, or between racial groups, then this factor ought to be taken into account in the organization of society. Since to the opponents of such research the mere consideration of the notion of hereditary determinants of intelligence, let alone taking it into account in social action, is an ethically inadmissible underpinning of racist ideology, they seem to feel morally obliged to deny outright the possibility of any connection between heredity and intelligence. Just like Christian Morgenstern's Palmström, they reason "pointedly, that which must not, cannot be."[14]

The proponents of research in hereditary determinants of intelligence, on the other hand, appear to be convinced that the failure to give due recognition to the existence of hereditary differences has pernicious social consequences and that, therefore, every effort must be made to identify the genetic basis of intelligence in a scientifically valid manner. This conclusion is not, however, rationally self-evident. For instance, let us consider Society A, which falsely believes that there is no hereditary contribution to intelligence (if that belief were really false, that is) and utilizes its educational resources less efficiently than Society B, which "tracks" its pupils according to a scientifically validated familial or ethnic prognosis (if such a prognosis were possible, that is). Cultural anthropologists might easily conclude under these circumstances that the losses sustained by Society A due to its falsely based educational system are more than outweighed vis-à-vis Society B by a greater communal cohesion, fostered by the (false) belief in innate human equality.

The most serious deficiency of soft-core scientism, however, derives from its overestimation of the power of science to provide an authentic understanding of just those phenonema which are most relevant for the ethical domain. That is, the physical sciences whose propositions are the most solidly validated have the least bearing on the realization of moral aims, whereas the propositions of the human sciences, which have the most bearing on the realization of moral aims, are conspicuously devoid of objective validation. Biology occupies an intermediate position between these two extremes, with respect both to the validity and the moral relevance of its propositions. Although this difference between the laws of, say, physics and sociology is, of course, generally recognized, the deeper epistemological reasons why the "hard" sciences are more authentic than the "soft" sciences are less widely appreciated.[15]

Pareto Distributions

In doing his work the scientist has to recognize some common denominator, or structure, in an ensemble of events; this structure is the phenomenon which is to be explained in terms of a scientific law. An event that is unique, or at least that aspect of an event which makes it unique, cannot, therefore, be the subject of scientific investigation: an ensemble of unique events has no common denominator, is not a phenomenon, and there is nothing in it to explain. Such events are random, and the observer perceives them as noise. Since every real event incorporates some element of uniqueness, every ensemble of real events contains some noise. The basic problem of scientific observation, therefore, is to recognize a significant structure of an ensemble of events above its inevitable background noise. Most of the phenomena for which successful scientific theories had been worked out prior to about one hundred years ago are relatively noise-free. Such phenomena were explained in terms of deterministic laws, which assert that a given set of initial conditions (antecedent situation) can lead to one and only one final stage (consequent). Toward the end of the nineteenth century the methods of mathematical statistics came to be trained on previously inscrutable phenomena involving an appreciable element of noise. This development gave rise to the appearance of indeterministic laws of physics, such as the kinetic theory of gases and quantum mechanics. These indeterministic laws envisage that a given set of initial conditions can lead to several alternative final states. An indeterministic law is not devoid of predictive value, however, because to each of the several alternative final states there is assigned a probability of its realization. Indeed, a deterministic law can be regarded as a limiting case of a more general indeterministic law in which the chance of the occurrence of one of the alternative final states approaches certainty. The conventional touchstone of the validity of both deterministic and indeterministic laws is the realization of their predictions in future observations. If the predictions are realized, then the structure which the observer believes to have perceived in the original phenomenon can be considered to have been real.

But, as was pointed out by Benoit Mandelbrot,[16] many of those noisy phenomena which continue to elude successful theoretical understanding are not only inaccessible to analysis by deterministic theories, but have also proven refractory to explanation in terms of indeterministic theories. According to Mandelbrot, it is the statistical character of the noise presented by these phenomena, or their spontaneous activity, which renders them scientifically opaque. In almost all systems for which it has so far been possible to make successful indeterministic scientific theories, the spontaneous activity displays a statistical distribution such that the mean value of a series of observations converges rapidly toward a limit. That limit can be subjected to analysis of the classical deterministic type. For instance, in the successful kinetic theory of gases, the spontaneous activity of a gas satisfies this condition. Here the energy of individual molecules is subject to a very wide variation (thermal unrest), but the mean energy per molecule converges to a limit and is, therefore, for all practical purposes determined. But many of the phenomena for which it has not been possible to make successful scientific theories so far turn out to possess a spontaneous activity which displays quite a different kind of distribution, which is called "Pareto" distribution after the turn-of-the-century Italian economist who first observed it for the spread in incomes. For such phenomena the mean value of a series of observations converges only very slowly, or not at all, toward a limit. And here, it is very much more difficult to ascertain whether any structure the observer believes to have perceived is real, or whether the phenomenon is merely a figment of his imagination.

As Mandelbrot has pointed out, the "softness" of the human sciences arises from the predominance of Pareto distributions in the basic phenomena to which they must address their analysis. In economics, for instance, firm sizes and income and price fluctuations follow Pareto's law. In sociology, the sizes of "human agglomerations" have a similar distribution, which demonstrates that such common-sense terms as "cities," "towns," and "villages" are ambiguous, impressionistic structures. That our vocabulary contains these terms, nevertheless, is a reflection of our habit of providing a specific description of a world whose events are intuited in terms of converging mean-value statistics.

Hence, it is because of the intrinsically refractory statistical character of the phenomena in want of explanation that it is possible only in exceptional cases to ascertain whether the propositions of the human sciences represent reality or figments of the imagination. It is for just that reason that the human sciences are "soft," and their laws generally beyond the reach of validation. This is not to suggest by any means that the human sciences are worthless enterprises and that no attention need be paid to the insights they provide. On the contrary, we cannot do without them; just as we cannot do without morality. But these considerations do show that the scientistic claims on behalf of an authoritative role of science guiding moral action can themselves be doubted on scientific grounds.

Structuralism

That the human sciences are, in fact, unlikely to provide the authentic guide to the realization of moral aims envisaged by soft-core scientism has come to light with the emergence of the "structuralist" approach to the human mind and the decay of positivism as the philosophical infrastructure of modern science.[17] Structuralism transcends the limitation on the methodology, indeed on the agenda of permissible inquiry, of the human sciences imposed by positivism. Structuralism admits, as positivism does not, the possibility of innate knowledge not derived from direct experience. It represents, therefore, a return to Cartesian rationalist philosophy. Or, more exactly, structuralism embraces this feature of rationalism as it was later reworked by Kant for his philosophy of critical idealism. Kant held that the mind constructs reality from experience by use of innate categories, and thus, to understand man, it is indispensable to try to fathom the nature of his deep and universal cognitive endowment. Accordingly, structuralism not only permits propositions about behavior that are not directly inducible from observed data, but it even maintains that the relations between such data, or surface structures, are not by themselves explainable. According to this view the causal connections that determine behavior do not relate to surface structures at all. Instead, the overt behavorial phenomena are generated by covert deep structures, inaccessible to direct observation. Hence, any theoretical framework for understanding man must be based on the deep structures, whose discovery ought to be the real goal of the human sciences.

Universal Grammar

Linguistics is one of the human sciences in which the structuralist approach is currently very prominent. The older, positivist approach to linguistics addressed itself to the discovery of structural relations among the elements of spoken language. That is, it was concerned with the surface structures of linguistic performance, the patterns which can be observed as being in use by speakers of various languages. Since the patterns which such classificatory analysis reveals differ widely, it seemed reasonable to conclude that these patterns are arbitrary, or purely conventional, one linguistic group having chosen to adopt one, and another group having chosen to adopt another convention. There would be nothing that linguistics could be called on to explain, except for the taxonomic principles that account for the degree of historical relatedness of different peoples. By contrast, the structuralist approach to linguistics, according to its main modern proponent, Noam Chomsky, starts from the premise that linguistic patterns are not arbitrary.[18] Instead, all men are believed to possess an innate, a priori knowledge of a universal grammar, and despite their superficial differences, all natural languages are based on that same grammar. According to that view, the overt surface structure of speech, or the organization of sentences, is generated by the speaker from a covert deep structure. In his speech act, the speaker is thought to formulate first his proposition as an abstract deep structure that he transforms only secondarily according to a set of rules into the concrete surface structure of his utterance. The listener in turn fathoms the meaning of the speech act by just the inverse transformation of surface to deep structure. Chomsky holds that the grammar of a language is a system of transformational rules that determines a certain pairing of sound and meaning. It consists of a syntactic component, a semantic component, and a phonological component. The

surface structure contains the information relevant to the phonological component, whereas the deep structure contains the
information relevant to the semantic component, and the syntactic
component pairs surface and deep structures.

So far, it does not seem to have been possible to identify
clearly those aspects of the grammar of any one natural language
which are universal, and hence shared with all other natural
languages, in contrast to those aspects which are particular, and
hence responsible for differentiating that language from other
languages. Some success has been achieved at the sound level,
where a limited number of universal "distinctive features" has
been identified. Each feature takes on one of a very few discrete
values (such as "present" or "absent") in a given sound element
of speech. In other words, every symbol of a phonetic alphabet
can be regarded as a set of these features, each with a specified
value. Thus it should be possible to construct a universal phonetic script which would allow, in principle at least, a speaker of
any natural language to pronounce correctly a written text in any
other natural language.

Much less success has been achieved so far at the philosophically more interesting meaning level. Here the concept of a
universal grammar would suggest the existence of an ensemble of
universal semantic "distinctive features" and laws regarding their
interrelations and permitted variety. That is, every meaningful
concept would be fathomable as a set of semantic features, each
with a specified value. From this point of view, it should be
possible to construct a universal "semantic script," texts of which
all speakers of natural languages would understand. Unfortunately, it has proven difficult to put forward any specific proposals for or examples of the putative "semantic features," except
to conclude that they must be of a highly abstract nature. In any
case, if both the surface level of sound and the deep level of
meaning are universal aspects on which all natural languages are
based, then it must be the transformational components of grammar that have become greatly differentiated during the course of
human history, since the building of the Tower of Babel. But the
presumed constancy through time of the universal aspects cannot
be attributable to any cause other than an innate, hereditary

aspect of the mind. Hence, the general aim of structuralist linguistics is to discover those universal aspects.

The great strength of the structuralist human sciences is that they do offer a theoretical approach to understanding human behavior. Their great weakness, however, is that it is not possible to validate the propositions which they offer regarding the mental deep structures. The reason for this is not only the refractory statistical character of the surface structures, or phenomena to be observed, which is no less troublesome for the positivist than for the structuralist approach, but also the transformational relation between surface and deep structures, with which the positivist approach need not contend. Propositions about the deep structures are nearly impossible to falsify by empirical study of the surface structures, since it is almost always feasible to reconcile any apparent contradiction between theoretical prediction and observed fact by an appropriate adjustment of the transformational rules. Thus, the structuralist schools active in the human sciences do try to explain human behavior within a general theoretical framework, in contrast to their positivist counterparts who cannot, or rather refuse to try to do so. But there is no way of validating the structuralist theories in the manner in which the theories of physics can be validated through critical experiments or observations.

Biology and the Kantian a priori

As it turns out, however, the structuralist approach to the mind can draw support from the insights of modern biology. To secure this support, it is not necessary to embrace the position of extreme materialism which envisages that all conscious thought is "reducible" to neurophysiology. Instead, it suffices to hold the minimal position compatible with any scientific approach to the mind-body problem, namely, that there exists some isomorphism between cerebral and mental events. One example of a provision of support by biological insights for a structuralist tenet has been the resolution of an old dilemma posed by Kant's epistemology. As Kant set forth, sensations become experience, that is, gain meaning only after they are interpreted in terms of a priori concepts, such as time and space. Other a priori concepts, such as induction (or causality), allow the mind to construct reality from that experience. But if, as Kant alleges, we bring such concepts as time and space to sensation and causality to experience a priori, how is it that these transcendental concepts happen to fit our world so well? Considering all the ill-conceived notions we might have had about the world prior to experience, it seems nothing short of miraculous that our innate concepts just happen to be appropriate. Here the positivist view that all knowledge is derived from experience a posteriori would seem much more reasonable. It turns out, however, that the way to resolve this dilemma posed by the Kantian a priori has been open since Darwin put forward the theory of natural selection in the mid-nineteenth century. As Konrad Lorenz[19] has pointed out, the positivist argument that knowledge about the world can enter our mind only through experience is valid if we consider only the ontogenetic development of man from fertilized egg to adult. But once we take into account also the phylogenetic development of the human brain through evolutionary history, it becomes clear that individuals can also know something of the world innately, prior to and independent of their own experiences. After all, there is no biological reason why such knowledge cannot be passed on from generation to generation through the ensemble of genes that determines the structure and function of our nervous system. For that genetic ensemble came into being through the process of natural selection operating on our remote ancestors. According to Lorenz, "Experience has as little to do with the matching of a priori ideas with reality as does the matching of the fin structure of a fish with the properties of water." In other words, the Kantian notion of a priori knowledge is not implausible at all, but fully consonant with present mainstream evolutionary thought. The a priori concepts of time, space, and causality happen to suit the world because our brain—and hence, in view of its isomorphism with the brain, our mind—was selected for evolutionary fitness, just as were innate behavioral acts.

In addition to being fully consonant with modern evolutionary thought, the notion of Kantian a priori, and its latter-day, neo-Kantian structuralist elaboration, finds support from recent neurological findings which indicate that, in accord with those tenets, information about the world reaches the brain, not as raw data but as highly processed structures that are generated by a set of stepwise, preconscious informational transformations of the sensory input.[20] These neurological transformations proceed according to a program that preexists in the brain, and, in their initial stages, at least, consist of abstracting the vast amount of experiential data continuously fathered by the senses. In order to abstract, the brain destroys selectively portions of the input data and thus transforms these data into manageable categories, or structures that are meaningful.

One set of such neurological findings concerns the manner in which the nervous system of higher vertebrates, including man, transforms the light rays entering the eyes into a visual percept. This transformation begins in the retina at the back of the eye. There, a two-dimensional array of about a hundred million primary light receptor cells—the rods and the cones—converts the radiant energy of the image projected via the lens on the retina into a pattern of electrical signals, much as a television camera does. Since the electrical response of each light receptor cell depends on the intensity of light that happens to fall on it, the overall activity pattern of the light receptor cell array represents the light intensity existing at a hundred million different points in the visual space. The retina not only contains the input part of the visual sense, however, but also performs the first stage of the abstraction process. This first stage is carried out by another two-dimensional array of nerve cells, namely, the million or so ganglion cells. The ganglion cells receive the electrical signals generated by the hundred million light receptor cells and subject them to information processing. The result of this processing is that the activity pattern of the ganglion cells constitutes a more abstract representation of the visual space than the activity pattern of the light receptor cells. Instead of reporting the light intensity existing at a single point in the visual space, each ganglion cell signals the light-dark contrast which exists between the center and the edge of a circular receptive field in the visual space, with each receptive field consisting of about a hundred contiguous points monitored by individual light receptor cells. In this way, the point-by-point fine-grained light intensity information is boiled down to a somewhat coarser field-by-field light contrast representation. As can be readily appreciated, such light contrast information is essential for the recognition of shapes and forms in space, or visual perception.

For the next stage of processing the visual information leaves the retina via the nerve fibers of the ganglion cells. These fibers connect the eye with the brain, and after passing a way station in the forebrain the output signals of the ganglion cells reach the cerebral cortex at the lower back of the head. Here the signals converge on a set of cortical nerve cells. Study of the cortical nerve cells receiving the partially abstracted visual input has shown that each of them responds only to light rays reaching the eye from a limited set of contiguous points in the visual space. But the structure of the receptive fields of these cortical nerve cells is more complicated, and their size is larger than that of the receptive fields of the retinal ganglion cells. Instead of representing the light-dark contrast existing between the center and the edge of circular receptive fields, the cortical nerve cells signal the contrast which exists along straight line edges whose length amounts to many diameters of the circular ganglion cell receptive fields. A given cortical cell becomes active if a straight line edge of a particular orientation—horizontal, vertical, or oblique—formed by the border of contiguous areas of high and low light intensity is present in its receptive field. For instance, a vertical bar of light on a dark background in some part of the visual field may produce a vigorous response in a particular cortical nerve cell, and that response will cease if the bar is tilted away from the vertical or moved outside the receptive field. Thus the process of abstraction of the visual input begun in the retina is carried to higher levels in the cerebral cortex. At the first abstraction stage the data supplied by the retinal ganglion cells concerning the light-dark contrast within small circular receptive fields are transformed into the more abstract data structure of contrast present along sets of circular fields arranged in straight lines.

Toward a Structuralist Ethics

These findings thus support the structuralist dogma that explanations of behavior must be formulated in terms of deep structures and transformational processes. This biologically grounded reemergence of the Kantian concept of a priori knowledge in the guise of structuralist epistemology provides encouragement for developing also a neo-Kantian structuralist ethics. The purpose of such a project is not the scientistic objective to extend the authority of science to the ethical domain, but merely to illuminate the metaethical question of how morals are possible at all. Although science cannot justify moral values and is only of limited use for their realization, it may, all the same, be able to give an account of their biological basis. This account would not, of course, consist of functionalist explanations of the social role that morals play in human intercourse or the nature of the evolutionary "fitness" which morality may have conferred on *Homo sapiens*. There has been no shortage of such explanations since the rise of Darwinism a century ago, which, as I have said, have provided a cornerstone for the foundations of hard-core scientism.[21] Rather, instead of Darwin's recognition of the role of natural selection in evolution, the point of departure of this project would be Kant's recognition that the peculiar obligatoriness of moral principles can be explained only by their unrestricted universality, that is, by their independence of any existential facts. Thus, contrary to the tenets of utilitarianism, it is not to promote happiness, or to serve progress, but to accede to the demand of human reason that action be in accord with universal law that we feel obligated to obey moral principles. It is man's innate knowledge of this law, whose origin—it goes without saying—can readily be consigned to the evolutionary history of *Homo sapiens,* which gave rise to the possibility of a social existence in the first place. Moreover, the nature of that universal law determined the kind of social structures which eventually arose.

Some idea of what structuralist ethics would be like can be gained by extending Chomsky's approach to the nature of language to the ethical domain. Just as one of Chomsky's empirical starting points for the development of the transformational grammar concept was the creative aspect of human language, which provides a speaker with the capacity to produce a limitless number of meaningful statements, so any account of the nature of morality must begin with the empirical fact that there seems to be no limit to the number of significantly different social situations for which individuals can produce value judgments that appear reasonable to other men. So the empirical premise of structuralist ethics would be that moral judgments arise by a generative process involving transformational operations on a subconscious mental deep structure. This approach, therefore, acknowledges the subjective and intuitive nature of moral judgments. But despite their subjectivity, moral judgments would not be viewed as arbitrary or completely idiosyncratic, not for the trivial or functionalist reason that they must not be dysfunctional or give rise to unviable forms of social organization, but because they reflect an innate, a priori, universal ethical deep structure which all humans share. These universal deep structures would be more or less equivalent to Kant's concept of the categorical imperative, which he took to govern human action independently of any desired ends, including happiness. However, the neo-Kantian feature of the structuralist approach to morality is that it would posit a more complicated, or transformational, relation between the universal categorical imperative and particular moral judgments than the direct connection evidently envisaged by Kant.

From that neo-Kantian point of view, the overt ethical surface structures would consist of the concrete moral code of which a person is consciously aware and to which he can give verbal expression. This surface structure is reflected in the moral judgments made by that person, and hence is accessible to direct observation through his acts and statements. One obvious empirical fact, relevant to these surface structures, is that they can differ significantly between diverse social groups and among members of the same social group. The reason for these differences is that the particular moral code held by any individual is the product of a twofold historical process, namely, of the ethnic history of his social group and of his personal, ontogenetic history. The covert ethical deep structure, on the other hand, would consist of an abstract moral code, of which the person is not consciously aware and to which he cannot in general give verbal expression. This ethical deep structure is innate and common to all men, as members of the species *Homo sapiens*. The abstract ethical deep structure gives rise to the concrete moral code of the surface structure through a transformational process. According to this view, the empirically observable differences in extant moral codes would be attributable to differences in the rules by which particular individuals carry out the deep-to-surface transformational processes. In line with model psychological concepts, the primary course of the personal set of transformational rules would be the assimilation of parental moral authority by the child, just as in the acquisition of speech, the child assimilates the syntactical and phonological components of the grammar of its native language from the examples provided by parental speech. The child is able to assimilate these moral transformational rules only because, thanks to an innate possession of the universal, abstract, ethical deep structure, he already knows the abstract essence of human morality of which his own ethical system will be a particular concrete realization. In particular, it is thanks to the deep structure that the child has an a priori, intuitive understanding of the meaning of the unanalyzable, undefinable concepts of moral values, such as "good."

Thus, according to this structuralist concept, the extant moral systems all share certain fundamental features, of which the very notion of moral value is one of the most basic, because they are all rooted in the same universal ethical deep structure. Hence, the discovery and elucidation of the ethical deep structure ought to be the central goal of what J. M. Gustafson defined as "ethics," namely, "a human intellectual discipline which develops the principles which account for morality and moral action and the normative principles and values that are to guide human action."[22]

But just as the structuralist linguists have been more successful in demonstrating the plausibility of the existence of a universal grammar than in spelling out just what abstract linguistic principles it contains, so it is easier to adduce arguments in favor of the existence of a universal, deep ethical structure than to describe its abstract moral content. Kant thought, of course, that he had managed to identify that content, by proposing that there is one fundamental categorical imperative from which all specific moral duties can be derived, namely: "Act only according to that maxim which you can will to be universal law." It seems highly plausible that some such criterion of universalizability of the moral code is indeed contained in the deep ethical structures, in view of the empirical fact that the "golden rule," which is manifestly an expression of that principle, forms part of almost all the great religions. But it seems equally plausible that despite the fact that the criterion of universalizability may well be, as Kant claimed, a logical necessity for requiring universal obedience to a rule of action, this criterion cannot be contained in the deep structures in the strong form enunciated by him. For any such all-inclusive generalization would place too severe a limitation on the creative aspect of morality and limit the variety of social situations under which rational value judgments can be produced. Thus, it is clear that there are few if any moral rules that we would want to be followed without exception, for whose justifiable contravention we cannot imagine scenarios.

Here we reach what would appear to be the most significant aspect of the ethical deep structure, namely that its open-ended creative possibilities appear to be achieved at the expense of logical consistency. Whatever may be the abstract moral content of the deep structure, its nature is such that the transformations to which it is subject give rise to a set of judgments that are not necessarily logically compatible and hence are not necessarily reconcilable rationally. Indeed, the irreconcilable yet unavoidable coexistence of an authoritative science and an autonomous morality is most plausibly attributable to that feature of our a priori knowledge. Thus, from the structuralist viewpoint, the moral dilemmas and paradoxes with which we are wrestling today are not simply the result of unenlightened or irrational human attitudes but are, instead, reflections of the fundamental inconsistency of the ethical deep structure which underlies our morality in the first place. Thus the resolution of these dilemmas, if possible at all, is not likely to be achieved by merely calling attention to their existence or by any simple remedy short of changing human nature. But whether such a change is possible, or even desirable, as has long been maintained by Buddhism and some other Eastern philosophies, or whether we can only continue to muddle along as best we can with our paradoxical endowment is, in my opinion, the central ethical question of the future.

NOTES

I thank Georges Kowalski and Gonzalo Manévar for helpful suggestions and discussions during the writing of this essay.

1. Jacques Monod, *Chance and Necessity* (New York: Alfred A. Knopf, 1971).
2. Helmut Schoeck and James W. Wiggins, eds., *Scientism and Values* (Princeton, N.J.: Van Nostrand Co., 1960).
3. Herbert Spencer, *Principles of Ethics*, 2 vols. (London: Williams and Norgate, 1892-3). C. H. Waddington, in his *The Ethical Animal* (London: Allen and Unwin, 1960), finds that Spencer's ethical "theories have been so completely discredited that at this time little further needs to be said about them" (p. 23). But Waddington then produces a casuistic variant of Spencer's hard-core evolutionist ethics, namely, one that holds that although the notion of "good" cannot be simply identified with progress, a particular set of moral values can be judged to be good if it promotes "anagenesis," or evolutionary improvement (p. 202).
4. Konrad Lorenz, *On Aggression* (New York: Harcourt, Brace & World, 1966).
5. A (undoubtedly unintended) caricature of this approach can be found in Wolfgang Wickler, *Die Biologie der Zehn Gebote* (München: Piper Verlag, 1971).
6. Desmond Morris, *The Naked Ape* (New York: McGraw Hill Book Co., 1967).
7. Richard P. Michael, "Bisexuality and Ethics," in *Biology and Ethics*, F. J. Ebling, ed. (London: Academic Press, 1969), pp. 67-72.
8. James F. Crow, "The Dilemma of Nearly Neutral Mutations: How Important Are They For Evolution and Human Welfare?" *Journal of Heredity*, 63 (1972) 306-16.
9. T. S. Kuhn, *The Structure of Scientific Revolutions* (Chicago: University of Chicago Press, 1964).
10. Ernst Mayr, "Teleological and Teleonomic, a New Analysis," *Boston Studies in the Philosophy of Science* 14 (1974), 91-117.
11. Patrick Heelan, "Medical Praxis and Manifest Images of Man," in *Science, Ethics and Medicine*, H. T. Engelhardt, Jr. and Daniel Callahan, eds. (Hastings-on-Hudson: Institute of Society, Ethics and Life Sciences, 1976), pp. 218-24.
12. C. Galpérine, ed., *Biology and the Future of Man* (Paris: The Universities of Paris, 1976), pp. 377-415.

13. Bronislaw Malinowski, "Anthropology," in *Encyclopedia Britannica,* 13th ed. (New York: Encyclopedia Britannica Inc., 1926), Vol. 29, pp. 131-40.
14. Christian Morgenstern, "The Impossible Fact," in *Gallows Songs and Other Poems,* trans. Max Knight (München: Piper Verlag, 1972), p. 25.
15. Gunther S. Stent, *The Coming of the Golden Age. A View of the End of Progress* (Garden City, N.Y.: The Natural History Press, 1969), pp. 115-21.
16. Benoit Mandelbrot, *Les objets fractals* (Paris: Flammarion, 1975).
17. Gunther S. Stent, "Limits to the Scientific Understanding of Man," *Science* 187 (1975), 1052-57.
18. Noam Chomsky, "The Formal Nature of Language," in E. H. Lenneberg, *Biological Foundations of Language* (New York: John Wiley, 1967), pp. 397-442. *Language and Mind* (New York: Harcourt, Brace and World, 1968).
19. Konrad Lorenz, "Kant's Doctrine of the *a priori* in the light of contemporary biology," in *General Systems,* L. Bertalanffy and A. Rappaport, eds. (Ann Arbor: Soc. Gen. Systems Research, 1962).
20. Gunther S. Stent, "Cellular Communication," *Scientific American* 227 (September 1972), 42-51.
21. A collection of recent examples of this genre can be found in *Biology and Ethics,* F. J. Ebling, ed. (London: Academic Press, 1969).
22. J. M. Gustafson, unpublished draft manuscript prepared for discussion at the Hastings Center.

Natural Selection and Societal Laws

Richard D. Alexander

I believe that modern opposition, both overt and cryptic, to natural selection, still derives from the same sources that led to the now discredited theories of the nineteenth century. The opposition arises, as Darwin himself observed, not from what reason dictates but from the limits of what the imagination can accept. It is difficult for many people to imagine that an individual's role in evolution is entirely contained in its contribution to vital statistics. It is difficult to imagine that an acceptable moral order could arise from vital statistics, and difficult to dispense with belief in a moral order in living nature. It is difficult to imagine that the blind play of the genes could produce man.

—George C. Williams

Introduction

Ever since Darwin published his *Origin of Species* literate people have tended to regard the attributes of living things as outcomes of an evolutionary process, and to suppose that humans like other organisms are in some way derived through organic evolution. In terms of searches for explanation there are several meanings to this remark. Laboratory scientists, for example, may assume that common or similarly derived mechanisms underlie physiological phenomena observed even in widely different animals, and they may as a result use simpler or more easily studied organisms,

265

such as rats, to help understand complex species, such as humans, which are difficult to study in the laboratory. Primatologists may assume that humans are similar to other primates because of genetic similarity or a recent common ancestry; this assumption may be used in developing and testing theories about human behavior and its history, or about the phylogenetic derivation of humans. Paleontologists assume that the phylogenetic patterns they are able to trace across geological time are the result of mutation, selection, and isolation, as observable today, even though they are hardly ever able to reconstruct the environments in which the changes occurred well enough to understand the adaptive significance of ancient trends.

Biologists with a primary interest in the evolutionary process may seek generalizations about the nature of adaptation and extinction from the workings of that process now and in the immediate past, and develop and test hypotheses from this approach on whatever extant organisms seem best suited. They assume that if adaptation is a continuous process, and if generalizations can be extracted about adaptiveness of attributes common to many or most organisms—sex ratios, senescence, parental investment, sociality—then evidence of cumulative adaptive changes should appear in comparative analyses. At some point, with sufficient understanding of the evolutionary process and enough information about past environments, phylogenetic and other patterns from fossil evidence may be put together with adaptational information from the study of living forms in order to develop, as far as possible, both the actual reasons for long-term history and a greater predictability about the traits of living organisms.[1]

Here I wish to utilize the approach of generalizing and predicting from the process of adaptation as a vehicle for studying human sociality, especially to consider the nature and probable background of societal laws, norms, and traditions. The approach, as such, is not new. Since Darwin, it has been commonplace, at least in the Western world, to think even of human attributes in terms of natural selection. The reference, however, may be fleeting, only half-serious, or even principally humorous: "Ah, yes," we say with a smile, "Survival of the fittest!" Indeed, it is probably fair to say that in recent years most allusions to any relationship between human behavior and natural selection have been in jest. This may be partly because we are skeptical of the implication that what we do from day to day really has much to do with a process as simple and genetic as "survival of the fittest." It may be partly because we share the fears of others that evolutionary explanations imply an intolerable, robot-like determinism quite inconsistent with our views of our usual day-to-day, consciously planned, individualized existences. It may be partly because we sometimes recognize an irony in our identification of the "fittest" after the fact, because we know very well that we could have made it happen otherwise if we had intervened. It may partly stem from the suspicion that the purveyors of an evolutionary philosophy of life have some new brand of "social Darwinism" in mind—some notion that if natural selection lies behind human attributes then variations among people must be accepted as occurring along axes appropriately judged in terms of better versus worse, with such variations to be either allowed or caused to disappear by our deliberate contributions to the operation of some kind of "natural law" of survival of the fittest.

For these various reasons, applications of natural selection to human phenomena, and in fact as crucial explanations of biological phenomena in general, have drifted into neglect or at least a lack of centrality. This has happened despite unswerving recognition within biology that natural selection, or differential reproduction, is the principal guiding force in the evolutionary process.[2]

Some of the error and vagueness exists for unjustifiable reasons. Thus, genetic determinism is not in any sense a concomitant of the application of a selective model of human history. Genetic determinism implies long-term, irrevocable causation, but the elaboration of ontogenies and phenotypes which characterizes the evolution of life through natural selection is actually an opposite trend. Phenotypes and ontogenies—and especially behavior as an aspect of the phenotype—represent flexibilities that are opportunistically and strategically realized in the variable environments in which the organism lives out its life. In a sense, the most deterministic aspect of life is actually in the consistencies of the environments in which successive generations develop, and of course humans are masters at altering their environments far outside the limits represented by history. The existence and elaborateness of learning testifies to the absence of long-term causation in the environments of life, and therefore to the value of reliance upon immediate contingencies, especially in regard to social events. It is a curious fact that when genes are brought into the equation Genes + Environment → Behavior, as they must be, there is a widespread tendency to assume that the role of the environment is thereby necessarily underplayed and that of genes overemphasized. Even if this has been true in the past we have no choice but to leave genes in the formula and try to discover their role as well as that of their environment.

Similarly, there is no excuse for extrapolating from natural history to the development of value judgments about human attributes expressed in the present or future. Again, the opposite is more reasonable: To understand the past is not to bind ourselves to it but to deliver ourselves from its grip. Knowledge of the history of our own evolution should place us in the best possible position to cause the shaping of our future by human design, which in itself is inevitable, to proceed in desirable rather than undesirable directions.

I think, however, that fears of determinism and social Darwinism were not the real reasons why evolution, in the decades following Darwin, seemed to drift away from the front lines of biological investigation, and especially behavioral analysis. If evolutionary models had worked, they would have remained in the forefront. The reason they did not work was never squarely identified until George C. Williams published a dramatic refinement of Darwinism in his 1966 book *Adaptation and Natural Selection: A Critique of Some Modern Evolutionary Thought.* Williams's argument was that biologists had never clearly answered the question: Survival of the fittest *what?* For various reasons, they more often than not had assumed that the attributes of organisms have evolved because of their value in perpetuating the species, population, or social group. Williams showed that when the directions of change so indicated are contrary to those that would contribute to the survival of the genes of the individual organism, under nearly all conditions the latter will prevail.[3] What survives are the most reproductive sets of genes, and, concomitantly, the phenotypic potentials they have yielded in the environments of history (hence, that they may yield in the environments of the future).

This crucial refinement of Darwinism has generated a remarkable new surge of attention to evolutionary explanations, especially of behavior; and it promises to place natural selection once again in the forefront of every kind of biological investigation, including our efforts to understand ourselves through our history. Numerous authors have pointed out how this change in our thinking has rendered basic concepts and approaches obsolete in biology in general, and particularly in population genetics, ecology, ethology, and anthropology, because they depended upon selection operating principally at the population or group level.[4,5]

Darwinism, then, or the principle of differential reproduction, is a statement about why things are as they are with the entire world of life. It leads unmistakably to an attitude about the ultimate causes that lie behind the proximate mechanisms with which we, as individuals, must deal in our everyday, practical existences. Anyone who would challenge the philosophical implications of these statements must attack Darwinism at its base, which is to say, the entire idea and the universality of natural selection. For, as Darwin noted in 1859, to find an exception, an adaptation derived from some effect other than the cumulative influence of differential reproduction of variants, would not merely weaken his theory or reduce its overall significance but annihilate the entire idea. In the absence of any such challenge, we are not free to ignore the consequences of an evolutionary process, the cumulative effects of a continuing process of differential reproduction, upon all of natural history, including our own current attributes and tendencies. We are not free to deny such effects by assertion. We are not free to require that each scholar return to a defense of Darwinism before he develops a thesis on the assumption of its validity. In fact we are not free— any of us—to reject the evolutionary view of life. Logic, fact, and the absence of substantive challenges or reasonable alternatives clearly deny us any such frivolity. Whether we like it or not, and whether or not it has been a part of our personal educational, philosophical, social, or ideological backgrounds, we are required to accept that *background explanations for all activities of life, including our own behavior, will eventually be found in generalizations deriving from the cumulative effects of an inevitable and continuing process of differential reproduction of variants.*[6] The only question is their nature and the directness of their applicability.

From these introductory comments, I now proceed toward the particular discussion proposed for this chapter, the probable background of societal laws. Since laws are functions of societies, I shall do this by first discussing the probable backgrounds of societies and sociality.

Origins of Sociality

Once biologists had recognized that differential reproduction cannot easily be invoked to explain any attributes of organisms supposed to be good for the species or group as a whole, it quickly became commonplace to assume that attributes of organisms have evolved because in the past they helped the individual organism to maximize its reproduction. This interpretation has proved to be extraordinarily powerful in solving long-standing problems about altruism, population regulation, sex ratios, senescence, sexual dimorphism, parental investment, breeding systems, menopause, length of juvenile life, and a great many others.

The greatest impact of this revolution has been felt in the study of social behavior. Sociality can only exist in group-living organisms. Supposing that organisms do things because, in historical terms, they thereby help their own personal reproduction not only raised questions about all of the behavioral expressions commonly regarded as "social"—like cooperation, sharing, and all forms of altruism—but also changed our attitude toward voluntary group living. If groups were seen as forming, and the individuals within them interacting and cooperating, solely to help perpetuate the species, then deleterious consequences to individuals were to be expected and would not necessarily be minimized. Only the success of the group would be relevant. On the other hand, if behavior evolves to help individuals, we are suddenly aware that group living entails automatic expenses to individuals, such as increased competition for all resources, including mates, and increased likelihood of disease and parasite transmission. Accordingly we are made to wonder—for the first time, really—why animals should bother to live in groups. Why be social, beyond what is required to mate and raise a family? If the answer is that individuals living in groups reproduce *more* than individuals not living in groups, then, again for the first time, we are led to seek out the specific benefits that accrue from social life.

A few years ago, in the wake of this realization, I attempted an exhaustive list of such benefits for all organisms. To my surprise I was able to generate only three broad categories: (1) predator protection, either because of (a) group defense or (b) the opportunity to cause some other individuals to be more available to the predator; (2) nutritional gains when utilizing food, such as (a) large game, difficult to capture individually, or (b) clumped food difficult to locate; and (3) simple crowding on clumped resources.[7]

To my knowledge, no other reasons for group living, commensurate with the now well-established view that selection operates principally at and below the individual level, have been generated. It is a crucial point. Because individuals should tend to move apart, avoid competitors, and be nonsocial, large groups should appear only (a) when the resources of reproduction are so clumped that there is no alternative to close proximity (3, above) (a situation implying no cooperation, hence no special social organization), or (b) when cooperation contributes to individual reproduction in the population or species at large because of some extrinsic hostile force (1 and 2 above).[8]

Applying these hypothesized explanations to familiar organisms yields some interesting and surprising suggestions. Thus (2b) applies easily only to a few animals, like foraging vultures and sandpipers, and (2a) only to species like African hunting dogs, wolves, lions, group-fishing pelicans, and group-hunting fish. That leaves responses to predators as the probable evolutionary basis, or function, of all other actively formed groups, including most primate species and all of the great herds of ungulates and schools of fish.[9] Because laws are only made by humans living in the kinds of social groups we call societies, understanding group living is evidently closely related to understanding systems of laws.

Causes of Human Groupings

Everyone knows that early groups of humans are postulated to have been hunters of large game. Their predecessors almost certainly lived in groups for the reason that, probably like all modern group-living nonhuman primates, they were the hunted rather than the hunters. To all indications man is the only primate who became to some significant extent a group hunter—the only group-living primate who, at least for a time, escaped having his social organization essentially determined by large predators. In this light, it may not be so startling that dog and wolf packs and lion prides are social groups with which we empathize to a great degree—social groups that fascinate behaviorists because of parallels and complexities that are not clearly established elsewhere outside the human species. The human brand of sociality thus appears to be approached from two different directions—by various other primates because they are man's closest relatives, and by canines and cats because they most nearly do, socially, what humans did for some long time.

But the organization and maintenance of recent and large human social groups cannot be explained by a group-hunting hypothesis.[10] The reason is obvious: The upper size of a group in which each individual gained because of the group's ability to bring down large game would be rather small. As weapons and cooperative strategies improved, then, owing to the automatic expenses of group living, group sizes should have gone down. Instead they went up—right up to nations of hundreds of millions.

Human nations of millions of individuals, each potentially reproductive, appear to be unique in the history of the earth. There is no parallel, as often supposed in the past, with the social insects, in which one or a few females do all of the reproducing and the rest are closely related sterile workers and soldiers. Chimpanzees, baboons, and macaques are probably our closest counterparts in this regard, and their social organization likely never escaped strong effects from predators of other species (one of the most important of which may well have been our own ancestors).

What, then, did cause human groups to keep right on growing? If we hold to the arguments described above, what forces could possibly account for the rise of what anthropologists have called the "nation-state"? The uniqueness of human group sizes, as well as the uniqueness of humans, suggests that unique, truly remarkable causes may be involved.

One possibility is that the early benefits of group living (such as group hunting, cooperation in irrigation, and a host of others) were so powerful that they produced humans with such strong tendencies to group that they developed the huge modern nations of today as more or less incidental effects. This argument construes humans as being considerably less flexible in their behavior than I would like to allow. It says, in effect, that we are captives of our genetic history, and are such compulsive group livers that we pursue the habit relentlessly despite deleterious effects on ourselves and our children, and despite its hindering effects on the reproduction of ourselves and our close relatives. Perhaps such an argument does not seem too remote to those who have regarded reproduction as a triviality in human history, or to those who do not recognize the degree of opportunistic flexibility that typifies the human organism. Any such argument, however, seems entirely impotent to me. Moreover, should this be the real reason for human sociality, alternative hypotheses should not easily apply.

But there is an alternative hypothesis, one recently proposed by several different writers, and one which seems to me reasonable, appropriately unique, and clearly relevant to all efforts to understand, govern, and perpetuate ourselves.[11] I will call it the "Balance-of-Power Hypothesis." This hypothesis contends that at some early point in our history the actual function of human groups—their significance for their individual members—involved the competitive and predatory effects of other human groups and protection from them. The premise is that the necessary and sufficient forces to explain the maintenance of every kind and size of human group, extant today and throughout all but the earliest portions of human history, were (a) war, or intergroup competition and aggression, and (b) the maintenance of balances of power between such groups. I emphasize that this is hypothesis, not conclusion, and I state it in this simple radical form to make it maximally vulnerable to falsification.[12]

The model deriving from this argument would divide early human history into three periods of sociality, roughly as follows:

1. Small, polygynous, probably multi-male bands which stayed together for protection against large predators. (By polygyny is meant not necessarily the maintenance of

harems, but simply that fewer males than females were contributing genetically.)[13]

2. Small polygynous, multi-male bands which stayed together both for protection against large predators (probably through aggressive defense) and because of the ability to bring down large game (perhaps, at certain times, entirely because of one or the other of these reasons).

3. Increasingly larger polygynous, multi-male bands which stayed together largely or entirely because of the threat of other, similar, nearby groups of humans.

I suggest that expressions of human social organization today are derived from this sequence, with the relative importance of each stage in understanding sociality in modern humans dependent upon the duration of the stage, the intensity of selection during it, and where it occurs in the sequence. I also suppose that we have been in the third stage so long that the influences of the first two stages are relatively minor. The latter assumption departs dramatically from arguments of other writers, but that is not critical to the arguments that follow.

To relate the scenario I have just constructed to the thinking of archaeologists and anthropologists on the problem of the rise of nations, I would call attention to the recent review of Flannery (1972) on the evolution of civilizations, to Carneiro's (1970) paper, and to Webster's (1975) critique of Carneiro's argument.[14] Flannery describes the modern range of human societies from small hunting-gathering bands of fewer than two hundred individual affiliates through tribes and chiefdoms to huge industrial nations. He notes that all large nations had to pass through at least some of the smaller stages to reach their present condition, and shows that archaeological evidence regarding the earliest known dates for the three classes of societies larger than band societies suggests the appropriate chronology from small groups to large.[15] Then he asks what "prime mover" could account for the trend toward larger, more complex states and nations?

After reviewing many extrinsic possibilities and finding each either unnecessary or insufficient, Flannery seems to follow an approach frequently resorted to by biologists and social scientists alike in this kind of situation; he seems to seek the reasons for the nature of society in its internal workings. This approach leads to hypotheses like the one discarded earlier here—hypotheses of orthogenesis or genetic, physiological, or social "constraints" or "inertia." In biology it leads to what are termed arguments from physiological limitations—tendencies to explain each attribute as the maximum that could be achieved in a certain direction despite continued favoring of directional change. In effect, it requires that one explain ultimate causes by proximate causes rather than vice versa, and it is at best a vulnerable argument.[16]

Anyone who invokes proximate limitations to explain extant phenomena of life is in effect denying the power of the evolutionary process to produce some perceived or imagined effect. Sometimes there are valid arguments from adaptation for such explanations. An example is the argument that no more than two sexes exist because the presence of three or more would automatically cause an ecologically inferior sex to become less valuable as it became rare and eventually to disappear; with two sexes individuals of the rare sex automatically become more valuable.[17] But to deny adaptive significance because of supposed constraints on natural selection is perilously close to asserting either that marvels like humans and honeybees are impossible, or that they are entirely predictable. Moreover, the rapid directional changes induced by human selection, especially upon domestic animals and plants, and the diversity of effects achieved within species by different directions of selection in only a few generations, tend to deny any long-term significance of genetic constraints and attest to the potency of selection.

How, though, does Flannery dismiss the hypothesis suggested here, that of intergroup competition? He notes that intergroup aggression has evidently been continuous throughout history in many parts of the world where large nations have never evolved. Like Webster and others, he concludes from this that, while war may be necessary to explain the origin of the state, it is not sufficient.

But these authors do not explicitly consider the question of balances of power. Balances of power depend to some extent on physiographic and other extrinsic environmental circumstances, and they may as well exist between tiny New Guinea tribes as between nuclear powers.[18] Moreover, aspects of intergroup conflict among such people, which are commonly referred to as ceremonial or ritualistic, may actually reflect the importance of balances of power; examples are elaborate bluffing and the intensity of concern with avenging each death. Balances of power are also significant within groups, continually denying to individuals and subgroups the possibility of initiating individualistic reproductive strategies or fragmenting the larger group by secession or fission.

If, for whatever reasons, growing imbalance through one-sided expansions of some groups, or superiority in weapons or some other regard is not possible, then large nations may never appear. One test of a balance-of-power hypothesis would involve checking to see if physiographic or other barriers reduce the effectiveness of coalitions or the likelihood of unity across areas of increasing size, preserving the balance at low group sizes (Carneiro's "environmental circumscription"). Another test would be to see if empires have tended to develop in pairs or groups, or centrally nested inside multiple smaller competitors, and to disintegrate when they lacked suitable adversaries (Carneiro's "social conscription"). Even a very general knowledge of history suggests that these things have been true. Carneiro's hypothesis, and the analyses of Flannery and others, seem to me to put us on the brink of modifying to acceptability a hypothesis of just the sort discussed here (and in somewhat different forms by others).

Across the past several decades, failures in the social sciences to locate broad explanatory generalizations have led to the tendency to suppose that, since singular explanations have been singularly absent, it is more appropriate to seek or rely upon multiple causations than to accept singular ones—even, it seems, if one of the latter should appear sufficient! Perhaps it is vile and degrading to expect that singular explanations can be derived at any level for the complex phenomena of human behavior, but not nearly so much so as to deny them on that basis alone. The new evolutionary arguments about group living summarized above, for example, simultaneously cast doubt on the older "group-function" explanations and imply that a singular basis is both possible and likely.

Now let me review the steps by which I arrived at the hypothesis that the rise of the nation state depended on intergroup competition and aggression, and the maintenance of balances of power with increasing sizes of human groups. First, Williams's convincing argument that selection usually is effective only at individual or genic levels forced a search for reasons for group living that would balance its automatic costs to individuals. The available reasons have proved to be small in number, and only one, predator protection, appears applicable to large groups of organisms, including those of humans. For humans a principal "predator" is clearly other groups of humans, and it appears that no other species or set of species could possibly fulfill the function of forcing the ever-larger groups that have developed during human history. Carneiro[14] and Flannery[14] essentially eliminated as "prime movers" all of the other forces previously proposed to explain the rise of nations, and I think their arguments are reasonable. Flannery and Webster also eliminated intergroup competition as a prime or singular force, and they sought causes of the rise of nations within societal structure. This last procedure is here deemed unsatisfactory because it leads to the explanation of ultimate factors by proximate mechanisms rather than vice versa. Moreover, Flannery's rejection of intergroup aggression as necessary but not sufficient is deemed inadequate because he did not specifically consider intergroup aggression in terms of the maintenance of balances of power. His elimination of other factors may or may not be satisfactory; the fact is, in light of the realization that the automatic expenses to individuals which accompany group living are generally exacerbated as group sizes increase, none of the supposed causes for the rise of nations except balances of power seems even remotely appropriate; nor do they serve any better when grouped and regarded as multiply contributory.

The kind of argument I am making here cannot fail to be disconcerting, or even bizarre, to many modern scientists, philosophers, and humanists, especially those who are reasonably well satisfied with their present way of looking at things; it is too novel for anything else to be the case. There is only one acceptable basis for rejecting it, however, and that is by demonstrating its weaknesses or error. I believe that applying Williams's refinement of Darwinism, as I am attempting to do here, seriously threatens current philosophical thinking at its base and cannot fail to alter dramatically the theoretical underpinning of the social sciences, not in the sense often imputed to Wilson (1975)—that the formulation of normative ethics must depend upon and derive from biology—but in the sense that interpretations of history, and predictions about the future of humans not yet cognizant of these matters, will be facilitated by this kind of thinking more than by any other aspect of human understanding. Of course, if I am right, how any desired social, ethical, moral, philosophical, or legal situation is realized will also be massively affected by the analytical process proposed by evolutionary biology. My view of the potential flexibility of human behavior, however, causes me to deny any other necessary effects of knowledge of evolution upon the efforts of human beings to manipulate their future (see below).

Group Living and Rules

With these arguments and hypotheses about the history of human society, we may be in a position to develop a clearer overall view of the backgrounds and significance of societal rules and standards.

In the first place, we are led to hypothesize that rules in some fashion represent the wishes of individuals and relate to reproductive competition among individuals within groups, with the additional constraint that individual reproductive success within groups depends to some extent on the success or maintenance of the group as a whole. In other words, we might hypothesize that individuals behaving consistently in respect to the long evolutionary history of humans should work to preserve their group and keep it healthy while simultaneously striving, as far as possible, to convert their groups into clans of descendants and other genetic relatives related as closely as possible to themselves.

It is relevant that efforts to cause changes in the behavior of populations only work when the individuals in the population regard them as personally advantageous: It has to be to the *individual*'s advantage to reduce family size, conserve fuel, or treat his neighbor right; or it has to be to his disadvantage not to do so. Cooperative subgroups, like corporations, are not likely to follow courses that match the interests of the whole group, as in avoiding pollution, resource depletion, or profiteering, unless (a) the penalties imposed by the whole group are sufficient to eliminate the profit in selfish behavior, or (b) a threat external to the entire group makes it temporarily profitable to direct efforts primarily to sustaining it (not the least reason for which is the "public relations" effect from altruism or heroism in such situations).[19]

It is the purpose of laws to cause these things to be true, and to be regarded by individuals as having this function; individual members of a group tend to obey the laws and work for the common good with the least encouragement at times when a group is obviously threatened by external forces—indeed, these are the times when even huge nations form alliances with one another.

What Is Justice?

To relate these musings by a biologist to the thoughts of legal philosophers and sociologists, we can turn briefly to perhaps the most widely asked question about societal laws, the very prominence of which supports the individualistic interpretation of history being defended here. The question is, "What is justice?" I will start with an essay on that topic by Hans Kelsen, which opens his book of the same title.[20] Kelsen notes that:

> No other question has been discussed so passionately; no other question has caused so much precious blood and so many bitter tears to be shed; no other question has been the object of so much intensive thinking by the most illustrious thinkers from Plato to Kant; and yet, this question is today as unanswered as it ever was. It seems that it is one of those questions to which the resigned wisdom applies that man cannot find a definitive answer, but can only try to improve the question.

Kelsen goes on to define justice as "social happiness," and he says:

> It is obvious that there can be no "just" order, that is one affording happiness to everyone, as long as one defines the concept of happiness in its original, narrow sense of individual happiness, meaning by a man's happiness, what he himself considers it to be. For it is then inevitable that the happiness of one individual will, at some time, be directly in conflict with that of another.

> Where there is no conflict of interests, there is no need for justice. A conflict of interests exists when one interest can be satisfied only at the expense of the other; or, what amounts to the same, when there is a conflict between two values, and when it is not

possible to realize both at the same time; when the one can be realized only if the other is neglected; when it is necessary to prefer the realization of the one to that of the other; to decide which one is more important, or in other terms to decide which is the higher value, and finally: which is the highest value.

Kelsen notes that justice must be relative and incomplete, and can only be regarded as ideal or absolute if it is accepted (by everyone!) as having been determined by an ideal or absolute being, such as God—a view expressed by a long succession of philosophers.

Justice is necessarily incomplete, and laws are fluid, then, because people strive. To understand sociality and the sociology of law it would seem useful to know what people are striving for. This too is an old question. Kelsen, and the American Bill of Rights, say they are striving for happiness, and this is no doubt true. Happiness, though, as the different versions of a prevalent adage tell us, is many things. It is eating and sex and parenting and warmth and touching and ownership and giving and receiving and loving and being loved; it is eating when hungry, drinking when thirsty, coolness when it's hot, and warmth when it's cold; it is the cessation of pain and the onset of pleasure; it's finding a way to win; it's having a magnificent idea or a grandchild.

In some sense these are all biological things. There is probably nothing on the list that doesn't bring a happiness equivalent to at least one nonhuman organism as well as to humans.

Biologists ask another kind of question about the organisms they study: *Why* does that particular event or stimulus bring pleasure or happiness? As a result, biologists are able to generalize about happiness and see it eventually as an evolved means to an end. The neural connections that cause a bare foot to hurt when it comes down on a sharp object are not there accidentally; nor are those that cause a pleasurable sensation when a ripe fruit is placed inside the mouth. These are evolved correlations. Pleasure and happiness associate with events and stimuli that are beneficial to us in the usual environments of history.

Why should it be so? It should be so only if "beneficial" is defined, in terms of history, as leading to reproduction, i.e., as leading to genetic survival. Whatever, in the past, led to increased reproduction was likely to save itself, to cause its own perpetuation. Whatever did not was at least irrelevant, and, as such, deleterious to its own survival as an alternative to anything that correlated with reproduction. In this light we can understand why intense pleasure should be associated with the opportunity to benefit our offspring—or improve their situations by personal sacrifices—even, if necessary, by giving our lives for them in excruciatingly painful fashion.

Biologists divide the lives of organisms into two stages: resource-garnering (growing, maturing, becoming wealthy or powerful or clever) and resource-redistribution (reproduction, using power, wealth, and wisdom to produce and assist descendants and other relatives).

Now we can suggest that what humans have evolved to strive for is to reproduce and to reproduce maximally—indeed, to *out*-reproduce others.[21] Happiness, then, is an end for the individual only in the sense that it is achieved by acts leading to reproduction. Happiness is a means to reproduction. (That this is strictly true only in historical terms and that happiness can obviously be diverted from the goal of reproduction can be ignored for the moment.)

In other words, the striving of organisms can be generalized on solid grounds, and it is not hedonistic at all but reproductive; in historical terms hedonism is itself reproductive, and when it is not we expect it eventually to be abandoned.

I believe that these thoughts give us a way of understanding why human striving is incompatible with the concept of ideal, pure, or complete justice. First, humans strive as individuals or subgroups rather than united wholes. Second, there is no automatic finiteness to their striving because success can be measured in no way except in relation to one another: It follows that their separate strivings conflict, and sometimes involve direct thwarting of one another's efforts. Finally, they are continually altering their strivings to increase their success in the changing situations of life, and thereby introducing additional changes.

The differences of interest that legal philosophers discuss are thus based on differences of reproductive interest, and ultimately on genetic differences, and they are not likely to be resolved, in any absolute sense, by allowing given amounts of reward, payment, or returns on investments.

Our interests, then, are turned to several items, the first of which may be degrees of genetic relatedness or overlap among interacting individuals. We can even suggest that it is no accident that Kelsen's examples of the complexities of justice are: (a) two men in love with the same woman; (b) King Solomon's threat to divide a disputed child between the two women who claimed it, with the intent of giving it to the woman who loved it too much to allow it to be hurt; and (c) two men in competition for the same prestigious job.

The basis for conflicts of interest among individuals—hence, the basis for the unresolvability of the question of justice— evidently derives from our history of reproductive competition operating primarily at the individual level. I am saying bluntly that social conflict derives from biological facts. To me this suggests that our best chance for diminishing social conflict lies in better understanding of its biological basis.

Since most people today live in nation-states, we must also be interested in the nature of such societies and the possibility of generalizing the basis for the systems of law by which nation-states manage to function. Stein and Shand, in their 1974 book, *Legal Values in Western Society,* argue that order is "the primary value with which law is associated." But they answer the question, "What is law for?" by saying that the "three basic values of the legal system" are "order, justice, and personal freedom." From the arguments I have just made, and those that follow, I suggest instead that law is "for" but one thing: the preservation of order; and that justice and personal freedom, to whatever extent they are sought or approached, are also for the purpose of maintaining order. Order is valuable to everyone if extrinsic threats to the group are sufficiently severe, and the group is of no value if there are no such threats. In times of little or no extrinsic threat, on the other hand, laws are most valuable to those who lopsidedly control resources. These people generally include the wealthy and secure (versus the poor and insecure), parents (versus individual offspring), and older people (versus younger people). Revolutionaries (those willing to destroy order) must either (a) perceive themselves to be in a very bad position within society; (b) suppose that no significant threats to the group exist at the moment (so that internal dissension would not lead to worse troubles for themselves as a result of outside forces); or (c) have support from outside the group that seems to them to promise a better situation as a result of destruction of the existing order, and perhaps even their group as constituted.

And so we are returned to the biologist's view of organisms' lives being divisible into the activities of resource-garnering and resource-redistribution. I think we are talking about the basis for everyday phenomena such as the so-called "generation gap," inheritance laws, changes in occupation at midlife, racism, and reasons for racism's effects falling more heavily upon one sex (male) of the minority group than upon the other.

What I am saying, in many parts of this essay, I recognize to be essentially common sense. It seems to me that this is true to the extent that appropriate explanations are being approached. On the other hand, even common sense should become infinitely more sensible in the context of a history of differential reproduction, and I want to pursue that possibility further.

Reproductive Competition and Law-breaking

I have argued that the *function of laws is to regulate and render finite the reproductive strivings of individuals and sub-groups within societies, in the interest of preserving unity in the larger group* (all of "society" or the nation-state). Presumably, unity in the larger group feeds back beneficial effects on those segments or units which propose, maintain, adjust, and enforce the laws. Partly because of continual shifts of interests, changing coalitions, and power adjustments, it is not likely always to do so evenly, or in such fashion as to cause all individuals to benefit equally from group unity; hence, the value of "federal" government.

As a preliminary test of the general model that laws function to place limits on reproductive striving,[22] several obvious predictions may be considered. First, laws should be constructed so as to regulate competitive striving, and the severity of punishment should reflect the severity of deleterious effects on the reproduction of others. Capital punishment is generally correlated with murder, which destroys the victim's ability to reproduce; treason, which potentially lowers, at least slightly and perhaps massively, the reproductive fitnesses of everyone else in one's society; rape, which may directly interfere with a man's chances of reproducing via his spouse, sister, daughter, or other female relatives. Rape laws are particularly interesting to consider, since, because it is a nonfatal kind of assault, rape may not at first seem to be an appropriate transgression for the imposition of capital punishment.

If we were to select a category of striving that is centrally important, restricted to a definite part of the human life span, and more intense in one sex than the other, then we should be able to plot changes in the intensity of that striving—say, by age—against changes in the likelihood or rate of lawbreaking.

Suppose we choose sexual competition, or competition for mates, including all of the various activities involved in increasing one's desirability as a mate, hence, one's ability to select among a wider array of potential mates. First, sexual competition is demonstrably more intense among males than among females; and one can easily show from apparently accumulated differences between modern human males and females powerful evidence that this has consistently been the case during human history, and that a general consequence is that the entire life-history strategy of males is a higher-risk, higher-stakes adventure than that of females.[23] This finding leads to the prediction that lawbreaking will occur more frequently among males, which of course is already well known.[24] It also seems to predict that laws are chiefly made by men (as opposed to women) to control men (as opposed to women). That laws are made by men to control men is suggested over and over again in the structure and application of laws. As perhaps the prime example, it has become painfully clear because of attention recently brought to bear by women's groups on the application of laws against rape that the female victims are treated like pawns by the collections of (mostly) males who enforce the laws, judge and punish the offenders, and are indirectly wronged because of affinal or kin relationship to the victim. One might say that rape victims appear to be treated as if rape laws were designed to protect them only in the sense that rape wrongs the males to whom they "belong" or might have belonged and reduces their value or attractiveness to those males; and in the sense that, when rapists are free to act, the interests of all *men* are in jeopardy. It appears that the female victims of rape may be only incidental to the development and application of rape laws. Under current circumstances, the most pathetic of all rape victims is probably the female (1) without a male who has at that moment a proprietary interest in her welfare, such as a father, brother, husband, or sweetheart; (2) whose male defenders are already somewhat tentative in their allegiance to her; (3) who was raped by such a person or in such a circumstance as to pose little threat to other males in society; or (4) was raped in a fashion or circumstance that reflects particularly severely on her future desirability as a mate. It is relevant that in most states a man cannot be accused of raping his wife, and, until very recently, a man could kill his wife or her lover without being accused of murder while a wife could not.[25]

Lawbreaking is also expected to be concentrated at those periods in life, or those ages, when competitive striving is most intense or most crucial. Competition for mates is greatest just before the usual ages of marriage, and the extent to which an individual is able to begin effectively to climb the ladder of affluence may also be determined at about the same ages. Lawbreaking is strongly concentrated during ages 17-22 in technological nations.[26] These are also the precise ages at which Yanomamö Indians, and probably men in most societies, suffer their highest mortality, mostly from intergroup aggression, and also the ages of highest likelihood of military induction.[27] These ages immediately precede those at which marriage is most frequent.

Lawbreaking is expected to be higher in individuals or groups most inhibited from climbing the ladder of affluence or using the system legally to accumulate resources. Moreover, lawbreaking should be even more heavily concentrated in males who are more or less publicly identified as likely to have such difficulties. Thus:

(a) Lawbreaking should be, and is, higher in minority-group males than in majority-group males.[28]

(b) Lawbreaking should be, and is, higher in publicly (e.g., physically) identifiable minority-group males than in those not publicly identifiable.[28]

(c) In the absence of publicly identifiable minority groups, lawbreaking should be highest in young males whose families give them least assistance in climbing the ladder of affluence. The most dramatic correlation found by Ferracuti and Dinitz (1974) with delinquency in a racially homogenous Puerto Rican situation was with lowering social status of the boy's family.[29]

Lawbreaking is also higher in families lacking one parent—especially the father—in families that are less religious, and in families with less control over their children and who give their children less assistance, encouragement, and attention, but who punish them more often.[29]

Finally, we may consider alternative strategies of reproductive competition among males, their distribution, and their consequences for patterns of lawlessness. I assume that freedom of opportunity to "climb the ladder of affluence" is a crucial aspect of sexual competition which, when available, will supplant all others—that is, that males who are either affluent or have a very high likelihood of becoming affluent are among the most desirable mates. Such males are unlikely to be lawbreakers, except in the context of using the system to further their affluence illegally, such as by income tax tricks or misuse of power associated with affluence.

In contrast, one expects alternative strategies, such as behavior that can be considered under the general label of "machismo," or flash and braggadocio, to be concentrated in individuals or groups whose likelihood of climbing the ladder of affluence ("using the system" effectively) is lowest, and especially when this low likelihood is publicly projected by inescapable identification with a disadvantaged group, such as a minority that the system discriminates against. "Macho" strategies of sexual competition are at once declarations of desirable qualities other than affluence, denials of the value of affluence as usually measured, rejections of the system, and declarations of a degree of disdain and independence with regard to the rules of the system. Sexual competition by macho behavior is almost by definition a declaration of lawlessness, or willingness to break the law.

In summary, the predictions may be met that (a) macho behavior, such as flashy dressing and abandonment of spouses and families, and (b) lawbreaking will be concentrated in men who (i) are young, (ii) lack wealthy, influential, successful, or powerful relatives, and (iii) are recognizable as members of minority or other disadvantaged groups. It is an obvious corollary that somehow to equalize the possibilities of individual men of all classes and origins of "climbing the ladder of affluence"—at least in terms of personal capabilities (and how they are seen by their possessors)—would provide the most reliable if not the easiest way of reducing the problem of overcrowding in prisons. Perhaps not surprisingly, this conclusion is consistent with those arrived at from entirely different approaches, and after very extensive examinations of correlates of crime and delinquency.[30]

Nepotism and Reciprocity

At this point I think it is necessary to distinguish explicitly two general classes of social interactions which have different characteristics and different outcomes. Although their differences and similarities are thoroughly explored elsewhere,[31] their changing relationship to societal laws in different kinds and sizes of groups requires a brief summary here.

Nepotism implies that benefits are given by one individual to another without reciprocation, the gain to the first individual resulting from the genetic overlap between the two. Reciprocity implies that benefits are only given when there is a high likelihood of a compensating return to the phenotype of the benefit giver (but, conceivably, the return could be to the phenotypes of relatives of the benefit giver). Only reciprocity can evolve within groups of unrelated individuals. In groups of equally related individuals (or individuals who cannot respond to differences in degrees of relatedness and can only evolve to respond in terms of average relatedness), nepotism will also evolve such that only two kinds of individuals will be distinguished: group members and nongroup members. Reciprocity can also evolve in such groups.

What happens in groups of variously related individuals, within which the individuals can respond to the differences in relationships? Obviously, when reciprocity is unlikely, closer relatives should be favored in beneficence. But so should they if there is any doubt about reciprocity, as there must always be. One can better afford to lose, and less afford to cheat, in reciprocity with a relative, and more so with a closer relative than with a more distant one.

Even parental behavior is, like reciprocity, an investment involving the risk that it may not yield a suitable return. If acts of nepotism should be directed at one's closest relatives, among those with equal needs, so should acts of reciprocity, assuming no variation in cost-benefit ratios. This means that in groups of variously related individuals, nepotism and reciprocity will always tend to be intricated. Thus, reciprocity can evolve alone, but only in groups of unrelated individuals; but nepotism evidently cannot evolve independently of reciprocity because reciprocity will always be potentially a factor in the social interactions of groups within which nepotism can evolve. This fact may be responsible for many of the confusing aspects of human systems of kinship cooperation and altruism that have led social scientists to doubt their derivation from a history of differential reproduction.[32]

Elsewhere I have argued that nepotistic behavior toward non-descendant relatives evolves out of parent-offspring interactions, and that reciprocity derives from nepotism.[33] Here I suggest that authority, in regard to regulation of social interactions, originates in parental authority, and that parental control of resources is a major aspect of rule construction and enforcement. From this beginning the extension to nepotism is small in the forms of assisting relatives in efforts to obtain repayment of debts owed them, avenging wrongs done to relatives, and accepting responsibility for debts incurred by relatives.

The development of nation-states correlates with the suppression of nepotism, a rise of concern with law and order, a rise of belief in the authority of divine beings or rulers, and an acceptance of nobility and divinity in leaders and rulers. I ask whether there is a connection between these changes and the original parental authority, with the origins of divinity being reverence toward deceased powerful ancestors and the effort to use their presumed wishes and authority to promote order, and to use the ability to convince others of either special knowledge of such ancestors' wishes or communication with them to succeed to leadership and power (hence, I suppose, unusual reproductive opportunities). I do not suppose it an accident that God should have come to be regarded as a "Father in Heaven."

Changes in Rules with Development of Nation-States

I have already argued that the rise of nation-states occurred as a result of the interactions of neighboring competitive and hostile groups expanding their alliances and cementing unities in a balance-of-power race. Now I suggest that rather than the rise of the nation-state being understandable through knowledge of its internal workings,[34] the internal workings of the nation-state are understandable only in terms of the reasons for its appearance, namely, intergroup aggression and competition. Let us examine briefly the sources and kinds of rules in the different kinds of societies compared by Flannery and widely regarded as representing stages preceding the nation-state. They are bands, tribes, chiefdoms, and stratified societies. In drawing heavily from Flannery's review, which I find consistent with other writings on this topic, I note that Flannery wrote in total unawareness of the arguments I am making.

Flannery notes that the only "segments" of *bands* are "families or groups of related families" and their "means of integration are usually limited to familial bonds of kinship and marriage, plus common residence. Leadership is informal and ephemeral; division of labor is along the lines of age and sex; and concepts of territoriality, descent, or lineage are weakly developed."

In extant band societies there is little heritable wealth. Social interactions are said to be based largely on "reciprocity," but the term has been used by anthropologists who did not distinguish nepotism and reciprocity. Wiessner[35] has evidence that in Kalahari Bushmen "reciprocity" is essentially limited to known genetic relatives, and it is practiced more with closer relatives than with more distant ones.

What authority there is in band societies seems to derive largely from parents and collections of parents, especially older men. Relatives defend and avenge one another, and they are expected to do so. The social "cement" of band societies is clearly nepotism.

Tribes are larger groups "whose segments are groups of families related by common descent or by membership in a variety of kinbased groups (clans, lineages, descent lines, kindreds, etc.). . . . Ancestors are often revered, and it is believed that they continue to take part in the activities of the lineage even after death. . . . Since 'tribes,' like bands, have weak and ephemeral leadership, they are further integrated (and even, it has been argued, regulate their environmental and interpersonal relations) by elaborate ceremonies and rituals. Some of these are conducted by formal 'sodalities' or 'fraternal orders' in which members of many lineages participate. . . . 'Tribes' frequently have ceremonies which are regularly scheduled . . . [and] may help to maintain undegraded environments, limit intergroup raiding, adjust man-land ratios, facilitate trade, redistribute natural resources, and 'level' any differences in wealth which threaten societies' egalitarian structure. . . ."[36]

It seems to me that Flannery may be describing the rudiments of laws that hold together groups of not-so-close relatives by imposing and maintaining restrictions on reproductive competition. He describes from archaeological finds "pottery masks . . . countless figurines of dancers . . . incredible accumulations of shell rattles, deer scapula rasps, turtle shell drums, conch shell trumpets . . ." which suggest not only ceremony but significant differentials in heritable wealth.

Chagnon[37] has noted that Yanomamö Indians may not mention the dead. Yet the Yanomamö, he assures me, otherwise fit Flannery's usage of tribes. This sensitivity around the use of ancestors may indicate the difference between allowing and not allowing succession to power and influence by identification with powerful deceased relatives. The Yanomamö tend to fission when a powerful ancestor dies, with the sizes of groups at fissioning correlated with degree of genetic relatedness in the groups. Tribes discussed by Flannery revere such ancestors, and, one supposes, may use them to enhance unity in their societies of groups of related families. The power of parents and the unity of nepotism thus still appear the major source of authority and rules in the tribal societies to which Flannery refers.

Chiefdoms are still larger groups in which "lineages are 'ranked' with regard to each other, and men from birth are of 'chiefly' or 'commoner descent.' " Such chiefs "are not merely of noble birth, but usually divine; they have special relationships with the gods which are denied commoners and which legitimize their right to demand community support and tribute . . . the chief . . . may be a priest . . . the office of 'chief' exists apart from the man who occupies it, and on his death the office must be filled by one of equally noble descent; some chiefdoms, maintained elaborate genealogies to establish this . . ."

"Since lineages are also property-holding units, it is not surprising to find that in some chiefdoms the best agricultural land or the best fishing localities are 'owned' by the highest-ranking lineages . . . high-ranking members of chiefdoms reinforce their status with sumptuary goods, some of which archaeologists later recover in the form of 'art works' in jade, turquoise, alabaster, gold, lapis lazuli, and so on."[38]

In chiefdoms it would appear that sources of authority have become more significant than in small groups, sometimes shifting from parental authority to deceased ancestors to gods representing extensions of such deceased ancestors. One also notices that the "office" of chief has itself become a vehicle of potential reproductive success for the individual who attains it—hence, itself a sought-after position (i.e., it is no longer strictly a vehicle for nepotism to the entire subject group, as in the case of a family patriarch). This opportunity is accepted and allowed by group members, perhaps because of the value to them of competition for the position of chief, which increases the likelihood that their leader will be a capable one.

Finally, "The state is a type of very strong, usually highly centralized government, with a professional ruling class, largely divorced from the bonds of kinship which characterize simpler societies. It is highly stratified and extremely diversified internally, with residential patterns often based on occupational specialization rather than blood or affinal relationship. The state attempts to maintain a monopoly of force, and is characterized by true law; almost any crime may be considered a crime against the state, in which case punishment is meted out by the state according to codified procedures, rather than being the responsibility of the offended party or his kin, as in simpler societies. While individual citizens must forego violence the state can wage war; it can also draft soldiers, levy taxes, and exact tribute."[39]

Nepotism displays a peculiarly altered condition within the nation-state, as compared to the smaller kinds of human societies in which it may represent the basic social cement. Nepotism obviously cannot be the social cement of nation-states of millions or hundreds of millions of individuals; only reciprocity can fulfill this function; and, of course, the interactions of individuals in nation-states are always organized around barter, currency, and various kinds of legal obligations and documents which ensure that debts are paid. So, within large nation-states we retain ties chiefly to the immediate family, and we tend to identify as immediate family parents, offspring, and siblings. Because there is a correlation between the uniquely human phenomenon of socially imposed monogamy and the nation-state, everyone in the immediate family is related to Ego by 1/2; nephews, nieces, aunts, and uncles by 1/4; first cousins by 1/8. More distant relatives are generally classed just that way—as "distant relatives." We do not usually organize into clans, and when we do we are usually regarded as behaving outside the law. So nepotism in the nation-state seems focused on the individual and the immediate family, with its vestiges outside the family likely often "misdirected," in historical, reproductive terms (especially in modern societies with the high and novel degree of mobility of our own) to neighbors, roommates, or others whose social relationships to us mimic those of relatives in the past. The functional relationships between nepotism and reciprocity described earlier thus correspond to the roles and relative prominences of these two related aspects of sociality in the different kinds and sizes of human social systems extant today and believed roughly to correspond to stages in the development of the nation-state.[40]

It seems to me that the categories into which the laws of nation-states can be arranged are commensurate with the biological arguments made above: (1) those which prevent individuals or groups from too severely interfering with the reproductive success of others, (2) those which prevent individuals or groups from too dramatically enhancing their own reproductive success, and (3) those which promote industry and creativity in individuals and groups in ways that may be exploited or plagiarized by the larger collective. Examples of laws in these three categories, respectively, are those concerning:

a. murder, assault, rape, kidnapping, treason, theft, extortion, breach of contract.
b. polygamy, nepotism, tax evasion, draft evasion, monopolies.
c. patents, copyrights, wills.

As a final comment, I cannot resist noting that the Ten Commandments look like a legal prescription for the maintenance of a nation-state. I find it easy to interpret the first four, all of which deal with paying homage to God and not breaking his laws, as referring to the importance of preserving the large group. I am impressed that 40 percent of the rules seem concerned with this issue.

The fifth says that we should also honor our parents. This is commensurate with arguments advanced so far: Half of the commandments thus deal with respecting sources of authority or not tampering with current distributions of resource control. These are the commandments that include threats of retribution. Even the fifth concludes its admonishment with the phrase "that thy days may be long in the land which the Lord thy God giveth thee," probably, however, referring to the family's survival rather than that of the individual—hence, effectively referring to genes rather than individuals!

The next four commandments tell us not to kill, commit adultery, steal, or lie. The tenth tells us not even to think about it. I am particularly impressed with the tenth commandment because, in my experience, humans tend to regard as first novel and bizarre, then ludicrous and outrageous, the suggestion that their evolutionary history may have primed them to be wholly concerned with genetic reproduction (in the environments of history). How does it happen, that in the course of evolving consciousness as a state into or through which *some* of our behaviors are expressed, we are so emphatic (and public) about rejecting this seemingly ever-so-reasonable one? Simultaneously we seem to reject the possibility that what we are truly about could be something we hadn't really thought of—personally and individually. It makes one wonder, quite seriously, if there might not be something incompatible about telling young children all about natural selection and rearing them to be properly and effectively social in the ways that we always have.[41]

Evolution and Normative Ethics

The arguments given above, and the cited references, make it clear why I believe that evolution has more to say about why people do what they do than any other theory. In contrast, my answer to the question: "What does evolution have to say about normative ethics, or what people *ought* to be doing?" is: "Nothing whatsoever." Apparently this response is so startling that I am required to explain it.

I have two reasons for giving this answer. The first is that I regard humans as sufficiently plastic in their behavior to accomplish almost *whatever they wish*. The emphasis is on the final phrase because this is the crucial question.

There is an unfortunately prevalent attitude that to suppose an evolutionary background for behavior automatically supposes a predictable future into which we are helplessly cast as a consequence of the ontogenetic determinism produced in us by the history of selective action on our genes. The feeling seems to be that all evolution has to offer is information about our inevitable route through history. No one wants to know all about his future, unless the knowledge, paradoxically, promises to help him change it; and most people doubt anyway that such knowledge is possible. I am sure these feelings give rise to one kind of anti-evolutionism.

People who think this way are missing the fact that the life histories of individual organisms and the fates of species are predictable, in evolutionary terms, only to the extent that environments and their effects are predictable. For a species whose individual members possess cognitive and reflective ability, and the power of conscious prediction and testing of predictions, even the knowledge of its evolutionary history, and the interpretation of its individual tendencies in different ontogenetic environments on account of that history, become parts of the environment that determine its future. Indeed, I am contributing to this book solely because it seems to me that no other aspect of the human experience could possibly be so massively influential upon our future as a clear comprehension of the reasons, and therefore to some extent the nature, of the fine tuning of our personalities, individually and collectively, from the effects of an inexorable process of differential reproduction during our history.

I am saying that what a knowledge of evolution really offers us, in terms of the future, is an elaboration not a restricting of ontogenetic possibilities, of life history or life-style opportunities, and of collective potential for accomplishing whatever may be desired. It does this by telling us who we really are, and, therefore, how to become whatever we may want to become. Evolutionary understanding, then, more than anything, has the power to make humans sufficiently plastic to accomplish *whatever they wish*. This grandiose notion, of course, loses all its glamour if there is any doubt at all about the centrality of evolutionary theory as explanatory of human nature.

My second reason for denying that evolutionary understanding carries lessons about what we *ought* to be doing involves the background of such notions. Ethical structures have been developed throughout history without any extensive direct knowledge or conscious perception of the evolutionary process. If they have in any sense converged upon what might have generated in the presence of such understanding it has to be because individuals and collectives of individuals have identified rights and wrongs in terms of effects, ultimately, upon reproductive success. I have already argued that they have done so, and I think it is obvious that they have usually done so without any conscious knowledge of the relationship of reproductive success to either history or proximate rewards like sensations of pleasure or well being.

Does this mean, however, that opportunities for reproductive success necessarily must lie at the heart of our considerations of normative ethics for the future? I can see no reason for such an assumption.

So we are returned to proximate rewards, which have formed the basis for all systems of normative ethics anyway, without any particular evidence of their connections to ultimate reproductive success. No one needs evolutionary theory to identify proximate rewards in his own life, although such theory may clarify their significance to us. Moreover, anyone who rejects as a proximate reward to himself whatever may be identified as such from evolutionary considerations by definition cannot, in my opinion, be wrong.

However proper systems of normative ethics are identified, then, evolutionary considerations almost surely can help to achieve the goal. It must be obvious that I think that it can do this better than any other kind of knowledge. But evolutionary understanding has little or nothing to tell us about how to identify the goal. At most it may suggest that this question is destined to remain much more complex than we would like, that answers to it will change rather than become simple and static, and that it will never be answerable for all time at any particular time.[42]

NOTES

1. This step has been possible so far with very few traits of very few organisms, and only then on short-term bases or with rather low

levels of certainty. The truth is that we do not yet know with much confidence such things as why the dinosaurs became extinct. Attempts at syntheses of the sort implied here are likely, however, to be prominent features of evolutionary investigations in the future, and I think we may expect them to occur first in three areas: (1) the evolution of sterile castes in insects (because the underlying genetics in Hymenoptera—the major group involved—are asymmetrical owing to haplodiploid sex determination, and we understand them well); (2) the evolution of mating behavior in arthropods and vertebrates (because so much comparative analysis is possible and so much relevant information is available from related studies, like the use of genitalic morphology by taxonomists); and (3) the evolution of human social behavior (because we are so fascinated by it, and because paleontological and archaeological data continue to be gathered so rapidly).

2. The reasons for this assumption are not widely discussed. Some of them are the following: (1) altering directions of selection alters directions of genetic change in organisms; (2) the causes of mutations (chiefly radiation) and the causes of selection (Darwin's "hostile forces" of food shortages, climate, weather, predators, parasites, and diseases) are independent of one another; (3) only the causes of selection remain consistently directional for relatively long periods (thus could explain long-term directional changes); and (4) predictions based on the assumption that adaptiveness depends solely upon selection work. A prime example of the last is the history of sex ratio selection, traceable from the work of R. A. Fisher, *The Genetical Theory of Natural Selection,* New York: Dover, 1958; (1st ed. 1930), pp. 158-62; W. D. Hamilton, "Extraordinary Sex Ratios," *Science* 154 (1967): 477-88; R. L. Trivers and D. Willard, "Natural Selection of Parental Ability to Vary the Sex Ratio of Offspring," *Science* 179 (1973): 90-2; R. L. Trivers and H. Hare, "Haplodiploidy and the Evolution of the Social Insects," *Science* 191 (1976): 249-63; R. D. Alexander and P. W. Sherman, "Local Mate Competition and Parental Investment in Social Insects," *Science* 196 (1977): 494-500; R. D. Alexander, J. L. Hoogland, R. D. Howard, K. M. Noonan, and P. W. Sherman, "Sexual Dimorphisms and Breeding Systems in Pinnipeds, Ungulates, Primates, and Humans," to appear in *Evolutionary Biology and Human Social Behavior: An Anthropological Perspective,* ed. N. A. Chagnon and W. G. Irons, (North Scituate, Mass.: Duxbury Press).

3. See also R. C. Lewontin, "The Units of Selection," *Annual Review of Ecology and Systematics,* 1 (1970): 1-18; R. D. Alexander and

G. Borgia, "Group selection, altruism, and the hierarchical organization of life," *Annual Review of Ecology and Systematics* 9 (1978).
4. See references in the following: R. D. Alexander, "The Search for an Evolutionary Philosophy of Man," *Proceedings of the Royal Society of Victoria, 84 (1971): 99-120;* "The Evolution of Social Behavior," *Annual Review of Ecology and Systematics,* 5 (1974): 325-83; "The Search for a General Theory of Behavior," *Behavioral Science,* 20 (1975): 77-100; "Natural Selection and the Analysis of Human Sociality," in the *Changing Scenes in Natural Sciences,* 1776-1976. ed. C. E. Goulden, Philadelphia Academy of Natural Sciences Special Publication 12 (1977) 283-337. "Natural Selection and Social Exchange," in *Social Exchange in Developing Relationships,* ed. R. L. Burgess and T. L. Huston, (New York: Academic Press, 1978); "Evolution, Human Behavior, and Determinism," *Proceedings of the Biennial Meeting of the Philosophy of Science Association, 2 (1977): 3-21.*
5. Here I add a reservation about the enthusiasm which has occurred in the wake of Williams's 1966 book, and as a result of W. D. Hamilton's theory of inclusive fitness in "The Genetical Evolution of Social Behaviour, I, II," *Journal of Theoretical Biology, 7* (1964): 1-52 (later referred to generally as "kin selection"). Hamilton followed Fisher *(The Genetical Theory of Natural Selection)* and others in pointing out that organisms can reproduce genetically not only via their direct descendants but also through whatever other nondescendant relatives may be socially available to them. In other words, nepotism to any genetic relative may be part of an organism's strategy of reproduction through altruism to others (altruism being defined as acts that at some expense or risk to the actor contribute to the well being—actually the reproduction—of others). Since humans are more extensively and complexly nepotistic than any other organism, Hamilton's arguments are immediately interesting to anyone concerned with human behavior. Hamilton's arguments also focused attention on subgenotypic elements, since they deal with reproductive costs and benefits to anyone of helping relatives with different fractional genetic overlaps. My caution has to do with the fact that evolutionary biologists have followed the lure of simplified quantitative genetics, perhaps without due care, right to the gene level. A prime illustration is the recent book by Richard Dawkins titled *The Selfish Gene* (New York: Oxford University Press, 1976). The same trend followed the rediscovery of Mendel's results, and that approach was eventually termed "bean bag genetics." As Ernst Mayr put it ("The Unity of the Genotype,"

Biologisches Zentralblatt, 94 (1975): 377-88), "The approach . . . became entirely atomistic and, for the sake of convenience, each gene was treated as if it were quite independent of all others. In due time all sorts of phenomena were discovered which contradicted this interpretation, such as the linkage of genes, epistasis, pleiotropy, and polygeny, and yet in evolutionary discussions only lip service was paid to these complications. . . . The purely analytical school thought that . . . an integrative attitude was incompatible with a meaningful analysis and dangerously close to such a stultifying concept as holism." Sooner or later, I believe, we must return to the individual as the most potent level at which selection works (See Lewontin, "The Units of Selection"). This simply means that, whatever we decide about subgenotypic levels, we will be forced to consider at every step what is meant by the fact that genes do not produce their effects independently of their genetic environments and are not inherited separately. This question may seem largely academic for social scientists, since the interests of genes and genotypes are so often synonymous; however, the prominence of certain questions, like kin selection and the outcome of parent-offspring conflict (see R. L. Trivers, "Parent-Offspring Conflict," *American Zoologist,* 14 [1974]: 249-64; Alexander, "The Evolution of Social Behavior") indicates that subgenomic considerations cannot be ignored, even by social scientists. Moreover, useful parallels can be drawn between the effects of selection on organization at subgenomic and supragenomic (i.e., social) levels (see Alexander and Borgia, "Group Selection, Altruism, and the Hierarchical Organization of Life").

6. The potential significance of this approach is amply illustrated by several recent studies showing that, while culture clearly is *potentially* independent of the interests of the genes, in fact cultural patterns in regard to social activities like birth-spacing, infanticide, reciprocity, war, inheritance, and interactions of genetic kin reflect to a surprising degree the genetic interests of their perpetrators (Alexander, "Natural Selection and the Analysis of Human Sociality"; chapters by various authors in Chagnon and Irons, *Evolutionary Biology.* . .).

7. Some of my students suggested two special cases that do not fit well into these general categories: (4) communal winter clusters (e.g., of flying squirrels) which may chiefly gain from minimizing energy loss, and (5) the V-formation of migrating waterfowl in which individuals may gain from pooling their information about the long migratory route. W. J. Freeland ("Pathogens and the Evolution of Primate Sociality," *Biotropica,* 8 (1976): 12-24) ar-

gues that disease may be an alternative cause of group living, but his arguments seem more to involve modifications of group living, once other causes establish and maintain it, because of the expense of diseases under group living.

8. Relative food shortages are here regarded as a "hostile force of nature," as Darwin also regarded them.

9. I use the term "function" in this paper essentially in the sense of Williams, *Adaptation and Natural Selection* (Princeton, N.J.: Princeton University Press, 1966) (and now of evolutionary biology more or less generally) to mean *evolved adaptive significance.* In other words, I use it to refer to any contributing factor supposed or hypothesized to be responsible for the selective origin and maintenance of the phenomenon, as opposed to (1) effects (Williams's "incidental effects") or (2) contributing causes unable by themselves to account for the phenomenon. Thus, there is an implicit assumption that what I am calling the *function* of an act or other phenotypic expression is alone capable of producing and maintaining the phenomenon; or that is an hypothesis under consideration. In this sense I am searching for single causes, and I regard this procedure as a logical approach to causation in biological phenomena. Multiple causes should be accepted only when single ones prove insufficient. If the absence of truly broad generalizations in the search for understanding of human existence should happen to be attributable to our long-term failure to reconcile the search with the principles of organic evolution, then our reluctance to admit the possibility of "single causes" should at least be tempered somewhat when we enter into a stage of rapid and massive incorporation of evolutionary principles, as I believe is the case at the moment.

10. Alexander, "The Search for an Evolutionary Philosophy of Man," pp. 115-17.

11. A. Keith. *A New Theory of Human Evolution.* (New York: Philosophical Library, 1949); Alexander "The Search for an Evolutionary Philosophy of Man"; R. D. Alexander and D. W. Tinkle, "A Comparative Book Review of *On Aggression* by Konrad Lorenz and *The Territorial Imperative* by Robert Ardrey," *Bioscience,* 18 (1968): 245-48; R. S. Bigelow, *The Dawn Warriors* (Boston: Little, Brown, 1969); R. L. Carneiro, "Slash- and Burn-Cultivation among the Kuikuru and Its Implications for Cultural Development in the Amazon Basin," in *The Evolution of Horticultural Systems in Native South America: Causes and Consequences; A Symposium,* ed. J. Wilbert, *Antropologica* (Venezuela), Suppl. 2 (1961): 47-67; E. O. Wilson, "On the Queerness of Social Evolution," *Bulletin of the Entomological Society of America,* 19 (1973): 20-22; E. O. Wilson,

Sociobiology: The New Synthesis. (Cambridge, Mass.: Harvard University Press, 1975); W. H. Durham, "Resource Competition and Human Aggression. Part I. A Review of Primitive War." *Quarterly Review of Biology,* 51, (1976): 385-415.

12. I am not implying that no other forces *influence* group sizes and structures but that balances of power provide the basic sizes and kinds of groups upon which secondary forces like resource distribution, population densities, agricultural and technological developments, and effects of diseases exert their influences.

13. For a discussion of the multiple consequences of this situation, see R. D. Alexander *et al,* in Chagnon and Irons, *Evolutionary Biology.* . . .

14. K. Flannery, "The Evolution of Civilizations." *Annual Review of Ecology and Systematics,* 8 (1972): 399-426. R. L. Carneiro, "Slash- and Burn-Cultivation . . ."; D. Webster, "Warfare and the Evolution of the State: a Reconsideration." *American Antiquity* 40 (1975): 464-70.

15. The criticism is sometimes made that Flannery's (ibid.) kind of reconstruction assumes that a particular modern ethnographic example is an exact replicate of its archaeological (and extinct) counterpart, or even, in the extreme, that the ethnographic and archaeological examples are implied to give rise to one another, always progressing from simple to complex. This attitude implies a basic misunderstanding of comparative method. Comparative method, in biology or archaeology, assumes: (1) that sequences of change have occurred (genetic evolution and cultural change); (2) that parallel sequences of change occur in different places, at different times, and in different lines at the same times and places; (3) that some (but not all) of the attributes of different stages (but not the actual cases or even, necessarily, the actual sequences) will be represented in both extant and extinct forms, and (4) that appropriate comparisons of such attributes can yield information about the sequences of change and their causes. These assumptions allow interpretation of the past by studying the present, or vice versa, and comparative method, explicitly in the sense described here, represents the main source of evidence for both evolutionary biology and archaeology.

16. There *are* genetic and physiological constraints on natural selection: They are recognized by evolutionists under the term "specialization." An animal like a mole, specialized to live underground, is less likely to evolve wings than one, like a squirrel, which spends its time climbing and leaping from tree to tree. This is a very simple example, but the argument is essentially the same whether

one is considering subgenomic interactions or populational phenomena.

17. H. W. Power, "On Forces of Selection in the Evolution of Mating Types. *American Naturalist,* 110 (1976): 937-44.

18. Carneiro, "Slash- and Burn-Cultivation . . .," actually approached this argument with his concepts of environmental and social circumscription.

19. See Fisher, *The Genetical Theory* . . . on "Heroism and the Higher Human Faculties."

20. H. Kelsen. *What is Justice? Justice, Law, and Politics in the Mirror of Science; Collected Essays.* (Berkeley: University of California Press, 1957).

21. I am in no way arguing that all humans always behave so as to maximize reproduction but I am arguing that this is what they have *evolved* to do, in the *environments of* history, and that we must know ourselves in this way to understand best all of our inclinations and our motivations.

22. I would expect the function of laws (see footnote 9) to be the limitation of the reproductive striving of those *other than* the legislators and enforcers themselves; it is an incidental effect that legislators and enforcers are limited by the same laws—although from the viewpoint of those requiring legislators and enforcers to follow the same laws they have to follow (another form of enforcement), this "effect" in turn becomes a function.

23. R. D. Alexander *et al.,* "Sexual Dimorphisms and Breeding Systems . . ."

24. E. H. Sutherland and R. Cressey, *Principles of Criminology,* 7th ed. (New York: Lippincott, 1966), p. 26, note that: "The crime rate for men is greatly in excess of the rate for women—in all nations, all communities within a nation, all age groups, all periods of history for which organized statistics are available, and for all types of crime except those peculiar to women, such as infanticide and abortion."

25. Moreover, only very recently (e.g., Michigan Supreme Court ruling, 1977) has it been suggested formally that a woman has the right to choose sexual partners, in the sense that her sexual behavior in general cannot be used against her in court proceedings testing whether or not, in a specific instance, she has been raped.

26. D. J. Mulvihill and M. M. Tumin, *Crimes of Violence* (Washington, D.C.: U.S. Government Printing Office, 1969).

27. N. A. Chagnon, *Yanomamö: The Fierce People* (New York: Holt, Rinehart, and Winston, 1968); J. Himelhoch, "A Psychosocial Model for the Reduction of Lower-Class Youth Crime," in R. L.

Akers and E. Sagarin, eds., *Crime Prevention and Social Control* (New York: Praeger, 1972) pp. 3-14; Sutherland and Cressey, *Principles of Criminology*; Mulvihill and Tumin, *Crimes of Violence*.

28. F. Ferracuti and S. Dinitz. "Cross-cultural Aspects of Delinquent and Criminal Behavior," in M. Reidel and T. P. Thornberry, eds, *Crime and Delinquency: Dimensions of Deviance.* (New York: Praeger, 1974), pp. 18-34; see also B. M. Fleisher, *The Economics of Delinquency* (New York: Quadrangle Books 1966).

29. F. Ferracuti and S. Dinitz, "Cross-cultural Aspects . . ."; J. Himelhoch, "A Psychosocial model . . ."; J. B. Cortes and F. M. Gatti, *Delinquency and Crime: A Bio-psychosocial Approach.* (New York: Seminar Press, 1972); J. P. Clark and E. P. Wenninger, "Socioeconomic Class and Area as Correlates of Illegal Behavior among Juveniles." *American Sociological Review,* 27 (1962): 826-34. See also B. M. Fleisher, *The Economics of Delinquency.*

30. R. A. Cloward and L. E. Ohlin, *Delinquency and Opportunity* (Glencoe, Ill.: The Free Press, 1960); Fleisher, *Economics of Delinquency*; T. Hirschi, *Causes of Delinquency* (Berkeley: University of California Press, 1969); L. Radsinowski and M. E. Wolfgang, eds., *Crime and Justice. The Criminal in Society*, vol. 1; (New York: Basic Books, 1971); C. A. Hartjen, *Crime and Criminalization (New York: Praeger, 1974).*

31. Hamilton, "The Genetical Evolution . . ."; R. L. Trivers, "The Evolution of Reciprocal Altruism," 1971; M. J. West Eberhard, "The Evolution of Social Behavior by Kin Selection," *Quarterly Review of Biology,* 50 (1975): 1-33; Alexander, "The Evolution of Social Behavior"; "Natural Selection and the Analysis of Human Sociality" 1977; "Natural Selection and Social Exchange" 1978.

32. Trivers, ibid.; Alexander, ibid.

33. Alexander, ibid.; Alexander and Borgia, "Natural Selection and the Hierarchical Organization of Life."

34. Flannery, "The Evolution of Civilizations."

35. P. Wiessner, *Hxaro: A Regional System of Reciprocity among the !Kung San for Reducing Risk.* Ph.D. Thesis, University of Michigan (1977).

36. Flannery, "The Evolution of Civilizations."

37. N. A. Chagnon, *Yanomamö: The Fierce People;* "Genealogy, Solidarity, and Relatedness: Limits to Local Group Size and Patterns of Fission in Expanding Populations." *Yearbook of Physical Anthropology,* 19 (1975): 95-100; (1974).

38. Flannery, "The Evolution of Civilizations."

39. Flannery, Ibid.

40. P. Stein and J. Shand, *Legal Values in Western Society*. (Edinburgh: Edinburgh University Press, 1974), pp. 114-16, provide a closely parallel but evidently independent comment: "In the fellowship type of social relationship, the value of the individual as a person is secured by the mutual regard and affection of the members for each other. The nature of the relationship is such that every member can confidently rely on receiving respect from the others. Their mutual regard is the product of its personal character. Such a social group cushions its members against the impact of legal rules. For example, early Celtic society, which was largely pastoral, displayed marked fellowship features. The main social unit was the kindred, the *drebfhine* of Ireland and Gaelic Scotland, which extended for four generations. The act of one individual might affect all the members of the kindred, each could claim his share in any inheritance, and each was bound to assume his share of liability for any fines payable by any member. As Nora Chadwick says:

> There was no personal payment. The 'kindred' stood or fell together. In this way they were responsible for one another and would obviously keep a close eye on one another's doings. In this way too every 'kindred' group would see to it that the kindred did duty as both police and judges. There could have been no better way in such a society of keeping justice on an even keel, and this helps to explain the relative scarcity of legal machinery which a study of so many legal tracts implies.

"Traces of such group feeling can be found even today in closely knit family groups, which regard themselves as culturally distinct from the rest of society. Gypsies, for example, settle their disputes themselves according to their own customs, and will rarely have recourse to law, except in their dealings with outsiders. If a member of a gypsy family in East Anglia is accused of a motoring offence, it is common for his whole family to accompany him to court, and if he is convicted and fined they will all contribute as a matter of course to its payment.

"As societies develop into the nation-states, they cease to be collections of fellowship groups. These groups are replaced by less personal types of social relationship, in which the members feel no special regard for each other. In the newer relationships respect for persons cannot be taken for granted. Circumstances require that people be treated as individuals, and the position of the individual in society must be recognised by the law. Further, the precise character of the law is best adapted to a society whose members are treated as separate individuals rather than as members of groups. Historically, as laws have become more sophisticated, the more they have tended to make the individual rather than the group the focus of rights and duties. These considerations do not, however, imply the attribution of a particular value to the individual as against society.

"Ancient Roman society regarded property as belonging to the family, but quite early in its development it ascribed ownership to the head of the family, the *paterfamilias*. He could dispose of the family farm, for example, without the need to obtain the consent of other members of the family. The freedom of disposition applied both to alienations *inter vivos*, such as followed a sale of the property, and to those by will. Towards the end of the Republic, it is true, a testator was compelled to take into account the needs of his descendants when deciding the destination of his property after his death, but he was still allowed a very wide discretion. This aspect of the Roman law of property is sometimes cited as evidence of Roman dedication to the principle of individualism in the modern sense. Such an assumption is unwarranted. The freedom of disposition enjoyed by the Roman *paterfamilias* was legally and commercially convenient. Its exercise must be seen against the background of the strong social pressures of good faith, family piety, and neighbourly duty, summed up in the notion of *officium*. These pressures considerably inhibited the use which the *paterfamilias* made of his powers of disposition. Furthermore, what the Roman owner could do with his property, apart from his rights of disposition, was not so unrestricted as it has in modern times been declared to be. As we shall see, Roman law kept Roman owners within the limits of good neighbourliness, and the alleged 'absolute' character of Roman *dominium* has largely been read into the Roman texts by later generations of jurists imbued with non-Roman ideas. Had the Romans really been individualistic in the modern sense, they would have changed the rules whereby adult descendants, unless formally emancipated from the power of the *paterfamilias*, could own no property of their own in his lifetime. The law recognised their right to control what had come to them as a result of their own enterprise, such as military service, but anything they received by way of legacy or gift belonged to the *paterfamilias*, and was thus kept in the family funds of which he disposed."

41. I mean that our view of evolution may parallel our view of pornography, through reflections, conscious or not-so-conscious, about the effects of either on our children. Thus, we seem first to teach our children to be absolutely truthful—a way of operating that

clearly is incompatible with social, economic, and political success, probably in any society anywhere. *Then* we teach them to adjust the truth ever so slightly—and thereby successfully—to their own advantage. After they start telling Aunt Kate that she is fat, and such things, we begin to teach them to be what we so tactfully call tactful. Similarly, we seem first to teach our children that sex is an evil to be avoided—that too is a way of operating, for adults, at least, that is not usually compatible with either social or reproductive success. *Then* we teach them, or allow to develop, the circumstances in which sex is permissible and profitable; we allow them to learn that sex in these situations is enjoyable, and we try to teach them that sex in other situations is not. Perhaps, in each case, the sequence of learning is crucial; perhaps by these sequences alone we are able reliably to guide children to success in the sensitive business of sociality, sexuality, and morality. In each case a connection can be discerned between the education of children and the growth of understanding about evolution. In each case a possible explanation of the relationship between family stability and lawbreaking is discernible. Perhaps, without always being conscious of it, we tend to be repelled by evolutionary explanations, particularly of human sociality, because we somehow understand that full knowledge and acceptance of them would not be good for our children (see also R. D. Alexander. "Creation, Evolution, and Biology Teaching," *American Biology Teacher,* (Feb. 1978).

42. Donald Black's book, *The Behavior of Law* (New York: Academic Press, 1976) did not become available to me until the final draft of this manuscript was completed. Black's findings are relevant to my arguments and seem to support (even if inadvertently) the general viewpoint I have advocated. As his title suggests, for purposes of analysis, Black treats law as Leslie White, e.g., *The Science of Culture* (New York: Farrar, Straus, 1949) treated culture—as a thing apart from function, motivations, psychology, and individuals. He seeks correlates of the *quantity* of law (pp. 6-8) and tries to ascertain their effects. He defines law as "governmental social control" (p. 2), and quantifies it chiefly (p. 3) by "the number and scope of prohibitions, obligations, and other standards to which people are subject, and by the rate of legislation, litigation, and adjudication." He then examines the correlates of quantitative variations in law in different circumstances and societies, and emphasizes twenty-five or thirty such correlates, which may be condensed as follows: Law is "greater" (employed more often, or more effectively) in societies and social groups that are larger, more dense, more organized, more differentiated, more complex, more

stratified, and in circumstances in which there are fewer other social controls (e.g., less family control) and greater "relational" (social, genetic) distances among interactants (e.g., more during interactions between distant relatives, or nonrelatives, and "strangers"), than in the opposite kinds of societies, social groups, and circumstances. Within societies "more" law is directed (or law is directed more often and more effectively) at individuals and groups that are relatively low-ranking, uninfluential, transient, not "respectable," socially marginal, and more distantly related then in the opposite direction.

Black's approach treats law as a singular phenomenon whose traits can be analyzed and generalized. Because law is obviously not without function, and is not independent of the motivations of people, Black's success in locating a small number of general rules, despite the enormous variation in legal systems, suggests that a certain singularity of function, therefore of motivational background, may exist for law as a whole. That is also the argument made in my paper. Moreover, the particular correlates discovered by Black sometimes are the same as those I have emphasized, and his findings seem to support the arguments about the origins and functions of law described in my paper.

10

Evolution, Social Behavior, and Ethics

Richard D. Alexander

Introduction

NOTHING SEEMS LIKELY to influence analyses of the relationship between science and ethics as much as would a significant revision of our view of either science or ethics. Yet refinements of evolutionary theory within biology during the past twenty years seem to me to have provided a compelling new model of culture and human sociality which dramatically alters our interpretations of all human activities, including both science and ethics. This model has been developed elsewhere and the findings responsible for it described;[1] here I shall only summarize the attributes of the model, and the way in which it departs from earlier views, before discussing its apparent meaning for the current confrontation, or interaction, between science and ethics.

Culture theorists, philosophers, and historians have always wrestled with two related problems in their efforts to develop grand theories, the relationship between individual and group interests and the identification of function. Although various combinations of interpretations have been tried, the only one apparently consistent with modern evolutionary theory has not. Function, as *raison d'etre*, has characteristically been divided into proximate and ultimate forms. Proximate forms, such as satisfaction, pleasure, happiness, and avoidance of their alternatives, are more likely to be visualized as significant at the individual level; partly for this reason, psychology has developed with an emphasis on the individual. Some functions, such as efficiency of organization or operation, which could be regarded as either proximate or ultimate, are usually interpreted as group-level phenomena because social theorists have not commonly been concerned with genetic or physiological efficiency; this is especially true in anthropology, where explaining culture has been a principal focus; it is not so true in psychology, as Freudian theory indicates. Survival has often been regarded as the ultimate function and interpreted at either individual or group levels, although, because of frequent conflicts of interest, it obviously cannot always be interpreted at both levels.

The model recently developed within modern biology involves three assumptions: (a) proximate functions are never their own reasons for existence, but, in evolutionary terms, exist to serve ultimate function, hence, take their particular forms because of their contribution to ultimate function;[2] (b) ultimate function is invariably reproduction of the genetic materials because (i) no alternative to natural selection (differential reproduction of genetic alternatives) exists to explain the history of form and function in living things; (ii) natural selection proves both logically and empirically necessary and sufficient (in its present theoretical form); and (c) effects of natural selection on function are realized almost entirely, if not entirely, at the individual level or lower.[3]

As discussed later, and elsewhere,[4] this model returns the concept of function to survival, but to survival of genes (or polygenes, supergenes, and chromosomes)[5]—not of individuals (which clearly have not evolved to survive), and not of groups (which, however, give more of an illusion than do individuals of having the function of facilitating only their own survival).[6] Genes evidently have promoted their survival through effects leading to finiteness of individual lifetimes,[7] and, in social species, sometimes to indefinite prolongations of identifiable social groups. That this conclusion is discomforting to an organism with consciousness only at the individual level is not an appropriate reason for denying it.

The main element of the new view of sociality I have just described is clearly a return to a kind of individualistic and utilitarian view of history. It is, however, a view of individualism or utilitarianism never before held or advocated in efforts to explain human behavior and culture. Previous explanations of culture and human striving, as the outcome of individuals seeking to realize "their own best interests" or to "maximize their outcomes"[8] have never explicitly identified these "interests" and "outcomes," or else they have defined them in terms of either (a) proximate rewards, like happiness or (b) survival.[9] The view from evolutionary biology identifies "own best interest" in terms of reproductive success (or, in our current, novel, rapidly changing environment, surrogates of reproductive success), and hypothesizes that hedonistic rewards relate solely to such returns if they are interpreted in terms of the environments of history.[10] Growth, development, aid to reciprocating friends, and the acquisition of power are seen as the accumulation of resources; assistance to offspring and other relatives represents the redistribution of accumulated resources. Culture is seen as the cumulative effect of this "inclusive-fitness-maximizing" behavior[11] by all of the individuals who have lived during history. Culture, then, is the result of endless compromises, conflicts, power interactions, cooperative events, and formation and dissolution of coalitions. According to this view, there would be no single "function" of culture as a whole, as some anthropologists have supposed; nor should we expect even a few indentifiable functions.[12] Aside from those rare issues on which everyone agrees because everyone is aware (or behaves as though aware) that all of our interests are the same, I am suggesting that culture is an incidental effect of our separate, conflicting strivings in which success tends to be (in historical or evolutionary terms is invariably) measured in relative not absolute terms; that culture is the environment into which we are born and according to which we must achieve our goals; that cultural inertia, giving it the quality or appearance of being something greater than the humans responsible for it, is largely owing to the simultaneous effort of every one of us to use and manipulate it to serve our own interests, to keep everyone else from so using it when their efforts conflict with our own, and to extend (temporally and otherwise) our ability to redistribute resources according to our own interests.

At least eight major issues have clouded efforts to develop culture theory in this direction. First, reproduction involves altruism to other individuals, and in humans a bewildering array of genetic relatives of varying degree and varying needs is socially available to each individual. As a result, the altruism of nepotism gives an illusion of group function. On the other hand, the complexity and accuracy of knowledge of *differences* among kin support the idea that nepotism has been a major avenue of reproduction by *individuals*.[13]

Second, effects of the peculiarly human mode of reproductive striving, through group-living, persist as culture and technology long past individual lifetimes. This also gives an illusion of group function. As suggested earlier, much of this effect is also recognizable as a result of the striving of individuals to provide for relatives and descendants as far as possible into the future.

Third, as a part of group-living we are constantly forming and dissolving coalitions, or subgroups, of individuals who temporarily have common interests. Although this too gives an illusion of group function, the mere fact that coalitions are temporary and shifting indicates otherwise.

Fourth, we have turned our group-living and group-competitive behaviors to the development of nations within which reciprocal behaviors apparently derived historically from nepotistic interactions within clans and tribes form the social cement,[14] and within which extensive nepotism is both downplayed by law and thwarted by geographic mobility of individuals and families. This effect creates circumstances in which the altruism of nepotism is "misdirected," and others in which altruism with the function of maintaining acceptability in the group, or gaining status, and, hence, access to resources, again creates the illusion of group function.

Fifth, the accelerating rate of cultural innovation has caused massive novelty in our environment,[15] thwarting analyses based on function, except as interpreted in terms of past environments. Although this situation may lead to frequent errors, analyses of human behavior are still most likely to be accurate if they are developed from an understanding of the effects of a history of natural selection, with allowances for the particular kinds of environmental changes known or suspected to have occurred.[16]

Sixth, it has proved exceedingly difficult to trace the pathways between gene expressions and complex behaviors, so that the relationship of the latter to genetic reproduction, and therefore the importance of interactions among relatives, is still viewed with scepticism. The significance of this scepticism is much reduced by the knowledge that (a) the complete ontogeny is known for no behavior in any organism and (b) complex and accurate predictions about behavior have been made on a wide scale from a knowledge of selection alone.

Seventh, proximate mechanisms have not previously been hypothesized whereby altruistic nepotism and the altruism of reciprocity could be directed appropriately so as to maximize inclusive fitness (the reproduction of one's genes) and yet be commensurate with what is known about the plasticity of human behavior and theories of learning. At least in terms of reasonable theory I believe that this problem has been solved.[17]

Eighth, humans have found it difficult to evaluate with disinterest the suggestion that their evolutionary background has primed them to behave as the reproductive machinery of the genes. This fact seems to result in part from a tendency to self-deception which has its advantages in an extraordinary ability by humans to detect deliberate deception in others.[18]

Despite these difficulties, the theory that culture is no more or less than the outcome of inclusive-fitness-maximizing behavior by all of the individuals who have lived during history appears capable of surmounting the difficulties encountered by the older theories.[19] Although efforts have been made to describe this view of culture as "Hobbesian" or "utilitarian" in ways rendering it out of date, or as not different from other approaches that have already been tried and discarded, it is in fact distinct from any view previously generated. Although efforts have also been made to associate it with some particular ideology, such as social Darwinism, its testing is a procedure in natural history; regardless of what may be said, by either its proponents or its opponents, it is not properly ideological in nature.[20]

Science as a Social Enterprise

If my arguments to this point are acceptable, then science may be considered as a particular kind of activity of individuals, sometimes operating in groups, with certain unique characteristics and consequences. Its central attribute is its unusual degree of self-correction, induced by the criterion of repeatability of results. This aspect of scientific method, theoretically, at least, forces the practitioners of science to explain fully the methods by which they make their discoveries and reach their conclusion. The resulting tendency for scientific findings continually to approach correctness in explanation gives an illusion that scientists are devoted to a search for truth, hence, are somehow unusually humble and altruistic. Instead, the system of investigation called science, however it may have begun, *forces* its practitioners to report their methods as well as their results, or risk being exposed as unscientific and drummed out of their profession.[21] Scientists compete by striving to acquire authorship for as many of the best ideas as possible. This competition includes identifying and publishing the errors of others. As nearly all scientists are aware, the slightest taint of deliberate falsification of results or plagiarism is often enough to damage a career permanently, and may be vastly more significant than mere incompetence. I speculate that science, as a method of finding out about the universe, began as a consequence of competition among the ancients to prove their ability to comprehend cause and effect and to meet the challenges of one another for preeminence in this enterprise and the prestige and leadership that went with it. The requirement of repeatability is what distinguishes science, indeed, diametrically opposes it to dominance or prestige by virtue of claims of divine revelation or knowledge conferred by deities—although the two kinds of effort may exist for exactly the same reasons.

To understand why the public tolerates and supports scientists—even, sometimes, regarding science as the most prestigious of all enterprises—we must turn to the products or results of scientific investigation. These results are represented not only by all of the products of technology but by innumerable changes of attitude toward ourselves and our environment as a result of new knowledge. In some sense, essentially all of the reasons for societal affluence, and many of the reasons for our ability to achieve a modicum of serenity in the face of the uncertainties, complexities, and competitiveness engendered by the reasons for affluence, are seen as products of science. So, I suggest, science is supported for the same reason that copyright and patent laws are maintained to allow inventors to profit from their inventions. We evidently believe, individually and collectively (or we behave as though we believe), that the discoveries made by scientists are likely to benefit all of us sufficiently to make their support worthwhile. This view of science also contributes to the impression that scientists are humble truthseekers, in no way out to maximize personal gain. The truth, however, is something else, as is suggested by the enormous scale on which scientists are employed directly by organizations that exist for the sole purpose of making profits.

Now we can see that, so long as what scientists discover represents solutions to problems that face *all* humans, the relationship of science to any system of ethics regarded as functional and acceptable at the group level (that is, as helping everyone about equally) is clearly a harmonious one. Even a science practiced by individual scientists who are totally selfish in their reasons for doing it would tend to help the group involved, except when a discovery gave a scientist such personal power as to allow him to seek his own ends in conflict with those of everyone else or the group as a whole; or to the degree that scientists themselves form subgroups with common interests among themselves and different from those of others.

Scientists employed by subgroups, such as corporations, seeking their own profit rather than that either of the group (nation?) as a whole or of others in the society, are somewhat removed from the continual scrutiny and approval of the collective of individuals called the public. Given the view of science I have just presented, such scientists may be expected to develop and pursue lines of investigation that do not represent the interests of the group as a whole, or even of the majority of individuals within it. Technological and other products of science which create serious problems for society, I suggest, may frequently be expected to come from these kinds of scientific enterprises. Accordingly, in this particular realm, many problems in the relationship of science and ethics may be expected to occur. For example, what is the net value to society as a whole of new herbicides, insecticides, patent medicines, cosmetics, and particular trends in automobiles, farm, and industrial machinery, computers, appliances, office equipment, and so on? Trends in such products may frequently proceed in directions catering to individual needs, desires, whims, and weaknesses, such as susceptibility to novelty, desires to prolong the phenotype at whatever cost (even, in the eyes of relatives, using all of the resources one has saved during a lifetime), or desires to reserve, at great cost, the opportunity to reproduce far into the future (for example, through sperm banks). Given such propensities, and the readiness of people to accept placebos, some of the directions taken by corporation-dominated science are bound to be detrimental, not merely to most of the populace but to all users, while nevertheless profitable to their creators and manufacturers, and to the stockholders.

These assertions, of course, do not speak to the question of what proportion of the scientific discoveries useful to all members of the group are also likely to come from scientists employed by profit-seeking subgroups because of the profit incentive. Also, although government scientists, who may create weaponry raising the most serious of all ethical questions, may seem to be excluded, in the sense involved here they may also be regarded as employed by subgroups, since such weaponry is presumably developed explicitly for employment against the members of other similar groups (nations) when the interests of the different groups are sufficiently in conflict in the eyes of their leaders.

The above view of science is entirely compatible with the general theory of culture and sociality described earlier. It does not appear to me to be counterintuitive, though it is surely not the most widely held view of science.[22] I believe that it tends to resolve certain paradoxes in generally held views of science.

The next question is: What does the new view of human sociality mean for our understanding of ethics, and, in turn, what does the view of ethics so generated mean for the relationship of science and ethics?

The Biological Basis of Ethics

Consistent with the above arguments I hypothesize that ethical questions, and the study of morality or concepts of justice and right and wrong, derive solely from the existence of conflicts of interest. In social terms there are three categories of such conflict: (a) individual versus individual, (b) group versus group, and (c) individual versus group. In biological terms two kinds of returns are involved in judging conflicts of interest: (a) those coming to Ego's phenotype and (b) those coming to Ego's genotype, through the success of various kinds of relatives including offspring, and representing reproductive success. In evolutionary terms, all returns are of the second kind, and, as theories of senescence and reproductive effort indicate,[23] our efforts to garner the first kind of returns are expected to be shaped so as to maximize the second kind; there is no other reason for lifetimes having evolved to be finite.

The recent exacerbation of ethical questions has been caused by an accelerating tendency for discoveries from science to cause new kinds of conflict and to cause conflict in new contexts. This situation has caused us to reexamine the basis for ethical norms, seeking generalizations which may assist us in extrapolating to solve the new problems. The effort is actually urgent, since the difference between the processes of organic and cultural evolution are such that the latter continues to accelerate in relation to the former, so that we may be assured that new ethical questions will be generated at ever-increasing rates in the future.[24]

The two major contributions that evolutionary biology may be able to make to this problem are, first, to justify and promote the conscious realization that it is conflicts of interest concentrated at the individual level which lead to ethical questions, and, second, to help identify the nature and intensity of the conflicts of interest involved in specific cases. Undoubtedly the most dramatic and unnerving aspect of these contributions is the argument, or realization, that all conflicts of interest among individuals, in historical (evolutionary) terms, resolve to conflicts over the differential reproduction of genetic units, hence, that conflicts of interest exist solely because of genetic differences among individuals, or histories of genetic differences among individuals interacting in particular fashions. I emphasize that the major barrier to acceptance of this argument—absence of theories about proximate (physiological and ontogenetic) mechanisms acceptable in light of learning theory and the modifiability of human behavior—has been at least partly eliminated.[25]

The above arguments indicate that analyses of ethics, either from a descriptive approach or as an interpretation of the sources of normative ethics in the past, must be phrased from the individual's viewpoint and must bear on the problem of how the individual is most likely to maximize its inclusive fitness. This is true even if most concepts of right and wrong, most laws, norms, traditions, and reasons for courses of action, were established in generations past and are resistant to change. The inertia of culture does not remove the individual's historical reasons and tendencies to strive, it only restricts or alters the manner of striving and the degree to which the ends involved are likely to be achieved.

In the individual's terms, then, a statement by a biologically knowledgeable investigator about the normative ethics *of yesterday*, applicable in any cultural situation, might come out as follows[26]: I "should" treat others so as to maximize my inclusive fitness. My treatment of relatives "should" be more altruistic than my treatment of nonrelatives (that is, altruism to kin should be more likely than altruism to nonkin in situations in which phenotypic returns are unlikely). My treatment of both relatives and nonrelatives "should" be developed in terms of (a) effects of my actions on the reproduction of relatives (including offspring), hence, the reproduction of my genes; (b) effects of my actions on how I will be treated by those directly affected by my actions (how will interactants treat me subsequent to my actions toward them?); (c) effects of my actions on how my relatives will be treated by those affected by my actions; and (d) effects of my actions on how I will be treated by those only observing my actions, and either (i) likely to be interacting with me subsequently or (ii) likely to be affected by the success or failure of my actions because of the observation, and, hence, acceptance or rejection of them by still others. It is particularly perplexing that we must investigate the extent to which our behavior supports this hypothesis under the realization that, if such goals do guide our behavior, they are nevertheless not consciously perceived, and, if the hypothesis is correct, this means, paradoxically, that we are evolved to reject these goals whenever we are asked to evaluate them consciously. This does not mean that we *must* reject them, but that individuals not aware of all this are expected to behave as if these were their goals even if denying it is so, and that to convince them of self-deception may be difficult, and will be most difficult for the precise activities about which they deceive themselves, for the same reason that they do so. The question is testable: Do we or do we not behave as predicted, whether we think so or not, when we are not yet aware of the predictions? It is the same kind of question anthropologists always must ask when they undertake to analyze the structure of a culture alien to their own.

By these arguments the complexity of ethical issues derives not from their general basis but from the diversity and complexity of sources of conflict, and of the means by which they are altered.

We are led to a division of normative ethics into those of the past—before development of the realization that genetic interests underlie conflicts of interest—and those of the future, following conscious understanding of such arguments. It is crucial that this distinction be recognized; otherwise, what I have said above will be interpreted erroneously as naively deterministic, with new knowledge of the significance of history not acknowledged as having effects on the future of human sociality or the determination of ethical procedures.[27] I appreciate the way Albert Rosenfeld put this particular point:

> .. the individual who militantly seeks to have the quest for knowledge brought to a halt is often the same individual who is outraged by the sociobiological suggestion that we are more controlled by our genes than we realize. We *are* more controlled by our genes than we have realized [This is a reasonable assertion, since not too many years ago we hadn't even heard about their existence]; therefore, the more we discover about the mechanisms of genetic control, the better equipped we will be to escape these controls, through our enhanced awareness, to transcend them so that we may, for the first time in our history, work for ourselves, instead of for our genes, exercise truly free will and free choice, give free reign to our minds and spirits, attain something close to our full humanhood.[28]

Why should biologists, social scientists, philosophers, and historians find it so difficult, or distasteful, to accept what Rosenfeld has grasped so well? I am inclined to suggest that what is involved are the reasons for cultural inertia and the nature of science, already mentioned here. Leaving aside the obvious virtue of some conservatism about novelty, the emotionality of responses to this issue suggests to me that those of us who make our living in this subcultural arena are reluctant to accept new paradigms, which, if they succeed, represent someone else changing the rules in the middle of our game; we have learned how to use the system—in our own subarenas of science and humanism—to meet our own ends, and we resent the suggestion that we must in any sense start all over again.

Perhaps as well it has not for a long time been profitable for social scientists to entertain truly novel theories, partly because of the supposed relationship between new ways of viewing human activities and the potential for misusing them. Thus, someone has said that a natural scientist is remembered for his best ideas, a social scientist for his worst. Perhaps the new paradigm in evolutionary biology will be first absorbed into fields like economics, and by laymen, who are curious but lack the vested interests and other inhibitory baggage of much of academia.[29]

Justice, Happiness, and Keeping Up with the Joneses

Rawls developed the idea that justice correlates with happiness, and that happiness may be identified as follows: "A person is happy when he is in the way of a successful execution (more or less) of a rational plan of life drawn up under (more or less) favorable conditions, and he is reasonably confident that his intentions can be carried through . . . adding the rider that if he is mistaken or deluded, then by contingency and coincidence nothing transpires to disabuse him of his misconceptions."[30]

But Rawls fails to consider fully how individuals decide upon particular courses of action, thus, why there is any likelihood at all of selecting a plan of life that is *not* likely to be carried through, particularly in an affluent society where scarcely anyone is actually in danger of starving, freezing, or otherwise dying prematurely because of inability to secure necessary resources. In others words, he has failed to explain why people strive, and what he has left out seems to be the crux of the problem, and the source of the conflicts of interest that lead to ethical questions. I think we can be certain that, even in affluent societies—and, I would venture, *especially* in some such societies—there will be much evidence of unhappiness. Why should this be so?

It should be so because, again in historical terms, success is only measurable in relative terms. We set our goals and determine our plans of life in terms of what we observe others about us achieving; such goals are irrational, or likely to be inaccessible and thus to lead to unhappiness, when different individuals (a) strive from different resource bases, and fail to take this into account; (b) fail to consider the different sorts of obstacles placed in their ways (because of race, sex, physical or mental handicaps, or other bases for discrimination); (c) fail to consider trends in society that may eliminate possibilities open to others; or (d) fail to consider the extent to which achievements of others have required use of excessive power, influence, chicanery, or injustice against others (and the attendant risks). I think we can predict that unhappiness as a consequence of unlikely or irrational personal goals is likely to be most prevalent in societies that are hierarchically structured, so that lofty goals may be developed from observations of the success of others, and yet so constituted as to generate severe inequalities of opportunity so that the perceived goals are inaccessible for what are logically interpreted as unjust reasons.

In natural selection the likelihood of a genetic element persisting depends entirely on its rate of change in frequency *in relation* to its alternative; changes in absolute numbers are irrelevant. Among the attributes of living creatures, whatever can be shown to have resulted from the action of natural selection may be expected to bear this same relationship to its alternatives. This means that we should not be surprised to discover that the behavioral striving of individual humans during history has been explicitly formed in terms of relative success in reproductive competition. As I have noted elsewhere[31] this is the reason why justice is necessarily incomplete, why happiness is not a commodity easy to make universal, and why ethical questions continue to plague us, and can even become more severe when everything else seems to be going well.

Right and Wrong

Interpreting the concepts of right and wrong in terms of conflicts of interest is a difficult task. First, there is an implication of absoluteness about right and wrong which gives an illusion of group function to their invocation. This flavor is promoted by legislative bodies and law; by authority in the form of parents, organized religion, and other sources of power, influence, and leadership; by persistence of meanings across generations; and even by our use of the terms right and wrong in the context of correctness and incorrectness about decisions or answers, or understanding of factual matters (e.g., the *right* or *wrong* distance, direction, number, or answer; a *right* line is a straight line; the *right* hand is the correct one; *right* now means precisely at this time; and so on).

Yet all of the arguments I have presented so far suggest that this implication of absoluteness and group function has some significance other than actual unanimity of opinion or equality of return to all individuals. What is this significance?

Parents begin instilling the ideas of right and wrong in their children, and this is probably the normal origin of the concepts for most individuals. Initially, at least, right and wrong are for children whatever their parents say is right and wrong. What, though, are usual concepts of right and wrong in parents' views of their children's behavior? One might suppose that children are simply taught by their parents never to deceive, always to tell the truth, the whole truth, and nothing but the truth; therefore, that children are taught always to be altruistic toward others, to be certain that justice is afforded all those with whom they interact, and that their own interests are secondary to those of others or of the members of the group to which they belong.

Alas, it cannot be true. As we all know very well, children so taught, who also obeyed their parents' teaching faithfully, could not be successful, at least in this society; whatever they gained personally would immediately be lost. They would be the rubes of society, of whom advantage would be taken at every turn.[32]

I suggest something so different that it may at first sound pernicious: that parents actually teach their children how to "cheat" without getting caught. That is, that parents teach their children what is "right" and "wrong" behavior in the eyes of others, and what truth-telling and forthright behavior actually are, so that from this base of understanding children will know how to function successfully in a world in which some deceptions are sometimes profitable, some unforgivable, and hence expensive, and some are difficult to detect, others easy. I suggest that parents are more likely to punish children for (a) cheating close relatives, (b) cheating friends with much to offer the family in a continuing reciprocal interaction, or (c) cheating in an obvious, bungling fashion, sure to be detected, than they are to punish them for simply cheating (I am using the word "cheating" here in a very general way, referring to any kind of social deception or taking of advantage.) In other words, I suggest that the concepts of right and wrong are instilled into children in such fashion as to guide them toward inclusive-fitness-maximizing behavior in the particular societies and sub-societies within which they are growing up and are likely to live out their lives; that they are taught by parents accustomed to living by these rules; and that the courts and prisons are filled with individuals whose teachers failed, for one reason or another, to impart just these concepts of right and wrong.[33]

The reasons that the concepts of right and wrong assume an appearance of absoluteness and group-level uniformity of application, then, are that (a) on some issues there actually is virtual unanimity of opinion, especially when dire external threats exist, as during wartime, and (b) it is a major social strategy to assemble as a coalition those who agree, or who can be persuaded to behave as though they agree, and then promote the apparent agreement of the subgroup as gospel. On these accounts relatively few ethical questions actually *seem* to involve disagreements between *individuals*: In one fashion or another one or both individuals are likely to have made their grievance appear to be that of a group. This is relatively easy to accomplish if the presumed offender constitutes a potential threat to others not directly involved. We subscribe to laws against acts like murder, rape, robbery, and usury not so much because strangers are victims as because we have assessed, consciously or unconsciously, the probability that we or those on whom we depend, from whom we expect to receive assistance or resources, or through whom we expect to achieve reproductive success, may sometimes be in a position similar to that of the victim.

In this light one may ask about the source of the apparent recent rise of attention to issues like child abuse, rape, and the rights of minorities, women, and the mentally and physically handicapped. I suggest that, as individuals, we regard ourselves as more vulnerable in the modern, urban, technological, socially impersonal environment, in which we are increasingly surrounded by strangers, and in which bureaucracy, weaponry, and medical knowledge of new gadgetry and substances affecting the functioning of the human body and mind seem to place us increasingly at the mercy of others. I speculate that the recent rise of interest in the rights of even nonhuman organisms represents an extension of the same trend—an effort to preserve our own rights, before they are directly threatened, by singling out others whose rights are directly threatened and using their situation to develop the social machinery to protect ourselves.[34]

A Concluding Remark

I have been asked by the editor to discuss briefly the limitations of the approach I have attempted here. First, I would reiterate my opinion that evolutionary understanding (therefore, science) has little to contribute to the *identification* of goals in systems of ethics and morality.[35] Second, in regard to the analysis of human sociality—the "natural history" of activities like science and the formation and maintenance of systems of human behavior—I am willing to risk seeming unduly optimistic in supposing that evolutionary understanding represents *the central key*. Beyond this, I am impressed with the degree to which the conclusions of authors totally outside evolution seem to converge on those derived from modern evolutionary approaches. Thus, I agree with Friedmann that "The only general conclusion to be drawn is that, in any society that preserves a modicum of individual responsibility, there is a tension between individual ethics and social morality on the one part, and social morality and the legal order on the other part. How much these three spheres of normative order influence and modify each other is a question that cannot be answered in absolute terms."[36]

I believe that an evolutionary approach leads us to the same conclusion, but I also believe that it tells us, better than any other approach, why Friedmann's conclusion is reasonable and what are the likely degrees and patterns of expression of the interactions he discusses.

Mankind's self-interpretation, its conception of itself, its essence, and its destiny, is not without influence on what it then is.[37]

NOTES

1. See R. D. Alexander, "Natural Selection and the Analysis of Human Sociality," in *The Changing Scenes in the Natural Sciences, 1776-1976*, ed. C. E. Goulden, Philadelphia Academy of Natural Sciences Special Publication 12 (1977):283–337. In this paper I made a special effort to trace the sequence of changes in thinking responsible for the current model, because it seemed to me that much of the existing confusion about "sociobiology" stems from a failure by the authors of books in this area to identify and trace what has actually happened since 1957. For example, E. O. Wilson, in his massive and influential 1975 volume, *Sociobiology: The New Synthesis* (Cambridge, Mass.: Harvard University Press, 1975) defines sociobiology as "the systematic study of the biological basis of all social behavior." But this is not a new kind of study in biology. Moreover, the adjective "biological" when applied to behavior by social scientists all too often means "genetic," and it often is used explicitly to mean "other than social" in efforts to account for the ontogeny of behavior. Further, although Wilson says that "the organism is only DNA's way of making more DNA" and gives credit to W. D. Hamilton's (1964) theory of inclusive-fitness-maximizing (kin selection) (i.e., that *genetic reproduction can be enhanced by helping nondescendant as well as descendant relatives*) in explaining altruism, in my opinion he muddles the question of group selection which is crucial to understanding altruism. To make matters worse he refers to the seminal arguments of George C. Williams in *Adaptation and Natural Selection* (Princeton, N.J.: Princeton University Press, 1966) that *selection is highly unlikely to be effective above the level of the parent and its offspring* (regarded by many as responsible for the entire revolution) as Williams' "fallacy"! In effect, Wilson reintroduced genes into the formula, Genes plus Environment Yield Phenotype (including behavior), without clearly telling the reader why this can now be done satisfactorily; he persists in using the phrase "genetically determined" when referring to human behavior (even, sometimes, without specifying that he is referring to *differences* in behavior); and he gives the impression that the main change is simply a massive accumulation of very relevant data from field studies (later, in "Animal and Human Sociobiology," in *The Changing Scenes in the Natural Sciences 1776–1976*, pp. 273–81, he actually says this). But it is

not true: A massive *refinement of theory* reoriented the study of behavior. It may be difficult for outsiders to understand from accounts like Wilson's what is really new in evolutionary biology, and why it is important. The revolution was caused by the arguments of Williams and Hamilton, italicized above.

2. Gunther Stent, in a critical review of Richard Dawkin's *The Selfish Gene* (Oxford: Oxford University Press, 1976) recently published in the Hastings Center Report, has missed the point, in his distinction between deliberate and nondeliberate altruism, that "intent" is a proximate mechanism; a paradoxical aspect of its molding to contribute to ultimate function is that not all goals are conscious. This is not to suggest that "intent" is a trivial aspect of behavior or that it is not important to distinguish intentional and unintentional altruism and selfishness or kindness and cruelty. After all, intent is a central aspect of the definition of such terms, demonstrating its importance. It is crucial to ask *why* intent is so important to us, when it would seem that *consequences* are what count. The reason, I believe, is that intent has consequences outside the immediate circumstances. I think we *use* intent to enable us to predict about events additional to the ones in which we are immediately involved, just as we use information about whether associates follow the rules or play fair in trivial circumstances, or in games, to determine whether we should interact with them in more serious matters. We actually believe that he who is cruel or kind to others—or to animals, children, and other vulnerable beings—is likely to be cruel or kind to us as well. We are positive toward someone who *intends* to be altruistic for the same reason that we are negative toward someone who *intends* to be cruel: He may do it to us.

Stent also fails to grasp the all-important distinction, in evolutionary arguments, between incidental effects and evolved functions (well explained by Williams in *Adaptation and Natural Selection*). Stent's contention that evolutionary theory is not predictive is serious, not because it is true, but because he echoes a misconception prevalent among those accustomed to determining the nature of scientific predictiveness from theories dealing with nonliving phenomena. Stent, like some others, regards "the concept of 'fitness' [as] the Achilles' heel of Darwinism, for which a substitute has to be found if natural selection is to be upgraded from the status of a retrodictive historical theory to that of a predictive scientific theory." He acknowledges that "fully predictive evolutionary analyses are available" for "bounded situations in which the context can be completely specified," such as "the development of a drug-resistant bacterial strain from a drug-sensitive strain in a culture medium containing that drug." But he does not regard such predictions as adequate to give evolution "full standing as a theory in the natural sciences." He believes that what is needed is "some concept formally equivalent to fitness, but descriptive of an intrinsic quality." He remarks that "Dawkins evidently hit upon selfishness as a substitute for fitness." Maybe he did. But I would recommend to anyone interested in these questions (including both Dawkins and Stent) that they begin with Darwin, not Dawkins. The following is only one of his several grand challenges to falsification (C. Darwin, *On the Origin of Species. A Fascimile of the First Edition with an Introduction by Ernst Mayr.* (Cambridge, Mass.: Harvard University Press, 1967), p. 201, 1st ed., 1859.

> If it could be proved that any part of the structure of any one species has been formed for the exclusive good of another species, it would annihilate my theory, for such could not have been produced through natural selection.

Fitness is a *relative* concept, and it has no significance except in the environment of the organism. There is no such thing as absolute fitness, except in some trivial formulations of population genetics. Unlike non-living materials, living organisms actively compete, and their phenotypes, by definition, represent evolved capabilities to adjust in the face of particular kinds of competition. This does not mean that some kind of conceptual barrier to predictiveness is inherent in either an evolutionary theory based on fitness or the nature of living organisms. It only means that predictions about the evolution of life will be more difficult than predictions about nonliving phenomena, and that Stent's notion of an intrinsic quality equivalent to fitness and independent of immediate circumstances is irrelevant. There are no surprises in this for anyone who has truly considered the relative complexities of the aspects of the living and nonliving universe so far available to us.

One invariably predicts in what Stent calls "bounded situations." There are no theories which predict in the absence of assumptions. The only question is whether or not the predictions are useful in analyzing the phenomena under study. Stent may have developed his notion that evolution is not predictive partly from remarks by prominent evolutionists like Ernst Mayr and George G. Simpson to that effect; I have heard their statements cited to support such arguments. But Mayr and Simpson meant to refer to macroevolution, or the long-term patterning of life forms across geological time, which is essentially nonpredictive because we cannot reconstruct extinct enviroments in sufficient detail to understand the precise nature of adaptive change by natural selection that occurred prehistorically. This does not mean, however, that we cannot predict very extensively and with great accuracy about life from the assumption that the traits of extant organisms are the *cumulative results* of the microevolutionary process, guided chiefly by natural selection. The philosopher who wishes to understand how this is done ought to go to the current literature of evolutionary biology and not run the risk of generalizing from what he gratuitously refers to as a "vulgar popularization" by a mere "thirty-six-year-old student of animal behavior, [who] teaches at Oxford, and . . . seems to have published only one sociobiological paper . . ."

3. The reader should beware that, from this point on, when I use the term "function" I mean it in the sense of (b) above—as *evolved* or *adaptive* function, as distinguished from either "incidental effect" (see G.C. Williams, *Adaptation and Natural Selection*) or some assumption of physiological or other function in the individual that is not at least visualized as part of, or a contribution to, the ultimate function of reproductive maximization.

4. R. C. Lewontin, "The Units of Selection," *Annual Review of Ecology and Systematics* 1 (1970): 1–18; G. C. Williams, *Adaptation and Natural Selection*; E. C. Leigh, "How Does Selection Reconcile Individual Advantage with the Good of The Group?" *Proceedings of the National Academy of Sciences* 74 (1977): 4542–546; R. D. Alexander and G. Borgia, "Group Selection, Altruism, and the Hierarchical Organization of Life," *Annual Review of Ecology and Systematics* 9 (1978): 449–74.

5. There appears to be a feeling in some circles that a failure exists to define gene adequately for its use in discussions of behavioral evolution. The impression one gets is that if definitions were sharpened then implications of unacceptable determinism would disappear (or, alternatively, that evolutionary analyses of behavior would be shown to be inappropriate). Partly this feeling seems to derive from the error of supposing that such definition-sharpening would principally involve precision in describing gene function in terms of physiology or ontogeny— of generalizing about the connections between gene effects and behavior. But the generalization for this direction of definition, adequate for use of the concept of gene or genetic unit in evolutionary analyses, even of behavior, already exists: It is that genes always realize their effects in environments, and their effects change in different environments. I do not imply that all self-proclaimed evolutionists so use it, or use it appropriately or properly. Because the use of gene by evolutionary biologists actually refers principally to heritable or recombining units— or alternatives (and assumes the above physiological-ontogenetic-functional generalization or definition)—to refine the evolutionists' definitions (usages) would chiefly be a matter of describing the sizes and

divisibility of genetic units; this activity would not bear on the question of genetic determinism, as may be supposed. Genetic determinism, in its unacceptable forms, implies that only *some* behaviors are "genetically determined" (E. O. Wilson, "Human Decency is Animal," *New York Times Magazine*, October 12, 1975, pp. 38–50); that there are reasons for believing that some human social behavior is not learned (E. O. Wilson, "The Social Instinct," *Bulletin of the American Academy of Arts and Sciences* 30 (1976): 11–25); or that human behavioral variations like homosexual tendencies depend upon genetic variations which exist because of their contribution to homosexual behavior (thus, that the "capacity" for homosexuality exists only in "moderate frequencies" in the human population—E. O. Wilson, "Animal and Human Sociobiology"). In fact, either all human behavior is "genetically determined" or none of it is; unless learning is defined in a fashion dramatically more restrictive than its current usage in the social sciences there is no reasonable alternative to the hypothesis that all human social behaviors are learned; and even if some human behavioral *variations* are genetically determined (i.e., environmental variations are not involved in their expressions), there is, for example, no evidence that the capacity to behave either homosexually or heterosexually, even in rather ordinary environments, is absent in any human.

Biologists who develop general theories about behavior seem vulnerable to becoming the caricatures their adversaries initially make of them. Thus, many ethologists, originally interested in distinguishing behaviors with cryptic ontogenies from behaviors dependent upon obvious learning contingencies also were led eventually to defend them (as "innate" and "instinctive") as if they had virtually no ontogenies at all. The same thing need not have happened in the current circumstance, and this explains why some of us resent being called sociobiologists as long as to most nonbiologists the term expressly means acceptance of particular views about the ontogeny of behavior (see *Addendum 1*, pp. 150–52). It is surprising to me that Wilson, who has spent his life working on the social insects, in which the strikingly different castes are almost invariably determined by environmental variations, should seem so determined that such a vaguely defined behavioral variation as homosexuality in humans must depend upon a genetic polymorphism. Such causes were postulated for social insect castes, but they turned out to be wrong, at least in nearly every case.

6. Stent (Hastings Center Report) confuses the issue by referring to the efforts of molecular biologists to define genes in molecular terms as if theirs were the first efforts at useful definition of genetic units, with definitions functional in evolutionary analyses only coming along later

to "denature" the "meaningful and well-established central concept of genetics into a fuzzy and heuristically useless notion." This is nonsense. The gene concept was functional as a recombining unit, and highly useful as such, a half century before knowledge of DNA as its molecular basis; it has not ceased to be such a concept in evolutionary genetics, population genetics, and Mendelian genetics, despite Stent's assertion that for "all working geneticists" the concept is restricted to the unit of genetic material in which the amino acid sequence of a particular protein is encoded. Stent says that genes were "previously conceptualizable by classical genetics only in terms of differences or alleles." True enough, and they are still so conceptualized in studies outside molecular biology. The reason is that this is a very useful concept. We are back to the fact that fitness is only a matter of better versus worse in the immediate environment (Williams, *Adaptation and Natural Selection*). The important thing about genes is not what they are but what they do, and the most important thing they do is work together to produce organisms; we know very little yet about how they do that, and except for very few simple cases involving simple organisms what we know about it was not learned by studying either DNA or amino acid sequences. To behave as though all such things have to wait until we work up from the molecular level is to fail to comprehend that the secret of life is not DNA after all, but natural selection; the structure and integrity of the DNA molecule, as well as its relationship to the identity of the recombining units, are all products of natural selection. Satisfactory understanding of genetic units ultimately will involve connecting molecular-level structure and function with complex phenotypic effects, like behavior, the genetic basis of which will continue to be studied chiefly through recombination; such understanding is unlikely to be accomplished by either of these approaches alone.

7. G. C. Williams, "Pleiotropy, Natural Selection, and the Evolution of Senescence," *Evolution* 11 (1957): 398–411; W. D. Hamilton, "The Moulding of Senescence by Natural Selection," *Journal of Theoretical Biology*, 12 (1966): 12–45.

8. E. Walster and G. W. Walster, "Equity and Social Justice," *Journal of Social Issues* 31 (1975): 21–43.

9. A particularly good example is Jeremy Boissevain's approach in *Friends of Friends* (New York: St. Martin's Press, 1974). Another is B. F. Skinner, *Beyond Freedom and Dignity* (New York: Alfred A. Knopf, 1971), in which the author discusses positive and negative reinforcement in terms of *individuals* but skips to the group or species level to discuss cultural change (even though, curiously, moving back to the individual level to discuss *objections* to deliberate designing of culture through

conscious control of behavior). Never does Skinner hit upon the obvious: that *individuals* are evolved to *reproduce*: and this flaw, it seems to me, causes his entire theme (of behavioral control, design of culture, or search for "an optimal state of equilibrium in which everyone is maximally reinforced") to collapse.

10. For discussion of how the consideration of nepotism alters analyses of networks and systems of social exchange, see R. D. Alexander, "Natural Selection and Social Exchange," in *Social Exchange in Developing Relationships,*, ed. R. L. Burgess and T. L. Huston (New York: Academic Press, in press); "The Search for a General Theory of Behavior," *Behavioral Science* 20 (1975): 77–100; "Natural Selection and the Analysis of Human Sociality."

11. W. D. Hamilton, "The genetical evolution of social behaviour, I, II," *Journal of Theoretical Biology* 7 (1964): 1–52.

12. I am not suggesting that culture has no significance or value, but hypothesizing that the only *singular* thing about its significance, in historical terms, is that it derives incidentally from inclusive-fitness-maximizing behavior by individuals acting separately and in common-interest groups, and that its value—say, in terms of the present and future—will probably also be interpreted by individuals and common-interest groups on the basis of its ability to contribute to inclusive-fitness-maximizing and the surrogates of inclusive-fitness-maximizing in modern environments. This hypothesis, of course, remains to be tested.

13. To identify kin individually is to specify them as avenues of potential inclusive-fitness-maximizing by individuals. See R. D. Alexander, "Natural Selection and the Analysis of Human Sociality."

14. R. D. Alexander, "Natural Selection and Societal Laws," in *The Foundations of Ethics and Its Relationship to Science* vol. 3: *Morals, Science and Sociality* ed. H. Tristram Engelhardt and Daniel Callahan (Hastings-on-Hudson, New York: The Hastings Center, 1978).

15. For a discussion of the reasons why cultural evolution continues to accelerate in relation to organic evolution, and for other references, see R. D. Alexander, "Evolution and Culture," in *Evolutionary Biology and Human Social Behavior: An Anthropological Perspective*, ed. N. A. Chagnon and W. G. Irons (North Scituate, Mass: Duxbury Press 1979).

16. Thus, tendencies to become deleteriously obese or to seek "excessively" immediate pleasures, such as overconsuming sugar when it is abundant, are most likely to be understood by considering the kind of environment in which these propensities evolved.

17. See note 15 and references therein; also see R. D. Alexander, "Evolution, Human Behavior, and Determinism," *Proceedings of the Biennial Meeting of the Philosophy of Science Association* 2 (1976):

3–21; R. D. Alexander and G. Borgia, "Group selection, Altruism, and Levels of Organization of Life." Annual Review of Ecology and Systematics 9 (1978):449–74.

18. See R. D. Alexander, "The Search for a General Theory of Behavior," Behavioral Science 20 (1975):77–100; R. D. Alexander, "Evolution Human Behavior and Determinism,"; also R. D. Alexander and K. M. Noonan, "Concealed Ovulation and the Evolution of Human Sociality," In: Evolutionary Biology and Human Social Behavior.

19. See R. D. Alexander, Darwinism and Human Affairs (Seattle; University of Washington Press [in press]).

20. An evolutionary model does not deny that events contrary to inclusive-fitness-maximizing occur, only that when present they are most likely to be interpretable in terms of the history of environments in which they and their ontogenetic-physiological backgrounds were selected.

21. This does not exclude the possibility that some or even many scientists are, in fact, at least to the best of their ability to describe their motivations, devoted to a search for the truth. Repeated and sufficient positive social reinforcement for approaching this condition, and negative reinforcement for diverging from it, can surely bring it about.

22. Neither is it new. P. W. Bridgman, for example, expressed essentially this idea in Reflections of a Physicist (New York: Philosophical Library, p. 227), in these words: ". . . in scientific activity the necessity for continual checking against the inexorable facts of experience is so insistent, and the penalties for allowing the slightest element of rationalizing to creep in are so immediate, that it is obvious to the dullest that a high degree of intellectual honesty is the price of even a mediocre degree of success."

23. G. C. Williams, "Pleiotropy, Natural Selection, and the Evolution of Senescence: Evolution 11 (1957): 398–411; W. D. Hamilton, "The Moulding of Senescence by Natural Selection," Journal of Theoretical Biology, 12 (1966), 12–45.

24. R. D. Alexander, Darwinism and Human Affairs.

25. R. D. Alexander, Darwinism and Human Affairs.

26. Exactly the same set of statements could be developed into a set of predictions about the behavior of individuals in any extant society in which knowledge of the predictions does not exist.

27. Anyone incredulous about my acceptance of Rosenfeld's interpretation, or who fails to appreciate its extent (perhaps because of his own inability to visualize a compatibility between natural selection as a causal agent in human behavior and the kind of freedom of decision or will implied by Rosenfeld), will regard the inevitable paradox of more

and more profound self-analysis as something other than a problem for all analysts and observers; he may even see it as a special problem for the evolutionist. To the contrary, the problem will lie in the particular form of the bogey man of determinism seen in the mind's eye of such a critic, and will only disappear when his biological sophistication has exceeded the level indicated by his incredulity. A commentator on this paper, for example, suggested that I am guilty of the fallacy of self-referential inconsistency. An evolutionary view, however, may instead resolve this philosophical paradox. Thus, to say that humans have *evolved* to be nothing but inclusive-fitness-maximizing systems is not to say that in all environments they can *only* be such. Who can say what humans so evolved may do in an environment of both self-reference *and* knowledge of their evolutionary background?

28. Albert Rosenfeld, *Saturday Review*, December 10, 1977, pp. 19–20.

29. I am not arguing here that all cultural inertia has such causes, or that all cultural inertia is retrogressive; rather, only the obvious point that part of cultural inertia results from individuals and groups acting in their own personal interests, and that these interests may be realized by conserving essentially any aspect of culture, including demonstrably false ideas and interpretations.

30. John Rawls, *A Theory of Justice* (Cambridge, Mass.: Harvard University Press, 1971), pp. 548–49.

31. R. D. Alexander, "Natural Selection and Societal Laws."

32. It is worth considering in what kind of society this would not be so. I suggest that the criteria are not complex. A certain minimum contribution of each member to the common good must be specified. All material benefits and reproductive outlets (or their surrogates) above this minimum must be equalized among societal members, with graded rewards existing only in the form of differing degrees of social approval (indicated by entirely symbolic awards such as nontransferable and otherwise valueless medals, or by titles such as various orders of heroism). It would be a necessary concomitant that societal members not meeting the minimum contribution and otherwise accepting these criteria either be exiled to a less desirable circumstance or otherwise eliminated from society.

33. I allow for the essential certainty that in some circumstances, and perhaps for certain offspring more than others, parents actually manipulate offspring to maximize the parent's inclusive fitness rather than the offspring's own (See R. D. Alexander, "Evolution of Social Behavior," *Annual Review of Ecology and Systematics* 5 (1974):325–83. J. E. Blick, "Selection for Traits which Lower Individual Reproduc-

tion," *Journal of Theoretical Biology* 67 (1977):597–601, has noted that one part of my 1974 argument was wrong; this does not detract from the general asymmetry of the parent-offspring interaction, resulting from the phenotypic power difference and the facts that offspring depend on parents and parental care evolves to maximize the parent's reproductive success.

34. The advent of socialized medicine, at least in a society like our own, may actually exacerbate this problem in some respects, because it has the interesting consequence of causing medical care to become a burden on *society as a whole* which may sometimes lead to its validity or feasibility being judged in cost-benefit terms less directly relating to the welfare of the individual patients involved. Since none of us is likely to favor classes of discrimination likely to affect ourselves detrimentally, one might expect that common afflictions will sometimes be compensated when rare ones are not, or that medical compensation could become excessive in circumstances in which all in society feel threatened by the system.

35. See also R. D. Alexander, "Natural Selection and Societal Laws."

36. W. Friedmann, *Legal Theory*, 5th Edition, (London: Stevens and Sons, 1967), p. 47.

37. Michael Landman, *Philosophical Anthropology* (Philadelphia: The Westminster Press 1974), p. 22.

Addendum 1

DESPITE WILSON'S APPARENTLY erudite discussions in some parts of his 1975 book with respect to genetic and behavioral variations (e.g., pp. 26–27), several facts suggest a deficiency in his view of the relationship between genes and behavior which, although not unique to Wilson or even unusual among scientists, may underlie what I regard as a poor and confusing response to the critics of his book. Thus, although he carefully defines "instinct" (p. 587) and "innate behavior" (pp. 26–27), no definition or clear conception of the nature and limits of learning, which is treated as some kind of opposite, occurs in the book. Early in the book (p. 26) he notes that ". . . it is meaningless to ask whether blue eye color alone is determined by heredity or environment . . . . [because] Obviously both the genes for blue eye color and the environment contributed to the final product." Nevertheless, on p. 237, he asserts, with respect to birds, that "In some the male song is transmitted from generation to generation entirely by heredity, with no learning required." He probably *means* learning by listening to bird songs but that is not what he said; hence, he is implying that *songs* not *genes* are actually inherited and require no *ontogenies*, hence, no consistency in the developmental *environment*. The only way that I can imagine this argument to be defensible—and I doubt that it was Wilson's meaning—is through genes in the somatic cells being used as the *environment* of *development* for the behavior in question. Elsewhere *(Darwinism and Human Affairs)* I have postulated this selective background for the ontogeny of some insect sexual signals, in which there is no opportunity for the male to learn how to make the

333

signals from hearing them, or for the female to learn which ones to respond to. Similarly, on p. 151, Wilson contrasts with "directed" and "generalized" learners something called "the complete instinct-reflex machine." On p. 563, he speaks of "genetically-programmed sexual and parent-offspring conflict." Nowhere does he detail the proximate developmental or experiential mechanisms—even in the most general theoretical sense—by which behaviors appropriate to inclusive-fitness-maximizing by nepotism could evolve or be expressed in plastic organisms like humans. Of course, no one else had yet done so either though I call attention to passages in my 1971 and 1975 papers discussing this problem (R. D. Alexander, "The Search for an Evolutionary Philosophy of Man," *Proceedings of the Royal Society of Victoria,* Melbourne 84 (1971):99–120; "The Search for a General Theory of Behavior"). Few others had encountered this problem, because few others were claiming that human behavior was evolutionarily adaptive (but see R. D. Alexander, "The Search for an Evolutionary Philosophy of Man," "The Evolution of Social Behavior," *Annual Review of Ecology and Systematics* 5 (1974):325–83; "The Search for a General Theory of Behavior"; R. L. Trivers, The Evolution of Reciprocal Altruism," *Quarterly Review of Biology* (1971), 46:35–57; "Parent-Offspring Conflict," *American Zoologist* 14 (1971):249–64).

These different statements and omissions by Wilson, taken together, may in retrospect have presaged the type of defense he would develop in response to the charge of genetic determinism leveled by his critics. In fact, in parallel with other biologists before him who had experienced the same predicament, he seems to have *become* a genetic determinist, by defending the phrase and the kind of meaning his 1975 statement about blue eyes denies. In the *New York Times Magazine* of October 12, 1975 ("Human Decency is Animal"), pp. 39–50 (and elsewhere) he suggests that some of human social behavior may be genetically determined, without specifying explicitly, even in the emotion-charged atmosphere in which he was writing, that he meant some of the *variations* in human social behavior. Even that assertion is at least premature and misleading and probably indefensible—for example, it is entirely likely that even the differences between males and females that occur during their normal development because of their initial genetic differences can all (except for production of sperm and eggs) be reversed by changing their hormonal and social environments (e.g., see John Money and Anke A. Ehrhardt, *Man and Woman: Boy and Girl*, [Baltimore: The Johns Hopkins University Press, 1972].) Those of us sympathetic to Wilson's general situation of defending himself may want to give him credit for the meanings he should have specified. Others, however, did not, and on their side, unfortunately, are his various suggestions which support less acceptable meanings (Wilson, 1976, 1977, cited above).

Wilson, like everyone before him, evidently fails to understand how organisms like humans, who can learn by sitting alone and motionless and merely reflecting on their social circumstances, and whose learned behavior can itself be transmitted by learning, could possibly be expected consistently to develop and learn along lines that would maximize their individual inclusive fitnesses or genetic success. Of course they can do so only if their *environments of development* (ontogeny) and learning are consistent over long periods. This may seem to increase the importance of the genetic element. Perhaps it does so, in some sense, for explaining the past and present, but for modifying the future it does the opposite, by emphasizing the environment.

Only as a result of the discussions at these conferences has it become clear to me that the very general and widespread failure of understanding about the bases for the actual evolution of all ontogenies and learning ability is the crux of the problem faced by evolutionists in their efforts to develop and explain legitimate hypotheses about the evolution of all behavior, including and especially that of humans. Understanding this aspect of evolution, I believe, is also a problem for any other persons who wish to participate in the development of a human understanding of human behavior, and I mean explicitly to include philosophers and humanists as well as social scientists.

Addendum 2

AT THE LAST CONFERENCE someone remarked that science cannot contribute to the problem of understanding free will. Because of my impression that this kind of assumption underlies much of the resistance to biological-evolutionary interpretations of human tendencies, and because I regard it as an unwarranted assumption, I am appending this essay (expanded in *Darwinism and Human Affairs*) which I believe shows that reasonable and testable hypotheses can be generated about the biological nature and function of what we call "free will."

An integral aspect of consciousness is the phenomenon of self-awareness, and self-awareness, in turn, at least partly involves what Robert Burns called seeing ourselves as others see us. To a biologist—probably to almost anyone at all—this aspect of self-awareness is easily seen as crucial to success in social matters; in turn, biological (reproductive) success—the focus of the evolutionary biologist's interest—depends upon social success.

In some large part our conscious awareness of ourselves and our social circumstances is taken up with what might be called social "scenario-building." Almost continually we play out in our minds the possible and probable moves in the game of social living, which of course is not a game at all but the real thing. How can I write this paper (deliver this lecture, study for this examination, approach this policeman or judge or merchant or bully or friend) so as to achieve this or that personal goal? What will he or she do if I do this or that? What action by me will most likely cause my desired ends to be achieved? If I do this, and he does that, and then I do something else, then what?—and so on.

In such scenario-building we seem to see before us alternatives. We actually perceive beforehand—through, I believe, a marshalling of all the information available to us from the past and present—possible choices that we can make. We assume that we can take any one of those choices that we wish to take. We evaluate them, and we apparently take whichever one we decide is best (or preferred or whatever). We cherish the right to make the decision ourselves, on our own bases, and the additional right to keep the reasons private, and not even to review them consciously if we do not wish to.

This projecting and weighing of possibilities, it seems to me, has the obvious correlate that the most unpredictable aspect of our environment is the sets of other social individuals and collectives with which we must interact. They too are building scenarios, and, as in a game of chess, we will be best prepared to accomplish our purposes—whatever they may be—by knowing how to respond after *different* possible responses by our interactants to given events or circumstances.

I suggest that the essence of free will is the right to build our own scenarios and act on them for our own reasons without having to justify them—in other words, that free will involves nothing in particular about the causes of our behavior except our right to determine them—to weigh costs and benefits in our own terms.

To the extent that this is a correct interpretation, the problem of understanding free will resolves to that of understanding the bases on which we make our judgments of possible alternatives and why we cherish the right to be personal, private, and individual about such judgments.

The only background I can imagine for a compulsive adherence to such a privilege by every different individual—and at the same time an eminently reasonable one in biological terms—is that the reproductive interests of every individual are unique. Only monozygotic twins, among humans, share identical sets of relatives, and even they are unlikely to share identical sets of friends. Moreover, monozygotic twins likely have no significant social history in humans because of the evidence of prevalent infanticide of twins (R. D. Alexander, "The Evolution of Social Behavior").

This means that, in biological terms, the right to make our own personal decisions about our own futures is the ultimately precious possession of individual humans. Even if societal rules and obligations actually place enormous restrictions on this privilege, we strive for the right to apply and interpret these restrictions, as they affect us, by and for ourselves.

So we are brought to the question of how we actually make our cost-benefit assessments and arrive at decisions of the sort we term exercise of free will. Only if we know ahead of time that no sense can be made of this question would the assertion mentioned at the outset of this essay be appropriate. I do not think that we know this. Instead, I offer the hypothesis that these decisions— judged in terms of the environments of history—will tend to be those which maximize our inclusive fitnesses, that we have evolved to be exceptionally good at such decisions, and that this is the precise reason for the existence and nature of consciousness and self-awareness. I have offered elsewhere the further hypothesis that it is from just this kind of individual decision-making with respect to inclusive-fitness-maximizing, by the aggregate of all humans who have ever lived, that the phenomenon we call culture has generated. I am satisfied that this hypothesis is testable, and that such testing is already underway (e.g., Alexander, "Natural Selection and the Analysis of Human Sociality").

Thus, there is no reason to regard culture, consciousness, and free will as either outside or contrary to efforts to understand humans in evolutionary terms; instead, there appear to be good reasons for believing that our understanding of these attributes— uniquely expressed in humans, though in all likelihood shared by at least chimpanzees—will best be furthered by analyzing them in evolutionary biological terms.

11

Attitudes toward Eugenics in Germany and Soviet Russia in the 1920s: An Examination of Science and Values*

Loren R. Graham

THEORETICAL DISCUSSIONS of the relationship between science and values usually lead to the conclusion that, in a strict sense, science is value-free. If one confines one's attention to the intellectual content of scientific theory, and thereby excludes both the impact of technology on values and the influence of scientists as a political and social group, a persuasive case can be made that science is, indeed, neutral. There is no logical bridge between "is" and "ought."

It is obvious, however, that this form of exclusivist analysis of science overlooks some of the most historically important aspects of the relationship of science to modern culture. Explicitly, these examinations exclude links between science and technology as well as the connection between societal values and conditions for scientific research. Implicitly, these discussions exclude those arguments linking science to social value that are the most common in our imperfect world: the incomplete, semiscientific, possibly fallacious claims that often are advanced in the name of science, and the evaluations of these claims that every citizen has to make in order to decide about the relevance of science for social and political life.

In this essay I would like to examine and compare two separate but chronologically simultaneous episodes in the history of human genetics that involve all of these "second-order" links between science and values: the development in the 1920s of eugenic movements in Germany and Soviet Russia. Such a comparison produces unusual insights into the connections between science and political values.

The mention of the topic of human genetics in Germany and Russia in the early twentieth century will automatically bring to mind the issues of national socialist racial theories in Germany and Lysenko's theories of heredity in Soviet Russia. In the period which I am examining here, however, national socialism had not yet come to power in Germany and scientists of greatly differing political views discussed human genetics, including Marxists and socialists of various sorts, Catholics, liberals, and conservatives. In Soviet Russia, in the same years, no one had yet heard of Lysenko, and the spectrum of debate about human genetics was surprisingly broad. In Russia at this time there were Marxists who also were eugenists and saw no contradiction in their respective positions, and there were anti-Marxists who were Lamarckians. In both countries, then—Germany and Russia—I will be examining events in the periods before single-minded political concerns overruled scientific elements in the discussions about human heredity and its social implications.

How did it occur that this early complex period, in which so much uncertainty existed about the political value implications of theories of human heredity, was replaced in both countries by a later period in which Mendelian eugenic theories were usually linked to conservative views of society and Lamarckian theories were usually linked to left-wing socialist views of society? Was this process entirely a social and political phenomenon, essentially distinct from the scientific theories being discussed, or was there something intellectually inherent in each of the competing theories of heredity which supports a particular political ideology? If the answer to the latter question is affirmative, what do these inherent factors say about the allegedly value-free nature of science?

In both Weimar Germany and Soviet Russia, the peak of the debates over the social and political implications of theories of human genetics occurred in the mid-twenties, and reference was made in each case to ongoing debate in the other society. In both countries, moreover, Darwinism and social Darwinism had been familiar topics of discussion for decades, and the arguments of the twenties were set against this older background.

An example of the degree to which early German eugenists at first separated themselves from particular political viewpoints can be seen in the initial writings of Alfred Ploetz (1860-1940), a founder of the leading German eugenics journal and a central figure in the German eugenics movement of the twenties. As a young man Ploetz's interest in the genetic future of man was stronger than his commitment to any particular social or economic order, and he criticized both capitalism and socialism because of the contradictions which he saw between them and the ideals of eugenics. Ploetz, therefore, was no businessman or academic scholar defending economic competition on the basis of Darwinism, a model long familiar to us.[1] Ploetz was concerned to find a third way, a eugenic society that would put the good of the future above the comforts of the present.[2] Ploetz believed that socialism presented the prospect of a humanitarian society, and he praised the alleviation of economic suffering which he thought it could bring, but he saw it as thoroughly in contradiction with the principles of eugenics. If the "weak" were protected through social legislation guaranteeing employment, health, and life support, then they would propagate their kind in increasing numbers. On the other hand, Ploetz had little better to say for capitalism. Capitalism caused great human suffering—he cited Marx, Kautsky, Bebel and other socialists to that effect—and, furthermore, by giving advantages to the hereditary wealthy in the struggle for existence it hindered free natural selection.

From this analysis, one might guess that the most appealing form of society to Ploetz would be a somewhat softened capitalism in which individual competition still played the major role in determining success in any one generation. Ploetz, however, was both too complex and too humane to propose such a society. He seemed to favor all aspects of socialism except its alleged genetic consequences. The specter of open competition within each generation was offensive to him. Therefore, he struggled to find a way of combining the humanitarian and egalitarian ideals of socialism with the eugenic goal of a constantly improving biological base for society.

It might seem that in calling for a humane, eugenic, socialist society Ploetz was attempting to square a circle. However, he believed that he had found a way to reconcile his contradictory demands; he proposed that all people be protected by welfare legislation from the raw struggle for survival inherent in pure capitalism, as the socialists demanded, but at the same time he would ensure that each generation consisted of genetically healthy individuals by having each married couple select the "best" of their own germ cells for fertilization. Ploetz noted that the germ cells, or gametes, of each couple vary greatly in their genetic constitution; the important thing, from the standpoint of eugenics, was that the children be at least genetically equal to their parents. By "shoving selection back" to the prefertilization stage he hoped to achieve eugenic goals without tampering with individual human rights or interfering with natural, legal parenthood. As he wrote:

> The more we can prevent the production of inferior variations, the less we need the struggle for existence to eliminate them. We would not need it at all if in each generation we were able to ensure that the totality of variations was qualitatively somewhat superior, on the average, to that of the parents.[3]

It is easy to say that Ploetz's suggestion was naive and entirely impractical from the standpoint of the biological science and technology of his time. No one in the early years of this century had the faintest idea how to give an overall evaluation of the genetic quality of different gametes (nor can it be done now).

Nonetheless, Ploetz was making an important point which is more interesting to us now than it was when he wrote. The parents who decide today to abort a fetus found to be mongoloid through amniocentesis are following Ploetz's policy of "shoving selection back" to the prebirth stage in the name of humane principles, although not to the gametes themselves. And a few recent efforts have been made even to extend selection back to the gametes, as Ploetz suggested, not only for the determination of sex, but also for other specific genetic reasons. Controversial as some of these proposals are, we must grant that Ploetz was an early person to see that value consequences of applying the science of human heredity depend more on *when* and *how* it is applied than on the question of what is inherent in the science itself.

In the middle twenties, academic geneticists, anthropologists, and eugenists in Germany disagreed sharply over terminological issues concerning human heredity and race. Although these disputes may seem somewhat scholastic at first glance, they formed the essential theoretical background for the subsequent degradation of the science of human heredity in Germany. What occurred in this period was the gradual crystallization of political value links to specific biological interpretations.

The word eugenics is today usually considered a pejorative term and is even occasionally erroneously equated with national socialist doctrines. It is worthwhile noticing, therefore, that in Weimar Germany "eugenics" was considered by the protonational socialist publications and organizations as a kind of leftist deviation. The race hygienists followed the eugenics movements in other countries carefully, and pointed out frequently that the leaders of the movements there often failed to understand the racial significance of eugenics. Whether one used the term *"Rassenhygiene"* or *"Eugenik"* became in the late twenties a kind of political flag, with often the more right-wing members of the movement favoring the first term, the more left the latter.

The position of the German socialists and communists toward eugenics in the twenties was complex and interesting. Contrary to what we might assume, in the early and mid-twenties the leftist press did not define the debate as one over nature and nurture in which the nature side was inherently conservative from a political standpoint. The leftists noted that many of the eugenists opposed the traditionally conservative institutions of society—monarchies and the nobility—on the grounds that they were regressive from a genetic standpoint, with no correlation between influence and natural ability. And most Marxists prided themselves on their scientific outlook, with a knowledge of genetics a desirable goal. Furthermore, they were definitely in favor of reforming society, as were the eugenists. Therefore, many socialists and communists were supporters of eugenics.

The principle of responsibility to society as a whole lay at the basis of many of the German eugenic and early race-hygiene programs. The democratic socialist writers of the twenties often applauded this principle even when it was advanced by racist authors. Writing in 1923 in one of the oldest socialist journals, George Chaym observed, "Socialism certainly does not take a negative position toward race hygiene (*Rassenhygiene*), insofar as race hygiene concerns theoretical and practical measures for the improvement of the race or avoiding its debasement." Chaym continued that, correctly understood, race hygiene "belongs unconditionally in socialism's work program."[4]

If we examine the most prestigious journal of German social democracy in the twenties, *Die Gesellschaft,* we will find there many discussions of race hygiene and eugenics, and up to the end of the Weimar period the journal continued to support eugenics when it was divorced from extremist and racist interpretations.[5] Even the word *"Rassenhygiene"* continued to be used by many leftist writers.

The first major criticism of the race-hygiene movement to appear in *Die Gesellschaft* was an article in February, 1927, by Hugo Iltis, a biographer of Gregor Mendel.[6] The article revealed a great deal about socialist attitudes toward eugenics. Iltis was absolutely direct in his criticism of the majority of the German race hygienists. He said they were subverting science to politics, and he noted with regret that a number of prominent academic geneticists were among them. He criticized the typological description of races which was displacing the populational view and which attributed mental and ethical qualities to individual races. Iltis also saw clearly the dimensions of the threat; indeed, he said that "Race delusion was on the point of conquering German science." And he predicted that "The time will come when the race hatred and race obscurantism of our day will be what witchcraft and cannibalism are for us now: the sad vestiges of depraved barbarism."[7]

Surprisingly, not only did Iltis continue to support eugenics, but he even accepted the term *"Rassenhygiene."* He was convinced that the main problem with the field was the drawing of premature and inhumane conclusions on the basis of fragmentary data. In the future, he maintained, after "decades and perhaps centuries of hard work" we will create "the foundations of a genetic race hygiene," one that will serve the whole human race.[8]

Iltis also saw in Lamarckism a way of softening the hard facts of human genetics, and in that way he helped forge the links between leftist politics and Lamarckism that were growing in the twenties. He believed that only through the inheritance of acquired characteristics would it be possible to show that everything the socialists were working for—better education, better living conditions—would have a beneficial genetic effect.

Not all left-wing German eugenists supported Lamarckism, but the conservative race hygienists were delighted when they could hang the label of "Lamarckism" on their opponents; critics like Iltis became easy game for them. Fritz Lenz, one of the leaders of the German race hygienists, a person who would applaud Hitler even before he came to power, retaliated for the right-wing movement by dismissing the most prominent socialist and religious objectors to race hygiene as hopeless Lamarckians trying to dodge the facts of modern biology by creating the fiction of the inheritance of acquired characteristics.[9] Lenz was an academically qualified geneticist, and on the question of Lamarckism he exploited his advantage to the hilt. He pointed out that Paul Kammerer, a dedicated socialist and admirer of the Soviet Union, was trying to prove the inheritance of acquired characteristics with his experiments on the midwife toad. The experiments were exposed as fraudulent, after which Kammerer committed suicide. In the Soviet Union, Kammerer was made a hero, the subject of a popular film.

Lenz described all of this in his journal *Archive for Race and Social Biology,* and then turned the tables on his left-wing critics.[10] They accuse us, he said, of inserting our own values into biology, when actually they are the ones guilty of maintaining that biology contains humane principles, those of Lamarckism. *We* know, on the contrary, that science is value-free, he said.[11] We must follow the facts of human heredity wherever they take us, and those facts tell us that man will genetically degenerate unless the strong and the fit are given advantages in propagation.

The inheritance of acquired characteristics is a myth, he pronounced, and Mendelian laws alone govern human heredity.

Perhaps the most outspoken attack on the German race hygiene and eugenics movement to appear in the entire Weimar period was an article in 1928 in the communist journal *Under the Banner of Marxism*.[12] The author, Max Levien, presented a classical Marxist critique, simplistic but trenchant, and he avoided the Lamarckian trap. The central thesis of his long polemic was the view that the main current of German race hygiene was a bourgeois science which served the ruling class of German capitalists. The leading race hygienists preached a false theory of genetic degeneration because by portraying such a threat they hoped to justify imperial expansions against "inferior races and nations," particularly the eastern Slavs. Both of these goals were parts of their program of stemming the revolution already visible in the East.

Like the democratic socialists already discussed, the communist Levien believed that eugenics was a progressive, useful science. Once the revolution was victorious, eugenics could serve the proletariat as it had once served the capitalists. Levien said that German Marxists must not let the race hygenists do damage to "serious scientific efforts to create a people's eugenics (*Volkseugenik*) which considers the whole population of the earth."[13] Once race hatred has been deprived of its necessary base in the capitalist order, Levien asserted, man "will become a creative shaper of his own species; this advancement will bring about an upward surge in mankind's intellectual achievements and the power of science will thus enhance the rational, practical use of the laws of genetics for the development of an undreamt-of higher kind of man."[14] Levien's communist eugenics would be a part of an overall *Volkshygiene* program that would include both genetic and environmental improvement measures.

The relevance of Levien's argument for the Soviet Union is obvious. There the successful revolution he dreamed about had already occurred. The journal in which he wrote was the Western communist theoretical publication most widely circulated among Marxist intellectuals in the Soviet Union. Indeed, many of the articles were written by Soviet citizens. Would the Soviet Marxists, freed of the capitalist order, follow Levien's suggestion of developing a socialist eugenics? This will be one of the topics of the second part of this essay.

Observers of early Soviet history are frequently surprised to learn that Soviet Russia in the 1920s possessed a strong eugenics movement. One might have expected revolutionary Russia, which prided itself on its opposition to capitalist culture and aristocratic privilege, to have stood aside from the movement for "race betterment" which swept the world in those years, leading to the establishment of eugenics societies in several dozen different countries. To jump to this conclusion, however, is to carry back into the third decade of this century ideas both about eugenics and Soviet views of man which took clear form only in later years. Once again, as in Germany, we have the gradual formation of value links to scientific ideas, only in a very different political setting.[15]

In the first decades of the twentieth century, biologists in Russia had formed a center of outstanding genetics research. Around the figure of S. S. Chetverikov a school of population genetics was established which even yet is not fully appreciated by historians of biology, largely because it disappeared in later years when Lysenko took over Soviet genetics.[16] In addition to Chetverikov, outstanding early Soviet biologists included N. K. Kol'tsov, A. S. Serebrovskii, N. I. Vavilov, and Iu. A. Filipchenko. Several of these distinguished scientists were also heavily involved in the eugenics movement.[17] One of the outstanding younger Russian biologists would later emigrate to the United States, where he would become a world-famous scientist. He was Theodosius Dobzhansky, a scholar who began his career in Soviet Russia with a position in the Bureau of Eugenics of the Soviet Academy of Sciences.

The Russian eugenics movement was limited almost entirely to the years 1921 to 1930, and this period can be divided into two phases, with the division around the year 1925.[18] In the first phase, Russian eugenics developed along lines quite similar to the movement in a number of other countries. In the second phase, after 1925, Soviet eugenists made an effort to create a unique socialist eugenics of their own, an effort which met increasing opposition. Lysenko and the form of Stalinist genetics which later became notorious throughout the world were not involved in either of these phases, coming only in the late thirties and forties.

The two most important organizations in the Soviet eugenics movement were the Russian Eugenics Society and the Bureau of Eugenics of the Academy of Sciences, both created in 1921.[19] Each of them published a journal, the first entitled the *Russian Eugenics Journal,* the second (in its initial form) the *News of the Bureau of Eugenics.*

The historian who today leafs through the pages of the *Russian Eugenics Journal,* knowing well the class antagonisms and radical currents still waiting to be expressed in Soviet society, finds the naïveté and blindness to political complications of the early leaders of the movement quite striking. One of the early concerns of the authors in the journal in these years immediately after the Revolution was the genealogies of outstanding and aristocratic Russian families; investigations, complete with family tables, were made of princely families of exemplary achievements, as well as of all the members of the Academy of Sciences in the previous century. Several writers expressed dismay about the dysgenic effects of the Russian Revolution. The emigration of the nobility and of other upper-class families as a result of the Revolution was seen as a serious loss to the genetic reserves of Russia, requiring eugenic correction.

Several of the early Soviet eugenists showed that they were aware that their analysis and program were potentially inflammatory from the political standpoint. In the early spring of 1925 the Russian Eugenics Society debated eugenics proposals that had been advanced in other countries. Several Soviet participants objected to the "coarseness" and ill-defined quality of several of these proposals, some of which included plans for compulsory sterilization.[20]

The real significance of the Russian eugenics movement was not its relationship to Western eugenic proposals, but its place in the debates over the nature of man that were beginning to take place in Soviet Russia. How was the eugenics movement perceived by Soviet intellectuals outside the community of eugenists itself? What was the relation of the doctrines of eugenics to the ideas of Russian socialism and communism?

The great debate that eventually arose over the issue was rather slow in developing. The Commissar of Public Health, Nikolai Semashko, had given his approval to the eugenics movement, and the Commissariat of Internal Affairs (a police organization) formally accepted the charter of the Russian Eugenics Society. The Russian Eugenics Society received a small state subsidy.[21] These first official acts of recognition were probably not too significant in themselves, since in the early years the concept of eugenics was so new to most people in Soviet Russia, the essential issues so unexplored, that a sophisticated understanding of the movement by bureaucrats was hardly possible. To the extent that eugenics was understood it was thought to be the science for the collective improvement of mankind, and that was an activity that the young Soviet government automatically found interesting.

In 1925 the debate that had begun to simmer in lecture halls and in local publications spilled out into major Soviet intellectual journals. One of the first comprehensive and critical reviews of the eugenics movement was Vasilii Slepkov's article "Human Heredity and Selection: On the Theoretical Premises of Eugenics," which appeared in April, 1925, in the major Bolshevik theoretical journal.[22] Slepkov's point was that the eugenists were emphasizing biological determinants of human behavior to the total neglect of socioeconomic determinants. This point of view, said Slepkov, ignored the principles of Marxism, which demonstrated that social conditions determine consciousness. Slepkov quoted Engels on the importance of labor activity in the evolution of primates; Plekhanov on the view that conservative thinkers had always relied on explaining human behavior on the basis of innate qualities in order to avoid social analysis leading to revolutionary conclusions; and Marx to the effect that "people are a product of conditions and education and, consequently, changing people are a product of changing circumstances and different education."[23]

Slepkov did not deny, however, that individuals differ genetically. But in order to explain those differences he resorted to a view that was to have a long, and eventually tragic, influence on Soviet biology: the inheritance of acquired characteristics. He believed that social influence on the basis of conditioned reflexes, as he saw exemplified by Pavlov's research, was the best way of explaining the influence of environment on human behavior. And he pointed out that Pavlov believed that conditioned reflexes acquired during the lifetime of an organism could become, in some cases, permanently hereditable.

Despite Slepkov's emphasis, for many more years the inheritance of acquired characteristics remained as only a rather remote candidate for a replacement of classical genetics. As we will see, the geneticists and eugenists still had very powerful arguments at their disposal. Even in terms of politics, it was in the midtwenties still not assumed in the Soviet Union that Marxist socialism and eugenics were incompatible, nor that Marxism and Lamarckism were uniquely compatible.

Nonetheless, not only the eugenists with their arrogant programs for biological reforms of society, but also the more sober and scientific geneticists interested primarily in animal and plant heredity were beginning to meet stiff opposition from radical students in Soviet universities. One biologist with a political commitment to the new regime, B. M. Zavadovskii, wrote that each year when he gave lectures at the Sverdlov Communist University the radical students reacted in a hostile manner to his discussions of heredity, calling genetics "a bourgeois science" containing implications that were unacceptable to the proletariat. Voices in favor of Lamarckism are becoming "louder and stronger," he wrote in 1925, as is the belief that genetics contradicts Marxism and the social policy of the Communist Party.[24] "This point of view is receiving support in the psychology of the masses," he wrote, "whose first reaction to genetics is negative." Zavadovskii feared that in dispensing with the erroneous views of the eugenists, Marxists might "throw out the baby with the bath" and eliminate the science of genetics as well. Marxists, he observed, have been "frightened" by the conclusions of the bourgeois eugenists.[25]

By 1925, then, the first crisis in the debate between Mendelian or classical genetics and Lamarckism was coming to a head, and the eugenists were in the middle of it. The eugenists began to defend both genetics and eugenics simultaneously, and they considered the Lamarckians to be one of the most important groups of their opponents.

Several of the eugenists realized that the criticisms being advanced against them were so serious that unless some way could be found of reconciling their understanding of human heredity with Marxist aspirations not only was the eugenic movement in danger, but genetics as well. Iu. A. Filipchenko, one of the brightest of the eugenists, found an argument in favor of genetics that carried great weight, and for a time was thought by some observers to have outmaneuvered the radical critics of genetics.[26] Let us assume for a moment, said Filipchenko, that the Lamarckians are correct, and the Mendelians incorrect, even though scientific evidence at the moment all points in favor of the classical Mendelian theory. What would be the result for the proletariat, for lower classes in general, and for the cause of social revolution if acquired characteristics were inherited? Most people seem to believe, Filipchenko observed, that such a theory points to rapid social reform. The same people usually consider classical genetics, with its stable genotype, as inherently conservative in its social implications.

This view is actually superficial and false, said Filipchenko, because it assumes that only "good" environments have heritable effects, while a consistent interpretation of the inheritance of acquired characteristics would show that "bad" environments have effects also. Therefore, all socially or physically deprived groups, races, and classes of people, such as the proletariat and peasantry and the nonwhite races, would have inherited the debilitating effects of having lived for centuries under deprived conditions. Far from promising rapid social reform, the inheritance of acquired characteristics would mean that the upper classes are not only socially and economically advantaged, but genetically privileged as well, a result of centuries of living in a beneficial environment, and one could never hope that the proletariat in Soviet Russia would be capable of running the state. It would be lamed genetically by the inheritance of the effects of its poverty.

If the classical geneticists were correct, on the other hand, said Filipchenko, then that would mean that distributed throughout the genes of the lower classes were combinations of genes that would give the individuals possessing them all the possibilities for being great scientists, musicians, artists, or whatever they might wish to be, if only the exploitative conditions hindering them up to this time were eliminated.

The logic of Filipchenko's arguments seems to have caused a hesitation in the criticism being advanced against the geneticists. Several radical journals ran articles maintaining that it was really the inheritance of acquired characteristics, not Mendelian genetics, that was counter-revolutionary. One author in such a publication stated that the international bourgeoisie constantly renewed efforts to establish the inheritance of acquired characteristics in order to show its own genetic superority, but the proletariat was learning that science spoke against them. Another author, writing in *The Red Journal for All People,* said that every social reformer must read Filipchenko's argument in order to be armed for the political struggle.[27]

Filipchenko's argument was not persuasive enough, however, to stem permanently the popular belief that the inheritance of acquired characteristics was more congenial to the idea of creating a new society and a new culture than Mendelian genetics. And it should be noted that even those relatively few scientifically educated Soviet participants in the debate who listened to Filipchenko's view were not all convinced, some for fairly good reasons. After all, if Filipchenko *was* correct about the debilitating effects of an assumed inheritance of acquired characteristics on the lower classes, a great deal would depend on how long it would take to erase those effects—many generations or one or two. And, furthermore, the most that Filipchenko could promise on the basis of his classical genetics was that *some* members of the proletariat could excel because of their fortuitous possession of the right genes. The eventual result would be a class society based on innate, unchangeable ability, a meritocracy. The inheritance of acquired characteristics held a more radical, democratic prospect: *all* members of the lower classes and their progeny might advance equally because of their social environment, and, given sufficient time, there was no reason for the former lower class to be at any genetic disadvantage to the former upper class.

The overall result of these debates of the twenties was essentially a draw on the issue of whether the inheritance of acquired characteristics was theoretically more consonant with Marxism than classical genetics, although on a popular level, the belief among lay people and students that genetics was a bourgeois science continued to be strong and even grew as social conflict increased at the end of the decade with the commencement of the five-year plans.

The obvious losers in the debate were the Russian eugenists who defined their field in terms of the Western eugenics movement. They were not only supporters of classical genetics, with all the controversy that field attracted in the Soviet Union, but they went far beyond these theoretical principles to an extrapolation of biology to society, and in these extrapolations they had included a host of assumptions about the future of society, the nature of races and classes, and the relative influence of nature vs. nurture that did, indeed, conflict with prevalent views among the politically active elements of Soviet society.

The eugenists recognized that they must either abandon their concerns, or change radically their activities in order to demonstrate that they actually had the interests of Soviet socialism at heart, not Western capitalism. The scientists in the Bureau of Eugenics at the Academy of Sciences chose the prudent path of abandoning the field. Between 1925 and 1928 they shifted from a concern with human heredity and eugenics to a concern with the genetics of plants and animals.

The Russian Eugenics Society chose a more heroic and foolhardy path. The leaders of the journal decided to change their emphases, to show how eugenics could be fitted to the purposes of social revolution and Marxism. Turning away from their genealogical studies of the nobility, they began making studies of the reformers and revolutionaries of Russian history, beginning with the Decembrists of 1825, but continuing right up to contemporary Communist party leaders, whom they noted were not reproducing at an adequate rate.[28] Kol'tsov did a study of the genetic sources of the talented young proletarians being promoted up through the ranks of the universities and institutions of the Soviet Union.[29] Other eugenists began developing extended justifications of a unification of the goals of Soviet socialism and eugenics. But the whole effort became increasingly artificial and strained.[30] The eugenists, with their histories of connections with the international movement, including German race hygiene with

354   LOREN R. GRAHAM

its ever-clearer links to national socialism, could never justify themselves by trying to be more radical than their critics, or even equally radical, much as they were now trying. A scholar such as Filipchenko could win individual debates through the strength of his arguments about the social implications of an assumed inheritance of acquired characteristics, but by style and background he was always a middle-class *intelligent* to his critics.

By 1930 the eugenics movement in the Soviet Union was finished. These were years in which political controls in the Soviet Union were imposed in many scholarly institutions, and collectivization was violently enforced in the countryside. The Russian Eugenics Society was closed, and its publications suspended. By 1931, when the *Large Soviet Encyclopedia* published the volume of its first edition with an article on "Eugenics," the field was simply condemned as a "bourgeois doctrine."[31] By this moment in Soviet history the logical possibility of linking the Marxist desire to transform man with the eugenic desire to improve him had irretrievably disappeared.

By the early thirties the process of the gradual crystallization of value links to conflicting concepts of heredity—links that were at first by no means clear or inevitable—was far advanced in the two countries being studied here, Germany and Russia. Eventually the two societies went opposite directions in their interpretations of the nature-nurture controversy.

These two chronologically simultaneous episodes with contrasting results are probably as close to actual historical "test cases" on a large order of the question of whether different values are inherent in different theories of heredity as our very confused and inexact world is going to present to us. What do these examples tell us about the relationship between science and sociopolitical values?

Standing in our position today, it may appear that there is a natural alliance between eugenics and conservative, even fascist, sentiments. That link was not logically preordained, however, and was not perceived in the early twenties by large numbers of radical critics of society. Marxists and socialists of many types gave their support to eugenics in the early years, as did liberals, progressives, and conservatives. In the early twenties eugenics found response in both Weimar Germany and Soviet Russia across a rather wide range of political sentiment.

Eugenics in these early years was a faddish doctrine that was often considered progressive, the latest application of science for the benefit of humankind. If it was sometimes supported by aristocratic devotees of genealogical tables or middle-class members of social clubs, it was also on occasion given support by committed socialists who believed that a cultivation of true talent, rather than mere economic privilege, would destroy class society as it was known until that time. Both Weimar Germany and Soviet Russia were revolutionary states standing in the places of recent monarchies. Both in the twenties were going through eclectic periods when the full range of possible political implications of the latest scientific hypotheses had still not been formulated.

Was the passing of these early heterodox periods and the emergence of high degrees of consensus about the correlations between theories of heredity and political world views a phenomenon that touches science itself, or was it only an epiphenomenon of social and political turmoil? Do different theories of heredity intrinsically contain different value implications? The answers to these questions depend on what one considers the main rival theories to be. If one defines the contending theories in terms of their post-1933 vulgarized and absolutized forms (i.e., a national socialist theory of the "overall" values of different categories of humans, with Jews, gypsies, and certain types of "social misfits" genetically condemned to the bottom of the heap, and a Soviet alternative which opposes this view with a dogmatically environmental one), then it is obvious that the scientific "theories" in themselves contained by definition clear value components.

One can easily point out that these absolutized explanations, encased in official ideology and supported by the respective governments, can hardly be classified as "science." We will not use that fact, however, for a convenient exit from our dilemma about the relationship of science and values. We have purposely restricted ourselves in this study to the period before 1930, when professional geneticists and eugenists in both Germany and Russia usually defined the contrasting theories in much more academic terms. They often saw the difference between vulgarized extrapolations and core theories.

During the German Weimar and Soviet New Economic Policy (NEP) periods being considered here, the rival theories, stated in their scientific forms, did not explicitly contain value statements. The rival theories were those of Mendelian genetics and Lamarckism, viewed as scientific alternatives. Yet to many people they seemed to contain strikingly different value implications.

One of the several reasons for these apparent different value connotations stems from the state of genetics in the twenties as a pure and an applied science. Whether or not science *qua* science contains values, most people will agree that technology does have value impacts. Therefore, the significance for values of a particular science will vary as the associated technology for that science develops. One of the interesting aspects of the period of human genetics being studied here is that not only was human heredity understood in an exceedingly inexact fashion, allowing much room for speculation based on social and class motives, but there was no technology available for controlling the genetic constitution of organisms except by selection on the basis of phenotypes. Such selection was offensive to existing values when applied to people, and therefore humane individuals wished for an alternative even if they accepted the goal of more control over human genetics.

For this reason we take particular notice of the argument of the young Alfred Ploetz, still in his humanistic phase. He emphasized the fact that if the time ever came when selection could be shoved back before birth it might be possible to develop eugenic measures that were less offensive to traditional values than many of the proposals advanced in his day. We are now at a time when Ploetz's observation has a bit more meaning than it did when he wrote, at least for specific genetic defects. The differential impacts on values of various technologies thus serve as a further warning to us not to attribute values easily to scientific knowledge itself; the more important value-determinant is likely to be the technology derived from that knowledge.

The relatively few geneticists who did not fall prey to the political ideologies of the time in Germany and Russia were left with a very undramatic argument, one unable to carry their audiences in times of great social stress, of times when the active political elements were striving for answers to societal problems. The rigorous geneticists were saying, in effect: "Yes, the science of genetics is in principle applicable to man. However, genetics is so immature as a science that any effort to apply it to man now would have disastrous and unpredictable effects. Therefore, do not try to apply human genetics as a science, although continue to believe us when we tell you that science is ultimately the best hope for man."

In revolutionary moments popular audiences are not likely to find such an argument very persuasive. Both Germany and Russia were undergoing social and political upheaval, and the audiences turned toward more radical, although quite different, answers to the problem of heredity, answers that contained possibilities for application.

The German academic eugenists (as opposed to the race hygiene anthropologists), such as Fritz Lenz, were closer to science, as it existed at that time, when they attacked Lamarckists for their sentimental biology, than the Soviet Marxists who rejected genetics along with eugenics. The tragedy is that those scientists who—contrary to Lenz—remained loyal to genetics as a scientific theory while rejecting the growing inhumane and antirational extrapolations of German race hygiene were unable to find appreciative audiences in either Germany or Russia.

The reason for their failures was no doubt largely because of the social, political, and economic strains both societies were undergoing. To detail those strains would require a long digression into the social and political histories of Weimar Germany and Soviet Russia. But the existence of these strains was only a necessary, not sufficient condition for the emergence of radically different attitudes toward heredity. Science also was involved, a science of heredity that was so immature that it allowed room for wide speculation while offering few applications that were both reliable and ethical.

We are now approaching the core issue in the question of the relationship of science to values as revealed in our study of Germany and Russia in the twenties. We have already separated the question of political and social motivations from those of scientific inquiry to the maximum degree that is possible (it is never entirely possible) by focusing on more academic debates of the twenties, not the ideological exhortations of the thirties. We have separately considered the question of technology, trying to show where it had differential impacts on value that are distinguishable from those of scientific theory. Peeling away the layers of this problem, the central question emerges, one that relates to scientific theory alone: Was there something inherent in a hypothetical Lamarckian theory of heredity that made it a substantial buttress for egalitarian political values, and something within the Mendelian theory of heredity that lent support to elitist views of society?

Iurii Filipchenko tried to come to grips with this problem in 1926 when he maintained, with some success, that a hypothetical Lamarckian theory of heredity, followed to its conclusions, would mean the genetic impairment of those social classes whom left-wing social reformers wanted to help. The existence for many generations of the deprived classes in poor environmental conditions would supposedly have resulted in the acquisition of hereditary characteristics which would genetically impair them.

This argument was also used by the American geneticist and socialist, H. J. Muller, in his criticism of Lamarckism. (Muller and Filipchenko knew each other and the connection may not be coincidental). Yet we should admit that the argument by itself means very little. First of all, it is not completely clear that, in our hypothetical case of an assumed Lamarckism, deprived environments would lead uniquely to genetic damage; some people might maintain the reverse, seeing a sharp selection of the "fittest." Since Lamarckism is a doctrine without empirical support, there is no way of knowing how a hypothetical Lamarckism would fit with normal Darwinian selection. Furthermore, one would like to know how many generations would be required for a hypothetical Lamarckism to overcome the effects of earlier genetic impairment. Again, there is no way of knowing because we are not dealing with facts or testable hypotheses.

The assumptions that were carried by most Lamarckists into the debates in the Soviet Union of the twenties over human heredity were either (a) deprived environments do *not* result in impaired heredity, or (b) if deprived environments *do* result in impaired heredity, this impairment can be easily erased in a generation or two in the future through Lamarckian inheritance in improved conditions. *If* one makes these assumptions, then Lamarckian views truly fitted more comfortably with social reformism than Mendelian genetics, and this "science" contains real value implications. The Lamarckians could then promise the quick advent of a bright genetic future for all members of the proletariat (or any other group) while the Mendelians could promise such a future only to the fortunate few. This is the way the argument was usually seen by the thirties in the Soviet Union. Filipchenko lost the debate, the Lamarckians eventually won. But it should be clear that the chains of assumptions here took both of them into unreal worlds.

When we examine the relative value ingredients supposedly inherent in different theories of heredity, we should see that Filipchenko was not the only person to maintain that positive, humane values are inherent in theories of heredity that postulate a relatively stable genetic material, and that negative values lurk in the supposedly humane Lamarckian view of a malleable genetic base. Noam Chomsky has recently taken the view that man's relative immalleability is a protection for him against potential tyrants:[32]

> One can easily see why reformers and revolutionaries should become radical environmentalists, and there is no doubt that concepts of immutable human nature can be and have been employed to erect barriers against social change and to defend established privilege.
>
> But a deeper look will show that the concept of the "empty organism," plastic and unstructured, apart from being false, also serves naturally as the support for the most reactionary social doctrines. If people are, in fact, malleable and plastic beings with no essential psychological nature, then why should they not be controlled and coerced by those who claim authority, special knowledge, and a unique insight into what is best for those less enlightened?

This statement contains not only an observation on aspiring genetic manipulators of man, but also the concern of a more recent generation about the control of the behavior of man. From the standpoint of Chomsky's position, both the eugenic selectionists of Germany and the Soviet "makers of a new Soviet man" represented threats of a fundamental sort to human freedom. Yet it is clear that Chomsky's observation, valuable though it is, presents only one more insight, and is not an attempt to give an ultimate analysis of whether putative theories about the mutability of man, genetic or behavioral, contain inherently positive or negative value. He admits that the theories can work both ways, with hypothetical immutability "employed to erect barriers against social change and to defend established privilege" and hypothetical mutability serving as "the support for the most reactionary social doctrines." *Which* way the theories would work in a given historical situation depends on the values of the political and scientific authorities who disposed of the theories and the associated technology.

It is my opinion that in our present state of knowledge of human heredity the question of whether available theories have in themselves positive or negative value content simply cannot be answered on an abstract level, apart from reference to the existing sets of social forces and to the available technologies. However, in a given historical situation, such as the ones we have been studying here, rival scientific theories always exist within the context of given sets of social and political circumstances, of competing political ideologies, and economic motives, and of existing systems of technological capabilities. Within those frameworks of external factors, rival scientific theories *do* have differential value implications, but they derive their value meaning much more from their relationships to these external factors than from anything inherent in the science.

In terms of impact, then, we are not asking the right question when we ask, "Do scientific theories contain in themselves social or political values?" Instead, we should pay more attention to what I called at the beginning of this paper the "second-order" links between science and values, those which are contingent on existing political and social situations, current technological capabilities, and the persuasiveness of current ideologies, flawed in an intellectual sense as they may be.

If we look back at Germany and Russia in the twenties with these overall extra-scientific frameworks in mind, it is clearly far from accidental that the societies eventually ended up on the particular opposite sides of the nature-nurture dispute with which we now associate them. Arguments for radical egalitarianism *could* be made more easily and more persuasively in accordance with Lamarckian environmentalism, and arguments for hierarchies of social and racial values *could* be placed more comfortably within the Mendelian system. The more obvious points of debate leaned in these directions, while the more subtle ones were not heard at moments of social and political trial. In this global, approximate, and intellectually flawed sense, then, these rival scientific theories *did* contribute heavily to arguments about values. These value implications derived from the relationships of the theories to their social and economic milieus, but that is normally the situation with science.

Since I have maintained in this essay that the theories of human heredity current in Soviet Russia and Weimar Germany in the twenties contained in themselves much less inherent value component than is often considered to be the case, my viewpoint might easily be considered as a buttress for the argument that science is really value-free. My interpretation might even be used to attempt to free scientists from a sense of responsibility to society. My reply to this misunderstanding of my analysis would be to point out that the value-free interpretation of these theories of human heredity is persuasive only if the links of science and society are severed, and if science is viewed in abstract isolation from its setting. In actual fact, every scientific theory and every technological innovation *always* exists in a social and political setting, and the value impacts of these combinations can be massive.

Nuclear science is, seen in isolation, value-free. If, however, Nazi Germany had developed and employed atomic weapons in 1942, the configuration of our world might be very different today, and the effects on our values would probably be incalculable. Scientific descriptions of our universe—e.g., the Copernican or Ptolemaic alternatives—are, in the abstract, value-free, but the new and successful Copernican variant had a very large value impact when absorbed by a European civilization at a time when the older variant was firmly interwoven with religion and culture.

Scientific theories and technological innovations are thrust upon societies in which they may either buttress or counter existing value preferences. The powerful groups in society are usually more successful in turning science and technology to their advantage than the weak ones, so there is a natural tendency for science and technology to buttress the values of ruling classes or political groups. In both Germany and Russia by the thirties these links between ruling value systems and contrasting theories of heredity had been successfully forged, after some initial uncertainties, and the links then became powerful weapons of propaganda.

The responsibility of scientists for their creations is not less because of the fact that the value impacts of their work usually derive from a changing relationship between science and society, but greater. They must not only try to judge what *can* be done on the basis of their work but what, in all probability, *will* be done in view of the existing social forces.

As a hypothetical case, let me assume, somewhat grandiosely, that I am a scientist in Nazi Germany and that I have just discovered Tay-Sachs disease, a disorder with genetic causes that is more common among Jews than other groups of the population.[33] Whether I should publish my research and to whom I should send reprints (Hitler?) become moral acts, not because of values inherent in my scientific work, but because of the possible impact in that particular political setting of this purely scientific (not technological) finding.

When physicists speak of physical forces, they often speak of "strong" and "weak" forces. It might be useful for us to consider, for a moment, "strong" and "weak" value components in scientific theories. From the standpoint of a philosopher, the value components that I have found in scientific theories are weak, since they come not from the scientific theory itself, but from the relationship of the theories to society. Thus, Kenneth Schaffner commented on an earlier version of my essay:

> Professor Graham's view of the relations between science and values then seems to me to be an extremely *weak* one. Perhaps this is the one which he would in fact wish to defend. In my view, a much stronger thesis of the non-value-free character of science, including *basic* science, is defensible, but I do not have the time, nor would it be appropriate to develop my views here.

Since Professor Schaffner does not go on with his stronger

thesis, I can only speculate on what it might be. Certainly, if one can identify value components within science itself (and not in its relationship to society), this identification would result in a stronger case in philosophical terms (although we do not yet know whether the social significance of this value ingredient would be great or small). I suspect that such internal value components in some types of scientific theories *can* be identified. I am not, therefore, maintaining that science qua science is value-free. When, as others in this book have pointed out, scientists use terms such as "normal" and "abnormal" in physiology or psychology the importation of values seems likely. And doubtless there are other examples of diverse kinds in which value terms reside in the core of science itself.

Although I agree that the discovery of value components internal to science would be a stronger case in terms of philosophical considerations than the "contingent" or "relational" argument I have made here, I maintain that the value impacts on society coming from science of the type I have been examining are far stronger in terms of the concerns of historians or sociologists. In other words, I question the social importance of the value components that may be truly internal to science, but I underline the importance of those that derive from the relationship of science to society.

Thus, I suspect that Professor Schaffner and I are using the terms "strong" and "weak" in two different ways. He is interested primarily, it seems, in strong arguments showing value ingredients in science, whatever the social significance of those components may be. I am interested in strong value impacts of science and technology on society. Therefore, in many cases, what he would call "strong" I would call "weak" and vice versa.

In my opinion, the really massive impacts of science and technology on social values are all of the type I have described here, i.e., the impacts that derive from the relationship of a particular scientific theory or technical innovation to a particular society in a particular historical setting. These impacts are the type that change history: they result in life and death, in vast changes in social mores, in changing attitudes toward the scientific enterprise itself. On the other hand, those values that may be truly inherent in science, built into its structure, are, in my opinion, of less significance, so much so that I would call them "weak."

One last word on the relevance of the episodes in Weimar Germany and Soviet Russia to the present day. . . . I have emphasized that the value contributions or inputs of the rival scientific theories depended much more on external social forces and available technologies than they did on anything inherent in the theories. We now live in a time when the social circumstances and available technology connected with the science of human genetics are very different from what they were in the twenties. We should not assume, therefore, that the value links of our time on the nature-nurture issue are identical to what they were in the twenties. To ignore the genetic basis of human beings at the present time, when we understand that basis much better and are in some instances able to affect it in reliable ways or alleviate great suffering, would be quite inhumane. Eugenics is now a word in disrepute, but the use of genetic knowledge to benefit mankind is a far more viable possibility now than ever before. On the other hand, some of the dangers of the twenties are still with us. We need to examine each issue relating to human genetics separately, considering the whole context of second-order value links, and decide the issues without a priori ideological commitments.

NOTES

* I would like to express my appreciation to the Rockefeller Foundation for a Humanities Fellowship for 1976-1977, during which time I did research on the relationship of science and sociopolitical values, including this article. I would also like to thank Harvard University for providing research facilities during the year, particularly the Program on Science and International Affairs, the History of Science Department, and the Russian Research Center. A longer and somewhat different version of this chapter appeared in December, 1977, in the *American Historical Review*.

1. There is a very large literature on Darwinism and social Darwinism in Germany. See, particularly, Hans-Günter Zmarzlik, "Der Sozialdarwinismus in Deutschland als Geschichtliches Problem," *Vierteljahrshefte für Zeitgeschichte* no. 11 (1963), 246-73; and the

same author's "Der Sozialdarwinismus in Deutschland—Ein Beispiel für den gesellschaftspolitischen Missbrauch naturwissenschaftlicher Erkenntnisse," in Günter Altner, ed., *Kreatur Mensch: Moderne Wissenschaft auf der Suche nach dem Humanum* (Munich: Moos, 1973), pp. 289-311. Also, see William M. Montgomery, "Germany," in Thomas Glick, ed., *The Comparative Reception of Darwinism* (Austin: The University of Texas Press, 1974), pp. 81-116; Gerhard Heberer and Franz Schwanitz, eds., *Hundert Jahre Evolutionsforschung: Das wissenschaftliche Vermächtnis Charles Darwins* (Stuttgart, 1960); and Hedwig Conrad-Martius, *Utopien der Menschenzüchtung: Der Sozialdarwinismus und seine Fölgen* (Munich: Kösel-Verlag, 1955). An interesting but somewhat simplified account is Daniel Gasman, *The Scientific Origins of National Socialism: Social Darwinism in Ernst Haeckel and the German Monist League* (New York: American Elsevier, Inc., 1971). Also, Niles R. Holt, "Monists & Nazis: a Question of Scientific Responsibility," *The Hastings Center Report*, 5, no. 2 (April, 1975): 37-43.

2. Alfred Ploetz, *Die Tüchtigkeit unserer Rasse und der Schutz der Schwachen: Ein Versuch über Rassenhygiene und ihr Verhältnis zu den humanen Idealen, besonders zum Sozialismus,* (Berlin: S. Fischer, 1895).

3. Ibid., pp. 224-25.

4. *Sozialistische Monatshefte,* 10 (1923): 638.

5. In addition to the articles and reviews specifically discussed in the text, see the following reviews in *Die Gesellschaft*: R.F. Fuchs, review of A. Basler, *Einführung in die Rassen- und Gesellschafts-Physiologie,* 3, no. 3 (March, 1926): 283-86; Karl Kautsky, review of Alfred Grotjähn, *Die Hygiene der menschlichen Fortpflanzung: Versuch einer praktischen Eugenik,* 4, no. 4 (April, 1927): 381-82; M. Kantorowicz-Kroll, review of Robert Sommer, *Familienforschung, Vererbungs- und Rassenlehre,* 5, no. 7 (July, 1928): 92-4; Miron Kantorowicz, review of Ernst Neumann, *Individual-Rassen- und Volkshygiene,* 8, no. 9 (September, 1931): 288.

6. Hugo Iltis, "Rassenwissenschaft und Rassenwahn," *Die Gesellschaft,* 4, no. 2 (February, 1927): 97-114.

7. Ibid., pp. 108, 114.

8. Ibid., p. 113.

9. For examples of Lenz's attacks on Lamarckism see: review of Hermann Paull, *Wir und das kommende Geschlecht, Archiv für Rassen- und Gesellschaftsbiologie,* 15, no. 3 (1924): 330-32; review of Wilhelm Schmidt, *Rasse und Volk, Archiv für Rassen- und*

Gesellschaftsbiologie, 21, no. 1 (1928), 111-15; review of Friedrich Hertz, *Rasse und Kultur, Archiv für Rassen- und Gesellschaftsbiologie*, 18, no. 1 (1926): 109-14. An example of Lenz's praise of Hitler before national socialism came to power is the following 1931 statement: "Hitler ist der erste Politiker von wirklich grossem Einfluss, der die Rassenhygiene als eine zentrale Aufgabe aller Politik erkannt hat und der sich tatkräftig dafür einsetzen will." Fritz Lenz, "Die Stellung des Nationalsozialismus zur Rassenhygiene," *Archiv für Rassen- und Gesellschaftsbiologie*, 25, no. 3 (1931): 300-308.

10. F. Lenz, "Der Fall Kammerer und seine Umfilmung durch Lunatscharsky," *Archiv für Rassen- und Gesellschaftsbiologie*, 21, no. 3 (1929): 311-18.

11. Lenz many times made the argument that science was value-free. For example, in 1921 he said, "Die Natur verlangt überhaupt nichts; die Naturwissenschaft kann nur zeigen, was geschieht, nicht was geschehen soll." *Archiv für Rassen- und Gesellschaftsbiologie*, 13, no. 1 (1921): 112.

12. Max Levien, "Stimmen aus dem teutschen Urwalde (Zwei neue Apostel des Rassenhasses), "*Unter dem Banner des Marxismus*, 2, no. 1/2 [4/5] (1928): pp. 150-95. The article is a criticism of the views of H.F.K. Günther and A. Basler.

13. Ibid., p. 155.

14. Ibid., p. 163.

15. For background on the reception of Darwinism in Russia, see James Allen Rogers, "Charles Darwin and Russian Scientists," *The Russian Review*, 19 (1960): 382. There was even an early advocate in Russia of improvement of humans through selection: V.M. Florinskii, *Usovershenstvovanie i vyrozhdenie chelovecheskogo roda* (St. Petersburg, 1866). For a discussion of this book by an early Soviet eugenist, see M.V. Volotskoi, "K istorii evgenicheskogo dvizheniia," *Russkii evgenicheskii zhurnal*, 2, no. 1 (1924): 50-55. Also see George Kline, "Darwinism and the Russian Orthodox Church," in Ernest J. Simmons, ed., *Continuity and Change in Russian and Soviet Thought* (Cambridge, Massachusetts: Harvard University Press, 1955), pp. 307-28; N. Danilevskii, *Darvinizm, kriticheskoe issledovanie* (St. Petersburg, 1889); K.A. Timiriazev, *Charlz Darvin i ego uchenie* 3rd ed. (Moscow, 1894); Alexander Vucinich, "Russia: Biological Sciences," and James Allen Rogers, "Russia: Social Sciences," in Thomas F. Glick, ed., *The Comparative Reception of Darwinism* (Austin: University of Texas Press, 1972), pp. 227-68.

16. See Mark B. Adams, "The Founding of Population Genetics: Con-

tributions of the Chetverikov School, 1924-1934," *Journal of the History of Biology*, 1, no. 1 (1968): 23-39; "Towards a Synthesis: Population Concepts in Russian Biological Thought, 1925-1935," *Journal of the History of Biology*, 3, no. 1 (1970): pp. 107-29.

17. N.K. Kol'tsov was president of the Russian Eugenics Society. Iu. A. Filipchenko was the director of the Bureau of Eugenics of the Academy of Sciences. A.S. Serebrovskii was a member of the permanent bureau of the Russian Eugenic Society, and a contributor to its journal. For his great hopes for the eugenic movement, see A.S. Serebrovskii, "O zadachakh i putiakh antropogenetiki," *Russkii evgenicheskii zhurnal*, 1, no. 2 (1923): 107-16, especially p. 112. Ironically, N.I. Vavilov, who ultimately suffered the most at the hands of Soviet authorities, apparently steered clear of eugenics. Vavilov became a foe of Lysenko in the late thirties and died in 1940 in Siberian exile.

18. A good bibliography of Russian eugenic literature is K. Gurvich, "Ukazatel' literatury po voprosam evgeniki, nasledstvennosti i selektsii i sopredel'nykh oblastei, opublikovannoi na russkom iazike do 1/I 1928 g.," *Russkii evgenicheskii zhurnal*, 6, nos. 2-3 (1928): 121-143.

19. For accounts of the founding and early activities of the Russian Eugenics Society, see "O deiatel'nosti Russkogo Evgenicheskogo Obshchestva za 1921 god," *Russkii evgenicheskii zhurnal*, 1, no. 1 (1922): 99-101 and similar descriptions in succeeding volumes of the same publication. For an interesting but somewhat one-sided recent Soviet interpretation of these early eugenic interests, see N.P. Dubinin, *Vechnoe dvizhenie* (Moscow: 1973).

20. "Obsuzhdenie Norvezhskoi evgenicheskoi programmy na zasedaniiakh Leningradskoi Otdeleniia R.E.O.," *Russkii evgenicheskii zhurnal*, 3, no. 2 (1925): 139-43. The particular eugenic program that was at the basis of this discussion was that of the Norwegian J.A. Mjöen. This discussion of the Russian Eugenics Society is very interesting, with separate consideration of "positive and negative race hygiene proposals," and identification by speakers of wide disagreements on issues such as racially mixed marriages and mandatory sterilization.

21. For approval by the commissariats of health and education, as well as for announcement of the subsidy, see "Iz otcheta o deiatel'nosti Russkogo Evgenicheskogo Obshchestva za 1923 g.," *Russkii evgenicheskii zhurnal*, 2, no. 1 (1924): 4. For approval of the society's charter by the Commissariat of Internal Affairs, see "Evgenicheskie zametki," *Russkii evgenicheskii zhurnal*, 2, no. 1 (1924): 58.

22. V. Slepkov, "Nasledstvennost' i otbor u cheloveka (Po povodu

teoreticheskikh predposylok evgeniki)," *Pod znamenem marksizma,* no. 10-11 (October-November, 1925), pp. 79-114.

23. Ibid., p. 113.
24. B.M. Zavadovskii, "Darvinizm i lamarkizm i problema nasledo-vaniia priobretennykh priznakov," *Pod znamenem marksizma,* no. 10-11 (October-November, 1925), pp. 79-114.
25. Ibid., p. 101.
26. See the discussion of the impact of Filipchenko's argument in "Spornye voprosy evgeniki," *Vestnik kommunisticheskoi akademii* 20 (1927): especially 224-25.
27. "Spornye voprosy evgeniki," *Vestnik kommunisticheskoi akademii* 20 (1927): 225.
28. Kol'tsov observed in a 1924 article, "If we calculate the average number of children in the family of each member of the Russian Communist Party that number will no doubt be far from what Gruber cites as necessary for a population group to preserve itself in the overall population. What would we say about a stock-breeder who every year castrated his most valuable producers, not permitting them to multiply? But in cultured society approximately the same thing is occurring before our eyes!" N.K. Kol'tsov, "Vliianie kul'tury na otbor v chelovechestve," *Russkii evgenicheskii zhurnal,* 2, no. 1 (1924): 15. The reference is to Max Gruber, *Ursache und Bekämpfung des Geburtenrückgange im deutschen Reiche* (Munich, 1914).
29. N.K. Kol'tsov, "Rodoslovnye nashikh vydvizhentsev," *Russkii evgenicheskii zhurnal,* 4, nos. 3-4 (1926): 103-43; for other examples of this kind of article, see N.P. Chulkov, "Genealogiia dekabristov Murav'evykh," *Russkii evgenicheskii zhurnal,* 5, no. 1 (1927): 3-20.
30. The difficulty of the position of the academic eugenists was illustrated by Serebrovskii when he called for a socialist eugenics and then observed: "Every class must create its own eugenics. However, this slogan . . . must in no way be understood in the manner of several of our comrades, especially in Moscow, who maintain that the whole base of Morganist-Mendelian theory is an invention of the Western bourgeoisie, and that the proletariat, creating its own eugenics, must base itself on Lamarckism." A.S. Serebrovskii, "Teoriia nasledstvennosti Morgana i Mendelia i marksisty," *Pod znamenem marksizma,* no. 3 (March, 1926), p. 113.
31. "Evgenika," *Bol'shaia Sovetskaia Entsiklopediia,* 23 (Moscow: 1931), cols. 812-9.

32. Noam Chomsky, *Reflections On Language* (New York: Pantheon Books, 1975), p. 132.
33. I am grateful to Professor Noretta Koertge of Indiana University for suggesting this example.

Knowing and Valuing

12

Are Science and Ethics Compatible?

John Ladd

THE TRADITION THAT SCIENCE is one of the highest, if not the highest, human enterprise goes back to the ancient Greeks and has continued virtually unchallenged to the present. At one time, perhaps, the exaltation of science was accepted only by a minority of insiders. But today it is obviously part of the public faith of the scientific establishment, if not of our society at large. As Philip Handler puts it, "The search for truth is man's noblest enterprise."(1) Further, scientists comprise "The world's greatest army devoted to good works... for the scientists attack falseness of every kind and accept no doctrine until the last doubt has been disposed of."(2) In this paper, I want to discuss some philosophical questions concerning the supposedly superior moral status of scientific activity.

The attitude I want to examine may be illustrated by an anecdote. Once I attended a course in genetics in which some of the moral issues raised by recent advances were examined. During a discussion of serious genetic defects, the question of what should be done with newborn infants suffering from such defects was raised. Should an infant born with Tay-Sachs or Lesch Nayan disease be kept alive at all costs as long as possible? Yes, said one student. Why? asked the instructor.

Answer: by keeping the infant alive, scientists would be able to make fruitful observations of the development of the disease, thereby advancing our understanding of the disease and of genetic diseases in general.(3)

I do not think that this attitude is atypical: prolonging a miserable existence is good for science and science is good. Our universities and medical schools constantly indoctrinate students with the idea that they have a moral duty to advance science and that this duty takes priority over other considerations in their professional conduct. Their role gives scientists special rights over others, such as experimental subjects, as well as a right to a substantial part of society's resources. The advancement of science is considered more important than almost anything else.

My aim in this paper is not to denigrate science as such, or scientists. Rather, it is to examine critically the lofty claims made on behalf of science, claims that might be subsumed under the title "Ideology of Science." The doctrine that the pursuit of science is a highly moral activity is used to justify many of the demands made on behalf of science, both on individuals and on society at large. Individuals with scientific talents and training are expected to dedicate their lives to the cause of science as a "vocation," for which they are honored and rewarded. Society, for its part, is expected to make huge expenditures for the advancement of science. A mark of the exalted status assigned to science is the common assumption that moral considerations of other sorts—honesty, integrity, compassion, social responsibility, and justice—must give way to the objectives of scientific research in case of conflict.

Can these claims to special and superior moral status be substantiated? And if they can, what follows? But if they cannot, what follows instead? Are ethics and science compatible or incompatible? In what sense might they be incompatible?

The first part of this paper will consist of an examination of the theoretical basis for the kind of claims just mentioned: for a proper evaluation of these claims is a necessary preliminary to any attempt to answer the question of the compatibility of science and ethics.

The approach I shall adopt toward these claims is skeptical. The claims for a moral status for science will be evaluated on their own terms rather than by reference to extrinsic considerations. For, as I shall try to show later, it is logically possible to refute a set of moral claims without having to deploy positive counterarguments against them. Hence it is not necessary, for example, to show that science is evil in order to defeat the moral claims made for it. So, for purposes of this paper, I do not need to dwell on the particular sins of particular scientists or on particular evils that science has ostensibly perpetrated on society.

This general approach to moral claims, which might be called *methodological skepticism*, is in the final analysis logically more devastating to a claim than the deployment of positive counterarguments against it. The latter procedure is weaker for many reasons: it is more dogmatic, since it requires arguing from a preset position; and it ignores the ambiguous nature of the concept of incompatibility as it is used in ethics.

Having assessed the claims of science to be a moral activity, I shall then turn to an examination of the problem of the compatibility of science and ethics. This problem, again, raises many different questions relating to the nature, source, and consequences of ethical compatibility and incompatibility. As we shall see, one kind of incompatibility, which I call "contingent incompatibility," between certain specific requirements of science and certain specific requirements of morality is not inconsistent with the claims of science to be a moral activity. In contrast, another kind of incompatibility, which I call "logical incompatibility," if it can be shown to exist between the claims of science and the claims of morality, has very significant consequences for the relationship between science and ethics.

I do not pretend to offer any definitive answers to the questions I shall discuss. My principal aim is to call attention to some of the issues that need to be explored in answering the question of the compatibility of science and ethics. As a philosopher, I conceive my first task to be to disentangle the theoretical issues that are involved in this question.

We must begin by noting that science, like other institutionally defined activities, roles, and professions, is subject to abuse. There can be evils attendant on how science is pursued, how it is used, or what it is used for. As a social institution, science often leads to interpersonal animosities, jealousies, and deceptions, because of the excessive competitiveness in the contest to be the first to discover something, the race for the Nobel Prize, or the scramble to get into medical school. The institutionalization of science often makes it profitable, or at least tempting, to cut corners morally and legally in the pursuit of science, as in human experimentation. And science, as a source of power, has often been used for unjust political and military purposes, for instance, by the Nazis or by the military in Vietnam. In addition to such moral abuses, scientists sometimes violate the norms of their own professional ethics: they are often guilty of plagiarism, misrepresentation of results, fabrication of evidence, and so on.(4)

Against all these acknowledged evils, one can reply that *abusus non tollit usum* (an abuse does not derogate from the proper use). All these abuses arise out of the institutionalization of science and are not due to the nature of science itself, that is, science *qua* science. The "proper use" of science is for the discovery of scientific truth. In this sense, science must be considered the activity of scientists *qua* scientists, that is, activity in the pursuit of scientific knowledge rather than as a social institution. Although sociological considerations may be important for other reasons, our present concern is with scientific activity as it occurs in observation, experimentation, the construction and testing of hypotheses, and calculations, insofar as they pertain to obtaining scientific knowledge. When we ask about the moral status of science, we refer therefore to this kind of scientific activity, defined by its purpose. Let us call it "science *per se*."

At the risk of oversimplification we might then accept as the supreme practical principle of science *per se* something like the scientific imperative: "Do everything in your power to maximize scientific knowledge!" Insofar as we are concerned with the moral status of science *per se*, we are in effect asking about the moral status of the scientific imperative. Does it have a moral basis? If it does not, is it compatible or incompatible with morality?

I. Liberal Ethics: The Values Approach

Most current discussions of the relationship between science and ethics approach the moral issues involved through a theory of values. The issues are formulated in terms of values, in particular, possible conflicts of values. Science *per se* is assumed to be a value and all the moral problems relating to science are conceived of as essentially questions of the relationship between one kind of value (e.g., science) and other kinds of value.

Thus, for example, it is taken for granted throughout Katz's impressive collection of materials relating to human experimentation that every moral issue concerning experimentation arises out of a conflict of values (or interests) such as the conflict between the interests of the individual subject and the interests of society.(5) In general, the values approach typically construes moral problems as problems of how to reconcile, balance, or weigh multiple, ostensibly conflicting values or interests. Moral problems take the form: what is the optimal or fairest solution? This way of conceiving of moral problems, which might be called the "dogma of liberalism," is implied in Mill's classical utilitarianism, in welfare economics (Arrow's theory of social choice), in Rawls's contractarianism, and in most other liberal theories of value subscribed to by political theorists and social scientists. The job of ethics, according to the liberal theory, is to arbitrate between conflicting values (or interests). Thus, Rawls writes: "Perhaps the principal aim of ethics is the formulation of justifiable principles which may be used in cases wherein there are conflicting interests to determine which one of them should be given preference."(6) In Perry's words, the subject-matter of ethics is the "moral economy."(7)

Basic to this conception of ethics is a distinction between two sorts of questions: (1) what has value? (Perry calls this the question of "generic value"); and (2) how should values be ordered? (Perry calls this the question of "comparative value").

The value-theoretical approach in what I have called the liberal theory focuses on questions of the latter sort, which are often conceived of, for example, as questions of distributive justice.

However, the value-theoretical approach to ethics begs important philosophical questions at the outset and forces us to deal with the moral issues in the relation of science and ethics in a misleading way. Thus, it assumes as an unquestioned premise of the argument that science *per se* is a value and as such has a *prima facie* claim to moral status. But this premise is precisely the one at issue, the one that we need to examine critically. Not only is the premise questionable, but the value-theoretical framework forces us to view the relevant moral issues as simply issues of adjudicating between values (or interests), that is, as questions of comparative value. The net effect is to trivialize the important issues.

The appeal of the liberal model of ethics lies, of course, in its catholicity, its comprehensiveness and all-inclusiveness. Almost anything that people want can be counted as a value.(8) For Perry, for example, any object of any interest to any person is a value. In this inclusive sense, not only are science, art, health, honesty, self-esteem, and freedom values, but so also are money, drugs, fame, and cockfighting. The key point should not be missed: as values, every one of them must in principle be taken into account in the ethical decision process and, in this sense, every value has what might be called a *prima facie* moral status. Essentially, and in practice, the distinction between real and apparent values, or true and false values, is blurred if not repudiated outright. (In view of the variety of theories of value, some qualification of this last statement may be required. No liberal theoretician, however, is likely to maintain that science is an apparent or false value!)

The liberal approach to ethics achieves much of its plausibility from an equivocation on the term "value." Without going into theory of value in detail, it suffices to point out that the term "value" is used in two quite different senses. First, it is used to refer to things, or kinds of things, of value, e.g., material or immaterial goods such as health, knowledge, or friends. Perry's theory that value is any object of any interest to anyone and hedonism are general theories of value in this sense. Second, "value" is also used to refer to a person's (or group of persons') beliefs about what has value (in sense one). In the second sense, we speak of *someone's* values, meaning, for example, his aspirations or ideals; and when doing so we must always specify *whose* values we are referring to, e.g., Smith's or Jones's values, Mormon values, middle-class American values, or a scientist's values. For to be a value in this sense always means to be valued by someone, just as to be a belief means to be believed by someone. The situation is complicated by the fact that we also use the phrase "value for *X*" ambiguously, meaning that something *is* good for *X*, e.g., a particular medical treatment, or that *X believes* that something is good. The first proposition is objective in the sense that the value obtains regardless of who believes or asserts it, whereas the second proposition is subjective or relative in the sense that it depends on someone's believing it. By the same token, whenever we speak of values in the first sense, we *ipso facto* agree to the valuableness of what we are talking about; whereas, when we speak of values in the second sense, we can and often do mean to disown them; for example, we can talk about Mormon values without accepting them.

It should be clear that these two senses of value generate two entirely different kinds of conflict of values. A conflict of the first kind pertains only to elements that are in themselves truly and genuinely valuable (regardless of what anyone thinks). A resolution of the conflict does not require the denial of the valuableness *per se* of any of the conflicting elements; it simply requires an ordering of them, a harmonizing, balancing, or ranking. Although *X* and *Y* are both values, in situation *S, X* has *more* value than *Y*. It is important to note that the need to order values occurs only when an individual (or group) has to choose between two values or two good things—between life and freedom.

A conflict of values in the second sense is logically quite different; it is essentially a conflict of beliefs or attitudes. Here the resolution of the conflict entails the rejection of one of the conflicting values, just as in general the resolution of a conflict between two beliefs entails the rejection of one of them. An example of a conflict of value-beliefs would be a disagreement about the rightness of blood transfusions between, say, a Jehovah's Witness and a Unitarian. A conflict of this type cannot be resolved by "balancing"; it can only be resolved through persuasion, the use of force, or some other measure that results in the giving up of one value-belief and the adoption of the other.

As I have said, the liberal usually tries to reduce all conflicts to the first sort. He tries to take care of the second kind of value conflict by turning a conflict of opinions into a conflict of interests. In order to make this move plausible, however, he has to make an additional assumption, namely, that everyone's opinion about value, regardless of logical incompatibility, is *per se* something of value because, say, it is a reflection of interest. The reduction of beliefs, commitments, concerns, and ideological loyalties to interests is perhaps a politically expedient move in a democracy, where it is necessary to blunt the impact of ideological differences. For obvious reasons, that kind of move takes the impact out of radical criticisms of our society. But the interpretation of the issue of science and ethics along these lines, i.e., as an occasional conflict of value (*read* interest), as with many other basic ideological conflicts, solves the problem by sweeping it under the carpet.

There are also ethical objections to the reduction of conflicts of value-beliefs to conflicts of values or interests. The reduction trivializes important moral differences between people. Not only does it blind us to the seriousness with which people adhere to their ethical beliefs but, by assimilating deeply held ideological differences to differences of taste, it also represents a supercilious and disparaging attitude toward people with whom one has serious ideological disagreements. There are other ethical objections to the identification of value-beliefs with interests (values, sense 1). For example, it leads to an entirely fallacious notion of moral evil. In the liberal view moral evil is, as it is for the Aristotelian-Thomist, simply the choice of a lesser good over a greater good. Thus, one could say of Southam's injection of patients with live cancer cells without their consent, that what he did was wrong, because he preferred the good he hoped to achieve through his scientific experiment, a lesser good, over the greater good of "self-determination" of his subjects: both things were good, but one was comparatively better than the other. His mistake was one of ordering.

But moral evil is often something more radical than this; when, for example, it involves denying the goodness of what is good and the evilness of what is evil. Like Aristotle's vicious man who does not know what is right, the Nazi doctors were vicious, not simply because they preferred a lesser good to a greater good, but because they saw nothing wrong in what they were doing. The student mentioned at the beginning of this paper saw nothing wrong in prolonging the life (and suffering) of an infant merely for scientific purposes. It is simply not enough to say that it was a mistake in ordering or in priorities.

The whole issue of science and ethics comes into a new light once it is recognized that the relationship might involve more than occasional conflicts of values that are resolvable by a proper ordering. A possible conflict between science and ethics, either in general or in particular situations, might be more basic than a conflict of values or interests. It might be a conflict between what is moral and what is immoral, or between different conceptions of morality, and so on. Underlying all these possible conflicts is the notion of incompatibility. Therefore, our next task will be to examine this notion as it applies in ethical discourse.

II. Two Kinds of Incompatibility of Value

The two conceptions of conflicts of values just mentioned arise out of two different kinds of incompatibility, which I shall call "contingent" and "logical" incompatibility, respectively. Generally, contingent incompatibility obtains when two states of affairs (or actions) that are desired or desirable cannot, for contingent reasons, coexist. Two values (or duties) conflict—are contingently incompatible—inasmuch as they cannot both be realized (or performed) because of particular, contingent circumstances.

Logical incompatibility, on the other hand, holds between the assertion of a value and the denial of that value. In this sense, logical incompatibility is like a straightforward contradiction. The position that, for example, extramarital intercourse is wrong, is logically incompatible with the position that it is not wrong. Note that we are speaking here of the *negations* of moral propositions, not of assertions of the opposite. The negation of "*X* is wrong" is "*X* is not wrong," and the negation of "*X* is good" is "*X* is not good." To assert to someone who says "*X* is wrong" that *X* is right, or to someone who says "*X* is good" that *X* is bad, is not, strictly speaking, a denial. It is a counterassertion. Assertions and counterassertions are not logically incompatible in the sense intended here.

Contingent incompatibility is the source of moral and practical dilemmas of one sort or another: not only conflicts of interest and of value, but also conflicts of obligations, conflicts of loyalties, and so on. The dilemma faced by Sartre's young man who had to choose between joining the Resistance movement and staying home and taking care of his mother was due to the contingent incompatibility of the two courses of action: he couldn't do both. In other circumstances the two courses of action might have been compatible, if, for example, the Resistance forces had been located in the vicinity in which his mother lived. Similarly, the troubling dilemma of whether to save the mother or the child arises out of contingent facts about a particular mother and a particular pregnancy; under other circumstances—where pregnancy is normal—there is no dilemma. Again, the need to choose between spending limited resources on treatment or on research arises out of the contingent fact that resources are limited. Indeed, all dilemmas that involve weighing costs and benefits are due to contingent incompatibilities of one sort or another.

Dilemmas like these have both a practical and a logical side.(9) Although many philosophers frequently admit that, as a matter of practical reality, such dilemmas do arise, they mistakenly believe that such dilemmas are also logically absurd, that it is logically impossible for two contingently incompatible courses of action both to be right. They argue that, if I cannot keep one promise without breaking another, then it is not wrong to break one of them. And, by the same token, if I cannot save one life without destroying another, then it is not wrong to destroy one of the lives. Or, returning to our subject, if I cannot pursue a scientific investigation without resorting to deception, and if I have a duty to pursue this investigation, then it is not wrong to deceive. This position is, in my opinion, quite mistaken.

The basic premise in this sort of argument is the principle that X is wrong implies that X is not right and that X is right implies that X is not wrong. This follows from the assumption that opposites like right and wrong, good and bad, have the logical properties of contraries in the traditional square of opposition. In terms of deontic logic: $O(\text{not-}A) \to \text{not } (OA)$. I have argued elsewhere that this is an unacceptable principle and two distinguished writers have recently joined me in rejecting it.(10) There is no reason for saying that a particular act ceases to be a duty because, for contingent reasons, I cannot perform it, because, say, the performance of some other duty is more pressing. To assert this principle, then, amounts to denying that what Ross calls *prima facie* duties are duties at all. In the case of values, the absurdity of this principle is even clearer: the fact that under particular circumstances I cannot have both freedom and life does not imply that one of them is not a value.

Once it is admitted that it is possible for something to be right or good, that, for contingent reasons, cannot be done or had, some other moral consequences of an act's being right or good can be accounted for, namely, consequences that obtain when the act in question cannot be performed. These might be called "secondary moral consequences." For example, if I have to break a promise because of a conflict of obligations, I should, if possible, try to explain my action to the promisee and make some kind of recompense to him; it would not be inappropriate to say: "I am sorry that I couldn't keep the promise!" Sorrow, remorse, and regret are always appropriate, even if the action in question was unavoidable. The fact that I could not do what I had a duty to do does not wipe the slate clean. Yet that is what the position under attack requires us to believe.(11)

The point of this discussion is that logical incompatibility cannot be derived from contingent incompatibility. The fact that for some contingent reason I cannot do my duty (or avoid doing something wrong), does not imply that it was *not* a duty (or *not* wrong).

Hence a contingent incompatibility cannot be used to prove a logical incompatibility. For example, it is incorrect to infer from the fact that sometimes one has a duty to lie, say, to save a life, that lying is not wrong *per se*. From the contingent incompatibility in this case of saving a life and telling the truth, it does not follow that one of them is not right. I argue that to conclude that it does is unwarranted and that such cases reflect only contingent incompatibilities. One still has a duty not to lie and a duty to save a life, although by the nature of things one cannot do both. Just as one cannot do everything one wants to do, so one cannot do everything that one ought to do. It follows that for contingent reasons sometimes one has a duty to do something that is *per se* wrong, such as to lie or kill. Thus, a contingent incompatibility is neither sufficient nor, as I shall presently show, is it necessary to prove a logical incompatibility. In other words, I do not have to show that an action is right in order to prove that it is not wrong or to show that it is wrong in order to prove that it is not right (not a duty).

The application of the argument presented here to the question of science and ethics should be obvious. From the fact that in particular instances there is a contingent incompatibility between the demands of science and (other?) demands of morality nothing follows whatsoever concerning the general relationship between science and ethics. Since moral requirements are sometimes contingently incompatible with each other, the demands of science might or might not be moral. Contingent incompatibilities prove nothing in that regard. We must therefore look beyond contingent incompatibilities as reflected in particular cases or particular areas for an understanding of the relationship or lack of relationship between science and ethics. In order to do so, we must examine in more detail the notions of logical incompatibility and logical negation.

III. Ethical Negation and Ethical Neutrality

Logical incompatibility, as I have defined it, is a logical relationship between moral beliefs and attitudes or moral propositions, in which one of them is the denial or negation of the other. A few remarks concerning ethical negation are necessary as a preliminary to a discussion of logical incompatibility in connection with the relationship of science and ethics.

The logic of ethical negation has received much less attention than it deserves. This neglect is attributable, in part at least, to the fact that the category of negation is so often mistakenly assimilated to the category of opposites, as I have just pointed out. The concept of ethical negation, on the other hand, is important for an understanding of ethical controversy and ethical differences in general: that is, situations in which one party asserts, for example, that X is wrong, and the other party denies it, asserts that X is not wrong, without making any counterassertion about its rightness.

What we need, therefore, is a theoretical analysis of what a person is doing when he denies the rightness or wrongness of something, that is, when he asserts an ethical negation. And then we need an analysis of how an ethical negation can be supported or established. An adequate treatment of these two questions goes far beyond the scope of this paper. I must therefore limit myself to a few observations.

Let us begin with the most important and interesting ethical negations, namely, those which negate both the rightness and the wrongness of an act or activity—assertions to the effect that something is neither right nor wrong. This category is sometimes referred to as "moral indifference." I prefer to call it "moral neutrality." Aquinas gives as an example picking up a piece of straw while taking a walk. A large proportion of our everyday activities obviously come under this category. There may even be acts or activities that are universally held to be morally neutral.

Many of the most vehement moral disagreements in our society are between those who believe that a certain kind of conduct is wrong (or right) and those who believe it to be morally neutral. One example is the abortion controversy, which is usually between antiabortionists, who hold abortion to be morally wrong, and their opponents, who regard it as morally neutral; the same sort of division exists with regard to extramarital intercourse, pornography, smoking pot, and even racism, torture, the denial of liberty, the refusal of self-determination, ripoffs, and so on. In each of these controversies, one of the parties denies the wrongness of the thing in question without making any counterassertion as to its rightness. It is held to be morally neutral. Indeed, as I have already argued at length, no moral counterassertion would be sufficient to establish the negation of the original moral proposition. The failure to see this point explains why one cannot convince an antiabortionist that abortion is not wrong (morally neutral) by getting him to admit that there might be situations in which, for some special reason, it might be right (for example, in order to save the mother's life).

There are various kinds of assertions of moral neutrality: some are uncontroversial and others are controversial. The uncontroversial cases are those acts or activities that are regarded by all parties as compatible with morality but not required by it (Aquinas's picking up straw). The controversial cases, on the other hand, arise when moral assertions concerning them are logically incompatible, or when one party holds that the act or activity in question comes under the mantle of morality while the other party denies it. The claim that science is a moral activity clearly involves a controversial kind of assertion.

The positions that scientific activity *per se* is morally neutral or, on the other hand, that it is in some sense a moral activity, say, that it is morally right, morally valuable, or morally worthy are, of course, logically incompatible.

One might ask: what difference does it make how we answer this question, especially since it is framed in such general terms? One consequence of accepting science as a moral activity is that it would then be possible to have a moral justification for doing some things for the advancement of science that require the violation of certain ordinary precepts of morality; for example, the duty to advance science might, in certain cases, override the duty of truthfulness in the same way that the duty to save a life might, in certain cases, override the duty of truthfulness. On the other hand, if science *per se* is morally neutral, then there could be no such justification for overriding ordinary moral requirements like the duty of truthfulness.

IV. How is Moral Neutrality Established?

Before turning to the question of whether science is morally neutral, a few further remarks are necessary concerning the logic of ethical negations. It is possible to give only a brief outline of the logical principles that I shall use: a full exposition and justification of these principles must be given elsewhere. Basically, the form of argumentation used to establish the moral neutrality of an act or activity is, like all ethical argumentation, dialectical. In this regard, my conception of ethical argumentation is quite similar to that of Perelman and Olbrechts-Tyteca in their book, *The New Rhetoric: A Treatise on Argumentation.*(12)

The basic rule for establishing moral neutrality is what I call the *onus probandi* rule. According to this rule, the *onus probandi* in ethical disputes always rests on the person who asserts something to be morally right or wrong, good or evil. He must always be prepared to say what makes it right or wrong, good or evil, when and if his assertion is challenged. If he cannot meet the challenge by giving a reason or if the reason he gives is unacceptable (false or unfounded), then the thing in question must be presumed to be morally neutral. There is a kind of presumption of "innocent until proved guilty"— "neutral until proved right or wrong"—that provides the framework of ethical discourse. The reason is that if there is nothing to make an act or activity right or wrong, good or evil, then for logical reasons, it cannot be right or wrong, good or evil. If reasons cannot be given, it must be presumed that there are none.

It follows from this rule, as outlined, that appeals to self-evidence, intuitions, gut-feelings, or authority, i.e., *ipse dixits* of various sorts, are an *ignoratio elenchi*, or beside the point. For none of these *ipse dixits* can function as a right-making or wrong-making characteristic. There are, of course, other reasons for rejecting them as premises in an ethical argument.(13)

The dialectical nature of ethical argumentation is reflected in the fact that it proceeds developmentally, through a series of assertions and challenges. Unlike some other intellectual procedures, such as the solving of puzzles, the procedure involved here does not start from a question or a state of doubt. It always begins with an assertion or claim, which in turn is subjected to challenge. As the dialectic develops, if a challenge cannot be met, the original assertion loses its support and is thereby defeated, or negated. (The analogies to law are obvious: if a claim cannot be defended when challenged, then it must be rejected.) On the other hand, if the challenges are met, then the assertion in question may be regarded as established.

It is clear that in adopting this procedure we are using a logical rule that is inconsistent with the ordinary rule of formal logic known as the fallacy of denying the antecedent, i.e., fallacious inference from the falsity of the premises of an argument to the falsity of the conclusion. The new rule is in that sense clearly incompatible with the rules, say, of an extensional logic. That is why the present procedure is called "dialectical."(14)

In defense of the *onus probandi* rule, as presented here, I would argue that this is the natural, normal way we use to refute moral claims of one sort or another. Since I have already excluded the possibility of arguing from opposites, that way is not open to us. A purely negative argument must operate differently, e.g., by the *onus probandi* rule. Consider, for example, how you would argue against someone who claimed that walking on the cracks on a sidewalk was morally wrong. Would not, in the end, the only argument be a question: why should it be wrong? For want of a reason, the claim collapses. (To say, in response, that it will break your grandma's back is not a good reason simply because it is empirically false.)

Applying the *onus probandi* rule to the claim that scientific activity is a moral activity means that we must begin by asking: why? what makes it moral? And then, we must scrutinize each of the answers in turn, weighing its credibility—its empirical confirmability and warrant. Considering the immensity of the present subject and the generality of the claim, it will be impossible to deal with the question of the morality of science in the detail that it deserves. Therefore, what follows must be viewed as programmatic rather than definitive.

With this proviso, there seem to be two different kinds of argument that need to be considered for the position that science is a moral activity. The first argues from the almost invariable benefits of scientific knowledge and the second argues from the intrinsic worth to man of scientific activity considered as an intellectual activity. I shall discuss each of these arguments in turn.

V. Argument from the Universal Benefits of Science

We may regard scientific activity as a kind of intellectual activity aimed at producing scientific knowledge. In this sense, science is what Aristotle called a *poiesis*—a making or production—rather than a *praxis*—an activity valued for its own sake.(15) (Of course, it might be both, as Plato thought when he included science under things valued both for their own sake and for the sake of their consequences.) When regarded in this light, the value of scientific activity is a function of the value of its product, scientific knowledge. Accordingly, a good scientist is someone who produces good science; a worthwhile scientific project is one that leads directly or indirectly to good science; good scientific hypotheses, experiments, and observations are good if and only if they lead to good scientific results. People, their actions, thoughts, and relationships—all their activities in relation to science—are evaluated in terms of their scientific productivity. As in other examples of productive activity, the personality and motivation of the producer, and his moral character, are, strictly speaking, irrelevant to the quality of the product. The moral quality of the activity derives from the moral value of the product, and it is assumed as far as science is concerned that the product is always valuable!

One way of stating the argument in question is to say that all scientific knowledge is useful, either directly or indirectly, by leading to other scientific knowledge which in turn is useful. And in the long run scientific knowledge itself is almost invariably useful for mankind. In this regard science is like some other good things such as food or health.

It should be observed that the claim for science is quite comprehensive: it applies to *all* science. Other things being equal, scientific knowledge *per se* is good, for there is a high probability that almost any bit of successful scientific activity will turn out to be beneficial. Therefore, in order to vindicate this extreme claim, it is not enough to show that some scientific knowledge, such as certain medical discoveries, has been beneficial in the past. We are asked to accept the proposition that the pursuit of science is invariably worthwhile on the grounds that in the long run it will inevitably lead to worthwhile results. Since the claim to be moral is a wholesale claim, the support for it must be wholesale also.

To support the wholesale claim, its advocates point to spectacular discoveries in the past due to the accidental discovery of something else that had seemed at the time to be trivial or irrelevant. The unpredictability of future scientific discoveries may be granted. The question is whether or not it is sufficient to justify the general claim under consideration. Claims for long-range benefits are notoriously plausible for believers and implausible for nonbelievers. They are like Pascal's wager; you cannot lose. How much of this is blind faith is an open question; surely even the most optimistic defender of science must admit to the largely unempirical basis of his prediction of the inevitable benefits of science.

There are two parts to the hypothesis of expected benefits; first, what might be called the chain-reaction thesis—that one advance in science inevitably leads to further advances of science and that any discovery, however trivial, tends not only to increase the sum total of knowledge but to contribute to the growth of knowledge in depth as well. Whether or not science always develops in this way is a question that is beyond my competence to decide. But the fact that in some areas, such as molecular biology, one discovery has led to another cannot be used to establish the more general and all-encompassing thesis that any bit of scientific knowledge will be useful in the advance of science.

The second part of the hypothesis is that the scientific knowledge acquired will be beneficial to mankind. Here we are asked to consider the long-range rather than the short-range benefits. Nuclear physics, it is true, may have brought us the atomic bomb and the tragedy of Hiroshima, but we are asked to disregard them and to think instead of the long-range benefits from the use of nuclear energy in more constructive areas. The harmful side effects of scientific discoveries are systematically discounted.

The claim that science almost invariably brings benefits to mankind raises further questions: what kinds of benefits does it bring? It is easy to see that certain medical advances are good for mankind, although many of these advances—the elimination of certain diseases—create new social problems, such as overpopulation. It is not easy to know where we stand concerning the costs and benefits to society at large of much of science.

I suspect that underlying the optimistic view of science is an argument somewhat like the following: (1) The more we can control natural processes, the better it is for mankind; for then we can bend nature to our will and use it for our own welfare. (2) Science gives us progressively greater control over nature. (3) Therefore, science is good for mankind. This kind of argument is discussed at length by Passmore in his *Man's Responsibility for Nature*. He calls it the Baconian-Cartesian approach to nature, which he traces to the earlier Stoic-Christian doctrine that nature exists to serve man.(16) The argument that whatever is useful for man is good and that science is useful for man, QED, is so slippery that only someone already convinced would find it plausible.

In sum, it is not very difficult to think of many unanswerable questions regarding the thesis of the invariable beneficial character of science, if it is taken as a universal and all-encompassing claim. It seems more plausible to suppose that science *per se* is morally neutral and that sometimes it is beneficial and sometimes not. Indeed, the same bit of scientific information may at one time be beneficial, and at other times injurious.

Other questions appear at this point: for example, whether certain kinds of scientific endeavors may not themselves be intrinsically moral or, on the other hand, intrinsically immoral. Logically some of the activities we call science may involve reference to the purposes for which they are pursued, for example, science in the area of biological warfare or behavior control. But an adequate treatment of these issues would require a more extensive discussion of what science is, something that I am not prepared to undertake here. In any case, we may tentatively conclude that the benefits-to-mankind argument has serious holes.

VI. Argument from the Intrinsic Value of Scientific Activity

We still have to consider the other half of the argument for the moral value of scientific activity, namely, that science as an intellectual activity is good for its own sake. The *locus classicus* for this position is, of course, Book X of Aristotle's *Ethics*. I need not repeat the arguments; the main contention is that science (*theoria*) is a distinctly human activity and makes men like the gods.(17) Later versions emphasize the concepts of self-fulfillment, self-realization, perfecting human nature, and so on. All of them maintain that "Science is man's noblest pursuit." Not only is science what distinguishes man from the animals but it also distinguishes the civilized world from the world of the barbarians, and makes us morally superior to the cave man and to primitive people in general.

I find all these conceptions distressingly vague and confused. It is easy to understand that scientific discovery and creativity, or simply the possession of scientific knowledge, might be highly satisfying, exhilarating, exciting, moving, awesome, and wonderful in many ways that would be of great value to many individuals. But in this regard scientific activity is not unique; music, art, and other sorts of cultural activities have the same features. Furthermore, excitement is not restricted to scientific discoveries like that of the double helix; exploits like Lindbergh's flight across the Atlantic are equally exciting. Creativity in the arts may be as rare and wonderful as it is in the sciences. Mozart is not second to Newton in this regard. There is no reason why science should have the first place in things of the human spirit as Aristotle thinks it has. In any case we need further argument to convince us that science has a morally superior status that is in some respects unique.

At this point, one is tempted to ask: what *kinds* of arguments would be convincing, and what would they prove? Since we have separated the argument from intrinsic value from the argument from benefits to mankind, we must be careful not to slip from one of these arguments to the other when one of them begins to appear weak. Panegyrics apart, a survey of the history of philosophy, including philosophers like Plato and Spinoza, indicates that most of the arguments for the intrinsic value of science conceive of it as bringing salvation or liberation for the possessor. Possibly this kind of rationale for science may be out of date, if one considers the highly technical nature of modern science.

Obviously, a much more detailed study of these arguments and of other possible ones would be required before reaching any sort of definitive conclusion. Two preliminary philosophical questions might be mentioned that relate to the question of the intrinsic value of scientific activity. First, one might ask whether or not some sort of distinction ought be drawn between types or realms of values (moral values and spiritual values); if so, then one might admit that science is not a moral value, but nevertheless claim that it has an intrinsic value of a very high order (like art or religion)? Perhaps that is what is meant by calling it "man's noblest pursuit."

Closely related is the second question: does not the exaltation of science as a moral activity in itself reflect an élitist conception of ethics? Historically, as in the case of Plato, the scientist often regarded himself as a member of an ethical élite and not of *hoi polloi*; perhaps he ought to be regarded as a secular saint or an intellectual hero. One could well ask whether or not this kind of superior status is an acceptable ethical category.

To conclude this part of the paper, I want to stress that all that I have tried to do here is to indicate what kinds of questions someone who advocates the position that science *per se* is a moral activity ought to be prepared to answer. If these questions cannot be answered satisfactorily, we must conclude that science *per se* is morally neutral.

VII. Logical Incompatibility Between Conduct-Systems

We now come to our last question. If science *per se* is not a moral activity, as I have tentatively concluded, then is it logically compatible with morality (simply morally neutral), or is it logically incompatible with it? If it is logically incompatible, then some of the things required by pursuit of science, such as the scientific imperative, would be inconsistent with the requirements of morality. Does the scientific imperative require the *denial* of some of the precepts of morality?

In order to understand the issue involved, a few further observations concerning logical incompatibility will be required. What we need to show is that the acceptance of one set of precepts entails the denial of another set of precepts. For example, science (in the sense of what is prescribed by the scientific imperative) and morality would be logically incompatible if the scientific imperative meant that certain morally wrong acts or activities are not morally wrong and that certain morally neutral acts or activities are required to be done or omitted. Underlying the notion of logical incompatibility is the systematic character of "systems" like morality and the scientific ethos. By their "systematic character" I mean that they comprise sets of precepts, rules, principles, and categories that are interrelated logically through relationships of derivation, and so on.(18)

The way in which the notion of logical incompatibility functions can be understood most easily if we examine it in connection with moral conduct in the playing of games. Many games, especially competitive ones, permit or even require acts that are ordinarily prohibited by morality, for example, hitting, deceiving, or "doing one's opponent in." Such acts, although *per se* wrong morally, cease to be wrong when performed in the game. In James's words, while playing a game one goes on a "moral holiday." There is a kind of "suspension of the ethical," to use another well-known phrase, even in a supposedly tame game like croquet! The rules for games such as boxing, poker, and wrestling, often are, strictly speaking, logically incompatible with morality. Not only is there a logical incompatibility between the respective rules relating to overt acts, but also with regard to their general evaluation of conduct and of persons. A "good" poker player excels at deceiving others; a "good" boxer is one who knocks out his opponent.

It might be contended that the motive makes a difference; in playing a game the motives for performing certain acts are different from those in "real life." In the game, one player hits another only in order to win the game, rather than to hurt him. In fact, however, if one distinguishes between actual motives and supposed motives, it is clear that being "in a game" is often used to cover up bad motives; being in a game provides a good excuse for undesirable behavior. For example, one can legitimately lose one's temper at one's opponent in a game; in fact, it may help one to win. It is only too obvious that people often use the game as an outlet for their suppressed feelings of hostility and aggression or, as the case may be, for their greediness or suppressed sexual desires. All of this, however, simply confirms my thesis, namely, that things are permitted in games that are forbidden in real life: the ethical is suspended.

There is indeed a trivial sense in which conduct in compliance with the rules and objectives of a game might be construed as moral: a player might have entered into the game for moral reasons of one sort or another—through having promised to play the game, or in order to make someone else happy. In such cases the derivatively moral character of game-playing might make some of our examples cases of contingent rather than logical incompatibility. For present purposes, let us disregard ramifications of this sort.

The saving grace is, of course, that playing a game is restricted activity; it is circumscribed as to time and place, the role that it plays in a person's life, the seriousness with which it is undertaken, and the kind of injuries permitted. (If one includes dueling and Russian roulette, the injuries might be considerable!) The moral holiday that one takes in playing a game is ordinarily a brief one.

Nevertheless, disregarding these limitations, rules relating to playing a game (of these sorts) and those relating to morality are strictly speaking logically incompatible; that is, within the game acts are permitted (and approved) that are prohibited by morality and acts permitted morally are forbidden (and disapproved) in the game. We are dealing here with logical, not contingent incompatibility, for they involve two different and logically incompatible sets of rules, standards, and criteria for the evaluation of conduct. I shall refer to such a set of rules, standards and criteria of evaluation as a "conduct-system," where "conduct" is intended to designate not only acts and activities but also attitudes, purposes, goals, motives, and all the other kinds of things that are subject to prescription and evaluation in the context of action.

There are many different varieties of conduct-system in this broad sense. They differ in structure and in their interrelationships. Some systems are highly structured and articulated (such as chess); others are vague and fuzzy (such as etiquette). Some systems are open systems and others are closed. They are closed in the sense that there are decision procedures by which it can be determined what does and what does not belong to the system. Morality and law are typical instances of open conduct-systems; games, on the other hand, are typical instances of closed conduct-systems.

One variety of conduct-system that is particularly noteworthy consists of those conduct-systems that make absolute and categorical demands on a person's conduct and that, as such, have no built-in limitations like those possessed by games. Such conduct-systems are sometimes called "alternate moralities," "ideologies," or "value-systems." Elsewhere I have called them "moral codes." (19) Such conduct-systems would include the conduct-systems of the Mayans, Nazis, Hindus, Navahos, and so on. Since each of these systems claims absolute allegiance, as it were, they are logically incompatible with each other; for the acceptance of the precepts and norms of one entails the denial of the precepts and norms of the other, if only in the sense that the denial is a denial of the absoluteness of another system's claims.

The essential difference between unrestricted conduct-systems and games is that the former are mutually exclusive, unconditional, and absolute. They demand that their rules and principles be given priority over other rules and principles, personal preferences, and so on. Therefore in an important sense it is logically impossible to be a good Mayan and, say, a good Christian; although, by contrast, it is possible for both a Mayan and a Christian to play the same game. The reason is that most people are willing to subordinate the demands of a game to the demands of morality (or their supreme conduct-system).

It is impossible in the present paper to provide a complete analysis of the notion of logical incompatibility that is involved here; for to do so would require a thoroughgoing analysis of the logical structure of systems of this type. As I have already suggested, systems like natural moralities are open systems and the relationship between various elements in the system is loose and variable. Consequently, there are in actuality overlappings and crossings that make fruitful communication between adherents of natural alternate systems entirely feasible. The more structured and closed a system, the more stringent is the logical incompatibility between the elements of that system and those of another system. Thus, some versions of utilitarianism, which represent closed systems of this type, are more likely to comprise elements that are logically incompatible with other supreme conduct-systems.

As I have suggested, science may be conceived as a conduct-system, that is, as a system of rules, principles, standards, and evaluations based on the scientific imperative. As such, in comparison to "natural moralities," the system is relatively closed. If it is established that its requirements are not moral requirements, as I have suggested might be the case, then we must ask whether this system is or is not logically incompatible with morality. If it is, we must ask whether it is incompatible with morality only in the restricted sense in which some games are incompatible with it or in the broader sense, in which, say, Mayan cannibalism is incompatible with morality. The last question amounts to asking: is the ideology of science an alternative morality, a substitute for ordinary morality?

In view of the slipperiness of the subject, it is difficult to find any clear-cut, systematic statements of the position which we would have to examine in order to be able to answer these questions. Writers on science who make exalted claims and demands for science are not at all clear about what they are trying to do. Hence, at this point, it is easier to leave the reader with a set of questions to be answered rather than with speculative conclusions. The only thing that can be said in this regard is that the categorical claims and demands made on behalf of science make sense in general only if they are understood as part of a supreme conduct-system based on the scientific imperative. If that is so, then the legitimation of deception, abridgment of liberty or privacy, and so on, as approved, advocated, and practiced for the sake of science is an essential, rather than an accidental, feature of the scientific conduct-system. More likely than not, then, we are faced with a set of demands and claims that are logically incompatible with ordinary morality. The ideology of science asks us, then, to give up our old morality and to accept a new one—the morality of science.

The denial of the absolute claim for science, what I have called the "ideology of science," by no means entails that science *per se* is immoral or even that it is for the most part immoral. It is quite possible to accept science *per se* as morally neutral. If science is morally neutral, like all other morally neutral activities, it is subject to the constraints of morality. In particular, when the scientific enterprise demands that certain moral considerations be set aside in the interests of the advancement of science, the demand should be rejected as immoral. In a sense, therefore, we are dealing with a rather strong requirement; for it appears to call into question the morality of many scientific enterprises. Most important of all, however, is the obligation that it imposes on all scientists to reflect on the moral implications of what they are doing in general, and in particular and in detail. A scientist must always be prepared to answer the question: what are you trying to find out? why? and for what purpose? In this regard the appeal to self-evidence or intuition is not enough; indeed, as I have argued, it is an *ignoratio elenchi*.

VIII. Why Science Cannot be a Moral Activity

I should like to offer a few observations in closing on why science cannot be a moral activity in itself. My purpose here is to provide an explanation of the moral neutrality of science for which I have already argued. In my view, there are certain key elements missing in science that are essential for morality. Clearly, what I have to say in this regard is based on my own conception of morality. It is not possible to defend this conception of morality here, although I think that a detailed defense is possible. Indeed, according to the *onus probandi* rule mentioned earlier, the conception would be legitimate only if I can provide good reasons for accepting it and I believe that I can do so, although not in the present essay. Accordingly, my remarks may be taken hypothetically, that is, if a certain conception of morality, which I shall provisionally call Kantian, is valid, then we can see why science cannot itself be a moral activity. (Of course, I do not wish to deny that, like many other things, it can be used for moral purposes.)

To begin with, scientific activity, unlike morality itself, is achievement-oriented. That is, it operates on the principle that the end justifies the means; the end, scientific knowledge, is good; therefore, other things being equal, the means to it are good and ought to be used. I think the case of the defective infant mentioned at the beginning is an example of the application of this principle. (Many other examples may be found in Katz.) The teleological ethics implied here is subject to all the customary objections to that type of ethics. It makes persons, their conduct, and their morality into mere means rather than ends in themselves.

Another difficulty in squaring science and morality is that they employ entirely different categories. Science and the norms governing scientific activity make no place for the essential categories of morality, such as the categories of person, motive, social relationship, and responsibility. The concept of a person, for example, which is basic to ethics, is not a possible concept in medical *science* (as contrasted with clinical practice); the subject matter of medical science is always organisms of some kind: diseases, bodies, or organs. That is why doctors are often said to treat cases, not persons. As scientists no other alternative is possible. By the same token, science does not need to use the categories of motive, character, and social relationship in the evaluation of scientific conduct. Unlike morality, success is all that counts in science.

Finally, if we take science as a conduct-system, we find that it excludes the concept of responsibility in the sense of social responsibility.(20) A scientist *qua* scientist is required to ignore the wider ramifications of what he is doing. In this sense, a scientist must be "irresponsible." A good scientist has to give his exclusive attention to what he is doing, to his theorizing and experimentation; he must follow the thread without regard to where it leads. It is easy, therefore, for a scientist to disengage himself from the consequences of his discoveries. He says: "My job is to do science, it is the discovery of truth; what is done with what I discover is someone else's business, not mine." This attitude, which is not atypical, is about as irresponsible as leaving time bombs around to explode.

Morality, as I conceive it, arises out of and is directed toward relationships between persons. Science, on the other hand, is concerned with things, nonpersons. One could say that we are dealing with two entirely different sets of concepts, or languages: the language of morality and the language of science. Moral virtues such as compassion and concern as well as moral vices such as cruelty and indifference are outside the conceptual framework of science. Unlike science, however, these categories do enter into law and politics. And in contradistinction to medical science, they also enter into the practice of medicine.

In our culture there are many spheres of activity, like games, that demand and receive moral immunity of a certain sort. Their moral immunity makes them free from moral criticism and evaluation. This culturally approved mechanism for freeing oneself from moral and social responsibility by taking on a role is pervasive throughout our society. It represents one of the threats to its integrity. The excuse of role-playing was used by those participating in the Vietnam war, even though in private they had doubts about its rightness. It appeared again in the Watergate plots. These political fiascos have forced us to rethink the question of the immunity of government and its officials from moral accountability. Perhaps the time has come to reexamine the pretensions of scientists to the same kind of immunity that was claimed by our politicians.

NOTES

1. "... and what better basis is there for the moral imperatives which guide our society?" Interview with Philip Handler, reprinted in Jay Katz, *Experimentation with Human Beings* (New York: Russell Sage Foundation, 1972), p. 121. This section of Katz's collection contains many such statements. Further documentation seems unnecessary.

2. *Dictionary of Quotable Definitions* (Englewood Cliffs, N.J.: Prentice-Hall, 1970), p. 514.

3. Precisely the same position is echoed in a letter to *The New York Times Magazine*, June 8, 1975, p. 50.

4. A discussion of the "morality" of institutions may be found in my "Morality and the Ideal of Rationality in Formal Organizations," MONIST 54:4 (October 1970), 488-516. The "bureaucratization" of science is the basic theme of Harvey Wheeler's "Science's Slippery Slope," *The Center Magazine* VIII:1 (January-February 1975), 64-67. "There is hardly any but the bureaucratic way to do contemporary science" (p. 66).

5. The opening sentence of Katz, *Experimentation with Human Beings*, begins: "When science takes man as its subject, tensions arise between two values basic to western society..." (p. 1). Note the play on the word "value," which is noted in the following paragraphs of this paper.

6. John Rawls, "Outline of a Decision Procedure for Ethics," *Philosophical Review* 66 (1957), 177-97. Reprinted in Judith J. Thomson and Gerald Dworkin, *Ethics* (New York: Harper & Row, 1968), p. 59.

7. See Ralph Barton Perry, *General Theory of Value* (Cambridge, Mass.: Harvard University Press, 1926), *passim*. One of Perry's early books was entitled *The Moral Economy* (New York: Scribner's, 1909).

8. In Brian Barry's terms this dogma treats *wants* as the unit of social evaluation. See his *The Liberal Theory of Justice; A Critical Examination of the Principal Doctrines in "A Theory of Justice" by John Rawls* (Oxford: Clarendon Press, 1973), p. 21 and *passim*.

9. This distinction is set forth in greater detail in my "Remarks on the Conflict of Obligations," *Journal of Philosophy* 55 (September 11, 1958) Some of the present discussion makes use of ideas presented in that article.

10. See Michael Walzer, "Political Action: The Problem of Dirty Hands," *Philosophy and Public Affairs* 2:2 (Winter 1973); and Bas van Fraasen, "Values and the Heart's Command," *Journal of Philosophy* 70 (January 11, 1973), p. 166.

11. See Walzer, "Political Action," p. 166. "We know he is doing right when he makes the deal because he knows he is doing wrong. . . . If he is the good man I am imagining him to be, he will feel guilty, that is, he will believe himself to be guilty. That is what it means to have dirty hands."

12. Chaim Perelman and L. Olbrechts-Tyteca, *The New Rhetoric: A Treatise on Argumentation*, J. Wilkinson and P. Weaver, trans. (Notre Dame: University of Notre Dame Press, 1971).

13. "The self-evident, as the criterion of validity, is the authority for discrediting all *argumentation*. . . ." Perelman and Olbrechts-Tyteca, *The New Rhetoric*, p. 464. See also pp. 3, 11, 510.

14. It should be observed that the term "dialectical" is used here in a classical, Aristotelian rather than in a Hegelian-Marxian sense. See, for example, Aristotle, *Topics* 100^a30 and *Rhetoric* 1354^a 1-20. Perelman and Olbrechts-Tyteca prefer the term "rhetoric" in order to avoid the Hegelian connotations of "dialectic." For an English-speaking audience, on the other hand, the term "rhetoric" has undesirable connotations, whereas the term "dialectical" is relatively innocuous.

15. Aristotle, *Nicomachean Ethics*, Bk 1, Ch. 1 and Bk VI, Ch. 4.

16. John Passmore, *Man's Responsibility for Nature* (New York: Charles Scribner's Sons, 1974), Chapter I, "Man as Despot."

17. "The life of the intellect is the best and pleasantest for man, because the intellect more than anything else *is* man." Aristotle, *Nicomachean Ethics*, 1178^a5.

18. For some of the conceptions used in this section, I have drawn on my work, *The Structure of a Moral Code*. (Cambridge, Mass: Harvard University Press, 1957). For additional remarks on the game analogy, see my "Legal and Moral Obligation," in J. Roland Pennock and John W. Chapman, eds. *Political and Legal Obligation*: NOMOS XII (New York: Atherton Press, 1970).

19. See Ladd, *The Structure of a Moral Code*.

20. I have tried to explain this concept of responsibility—responsibility in the normative sense—in my "The Ethics of Participation" in J. Roland Pennock and John W. Chapman, eds. *Participation*: NOMOS XVI. (New York: Atherton-Lieber Press, 1975).

13

How Can We Reconnect The Sciences with the Foundations of Ethics?

By Stephen Toulmin

ANYONE FAMILIAR WITH THE contemporary literature on the philosophical foundations of ethics—say, from John Rawls's *Theory of Justice* (1972) up to Alan Donagan's *Theory of Morality* (1977) and Ronald Dworkin's *Taking Rights Seriously* (1977)—will know how little attention such books give to "science," or at least to "the natural and social sciences," as they are conceived of at the present time in the English-speaking world.[1]

The question is, "How far does this lack of attention reflect some immutable verities about the *essential* relations between science and ethics? And how far is it, rather, a temporary—even, transient—fact about their *actual* relation in our own day?" At other times, certainly, both "science" and "ethics" have been conceived of in other ways, and their interactions have been both more obvious and more vigorous. By recognizing how those interactions have been minimized over the last 100 or 150 years, we should be able to recognize also how they might be re-established and reactivated. Even to agree on that diagnosis would be to achieve something substantial. The arguments in this paper will therefore be partly historical and partly diagnostic.

The Purist View of Science

From a strict philosophical point of view, all attempts to insulate the sciences from ethics can easily be undercut. This is true whether our focus of discussion is intellectual, sociological, or psychological: the basic concepts of the sciences, the institutions and collective conduct of the scientific profession, or the personal motives of individual scientists.

As to the concept of science: so long as we restrict ourselves to the physicochemical sciences, our basic notions and hypotheses (e.g., hadron, field gradient, and amino acid) may have no obvious evaluative implications. But the physiological, to say nothing of the psychological and social sciences, employ whole families of concepts, for instance, those associated with functionality and adaptedness, and their cognates, which raise evaluative issues directly, both within the relevant scientific theories and in their broader implications.[2]

As to the scientific profession: the codes of good intellectual practice, and the criteria of professional judgment in the sciences, may once upon a time have looked to the needs of effective inquiry alone, rather than to broader "ethical" considerations. But it is by now no longer possible to draw so clear or sharp a line between the intellectual demands of good science and the ethical demands of the good life. The increasingly close links between basic science and its practical applications expose working scientists more and more to ethical problems and public accountability of sorts that are commonplace in service professions such as medicine and law.[3] A strong case can also be made for seeing the professional enterprises of natural science as creating, and even defining, certain basic ethical modes of life and conduct having their own characteristic virtues, duties, and obligations.[4]

Finally, as to the individual motives that operate for scientists in their work: though the "ideal" spring of action for scientific inquiry may be a pure respect for the rationality of the inquiry itself, such a "pure respect" is at best an aspiration, and a *moral* aspiration at that. Furthermore, it is something that can be developed in the course of any individual's lifetime, only as a somewhat refined product of moral education.[5]

Yet, despite these powerful objections, the notion that the intellectual activities of science are carried on at a level that sets them, if not above, then at any rate beside and on a par with the moral law, continues to have its charms; and we must try to understand its seductive power. One potent source, I suggest, has

been scientists' fear of relativism. During a period when exploration and anthropology were encouraging a sense of *pluralism* in
human affairs, and so generating a kind of moral relativism and
subjectivism that put the very foundations of ethics in doubt,* it
was understandable that scientists should have resisted the intrusion of ethics into the business of science; and that, in return,
they should have insisted that the concerns of science—unlike
those of ethics—were entirely objective, and in no sense "matters
of taste or feeling." Furthermore, the fact that scientific issues
could plausibly be depicted as public and intersubjective (rational) made it possible, also, to define the intellectual demands
of the scientific life in a similarly objective way. So, both the
collective conduct of the scientific profession and the personal
choices of individual scientists were apparently freed from the
existential arbitrariness and ambiguity of the ethical realm.

At this point, it might have been better if philosophers and
scientists alike had emphasized the similarities between science
and ethics, and had used the "rational objectivity" of science as a
model in seeking to reestablish the claims of moral objectivity, as
well. The argument that ethical issues are, in their own proper
ways, as public and intersubjective as scientific issues (and so
equally "rational") was thus abandoned too quickly and lightly.
But many scientists, lacking any sense of joint intellectual responsibility and interest with the moral philosophers, were happy
enough to disown relativism in science and bolt for cover on their

---

*In discussion, Paul Ramsey queried whether the natural sciences have in
fact been affected by the debate about subjectivism and relativism carried on
within philosophy over the last fifty or one hundred years. That, of course,
would be highly questionable. The point of my present argument is that the
recognition of anthropological diversity led, by around 1800, to a widespread
sense—not by any means confined to philosophers—that ethical beliefs and
practices vary arbitrarily from culture to culture. Earlier in the eighteenth
century it had still been possible for Voltaire to declare, "There is only one
morality, as there is only one geometry"; but, from 1800 on, cultural relativism
became a force to reckon with in general thinking about ethical matters. The
corresponding doubts about "objectivity" in natural science did not become
serious until the present century: first, following the collapse of the classical
Newtonian/Euclidean synthesis on which Kant had rested his case, and more
recently with the widespread adoption of Thomas Kuhn's theory of "paradigms"
as justifying a similar diversity in "views of Nature."

own. For so long as relativism and subjectivism remained viable options in philosophical ethics, most scientists understandably felt that it was more important to emphasize the distinctively intellectual—and so, presumably, "value-neutral"—character of their own enterprises. Provided they could preserve the autonomy of the scientific community against all outsiders, they did not mind letting the moral philosophers sink or swim by themselves.

By now, however, the "rationality" of science—the objectivity of scientific issues, the autonomy of the scientific professions, and the categorical claims of the scientific life—can no longer be used to differentiate science entirely from the rest of thought and morality. We are faced, on every level, not by a hard and fast distinction, but by a spectrum.

- The basic concepts of the sciences range along a spectrum from the effectively "value-free" to the irretrievably "value-laden";
- The goals of the scientific enterprise range along a spectrum from a purely abstract interest in theoretical speculations to a direct concern with human good and ill;
- The professional responsibilities of the scientific community range along a spectrum from the strictly internal and intellectual to the most public and practical.

Nonetheless, as recently as the 1930s, when I first acquired my ideas about "science," the most characteristic mark of the scientific attitude and the scientific task was to select as one's preferred center of attention the purest, the most intellectual, the most autonomous, and the least ethically implicated extreme on each of these different spectrums.

No doubt this "puristic" view of science was an extreme one, and by no means universally shared by working scientists, to say nothing of the outside social commentators who wrote about the scientific scene. Yet it is a view that had, and continues to have, great attractions for many professional scientists. Since "rational objectivity" is an indispensable part of the scientific mission, and the intrusion of "values" into science had come to be regarded as incompatible with such objectivity, all concern with values (or other arbitrary, personal preferences) had to be foresworn in the higher interest of rationality. Certainly, the professional institutions of science tended to be organized on this basis. The memberships of scientific academies, for instance, have for the last 75 or 100 years been increasingly recruited on the basis of the narrowly defined intellectual contributions of candidates alone,* without regard to their social perceptiveness, ethical sensitivity, or political wisdom. Indeed, the puristic view is still powerful today: consider, for instance, Arthur Kantrowitz's current proposals for a Science Court, whose duty would be to pronounce on the "factual implications" of science and technology for issues of public policy, without reference to the "values" at stake in each case.[6]

Accordingly, the purism of the views about science into which I was initiated was not merely a feature of the particular culture and time of my youth: one more local and temporary characteristic (so to say) of the factual, unemotional, antiphilosophical, class-structured, and role-oriented attitudes of the English professional classes between the two world wars. In part, the nature of that culture may have accentuated the larger tendency toward purism. Perhaps, if I had grown up in the United States rather than Britain (or even in Britain thirty years later) I would have acquired different views, both about science itself, and about its ethical significance. Certainly, there have not always been the kinds of barriers between ethics and science that I grew up with; nor need there always be such barriers in the future. Still, I seriously doubt whether this attitude was solely a local and temporary oddity of twentieth-century English upper-middle-class life and social structure. For many of the considerations advanced to explain and justify scientific purism have a force that carries them across national boundaries. These considerations—the intellectual reaction against ethical relativism, the collective desire for professional autonomy, the personal charms of an ethically unambiguous life plan—may have been felt with a special strength in the England of my youth, but they were by no means confined to it.

---

*Even in the second half of the nineteenth century, it was still accepted as a matter of common form that a poet such as Alfred Tennyson should be a Fellow of the Royal Society, and sit on important Royal Society committees. The restriction of membership in National Academies of Science to expert, full-time working scientists is thus largely a twentieth-century development.

The Professionalization of Science

What deeper explanation should we look for, then, to account for the emergence of this puristic view of science? Granted that, by the early twentieth century, relativism and subjectivism were beginning to pose an implicit threat to the objectivity of science as well as to ethics, how was it that scientists perceived and defined their own collective interests and self-image so clearly? How did they come to suppose that they could see science as capable of being the stronghold of reason by itself and on its own, in contradistinction to ethics, which had seemingly been unmasked as the plaything of emotion?

In part, these questions are issues for the history of ideas: in part, they will carry us deeper into the sociology and philosophy of science. Certainly, the distinction between an objective science and a subjective ethics may be traced back at least as far as the scientific positivism of Comte, in the early nineteenth century; and the same contrast helped to encourage the revival of scientific positivism in Vienna in the 1920s. But why was scientific positivism itself able to carry conviction from the early nineteenth century on, in a way that it had not done earlier? At this point, we should go behind the history of ideas, and consider these changes in "ideas" against their larger human background.

For our present purposes, I believe, the crucial development in the history of nineteenth-century science was the establishment of distinct scientific disciplines, professions and roles: that is, the process by which individual, sharply delimited special sciences began to crystallize from the larger and less-defined matrix of eighteenth-century natural philosophy. As a result of this change, scientific workers divided themselves up into new and self-organized collectivities, and acquired a collective consciousness of their specialized intellectual tasks, as contrasted with the broader concerns of philosophical, literary, and theological discussion more generally. In this way, it at last became possible to define the new individual role of "scientist." (This familiar word was coined as recently as 1840 by William Whewell, on the model of the much older term "artist," for his presidential address to the British Association for the Advancement of Science.)

In all these respects, scientific roles and writings, organizations and arguments dating from before 1830 differ sharply from anything to be found after around 1890. In the hands of the most distinguished eighteenth-century authors, scientific issues were always expanding into, and merging with, broader intellectual questions. In the writings of a John Ray or a Joseph Priestley, the doors between science, ethics, and religion are always open. "And why not?" they would have asked; "for natural philosophy must surely embrace within itself, not just mathematical and experimental philosophy, but also natural theology and natural morality." (Their sentiments were also those of Isaac Newton himself, for whom "to discourse of God" from a study of His Creation "does certainly belong to natural philosophy."[7]) Indeed, it took a series of deliberate and collective decisions to restrict the scope of scientific debate before these larger issues of philosophy and theology were effectively excluded from the professional debate about scientific issues. One such example was the resolution adopted by the Geological Society of London in 1807 to exclude from its Proceedings all arguments about the origin, antiquity, and creation of the earth, as being merely speculative, and to confine the Proceedings to papers based on direct observations of the earth's crust.[8] This is simply one early illustration of a trend that rapidly became general. During the rest of the nineteenth century, the intellectual concerns of the different special sciences were identified and defined in progressively sharper terms, setting them apart from the broader interests of philosophers, theologians, and the general reading public.

At this point, it would be helpful to develop a fuller understanding of the manner in which natural philosophy, as conceived in the seventeenth and eighteenth centuries, fell apart into its component elements, and the sciences (and scientists) were led to set up shop on their own. Even as late as the 1820s, Joseph Townsend could still present significant contributions to geological science in the guise of an argument vindicating *The Veracity of Moses as an Historian*.[9] By the end of the century, biblical history and geochronology had become entirely distinct disciplines, pursued by quite separate communities of scholars. Yet, even in this case, the transitions involved were protracted, hard-fought, and painful. Similarly, one major reason for the hostile reception that greeted Darwin's *Origin of Species* was the threat it seemingly posed to the traditional association between natural history and sacred history. Acknowledging a presentation copy of the book, Darwin's teacher Adam Sedgwick expressed sorrow and alarm at Darwin's disregard of the "essential link" between the moral and material order of the world. If natural historians no longer showed us how the hand of the Creator was exemplified in the living creatures that were his handiwork, how then could the human race be expected to retain its confidence in divine wisdom and providence?

In addition, it would be helpful to have more detailed studies of the institutional changes during the nineteenth century by the leading scientific academies and societies that had originally been founded from 1650 on. How did they move from being general associations of scholars, clerics, and gentlemen to being special-ized organizations of professional experts, with a narrowly de-fined scope and strict entrance qualifications? Before 1830, the Royal Society of London was still largely an association for the general discussion of issues in natural philosophy. By the 1890s, it had become the mode to pursue, not just art for art's sake, but also science for science's sake: even, electrical theory for electri-cal theory's sake, organic chemistry for organic chemistry's sake, botanical taxonomy for botanical taxonomy's sake. This was so because, by 1890, the self-defining disciplines and autonomous professions with which we are familiar today—each of them devoted to the special aims of one or another science—had finally established an existence independent of each other.

Once again, however, these institutional changes did not come automatically or easily. On the contrary, the intellectual and institutional claims of the special sciences faced continued resist-ance from the churches and elsewhere. So the collective experi-ence, interests, and self-perceptions of, for example, cell physiologists, historical geologists, and electromagnetic theorists led them to defend their newly won territories with some real jealousy, to act protectively toward the intellectual goals of their disciplines, and to resist any countermoves aimed at reabsorbing them into some larger system of philosophy or theology. Ernst Haeckel, the German zoologist and a leader of the German Monistic Alliance, is an interesting figure in this respect. He was perhaps the last representative of the older tradition, comprised of scientists who could maintain an acceptable balance between generalism and specialism, combining genuine expertise in a restricted field of study with a talent for larger-scale philosophical synthesis and exposition.

In short, if we are to understand how science came to part company from the foundations of ethics, we need to focus attention on the history of scientific specialization. It was the development of specialization and professionalization that was responsible for excluding ethical issues from the foundations of science, and so, though inadvertently, destroyed most of the links between science and the foundations of ethics, as well. During the hundred or so years beginning around 1840, the concepts and methods, collective organization, and individual roles of science were progressively sharpened and defined, in ways designed to insulate truly "scientific" issues and investigations from all external distractions. So defined, the task of "positive science" was to reveal how and in what respects, regardless of whether we like them or not, discoverable regularities, connections, and mechanisms are manifest in, or responsible for, the phenomena of the natural world.

This "positive" program for science was sometimes associated, but was never identical, with the philosophy of scientific positivism. It rested on a number of significant assumptions, which are worth spelling out here.

A scientific picture of the world differs radically from a metaphysico-religious picture. The former is realistically confined to demonstrable facts about the natural world: the latter embeds those demonstrable facts within a larger conceptual system, structured according to prejudices that are (from the scientific standpoint) arbitrary, externally motivated, and presumably wish-fulfilling.

A realistic view of the natural world is one that is kept free of irrelevant preferences and evaluations, and so depicts Nature as it is, "whether we like it or not."

If scientific work is to be effectively organized and prosecuted, questions of "demonstrable fact" must be investigated quite separately from all arbitrary, external, wish-fulfilling notions. Only in this way can we carry forward the technical inquiries of science proper, without being sidetracked into fruitless and inconclusive debates about rival values or *Weltanschauungen* to which individual scientists may happen (like anyone else) to be attracted for personal reasons, external to science, but which are not part of the collective agenda of science.

Thus, the deeper reasons for defining the scope and procedures of the special sciences in ways that keep ethical issues out of their foundations were connected with the basic methodological program of the modern scientific movement. In particular, they reflect the steps which have been taken over the last 100 years to give institutional expression to the maxims and ambitions of the founders of the Royal Society, through the professionalization of the scientific enterprise. Given the care and effort that the community of professional scientists has taken in this way to insulate the foundations of science from ethics, we should not therefore be surprised if they have made it that much the harder to preserve clear and significant connections between science and the foundations of ethics, as well.

Philosophical Justifications for Separating Ethics and Science

My argument* is aimed at showing how natural scientists worked to keep ethical considerations and preferences from operating within "the foundations of science"; so that, for instance, the tests for deciding whether one scientific theory or concept was "better" or "worse" than its rivals, from the scientific point of view, should be wholly divorced from issues about what was ethically "better" or "worse." It was a matter of great importance for scientists to be able to make the choice between alternative theories or concepts turn solely on "objective" or "factual"

---

*Against this background, it will be easier to analyze and deal with the points of difference between my own position in this paper and Loren Graham's, as presented in his commentary on my argument. For Professor Graham claims to find a far livelier and healthier interaction between science and ethics during the last hundred years than I here allow. Yet on closer examination (I believe) even his best and most carefully expanded example—that of the English astrophysicist and cosmologist, A.S. Eddington—will be found to support my conclusion.

considerations: they hoped to avoid having to face the question whether one theory or concept is morally preferable to, or more objectionable than, rival theories or concepts. (Can this divorce be preserved absolutely in psychiatry, for example? May it not be legitimate to raise moral objections to one or another theoretical formulation in the psychiatric field? Leaving aside all questions about their other rights and wrongs, we may still approve of Thomas Szasz's arguments for simply raising that issue.)

That kind of value neutrality is, of course, quite compatible with particular scientists adopting all sorts of ethical views and positions on their own responsibility. It is even compatible with one rather more general, collective view: namely, that we must begin by drawing a sharp line between matters of pure or real science and matters of applied science or—more precisely—of technology, after which it will become clear that questions of ethical desirability can arise only in the latter, technological area. (To put it crudely, anatomy is value-free, clinical medicine value-laden.) Above all, it is compatible with all sorts of philosophical discussions, as professional scientists seek to rationalize or justify their particular ethical positions, and square their personal views about ethics with their scientific interests and methodologies.

That is what seems to me to be happening in most of the cases that Loren Graham discusses in his commentary (see pp. 429–431). His exemplary scientists are not people who went out of their way to bring ethical considerations into their scientific work, to the detriment of the intellectual detachment at which professional scientists had aimed for so long. Rather, they were people with idiosyncratic views about the philosophical relevance of science to ethics, and vice versa. And, interestingly enough, several of them are people whose philosophical positions are ones that justify divorcing science from other realms of experience.

In this respect, Arthur Eddington in Britain resembles Pierre Duhem in France. Duhem combined a scientific expertise in the field of thermodynamics with a religious commitment to Roman Catholicism. He was anxious not merely to avoid, but actually to prevent, any conflict between those two parts of his thinking. So, he adopted early in his career a "phenomenalist" attitude toward scientific theories and ideas. In his view, it is not the business of scientists to aim at discovering the nature of reality, but only to formulate mathematical schematisms capable in practice of "saving the phenomena": this posture allowed him to reserve questions about reality to the pronouncements of the metaphysicians and theologians. For instance: when J.J. Thomson first argued for the existence of "electrons" less than 1/1000 as massive as the lightest chemical atoms, Duhem was very scornful. To publish speculative arguments of that sort was to take the pretensions of the atomistic manner of talking far more seriously than they deserved. (Thermodynamics was, of course, almost totally "phenomenalistic" in its methods of analysis.) And he went on to pursue his learned and classic researches into the history of astronomy—researches whose motto might well have been, *Osiander was right*. Finally, he published an essay in which he made his underlying program entirely clear, with the revealing title, *Physique d'un Croyant*, or *The Physics of a Believer*.

Both Duhem and Eddington were thus seeking to provide philosophical justifications for keeping science and ethics, or science and theology, at arm's length. Far from their example refuting my position, it tends only to confirm it. Both of them were in this respect people of their time, armed with a program for defining and pursuing the proper work of science in separation from ethical or religious thought. If they differed from the majority of their colleagues of the time, it was only in being more than wholly devout in their personal commitments to Catholicism or Quakerism. But their other commitments played their part in other areas of their lives, not within their science. They were, in short, both professional scientists and also religiously devout; not "religiously devout" in their actual ways of thinking about scientific issues. And, if that is a correct diagnosis, they were concerned to scrutinize the relations between science and ethics only for the sake of keeping them more securely apart.

The Limits of Positivism

In our own day, the accumulated successes of the "positive" methodology have carried science—and scientists—up against the limits of that program's validity, and in some places across them. As a preparation for answering my central question—"How can we set about reconnecting the sciences with the foundations of ethics?"—I can usefully begin by identifying certain points at which, during the last few years, the location of those limits has become apparent.

> To begin with, the positive program for science normally took for granted a sentimental view of ethics: this was used to justify excluding ethics—which was assumed to deal with labile and subjective matters of taste or feeling—from the systematic investigation of "demonstrable facts." It was assumed, in other words, that human values, valuations and preferences have no place within the world of nature that is the scientist's object of study.

During the twentieth century, by contrast, science has expanded into the realms of physiology and psychology, and in so doing has shown the limits of that assumption. As physiology and psychology have succeeded in securing their own positions as sciences, human beings have ceased to be onlookers contemplating a natural world to which they themselves are foreign and have become parts of (or participants within) that world. As a result, the makeup, operations, and activities of human beings themselves have become legitimate issues for scientific investigation. At the very least, the biochemical and physiological preconditions of *normal* functioning, and so of *good* health, can accordingly be discussed nowadays as problems for science, as well as for ethics.* With this crucial incursion by science into the foundations of ethics, we can recognize that not all *human* evaluations must necessarily be regarded, from the scientific point of view, as *irrelevant* evaluations. On the contrary, some of the processes and phenomena studied by natural sciences carry with them certain immediate evaluative implications for the "good and

---

*Notice, in this connection, John Stuart Mill's remark early on in *Utilitarianism* about the "goodness" of health. Health is in fact, for Mill, one of those paradigmatic "goods" about which utilitarian questions do not have to arise: it is "desirable," just because there would be something clearly paradoxical about people's not "desiring" it. (It should not have to be underlined that Mill was *not* committing G.E. Moore's "naturalistic fallacy" by this association of the "desirable" with "what is actually desired": on the contrary, what Mill sees is that any ethical system must rest on the existence of *some* things that anybody *may be presumed to* regard as "desirable," since they are the prerequisites—like health—for all other potentially "good" human experiences.)

ill" of human life. With this example before us, we are ready to take the first step in the direction hinted at earlier in this paper: that of using the "rational objectivity" of science as a model for reestablishing the claims of moral objectivity, as well.

> Given the increasingly close involvement of basic science with its applications to human welfare, notably in the area of medical research, it is meanwhile becoming clear that the professional organization and priorities of scientific work can no longer be concerned *solely* with considerations of intellectual content and merit, as contrasted with the ethical acceptability and social value, either of the research process itself, or of its practical consequences.

The very existence of the bioethics movement generally, is one indication of this change. The work of the National Commission for the Protection of Human Subjects, and of institutional review boards to review research involving human subjects, is another.

This being the case, the doors between science and the foundations of ethics can no longer be kept bolted from the scientific side, as they were in the heyday of positive science. Neither the disciplinary aspects of the sciences, their basic concepts and intellectual methods, nor the professional aspects of scientific work, the collective organization of science, and its criteria of professional judgment, can ever again be insulated against the "extraneous and irrelevant" influence of ethics, values, and preferences.

On what conditions, then, can we set about reestablishing the frayed links between science and ethics?

1. We should not attempt to reestablish these links by reviving outworn styles of natural theology. The kind of syncretistic cosmology to be found in Teilhard de Chardin, for example, is no improvement on its predecessors: this is indeed an area in which "demonstrable facts" are in real danger of being obscured by a larger wish-fulfilling framework of theological fantasies.[10] Instead, we should embark on a critical scientific and philosophical reexamination of humanity's place in nature, with special reference to the use of such terms as "function" and "adaptation," by which the ethical aspects of our involvement in the natural world are too easily obscured.

2. We should not attempt to force the pace, and insist on

seeing ethical significance in all of science, let alone require that every piece of scientific investigation should have a demonstrable human relevance. Though the enthusiasms of the 1960s "counter-culture" were intelligible enough in their historical context, that would be going too far in the opposite direction, and would land us in worse trouble than the positivist program itself.[11] Instead, we should pay critical attention to the respects in which, and the points at which, ethical issues enter into the conduct of scientific work, including its immediate practical consequences. The ethical aspects of human experimentation, and of such enterprises as sex research, are only samples, from a much larger group of possible issues.

3. We should not see this renewed interaction between science and ethics as threatening, or justifying, any attack on the proper autonomy of scientists within their own specific professional domains. The recent debate about recombinant DNA research generated rhetoric of two contrary kinds: both from scientists who saw the whole affair as a pretext for outside interference in the proper affairs of the scientific professions, and from laypersons who genuinely believed that those affairs were being carried on irresponsibly.[12] Instead, we should reconsider, in a more selective way, just what the proper scope and limits of professional autonomy are, and at what points scientists cross the line separating legitimate professional issues from matters of proper public concern, whether political or ethical.

4. We should not suppose that renewing diplomatic relations between science and ethics will do anything to throw doubt on the virtues, duties, and obligations of the scientific role or station. During the last decade, the antiscientific excesses of the radicals have sometimes made it appear necessary to apologize for being a scientist; and, as a reaction against this radical rhetoric, some professional scientists have developed, in turn, a kind of resentful truculence toward public discussions about the ethical and political involvements of the scientific life. Instead, we need to set about understanding better, both how the line between the narrowly professional and broader social responsibilities of scientists runs in the collective sphere, and also how individual scientists can balance their obligations within the overall demands of a morally acceptable life, as between their chosen

professional roles as neurophysiologists, for example, and the other obligations to which they are subject in other capacities as citizens, colleagues, lovers, parents, religious believers, or whatever.

Renegotiating the Connection between Science and Ethics

I have suggested that changes in the social and historical context of science could easily end the divorce of science from the foundations of ethics; and even that such changes may, already, in fact, be underway. There is indeed some evidence that this is already happening. During the last few years, the "purist" view of science—as a strictly autonomous intellectual enterprise, insulated against the influence of all merely human needs, wishes, and preferences—has lost its last shreds of plausibility. Whether we consider the basic concepts of the sciences, the collective enterprises of professional science, or the personal commitments and motivations of individual scientists, we can maintain a strictly value-free (or rather, ethics-free) position only by sticking arbitrarily to one extreme end of a long spectrum.

From that extreme point of view, the ideally scientific investigation would be a piece of strictly academic research on some application-proof project in theoretical physics, conducted by a friendless and stateless bachelor of independent means. There may have been a substantial body of science approximating this idea as recently as the 1880s and 1890s, but that is certainly not the case any longer. On the contrary, we can learn something about the foundations of ethics by reconsidering the character and content of the scientific enterprise on all three levels.

1. As a collective activity, any science is of significance for ethics on account of the ways in which it serves as an embodiment or exemplar of applied rationality. In this respect, the very objectivity of the goals at which scientists aim, both collectively and individually, provides us with the starting point for a counterattack against relativism and subjectivism in ethics, too; while the manner in which the sciences themselves, considered as "forms of life," define individual roles, with their own specific virtues, can

also be taken as a starting point for a much broader reconstruction of ethics.[13]

2. Correspondingly, the moral character of the scientist's personal motivation, particularly the way in which the Kantian "pure respect for rationality as such" grows out of the wider life of affect or "inclination"—what I have elsewhere called "the moral psychology of science"[14]—can teach us something about the nature of personal virtue and commitment in other areas of life as well.

3. Finally, the actual content of the sciences is at last contributing to a better understanding of the human locus within the natural world. This fact is well recognized in the physiological sciences, where the links betwen *normal* functioning and *good* health are comparatively unproblematic. But it is a matter of active dispute in several areas just at this time: for example, in the conflict over the relations between social psychology and sociobiology. And there are some other fields in which it should be the topic of much more active debate than it is: for example, in connection with the rivalry between psychotherapeutic and psychopharmacological modes of treatment in psychiatry.

This done, it should not be hard to indicate the points at which issues originating in the natural sciences can give rise to, and grow together with, evaluative issues—and not merely with issues that involve the values "intrinsic to" the scientific enterprise itself, but also larger human values of a more strictly ethical kind. For as we saw, the new phase of scientific development into which we are now moving requires us to reinsert human observers into the world of nature, so that we become not merely onlookers, but also participants in many of the natural phenomena and processes that are the subject matter of our scientific investigations. This is true across the whole spectrum of late twentieth-century science: all the way from quantum mechanics, where Heisenberg's Principle requires us to acknowledge the interdependence of the observer and the observed, to ecology, where the conduct of human beings is one crucial factor in any causal analysis of the condition of, say, Lake Erie, or to psychiatry, where the two-way interaction between the psychiatrist and his client is in sharp contrast to the one-way influence of nature on the human observer (but not *vice versa*) presupposed in classical nineteenth-century science.[15]

One likely outcome of this novel phase of science could well be the revival of interest in quasi-Stoic systems of ethics and philosophy, not to say, natural theology. The purist, or positivist, conception of science discussed earlier has a certain significant analogy with the Epicurean philosophy of late antiquity: both attempted to justify equanimity, or *ataraxia*, by pointing to the essential indifference ("value neutrality") of natural phenomena toward human affairs, and vice versa. By contrast, any improved understanding of the human locus *within* the natural world will presumably undercut this assumption of mutual indifference, and encourage people to move in a neo-Stoic direction—seeing human conduct as subject to ethical principles that must harmonize with the principles of the natural world.[16] Just as good health and physiological functioning are intrinsically linked together, so too human beings can presumably contribute to, or impair, the welfare of the natural ecosystems, or chains, within which they are links or elements.

Recognizing the interconnectedness of human conduct and natural phenomena may not by itself, of course, determine the direction in which those interconnections should point us. Acknowledging the need to establish some harmony between human conduct and natural processes is one thing: agreeing on what constitutes such a harmony is another, harder task. There was, for instance, a disagreement between Thomas Henry Huxley and his grandson, Julian, about the relations between human ethics and organic evolution.[17] (T.H. saw it a basic human obligation to fight against the cruelty and destructiveness of natural selection, whereas Julian saw the direction of human progress as a simple continuation of the direction of organic evolution.) What both Huxleys agreed about, however, was the need to see human ethics as having a place in the world of nature, and to arrive at a rational understanding of what that is.

It was with this need in mind that I referred, at the outset, to such concepts as function and adaptation as requiring particular scrutiny at the present time. For the question, "What is the true *function* of human beings?", is potentially as much a topic of debate today as it was in classical Athens, when Plato had Socrates raise it in the *Republic*. Likewise, the question, "How should our ways of acting change, in order to become *better adapted* to the novel situations in which we are finding ourselves?" is a question that also invites answers—sometimes, overly simple answers—based on a reading of contemporary biology and ecology. We are probably ripe for a revival of the organic theory of society and the state. And, though this is a topic that must be taken seriously, it is also one that is going to need to be handled with great caution and subtlety, if we are to avoid the crudely conservative emphases of earlier versions of the theory.[18] Starting from where we do, the answers we give to such questions will certainly need to be richer and more complex than those available in Plato's time; but, sharing Plato's questions, we are evidently back in a situation where our view of ethics and our view of nature are coming back together again.

To conclude: if there is one major field of discussion within which we should most urgently renegotiate the relations between the sciences and the foundations of ethics, that has to do with the concept of responsibility. There is a certain tension in all the sciences of human behavior at the present time, which I have discussed elsewhere under the heading of Townes's Paradox.[19] In thinking about the behavior of their research subjects, as objects of scientific study, psychologists and psychiatrists, neurophysiologists and the rest, are inclined to interpret their observations in a systematically *causal* manner. In thinking about their own behavior, as psychologists, psychiatrists, neurophysiologists or whatever, they are inclined to do so always in *rational* terms. They are prepared, that is, to take credit on their own behalf for a kind of rationality—a freedom to think, act, and write as they do for good reasons—that is missing from their accounts of the thoughts, actions, and expressions of their research subjects. And, since the human capacity to act "for good reasons" is a basic presupposition of all ethics (just as it is of any truly rational science) arriving at a satisfactory resolution of this tension between the causal and rational way of interpreting human conduct is a matter of some urgency, both for science and for the foundations of ethics.

NOTES

1. The point cannot be stated quite so crisply in French or German: Dworkin, at any rate, is certainly contributing to *Rechtswissenschaft*, or

les sciences du droit. But the differences in scope and sense between the English "science," French *science*, German *Wissenschaft*, Greek *episteme*, Arabic *'ilm* etc., provide too large and complex a topic to pursue here.

2. See, for instance, my paper, "Concepts of Function and Mechanism in Medicine and Medical Science," in *Evaluation and Explanation in the Biomedical Sciences*, ed. H.T. Engelhardt, Jr. and S.F. Spicker (Dordrecht: 1975), pp. 51-66.

3. See, for instance, my paper, "The Meaning of Professionalism," in *Knowledge, Value and Belief*, ed. H.T. Engelhardt, Jr. and Daniel Callahan (Hastings-on-Hudson, N.Y.: The Hastings Center, 1977), pp.25ff.

4. Cf. Alasdair MacIntyre, "Objectivity in Morality and Objectivity in Science," in *Morals, Science, and Sociality*, ed. H.T. Engelhardt, Jr., and Daniel Callahan (Hastings-on-Hudson, N.Y.: The Hastings Center, 1978), pp. 21-39.

5. See, for instance, my paper, "The Moral Psychology of Science," in *Morals, Science and Sociality*, pp. 48-67.

6. Arthur Kantrowitz, "The Science Court Experiment: An Interim Report," *Science*, 193 (1976), pp. 653 ff.

7. Cf: John Ray, *The Wisdom of God*, which is an indispensable source for the early history of botanical and zoological systematics; Joseph Priestley, *Disquisitions concerning Spirit and Matter*; and Isaac Newton, particularly his *Four Letters to Richard Bentley*.

8. Charles Gillispie's fascinating book, *Genesis and Geology* (New York: Harper & Row, 1959), is the classic source for this episode in the relations between geological science and natural theology.

9. See Gillispie, *Genesis and Geology*.

10. I have discussed this topic at greater length in an article about Teilhard de Chardin in *Commentary*, 39 (1965), 50 ff.

11. See for instance, my paper, "The historical background to the anti-science movement," in *Civilization and Science*, a Ciba Foundation Symposium, Amsterdam, 1972, pp. 23-32.

12. Cf. the National Academy of Science report on recombinant DNA research in February 1977.

13. Cf. Alasdair MacIntyre, "Objectivity in Morality and Morality in Science," and his forthcoming book, *Beyond Virtue*.

14. Cf. Toulmin "The Moral Psychology of Science."

15. Cf. Karl Popper's striking arguments in *On Clouds and Clocks*, (St. Louis: Washington University, 1966.)

16. It is interesting to consider Arthur Koestler's scientific writings as a kind of neo-Stoic reaction against the supposed Epicureanism of behaviorist psychology, neo-Darwinist biology etc. See, e.g., his *Janus* (London and New York: 1978).

17. The contributions of both men to this topic are conveniently printed together in the book, *Evolution and Ethics 1893-1943* (London: 1947), which comprises T.H. Huxley's original Romanes Lecture together with Julian's subsequent Herbert Spencer lecture.

18. See, for instance, my paper, "Ethics and Social Functioning," in *Science, Ethics and Medicine*, ed. H.T. Engelhardt, Jr. and Daniel Callahan (Hastings-on-Hudson N.Y.: The Hastings Center, 1976), which discusses the role of physiological analogies in the writings of such social theorists as Emile Durkheim and Talcott Parsons.

19. See my paper on "Reasons and Causes," in *Explanation in the Behavioural Sciences*, R. Borger and F. Cioffi, eds. (Cambridge, England: 1970). Hans Jonas has recently drawn my attention to similar arguments in his own writings: see, e.g., *The Phenomenon of Life* (New York: 1966), pp. 124-25, and his earlier paper in *Social Research* 20 (1953).

The Multiple Connections between Science and Ethics: Response to Stephen Toulmin

By Loren R. Graham

STEPHEN TOULMIN'S ATTEMPT to answer the question, "How can we reconnect the sciences with the foundations of ethics?" contains a great many observations with which I entirely agree. His belief that we have recently passed through a period (a generation or two) in which an extreme and historically conditioned effort was made to achieve a complete divorce between science and values is, in my opinion, correct. His observation (and prediction) that this era is now coming to an end, and will not soon be repeated, is supported by current controversies in many scientific fields. Equally helpful is his suggested alternative of a "series of spectra" to the "value-free" picture of science that has reigned in much of Western Europe and America in past decades.

He drew our attention to several points on these spectra which he thinks we should study more carefully, such as the scientific terms "function," "adaptation," the ethical aspects of human experimentation, the proper scope and limits of "professional autonomy," and the concept of "responsibility." Finally, Toulmin issued several crucial warnings about how *not* to go about the effort to investigate links between science and ethics: do not try to revive outworn styles of natural theology; do not

425

engage in such examinations in order to attack or defend the professional autonomy of scientists within their own specific domains.

With all of the above points I am in agreement. And yet, I must admit that I am troubled by what I see as a striking discrepancy between the actual, historical interaction of science and ethical values during our century and the relationship which he described. Is the century described by Toulmin the one in which I have been living? While he sees few connections between science and ethics in past decades, I see a multiplicity of such contacts. Indeed, I maintain that the interaction of science and ethics has been particularly intense through this century and that, at the present moment, it is probably greater than at any time in history.

Part of the explanation of this paradox can be found in the distinction between ethics as an academic discipline and ethics as the principles of conduct of an individual or a group. Toulmin is undoubtedly correct when he says that ethics as an academic discipline has recently been little affected by science. He began his essay by referring to the works of John Rawls, Alan Donagan, and Ronald Dworkin; he correctly noted that these works give scant attention to science. It would be a mistake, however, to consider ethics only as an academic field; our dictionaries give us various definitions of "ethics," and several of the main definitions place ethics squarely in a broad social rather than a narrow academic context. An example would be "the rules of conduct recognized in respect to a particular class of human actions or a particular group, culture. . . ."

I maintain that within the framework of this definition of ethics there has been during recent decades a massive influence of science upon ethics and *vice versa*. If the leading academic writers on the foundations of ethics have not wrestled adequately with this vigorous interaction, then an appropriate response would be "Why not?" instead of "Why are there so few contacts between science and ethics?" Or, returning to Toulmin's essay, it seems to me that a more helpful title would be, "How can we analyze the existing connections between the sciences and the foundations of ethics?" The problem we face is not in creating connections that earlier did not exist, but in recognizing and interpreting connections that have been there all along.

Ideally, an analysis of the connections of science and ethics or values should be broad enough to include most of the interactions we have observed in the history of modern science. Only in that way can we hope to understand how science has influenced our values and how values have influenced science. It is true that by casting our net so widely we will include within our analysis instances in which the concepts of science are connected with ethics and values by processes of poor reasoning and bad logic, but if these historical events had actual effects, they must be considered in order to meet our goal of understanding how society has been affected by science-value interactions. We cannot dismiss these cases by maintaining that individual authors were guilty of committing the "naturalistic fallacy." Scientific theories have often interacted with ethical and value systems at moments when a rigorous philosophical examination might result in the conclusion that the interaction was illegitimate. But just as illegitimate children need to be taken seriously by those who conceive them, so also must the interactions of the supposedly aloof systems of science and values be taken seriously by those who wish to understand history.

Throughout the history of science a great many attempts have been made to draw conclusions about ethical or socio-political values on the basis of science, and these attempts have differed greatly in approach and in quality of argument. Without attempting to classify exhaustively all of these efforts, I would like to point to two distinctly different classes of arguments about the relationship of science and values which I will call Expansionism and Restrictionism.

The Expansionist Approach

By Expansionism I mean that type of argument which cites evidence within the body of scientific theories and findings which can supposedly be used, either directly or indirectly, to support conclusions about ethical, sociopolitical, or religious values. I call this approach Expansionism because its result is to expand the boundaries of science in such a way that they include, at least by implication, value questions. A historically well-known type of interpretation in this category is an "argument by design" for the existence of God; the architecture of the universe, the structure of organisms, or the form of individual organs may be cited as evidence for the existence of some sort of a Supreme Architect. Numerous examples could easily be given, from Newton to Paley. A critic of religion who argues in the opposite direction—as, say, Clemence Royer did in the introduction to her French translation of Darwin's *Origin of Species*—is also using an Expansionist approach, for evidence found in the body of science is brought to bear on value questions.

Within Expansionism several different types of subclasses of arguments exist, which I will not be able to discuss in detail here. I will merely mention that the linkage between science and values constructed by Expansionist authors can be either direct or indirect. A direct linkage is one where the science is supposed to relate to values in a way that is not merely by suggestion or implication, but in a logical, confirming or denying fashion. Charles Gillispie's *Genesis and Geology* contains much discussion of this sort of argument. If a person is a Biblical literalist who takes the Genesis story as factually true—or even merely its main assumption of a historically describable divine creation—then the sciences of geology and biology should speak to that person in a direct way. On a more sophisticated and contemporary level, psychological behaviorists who believe that values are environmentally formed and can be created and controlled at will—once science is refined—are clearly Expansionists who are making direct linkages between science and values. An example of such a linkage is this statement of B.F. Skinner's:

> When we say that a value judgement is a matter not of fact but of how someone feels about a fact, we are simply distinguishing between a thing and its reinforcing effect. . . . Reinforcing effects of things are the province of behavioral science, which to the extent that it is concerned with operant reinforcement, is a science of values.[1]

E.O. Wilson in his *Sociobiology* opened the door leading to direct Expansionist linkages when he called for a "biologicization of ethics" but one remarkable aspect of that book was that, by and large, Wilson did not walk through the door; he only opened it and pointed through it. The reason, however, that the fields of sociobiology and animal behavior have excited interest among the educated lay public is that the members of that public correctly see these academic fields as efforts to expand natural science further into at least a partial explanation of human behavior, including ethics.

Expansionist authors may belong to a second subclass, that of indirect linkages. These are people who do not try to bring a particular piece of scientific evidence into immediate logical relationship with values, but instead work indirectly with the instruments of analogy, simile or metaphor. Social Darwinists who made apologies for industrial capitalism by pointing to the analogy between the struggle for existence in the biological world and competition in the economic world were following the line of argument of indirect linkage within the Expansionist approach. So was Friedrich Engels when he pointed to similar dialectical laws in chemistry and economics in his *Anti-Dühring*. And the astronomer James Jeans playfully pursued a similar type of argument in his popular writings when he spoke of the "finger of God" that started the planets in their orbits.

The Restrictionist Approach

The logical alternative to Expansionism is Restrictionism, an approach that confines science to a particular realm or a particular methodology and leaves values outside its boundaries. Although there are many types of values other than religious ones, Restrictionism is best known in debates about religion; Restrictionists often say "science and religion cannot possibly conflict, because they talk about entirely different things."

A strict adherence to this approach would mean that the relationship of science to ethical, sociopolitical, and religious values is neutral. Science can be used to support neither human selfishness nor human altruism, nor can it affirm or deny either religious belief or atheism. Science is simply neutral with respect to values.

Returning now to the analysis of recent attitudes toward science-value interactions given by Stephen Toulmin, we see that the view of science that he described as the attempt "to choose the purest, the most intellectual, the most autonomous, and the least ethically implicated extreme" on the spectra of science-value interactions was simply an unusually vigorous Restrictionism. Toulmin implies (and I agree) that the main error of this Restrictionism was not that it *never* is correct, but that it ignored almost everything that was happening at the other ends of the spectra, those topics in science, particularly in the biological and social sciences, where the basic concepts are irrevocably value-laden.

Before discussing why this view of science is now breaking down, I would like to examine one of its paradoxical features. As we have seen, strictly speaking, the adherence to Restrictionism that reigned in the thirties and forties should not have supported any particular value system, for it was based on the assumption that science and values belong to separate realms. But in order to understand the function of Restrictionism, we need to turn from abstract analysis to chronological and social analysis. Historically, the Restrictionism of those decades had a considerable impact on values, for its actual function was to protect two systems of values: the professional values of scientists and the predominant nonscientific ethical and sociopolitical values of society. For if science and values could not interact, then scientists were safe from incursions by critics who tried to submit scientific ideas and the scientific profession to social criticism; and ethicists and spokesmen for political or religious values were safe from attempts by scientists to show the relevance of science for their concerns. With the realms of science and values effectively insulated from each other, the historical effect of this demarcation of boundaries was to support existing institutional expressions of positions on science and values. Since I am a supporter of the scientific enterprise and also believe that society cannot exist without value systems, I believe that at least some of the effects of this demarcation were positive, but I also agree with Toulmin that it was a temporary historical product based on assumptions no longer tenable. Indeed, the negative effects of this compromise are now increasingly clear.

Let us look briefly at one well-known scientist who wrote extensively in the middle of the period between the two world wars, the generation upon which Toulmin concentrated in his description of the "value-free" era of science. The great British astrophysicist Arthur Stanley Eddington supported Restrictionism strongly and yet, simultaneously, he found it a useful foundation on which to support existing social values. He was well aware of the naturalistic fallacy and—contrary to the opinions of several of his critics—he never tried to support religion directly with the findings of science. He wrote:

> I repudiate the idea of proving the distinctive beliefs of religion either from the data of physical science or by the methods of physical science.[2]

Eddington realized that to give scientific arguments in favor of ethics or religion was simultaneously to provide the theoretical base for scientific arguments pointed in the opposite direction. Thus, he affirmed that "The religious person may well be content that I have not offered him a God revealed by the quantum theory, and therefore liable to be swept away in the next scientific revolution."[3] Eddington found Restrictionism a source of great security, for it left his religious preferences undisturbed.

His motivation for relying on Restrictionism emerges in the following quotation:

> . . . If you want to fill a vessel with anything you must make it hollow. . . . Any of the young theoretical physicists of today will tell you that what he is dragging to light on the basis of all the phenomena that come within his province is a scheme of symbols connected by mathematical equations. . . . Now a skeleton scheme of symbols is hollow enough to hold anything. It can be— nay, it cries out to be—filled with something to transform it from skeleton into being, from shadow into actuality, from symbols into the interpretation of symbols.[4]

Eddington was trying to create a thirst in his readers for values derived from nonscientific realms, and he was accomplishing that purpose by maintaining that science was merely a system of symbols with no relevance to the major questions of human existence. Far too sophisticated and subtle a person to engage in proselytizing for his own religion of Quakerism, he nonetheless pointed out that "Quakerism in dispensing with creeds holds out a hand to the scientist." Eddington confined science to a small realm of man's concerns and he then invited his readers to fill the remaining space with value systems based on religion. We thus see that in Eddington's hands Restrictionism was turned in on itself and became a justification for certain kinds of values.

It is my opinion that Eddington is only one example of a number of writers on science during the twenties and thirties who found the principle that science is value-free useful in defending their own value preferences. If science tells us nothing about values, then every person is free to defend values without fearing that science will interfere. I should add, of course, that the use of the value-free principle in this "value-laden" way says nothing about the particular values being defended, because the principle could be used to justify any values at all. In historical reality, however, the principle tended to support societal values already dominant.

In his paper Toulmin tends to discount the relevance of people such as Eddington for an understanding of the relationship between science and values in the last generation or two. Eddington, he says, was a person "with idiosyncratic views about the philosophical relevance of science to ethics, and *vice versa.*" For the moment I will leave aside the fact that Eddington was probably the most influential and popular writer on physics (for the educated English-speaking public, not for professional philosophers) of the middle decades of this century, and I will agree with Toulmin that Eddington was indeed idiosyncratic. However, I think that the example of Eddington is still instructive for us in our effort to understand the relationship between science and values in recent generations. Eddington made explicit in a specific and idiosyncratic way the social relevance of Restrictionism that was, in a more general and less idiosyncratic fashion, widely accepted elsewhere. That view can be summarized as follows: if you insist that science and values do not mix, then the antecedent values of society are protected.

This position can be defended until that point in time when the relevance of new scientific knowledge to antecedent social values becomes so overwhelming that their separation becomes obviously artificial. After several generations of brave efforts to keep the two realms separate we have now reached that point of artificiality and the whole question of the relationship of science to values has to be raised anew.

I agree with Toulmin that a historical reconstruction or reinterpretation of the ways in which science came to part company with ethics "needs to focus attention on the history of scientific specialization." However, too narrow a concentration on professionalization and specialization could be misleading, for they are merely the *modes* by which science was separated from ethics, they are not the *reasons*, or, as a biologist might say, they do not reveal the "adaptive value" of the separation. Restrictionism (a term I prefer to "Separationism," since a pure separation was never possible) protected science, but not only science. Restrictionism also protected society by making its values imperturbable by science.

Links of Science to Values

The move toward Restrictionism came not because of specialization but because the relevance of science to values seemed to be changing in a way that made such protection desirable. In the eighteenth century, science could be rather easily used as an apologia or justification of the values most widely accepted in society at large. "Arguments by design" were essentially the employment of science for the buttressing of orthodox value positions. When this kind of argument was readily available and fairly persuasive, it was in the interests of scientists (natural philosophers) to advance such views in an explicit fashion. However, when science began to undermine existing values (for example, historical geology versus Creationism; Darwinian evolution versus *a priori* moral systems), the motivation for being explicit about links between science and values disappeared. Professional societies restricted their memberships increasingly to working scientists who avoided value questions because it was much safer that way. However, implicit links between science and values continued to pile up, as in some secret bank account, as science continued to develop. One day the dimensions of the reserve would demand discussion. Twentieth-century science moved heavily into the fields of behavioral psychology, human genetics, biomedicine, and ethology; the impossibility of keeping the links between science and values outside the concerns of scientists and their institutions became increasingly apparent. We now must reckon with the account that was gradually accumulated, as well as define our position on its future growth. Viewing the situation from this standpoint, I think the need is not so much to "reconnect" the links of science to values as it is to evaluate the links that have been multiplying for decades.

The exaggeration of the value-free nature of science which reigned in the interwar period (1918-39) had many causes, both intellectual and social, and a full analysis of them will not be possible here. One important intellectual stimulus, however, was the revolutionary developments in physics in the first thirty years of this century. Physics was seen in these decades as the science *par excellence*; when many scientists and philosophers talked about "science" they often meant "physics." And one of the important effects of the crisis in physics leading to the emergence of relativity theory was the stress on the extreme value-free and assumption-free end of the spectrum of science-value interactions that Toulmin described. Not only did most people agree, then and now, that the concepts of physics are far from value considerations, but even *within physics* the effect of the advent of relativity was to push thinkers back to the absolute minimum of assumptions about the natural world. Einstein had insisted that each physical quantity be defined as the result of certain operations of measurement, and he showed that by examining these operations more closely than anyone before had done a logical opening appeared through which a new concept of time, or simultaneity, could be drawn. Scientists and philosophers of science were understandably impressed by the fruitfulness of this approach, and a generation of writing followed in which physics was the major influence in the philosophy of science, driving it toward an analogous minimum of value-free assumptions.

Our more recent concerns about the relationship of science and values have been shaped by events in scientific disciplines on the other end of the spectra of science-value interactions, those where the connections between science and values seem unavoidable, probably intrinsic. Increasingly the attempt in the interwar years to build a value-free concept of science based on physics seems constricted, even quaint, to our ears. The areas of science that have treaded most closely on human values in the last decades are not ones in which quantitative approaches or measurement theory are crucially important. To take one example, the science of animal behavior, recognized by the award of Nobel Prizes to three of its leading practitioners in 1973, attempts to explain animal and human behavior in ways that have obvious value significance. What would Konrad Lorenz—who rarely made measurements, once boasted that he had never drawn a graph in his life, and found mathematics largely incomprehensible—say to the assertions of a number of scientists and philosophers of the interwar years that the division between scientific and extrascientific realms is the same as the cleavage between the metrical and the nonmetrical? And in other areas where science-value interactions are currently important, as in behavioral psychology, human genetics, neurophysiology, the concepts of philosophy of science, which came largely from physics, are not very helpful in solving our problems.

We are obviously now in a new era in our understanding of science-value relationships, and this new period brings with it both novel opportunities and novel dangers. We must live in the middle range of the science-value spectra, recognizing the erroneousness of the value-free conception of science so prevalent in the previous generation, and the equal erroneousness of the countering view that "all of science" is value-laden.

We now recognize more openly than before that at least some of the concepts of science, especially those of the social and behavioral sciences, contain value elements. We also know that scientific theories and findings in areas such as psychology, genetics, neurophysiology, and animal behavior can have important value effects. It seems, furthermore, increasingly likely that some of the aspects of human behavior that were previously assigned to the ethical realm are influenced by genetic and physiological bases. As we learn more about what sociobiologists and others have called the "emotive centers of the hypothalamic-limbic system" we will probably see more clearly that genetics and physiology are relevant to discussions of ethics. And as our knowledge of these areas increases, our power of intervention often grows.

In chronological terms the most dangerous period of the development of a science is when enough is known to advance the first fruitful speculations and to try a few interventions, but not enough is known to bring discipline to those speculations or to predict the possible side effects or aftereffects of intervention. When the science of human genetics first began to develop at the end of the nineteenth century and the first decades of the twentieth it was so inexact and contained so many flawed conceptions, such as beliefs in single-gene determination of behavioral and psychological characteristics, that it allowed room for a rash of pseudo-scientific eugenic theories and practices in which social and political prejudices played important roles. As we move into the newer areas of science-value interactions on the basis of such still fairly recent sciences as sociobiology a little conservatism about accepting all the claims advanced by advocates is entirely warranted.

As we learn that aspects of our behavior which earlier seemed to be based solely on nonscientific ethical values are actually conditioned genetically, we should be cautious about shifting the entire weight of our attention to that sort of explanation. Some important part of our ethical values may not be well-explained genetically, and these cultural aspects of ethics may play valuable roles of which we are still unaware. Just as we wish to preserve our genetic reserves, so we should preserve our cultural ones as well. Human beings are probably wiser than they know; *both* the genetic bases of their behavior *and* the cultural, ethical bases of their behavior have been selectively tested throughout the evolution of civilization. This cultural and biological evolution has been successful (in the sense of reproductive success and its surrogates), but its mechanisms are not fully understood.

Anthropologists tell us that the beliefs and superstitions of primitive peoples, at first glance irrational, often serve very practical goals in preserving the security of the particular primitive society although the society itself may not be aware of the value of their customs. Our traditional value systems, hopelessly nonscientific, may still work in some similar ways. Despite the injustices of contemporary civilization, it works fairly well, and we should not attempt to change its underlying assumptions in a wholesale way when we are operating on the basis of very partial scientific knowledge. There is an argument for gradualism even when irrationality is being replaced by rationality.

Perhaps a somewhat simple analogy will help a bit here. A grade-school child is often superb at riding a bicycle even though he or she knows nothing of the principles of physics that permit one to ride a bicycle and that govern what can be done with it. Later he or she may learn the necessary physics at school. If the youth would on some fine day decide to relearn how to ride a bicycle on a scientific basis, applying these principles, his riding would at first gain nothing, and he might even have a wreck. Accumulated experience is more important here than science. In a similar way, it is quite likely that some of the values necessary for the continuation of civilization were learned on a nonscientific basis and are now encased in nonscientific or even irrational beliefs; as we learn what the scientific explanations for some of these values and ethical systems are, we should be intelligently cautious about attempting a sudden new way of keeping our equilibrium. Indeed, we are so far from having a scientific explanation of ethics that genuine skepticism about a "biologicization of ethics" is warranted.

We have left behind the view that science is value-free. We recognize the links that exist between many areas of science and our values and ethics. We are ready to benefit from the insights that science can bring to our understanding of these values. We know that we must live in the middle range of science-value interactions, seeing that the pure poles of "value-free science" and "science-free values" are diminishing in strength. But living on this particular slippery slope will require extreme caution. The major flaw in the view of the past generation described by Toulmin was to refuse to see where science was affected by values; we should guard against a possible future period in which we might fall into one of two possible different errors: the attempt to explain values exhaustively in terms of a science that is always incomplete, or the attempt to attack all science as being intrinsically value-laden.

Avoiding these extremes, much valuable work remains to be done. We need to examine the internal concepts of science, as Toulmin has suggested, to find how we might analyze the connections of the sciences with the foundations of ethics. We need to study more thoroughly the importance of genetic evolution for understanding our social behavior. We also need to re-examine the history of science to see where science-value interactions have occurred with important social effects, even though some of the concepts were, from our present point of view, faulty (the history of eugenics, the attempts to link quantum mechanical indeterminacy with concepts of free will, the relationship between Marxism and science, the relationship between religion and science). And of course we need to explore the ethical dimensions of present scientific research procedures and technological practices. By pursuing these different approaches we will learn much more about the great variety of ways in which science and values can interact.

NOTES

1. B.F. Skinner, *Beyond Freedom and Dignity* (New York: Alfred A. Knopf, 1971), p. 104.

2. A.S. Eddington, *The Nature of the Physical World* (Cambridge: Cambridge University Press, 1928), p. 333.

3. Eddington, *The Nature of the Physical World*, p. 353.

4. A.S. Eddington, *Science and Religion* (London: Friends Home Service Committee, 1931), pp. 9–10.

Index